The Big Spenders

The Big Spenders

The Epic Story of the Rich Rich,
the Grandees of America and the Magnificoes,
and How They Spent Their Fortunes

Lucius Beebe

Axios Press
P.O. Box 118
Mount Jackson, VA 22842
888.542.9467   info@axiospress.com

Distributed by NATIONAL BOOK NETWORK.

Library of Congress Cataloging-in-Publication Data

Beebe, Lucius.
      The big spenders / Lucius Beebe.
            p.   cm.
      Originally published: Garden City, N.Y. : Doubleday, 1966.
      Includes bibliographical references and index.
      ISBN 978-1-60419-006-9 (alk. paper) 1. United States—Social life and customs—1865-1918. 2. United States—Social conditions—1865-1918. 3. Upper class—United-States—History—19th century. 4. Upper class—United States—History—20thcentury. 5. Rich people—United States—History—19th century. 6. Rich people—United States—History—20th century. 7. Luxury—Social aspects—United States—History—19th century. 8. Luxury—Social aspects—United States—History—20th century. I. Title.
      E168.B43 2009
      973.8—dc22

                                                                            2008034480

Contents

Acknowledgement

For their assistance in the preparation of this book in the form of reminiscences, documentation, and editorial contributions generally, the author is in the debt of a number of courteous correspondents whose good offices are much appreciated and here acknowledged. They include Everett De Golyer of the De Golyer Foundation at Dallas; the late William M. Houghton of *New York Herald Tribune;* Merle Armitage of the Manzanita Press; Eugenia Sheppard (Mrs. Walter Millis), fashion editor of the *New York Herald Tribune;* Joseph J. O'Donohue IV; the late Gene Fowler; Schuyler Parsons; Alfred Barton; J. W. Ehrlich; Robert Kriendler of Jack & Charlie's "21" Club; Paul Mellon; Finis Farr; Joseph Bryan, Esq., of Brook Hill, Richmond; Frank X. Tolbert of the *Dallas News;* Cleveland Amory; Henry Sell; and Stephen Birmingham.

A bibliography of sources quoted and consulted will be found on page 492.

Illustrations will be found in a gallery the center of the book.

". . . the nuances of snobbery, the discrimination and cultivation of which have been the major contributions of the Anglo-Saxon people to civilization."

Wilmarth Lewis

Foreword

WHEN, IN THE wide-open New York that flowered in the years immediately after the Civil War, the town's biggest gambler and a political jeffe of consequence, John Morrissey, opened what were reputed to be the world's most lavish gaming rooms on Twenty-fourth Street opposite the chaste premises of the ultrarespectable Fifth Avenue Hotel, there were those of his neighbors who took offense. These fastidious cave dwellers, although not above patronizing Morrissey's games of chance or eating a dish of diamondback terrapin from his celebrated free buffet, maintained that his casino lowered the moral tone of the community, and their wives, when the Morrisseys attended grand opera at the Academy of Music, ostentatiously glared at Mrs. Morrissey through mother-of-pearl opera glasses.

On a to-hell-with-you basis of affront to these social dissidents, Morrissey ran for Congress. He won handily and just to be sure nobody missed the point, he ran a second time and was re-elected by an even wider margin.

To celebrate his second victory, he commanded from Lemaire of Paris, for his wife, what were probably the most ostentatious pair of opera glasses ever seen until that time. Their framework was in the form of a diamond and sapphire lyre and they cost

$75,000, which enabled the delighted Mrs. Morrissey to glare right back and in an even more expensive manner at her social detractors on opening nights.

Openhanded John Morrissey's pleasure in his wife's effulgence anticipated by only a few decades that of Potter Palmer, the Chicago hotel-man who kept his wife so loaded with jewels that observers following her progress through the restaurant of the Paris Ritz thought that she staggered visibly, not from any communion with the wine card, but from sheer weight of diamonds. "There she stands with half a million on her back," Potter Palmer used to say admiringly.

It was at Morrissey's, too, whose gaming rooms were so magnificently furnished that they reputedly outshone any and all European casinos of the time, that the senior August Belmont consumed at the midnight buffet what he proudly announced to be the most costly brace of canvasback ducks ever served in the United States. He had just lost $60,000 at baccarat, which tagged each duck at $30,000, a price he allowed was entirely in keeping with his station as the American representative of the House of Rothschild.

For sheer costliness for an entree, Belmont's ducks set a record that was to remain unchallenged until a century later when a single order of breast of chicken in aspic precipitated a lawsuit between Calouste Gulbenkian, the Iranian oil tycoon, and his son Nubar, the greatest magnifico of his age, in which the barristers' fees alone came to $150,000. The elder Gulbenkian took exception to his son's charge of luncheon on an expense account and the most expensive family falling out of the London generation followed.

Except, however, as they may furnish a frame of reference or solid-gold standard of comparison for parallel splendors nearer home, the caprices of foreign magnificoes are not the immediate concern of this book. A possible exception to this ruling may well be the case of the elegant Count Boni de Castellane whose flights of fancy relieved Anna Gould of $12,000,000 in half as many years, but this was, after all, American money and therefore in a position to command attention.

Asked to itemize some of his whims, Boni later deposed that he had spent the $12,000,000 sweated from the Missouri Pacific and other Gould railroads on such matters as "my general existence, my chateaux, my palaces, my *bibelots,* my race horses, my yachts, my traveling expenses, my political career, my charities, my fetes, my wife's jewels and loans to my friends. . . ," He added: "I claim to represent the best investment the Goulds ever made."

Who can say him no?

The purview of this inquiry inclines more closely to the film celebrity who, a few years back, attended the opening of a new ice-cream parlor by Wil Wright, Hollywood's and, therefore, the world's most expensive merchant of butterfat content. The name laid a crisp new $100 bill on the marble counter and said: "Couple of cones please, if that's sufficient."

"Associate with people of cultivated tastes and some of the culture may rub off on you," once remarked Stanley Walker, the celebrated city editor of the *New York Herald Tribune* in the 1930s. "Hang around musical folk and you may, with luck, get to know Brahms from Beethoven. But keep company with the very rich and you'll end picking up the check."

While this was, and is, a quotable aphorism and may in some cases be possessed of validity, it needn't be accepted as universal sooth. People who hung around with John D. Rockefeller, especially if their name was Flagler, Archbold, or Rogers, had no visible cause to regret it.

Those fortunate enough to find themselves in the company of William Collins Whitney may have had occasion to ponder their ways the next morning but while the association lasted, nobody had reason to complain. Whitney, the archmagnifico of the American scene at the turn of the century, was far and away the greatest champagne buyer in the house, not excepting George Kessler and Manny Chappelle, who were paid to push the stuff around.

If you consorted for any protracted period of time with Mrs. Stuyvesant Fish you were pretty apt to get your name in the society columns which, to a number of people at the time and place, represented the sum of all imaginable good.

On the other hand, if you hung around Bleeck's saloon next door to the *Herald Tribune* with Stanley Walker himself, you almost invariably ended picking up the tab, for the author of *Mrs. Astor's Horse* and *City Editor* was a match game player of accredited skill and ferocity. It wasn't associating with the rich that sent young reporters home on the subway instead of in a taxi. It was associating with the cultured cowboy from Lampasas, Texas.

"Anybody," said Jay Gould, "can make a fortune. It takes a genius to hold onto one."

"A man with a million dollars can be as happy nowadays as though he were rich," deposed Ward McAllister.

"Money has a tendency to buy happiness," wrote Damon Runyon.

"Money is something to be thrown off the back platform of moving trains," was the stated philosophy of Gene Fowler.

Each of the foregoing expressed at least a facet of the basic thinking of all but the most benighted men and women. There are proverbs and admonitions to the contrary, to be sure. "A fool and his money are soon parted" is learned by that mythical entity, every schoolboy, as early as he can read and write. Prudence and saving ways were advocated in ample abundance by Benjamin Franklin. The impending rainy day is part of every American's subconscious awareness as is attested by the hundreds of millions of dollars in savings banks. But, by and large, the American people are a spending people just as, by and large, the French are a saving people, unless, of course, they happen to have in hand somebody else's money.

On the basis of the existing record it is safe to assert that, in the great American credo, a rich man is the noblest handiwork of God, and the corollary of the aphorism is that how he spends his money is the measure of the rich man.

It is the purpose of this book to explore some of the ways in which Americans and, in a few cases, foreigners financed with American money have expressed the genius required for the rewarding expenditure of substantial sums of money.

When in the early 1920s an Armenian named Michael Arlen who was then living in England and later became an American citizen found himself on the way to almost overnight riches on the strength of a novel called *The Green Hat,* he was faced with the problem of how to spend the not inconsiderable sum represented by his first royalty check. His first impulse, which he happily was able to resist, was to pay his indebtedness to his tailor, who happened to be Henry Poole & Company Limited just off Burlington Gardens. He might also have paid his back rent which was mounting or even repaid some of the loans from kind friends on which he had been subsisting while waiting for fame to crown his slightly oriental brows.

With great strength of character he was able to restrain himself from indulging such urgings of middle-class probity and went out and spent the entire sum in hand on the biggest, flashiest Rolls-Royce touring car with a body by Park Ward, in blinding canary yellow.

"It gave me a new dimension," he said.

"All I want of the world is very little," he later explained as his basic philosophy of life. "I only want the best of everything and there is so little of that."

In similar if more modest vein was the revealing episode in the life of the above quoted Damon Runyon with the first pay check he received as a New York newspaper reporter fresh from the howling wilderness of Pueblo, Colorado, and still very damp behind the professional ears. Like Arlen, he owed for rent and was in arrears to friends, but as he strolled Fifth Avenue on that now distant day, his eye lighted in a shop window on the most elaborate and beautiful shoe trunk ever devised by a skilled leather merchant. Felt-lined compartments were provided for boots of whose very name and use he was in ignorance; the brass fittings gleamed like eighteen-karat gold; it was a lovely, costly, and, to the possessor of a single pair of button boots in the world, useless artifact. Its price was $47, which was precisely the amount of the first pay check then in his pocket, and without a moment's hesitation he bought the shoe trunk.

"It gave me a new dimension," he said afterward.

For some inscrutable reason, shoe trunks have exercised a compelling fascination for Hearst practitioners of beautiful letters at all levels in the literary hierarchy. When Henry Sell in the early 1920s was hired away from the book page of the *Chicago Daily News* to take over the management of *Harper's Bazaar* for William Randolph Hearst, Ben Hecht decided to accompany him to New York and see him safely emplaced in his new job. As they got off the *Twentieth Century Limited* at Grand Central and went for a taxi, the pair passed a luggage-shop window in which was prominently displayed an elaborately fitted and very costly shoe trunk.

"The first thing an important New York magazine editor needs," said Hecht, "is a shoe trunk."

Sell, in better financial case than Damon Runyon, owned four or five pairs of shoes, although not nearly enough to warrant a shoe trunk, so he bought it. He and Hecht, filled with a spirit of what Sell was later to describe as "expensive cheerfulness," also bought pearl-gray Homburg hats and varnished Malacca walking sticks. They then set out up Fifth Avenue to take New York by storm.

The gulf represented by the difference between Damon Runyon's $47 and Michael Aden's $27,000 is not as abysmal as it seems. The two were blood brothers in the closely bonded confraternity that believes that money is made to be spent and that allowing it to light a fire in one's pocket can result in painful burns. That it must be spent with a maximum of panache, in the greatest possible expression of the *beau geste,* is what differentiates the truly big spender from the merely expensive spender.

It is a philosophy most perfectly expressed in the magnificent gesture of an old-time ante-bellum New Orleans gambler, immortalized by Herbert Asbury, whose luck had finally turned against him to such a degree that his bankruptcy was known in every restaurant and café in the Vieux Carré, so that where he had once been welcomed as an openhanded magnifico he was now asked to show his money before being served even the humblest fare.

Finally, in desperation he pawned his overcoat and sword cane, the last vestigial remnants of happier times, and presented himself, in funds once more, at the most expensive restaurant in the Rue Royal where he ordered the most costly meal within the compass of the menu. Gulf oysters and terrapin, champagne in magnums, *filet de boeuf Mirabeau,* and hothouse asparagus—all were brought to his table by smiling servitors. When all was prepared the old fellow paid his bill with a handsome tip which consumed the last picayune in his pocket, threw every dish on the floor together with the crockery, silver, and table ornaments, retrieved his tall hat from the hat rack, and stalked disdainfully from the premises. Later that night he shot himself.

A true believer in the established faith of the big spenders and a magnifico to the last, he subscribed without reservation to Gene Fowler's dictum: "Money is something to be thrown off moving trains."

No player in the rich and variegated cast of characters that have peopled the drama of the United States has so endeared himself to posterity as the big spender, the openhanded grandee whose progress through the world was a dazzlement of wealth handsomely and promiscuously distributed. He appears in the identical guise in a number of folk myths, some of which have their basis in reality, a sure indication to students of history and of national character of his hold upon the imaginations of those successive generations of fellow Americans.

Witness the anecdote concerning the magnifico who, for a variety of reasons, usually a failure to recognize him on the part of a green desk clerk but sometimes attributable to the malice of the manager, is unable to get a room or suite in his accustomed hotel. Outraged, he disappears briefly into the night and returns with a deed to the property, having purchased the establishment, lock, stock, and barrel, and forthwith discharges the obnoxious flunkey and gets a good night's rest. Sometimes he makes a deserving bellman manager on the spot. In some versions he goes off to build a rival hotel which eventually puts the offending hostelry out of business. The episode, stylishly embellished, appears so frequently in the folklore of the old West as to assume the dignity of portions of the Icelandic sagas or the Arthurian legend.

The wish-fulfillment hotel purchase, already well established in the national mythology, can factually be traced to at least three authentic episodes in Denver, Butte, and Colorado Springs, respectively, a circumstance which must be viewed by the social historian with much the same satisfaction as is activated in a student of the *chansons de geste* by supporting evidence that there was in fact a Roland who did indeed blow his fated horn at Roncesvalles.

It may well be that the realms of gastronomy and architecture furnish the most fertile field for research in the matter of determined ostentation, although in point of actual expenditures involved they are worlds apart. Diamond Jim Brady's most dissolute skirmishes with the bill of fare at Rector's or Woodmanston Inn couldn't compare, say, with the eventual bill footed by George Washington Vanderbilt II for the construction of *Biltmore* at Asheville, North Carolina, but there can be a nobility of conduct among the plovers' eggs and magnums of Krug's Private Cuvée that must excite the admiration of connoisseurs.

Americans avid for recognition in the gastronomic sweepstakes had before them in Victorian and Edwardian times a wide range of inspiration from which to choose among the Russian grand dukes at Monte Carlo and the landed nobility of England. They could set their sights on the bravura performance, cited by Joseph Bryan II as a pure classic, of Count Apraxine who at the turn of the century was a welcome guest at Andre Sella's Hotel de Cap d'Antibes, rated by Mr. Bryan as the world's most expensive as well as aloof hostel, where "all the face-cards of the century stayed at one time or another."

Count Apraxine, in an age when out-of-season strawberries on the Riviera fetched approximately $2.50 apiece, gold, commanded a dozen to be brought to him on the terrace each day for breakfast. When they arrived, he would mash them to a pulp with a solid-gold fork, thoughtfully and thoroughly, and then return them uneaten to the kitchen.

Compared to the Count, Lillian Russell and Diamond Jim engaged in an eating competition at the United States Hotel in Saratoga that must have been vaguely reminiscent of Henry VIII entertaining Cardinal Wolsey at luncheon while the dogs under the royal table disputed among the rushes for the discarded carcasses of swans, geese, and venison. But if Diamond Jim and the other pets of the lobster palaces of his time seem crude in retrospect, there is the more elevated example of William Collins Whitney, perhaps the greatest magnifico of them all, who in his tenure of office as Cleveland's Secretary of the Navy ordered a light collation for a conference of department heads from a Washington caterer which involved 200 gallons of terrapin and eighty cases of champagne. Being a cabinet member meant something then.

Compared to such stimulating recollections of the *belle epoque* of big spending and the lavish gesture, the degenerate present, despite material abundance on a scale to dwarf the dreams of a Roman proconsul, offers a sorry comparison. Never have material prosperity and emergent good fortune in such radiant dimension crowned a nation's destinies; never have diffidence and timidity suggested their enjoyment on a scale of more debased mediocrity.

The details of what can only be regarded, by persons of taste and imagination, as an American tragedy came over the wires from Houston not long ago when a Texas oil tycoon named James M. West at last encountered the old fellow with the scythe. It wasn't the fact of Mr. West's demise, a matter we must all face sooner or later, that constituted tragedy: it was the details of his life as furnished by the Associated Press.

Mr. West left an estate of $100,000,000, take or leave a few dollars, $290,000 of it squirreled away in silver dollars in a secret cellar in his home. He also left a fleet of forty-one Cadillacs and his favorite relaxation, which was riding night patrol in squad cars with Houston policemen.

There you have the archetypal American millionaire of the years of the nation's greatest economic affluence: more high-priced motorcars than he could possibly use, a taste for Skid-road adventure vicariously achieved, and such a terror of the times that he couldn't feel secure without a hoard of hard cash in the cellar. His concern for minted coinage may have been prophetic but its suggestion of insecurity is none the less explicit.

If this were an isolated example of men of great wealth it would still be a matter for tears, but when you realize that, with only slight variations, it may be taken as typical of an entire generation of American millionaires it becomes a national catastrophe.

It may be argued that Texas millionaires are a specially inhibited and unimaginative breed, predisposed from birth to the inanities of football, drum majorettes, and private flying machines, and that elsewhere in the land rich men rise above this abysmal level of tastelessness and conformity, but the argument, alas, is not valid. Fords, Rockefellers, Morgans, Mellons, and Vanderbilts to a man are given to public good works and private lives of the most revolting probity. Among the inheritors of great names and great fortunes in America it is difficult if not impossible to find a living man who has given a dinner party at which nude chorus girls leaped from the innards of a lamb potpie. Few if any today imitate Wilson Mizner and openly smoke opium for kicks. Even alcoholic excess, long the most obvious and ingratiating of weaknesses, is in decline and the private lives, like the public careers of Whitneys, Stotesburys, and Carnegies, are an open book.

So too were the lives of a previous generation which included Bet-a-Million Gates, J. P. Morgan, William C. Whitney, and William Randolph Hearst, but the open book was, like as not, a turfman's odds book or *Fanny Hill*.

The great hallmarks of wealth and character that once set rich men apart from their inferiors—affairs with stage favorites, love nests aboard oceangoing yachts, private railroad cars, racing stables, vast retinues of domestics, collections of bogus old masters, membership at Colonel Edward Bradley's Beach Club at Palm Beach, titled sons-in-law, custom-made motorcars, cottages at Newport and mansions on Fifth Avenue, a nice taste in Madeira, and *fêtes champêtres* around swimming pools into which guests in evening dress precipitated themselves at frequent intervals—all are gone with the wind. And don't talk about poverty and income taxes and the hard lot of the well-to-do. There are men in Texas who could buy and sell J. P. Morgan, Jim Hill, and Jay Gould all rolled in one, but they are poltroons to a man, scared beyond measure of having fun. Instead of fancy-dress balls of revolting dimensions at the Waldorf-Astoria they are a pushover for family foundations. Instead of scandalous associations with French actresses, busted silk hats, and champagne bottles on the lawn, they prefer to be known as "plain as an old shoe."

In the year 1879, Saginaw, Michigan, was the lumber capital of the known universe, throbbing with prosperity and push, and to the greater glory of Saginaw there was opened in that year a magnificent new hotel, the Bancroft House, whose four stories, handsome cupola, private gasworks for illumination, and profusion of cut-glass chandeliers made it the talk of the countryside. To open this gorgeous hostelry there was a state banquet to which the timber barons were bidden to feast on Maryland terrapin and roast grouse washed down by Niagaras of champagne, claret, bourbon, and French cognac while a stringed orchestra, shielded behind potted palms, discoursed sweet music.

All the chivalry of Saginaw was invited, it seems, save Curt Emerson, already a millionaire many times over and a Michigan power to reckon with. Omitting his name was a mistake of the first magnitude. On the appointed evening, as the tycoons of the sawmill world were tucking their napkins into their boiled shirts and beginning to have at the terrapin à la Maryland, there arrived on the scene the unbidden Curt Emerson. With banshee screams of rage and indignation the lumber king leaped upon the snowy table-cloth, went into action with his heavy calked boots, and kicked his way from one end of the table to the other. A score of guests were maimed by splintered crockery, grouse took off to roost in the costly crystal chandeliers, and the banquet broke up. Next day Emerson paid $2000 for the broken dishes and torn linen and counted it money well spent. He was never again omitted from a guest list.

There is no moral to this recital of a few of the more lighthearted gestures of a departed generation of the millionaires except to point out that they will live in fragrant memory. There are ten times more millionaires today than there were when Morgans, Mellons, Hills, Astors, and first-generation Fords trod the earth but only the merest handful are known to the public, and there isn't an authentic magnifico in a carload.

Where now is the counterpart of Berry Wall, who once changed his attire at Saratoga Springs forty times in a day to become known as the "King of the Dudes," or of Boston's Mrs. Jack Gardner, who paid Paderewski $3000 to play at tea time for an elderly friend and herself on condition that he remain concealed behind a screen?

One looks in vain for the peer of the late Louis Hill of St. Paul, son of James J. Hill, the empire builder of the Northwest who, when guests were expected, sent two identical vintage Rolls-Royces with chauffeur and footmen to match to the railroad depot. Guests and their luggage were shown to one overpowering limousine while the other went on ahead empty. When guests inquired the reason, there was an answer: of the two identical cars, only one could make the hill at the edge of town. The staff never knew which was the underpowered car, so both were pressed into service.

A number of excuses are advanced for the decline of such spending, none of them valid. One is that taxes make expansive gestures impossible. This is demonstrably false, since today's men of wealth, instead of owning the ostentatious private Pullman car of tradition, have hangars full of B-29s at twenty times the cost of purchase and maintenance of a private railroad car. An airplane can be concealed on a private flying field, but a railroad car is not so easily hidden.

Then there is the school of thought contending that men of wealth have grown "more aware of their obligations to society." Nuts to this one, too. The rich man's debt to society is discharged when he has paid his federal taxes. Beyond these, he owes no farthing to the society that would confiscate his last dollar if allowed to.

There is also—and less valid—the theory maintaining that through some dispensation of Providence we have achieved higher standards of national taste, including the breed of rich men. This is the most ferociously preposterous of all theses advanced to account for the decline of rich men's whims. Will anyone undertake to demonstrate that there is better taste involved in the consumption of soft drinks and patent breakfast foods than champagne and *foie gras?* Will anyone maintain that a tieless sports shirt and plaid jacket could be sartorially or esthetically superior to a frock coat and top hat? Or that a television console fashioned in the likeness of a Chinese pagoda is a cut above the cast-iron stags that ornamented the lawns of the wealthy in the nineties? Or that French impressionists are superior to the Titians and Rembrandts featured in the golden age of American millionaires?

If it is argued, as sometimes happens, that the second half of the chronological disaster known as the twentieth century is not suited to personal magnificence and that it would be impossible in this degenerate time to approximate with social impunity the way of life that was maintained only yesterday by such practitioners of the *beau geste* as August Belmont, Spencer Penrose, and William C. Whitney, one has but to look to England for instant refutation of the argument.

Here amidst the noblest ruins of colonial imperialism and in the blight of a mildewed time there still flourishes in full luxuriance a small and select cadre of cavaliers banded together in confraternity of elegant amenities and spacious ways of life.

The gaze of approval will inevitably light on the bearded,

monocled, top-hatted, and orchid-buttonholed old gentleman of seventy named Nubar Gulbenkian who still rides point-to-point and who once undertook personally to consume twenty-five tons of fresh Beluga caviar left on his hands by a treacherous business associate. His father, Calouste Gulbenkian, was the architect of the Iraq Oil Company, known to the envious of his generation as Mr. Five Per Cent, and much of his enormous wealth is still intact and at the disposal of his son who admires to spend it in the fullest light of day and in the manner that has in all ages enjoyed the approval of Englishmen, namely on horse, hounds, haberdashery, and horticulture.

A well-lit production number and boon to the Sunday desks of London newspapers, where he has long since displaced the Loch Ness monster and Sir Bernard Docker's gold-plated Daimler, Gulbenkian a few years back undertook to have built to his own specifications a re-creation of the Vauxhall auto-taxi, and the English papers accorded the event full pictorial and editorial treatment. Their attitude was one of admiration but scarcely surprise since, even in a socialist generation, English approbation is universally extended to sporty old types of mature years and jaunty mien. As witness, only a generation gone, English preoccupation with the exclamatory persons of Lord Lonsdale, the Earl of Rosebery, and Lord Hartington who, when he entertained his royal master Edward VII at dinner, had his eighty house footmen newly outfitted in liveries of gold cloth so massively woven as to impede their movements and impart stateliness to their service.

The Vauxhall, in case you have forgotten, was the first London auto-taxi, an almost perpendicular vehicle, tall enough to accommodate without inconvenience a gentleman wearing a silk top hat and built with a wheel base so foreshortened as to facilitate the U-turns that, both then and now, are a part of London's well-ordered traffic. Contemporary taxis offer nowhere near the comfort of the Vauxhall and Mr. Gulbenkian, being not only well-to-do but a man who wears top hats rather more often than soft ones, felt a re-creation of his favorite conveyance was just the ticket.

When it was delivered, at formidable cost from the manufacturer, who had had to start all over again and build from the bottom up an artifact that hadn't been in request since before 1914, the proud new owner displayed it at a press conference at the Ritz. He demonstrated its availability to top-hat wearers, its commodious interior with a vase designed to hold just one American Beauty rose, and pointed out that, in traffic, it "could turn around on a sixpence." And added as an afterthought: "Whatever that may be!"

Students of the Gulbenkian legend see in this durable old gentleman the recapitulation of a long line of exquisites and cavaliers who have over the centuries, but most especially in modern times, peopled the English legend both factually and in literature. His role of country grandee has about it overtones of the celebrated spendthrift Squire John Mitton of the seventeenth century, though not Mitton's alcoholic dementia nor, hopefully, his bad end in debtors' prison. His orchids are in the direct tradition of such notable fanciers of these exotic and costly blooms as Jay Gould, Samuel Untermyer, Alfred de Rothschild, Nero Wolfe, and, oddly enough, Hetty Green's playboy son, one-legged Colonel Ned Green. The Gulbenkian single eyeglass derives from the best tradition of haughty and supercilious monocle wearers from Joseph Chamberlain to Joseph Conrad and from Benjamin Disraeli to George Arliss who portrayed Queen Victoria's favorite prime minister on the stage. His gray top hats and skirted frock coats at Lords are those worn only yesterday at Ascot and Auteuil by the late Evander Berry Wall, King of the Dudes, and his extra-length cigars without which he is seldom photographed, ahorse or afoot, are the properties of Lord Lonsdale and Winston Churchill.

There are, indeed, Londoners and amateurs of the Gulbenkian saga who, studying his likeness in the picture press as he feeds the swans in the ornamental waters of his country home at Hoggeston, shakes an admonitory finger at the Archbishop of Canterbury at Lambeth Palace, or drives his span of grays at the Richmond Horse

Show, wonder if, instead of being a favorite of the Sunday editors, Nubar Gulbenkian is not, rather, a figure of fiction out of one of the novels of the late E. Phillips Oppenheim.

Witnesses of his advent in the Gulbenkian custom-built Rolls-Royce, top-hatted, cigared, and attended by liveried servitors as he descends at the St. James Street entry of the Ritz, may be pardoned for imagining they are viewing a casting-agency creation directly from the Oppenheim syndrome whose components were quail for breakfast at the Hotel de Paris at Monte Carlo, prime ministers lunching at Claridge's in West Brook Street, *mille-franc* counters on the roulette tables at Cannes, and Sir Basil Zaharoff, favorite merchant of death of millions of Sunday supplement devotees, complete in Inverness cloak and deerstalker hat boarding the *Blue Train* for a secret destination on the Riviera.

There are flaws in the Gulbenkian production, but only such minor ones as will serve to lend it authenticity and remove it from the realm of truly ineffable perfection. The Gulbenkian Rolls-Royce was one. As all the world knows, the holy and untouchable aspects of "the Finest Car in the World" have been for the sixty-odd years of its existence the squared radiator, distinctive bonnet profile, and Spirit of Ecstasy mascot. In having his *sadenca de ville* styled by Hooper, The Last Magnifico committed the unpardonable offense of having a different and radically *moderne* bonnet incorporated in his car, and earned thereby the sneezes and jeers of True Believers in Rolls-Royce who are legion.

No less avid than their American opposite numbers for the picture-caption cliché, the English papers like to refer to Gulbenkian as "The Last Magnifico," although in a nation so fertile of individualists and so receptive of their caprices as England, it may be doubted if he is the last of anything.

And lest it be said that this chronicle of admiration of things English is biased in a masculine direction, it may be well to include mention of the emergence from amongst the pearl dog-collars and diamond stomachers of truly towering resources of a woman of sufficient character to justify being a repository of liberal means. Let mention be made of Nancy, Lady Astor, born Nancy Langhorne of Virginia, whose acid wit and unabashed wealth made her a picturesque and restive figure for two generations of English politics. Once when electioneering in a particularly depressed area near Liverpool, she took a wailing infant from the arms of a slatternly mother, whereupon the infant became quiet while fondling the peeress' rope of magnificent pearls. "You see," she told her listeners, "the way to keep a child quiet is always to have a pearl necklace or two handy."

The English folklore of wealth, which has the inestimable advantage over the mythology of money elsewhere in the world of having several resident Rothschilds as well as royal dukes who entertained so lavishly that a wine dispatcher was required to direct the distribution of champagne by platoons of footmen, also benefits from a reverse twist of humor, native to its national character and not common to American usage. This is the irony of austerity expressed in the understatement not available to transatlantic export and the creation of a sort of national antihero who suffers privations in the grand manner with which magnificoes of other traditions celebrate affluence.

One concerns the Duke of Devonshire, a favorite with the aforementioned Joseph Bryan as a connoisseur of the preposterous, who heard the cry of creditors baying at his heels and summoned accountants, actuaries, and men at law to devise economies which might banish his visions of Marshalsea gaol for debt and, ultimately, a pauper's grave. Several thousand pounds a year could be saved by a straighter economy in the kitchen; were three nationalities of pastry cooks, French, Danish, and Viennese, necessary?

"Good God," exclaimed the Duke in vexation, "can't a man have a biscuit if he wants it?"

There was also the great manor house afflicted of the times whose family consulted an efficiency expert who, after a prolonged survey, suggested closing the west and south wings and sharing of staff cars by the footmen. These and other unthinkable economies were considered and dismissed. In the end it was decided to suspend the supply of sealing wax in the guest bedrooms.

This type of folk myth, unhappily, has no counterpart in the American saga of riches. Like the Vouvray wines of the Loire, it doesn't travel well.

Confronted with a generation in whose character parsimony and poltroonishness struggle for mastery, we can still contemplate with envy and satisfaction those Americans of a vanished generation of magnificoes. When, as recently as in the automotive age, William K. Vanderbilt ordered the construction of a garage for his Long Island estate he thought not in terms of two cars that is today's hallmark of quivering mediocrity, but commanded space for an even 100 Rolls-Royces, De Dion Boutons, and Simplexes.

Let us rejoice, too, in the recollection of Montana's peerless Senator William Andrews Clark who, when seeking election to the United States Senate at the turn of the century, miscalculated by a comma the population of the city of Butte, Montana, and provided the free distribution among 45,000 enfranchised voters sufficient whisky for 450,000.

And as a salute to an age when rich men knew what they wanted and had no hesitation going after it, let us fire a rocket to the memory of James J. Hill, the greatest railroader of them all, the old bearded king of the Great Northern, who would map an empire of corn and wheat and lumber for generations unborn but would take no back talk from the peasantry. The Great Northern in years gone by ran through a community called Wayzata, Minnesota, a pretty resort village on the storied shores of Lake Minnetonka, patronized by conservative families from Minneapolis and St. Paul, which Hill personally remembered when it was called Pig Eye. Influential summer cottagers at Wayzata complained one day that Jim Hill's switching engines made night hideous near their villas; could he abate their noise? To put Wayzata in its place, which shortly was to be nowhere, Hill ordered the Great Northern's passenger operations to ignore the unhappy town. The depot was moved a mile down the tracks and the fast passenger trains scorched through in such smoke and glory that the first engine under the new order set fire to the town water tank. Wayzata languished on the vine, business went elsewhere, the summer tourists didn't come back. Wayzata was never the same again, thanks to James J. Hill.

Or let us contemplate briefly what, when they were spoken back in 1917, were beyond all argument the most expensive thirteen words ever uttered in the American record. The "I do" in marriage ceremonies may have accounted by indirection for the exchange, acquisition and distribution of greater sums, but for direct and immediate impact Allan Ryan's thirteen words, when brought to the attention of his father, Thomas Fortune Ryan, proved the most expensive.

Thomas Fortune Ryan's married life was not altogether a happy one. His wife, a countess of the Holy Roman Empire and a staunch Catholic like himself, was an invalid for many of the last years of her life, but neither side in the unhappy arrangement would consent to a divorce. In 1917, Mrs. Ryan died and Ryan, by now sixty-six years old, married again within seventeen days of the funeral.

The performance did not please Allan Ryan.

It was, he said at the time, "one of the most disrespectful, disgraceful, and indecent things I've ever heard of."

A decade later when the senior Ryan died leaving a fortune of $135,000,000, Allan Ryan was left two black pearl evening studs valued at perhaps $500. His sentiments about his father had cost him just upwards of $10,000,000 each for their thirteen words.

A short time afterward, however, Allan's brothers, John Barry and Clendenin, saw to it that their disinherited brother should receive $50,000 a year as long as he lived. John Barry Ryan could afford the gesture. At one time he bought Sendano, a two-year-old race horse, for $75,000, a set of six bronze paperweights representing mice, turtles, and donkeys for $6434, five sets of dice at $10 a set, and a gold-washed crucifix for $200.

Like the elder Ryan, the very rich are apt to be touchy about little things and sensitive to trifles. Back in 1930, Mrs. Lytton Ament divorced her husband, Colonel Lytton Ament, head of the Claims Department of the United States Veterans Bureau, in Reno, claiming that the Colonel had been "indifferent, domineering, dictatorial, and very unpleasant during bridge games." Married again and now Mrs. E. R. Thomas, the former Mrs. Ament took up residence in the expensive Pierre Hotel on Fifth Avenue, a millionaire trap of the first order and scene of some of the best-publicized jewel robberies of modern times. Upon one occasion she had to complain to the management of the Pierre about an uncommonly robust party that was being given in the suite above hers while she was giving a musical afternoon for a women's club. "Great masterpieces of art are being played," she said, "and the plaster from the ceiling is coming down on the piano."

Amid the melancholy tally of the rich in our time cowering in sanctimonious timidity behind the barriers of good works and twittering anonymity, there is another notable exception—the late Evalyn Walsh McLean. A woman to be sure, but one uninhibited by even the vaguest notion that it was wrong to have fun with wealth, who left behind her a legacy of magnificence that will live in memory when all the benefices of the Rockefeller Foundation are forgotten.

Evie McLean lived rich and died rich, the latter by a narrow and calculated margin. Her entertainments in Washington, Newport, and Colorado were the most splendid in the American record and no one had a better time at her parties than did the chatelaine of *Friendship,* her Washington mansion. She delighted in titles and tiaras, powdered footmen and ambassadorial protocol, private railway cars and limitless champagne, and she wasn't happy unless she was sharing these things with as many people as she might collect. She was a laugher, an easy touch, an abundant person—and we may not see her like again.

Only research beyond the purview of this volume can determine if the trend of spending in the current generation by Institutions, family foundations, and vast corporations has replaced, in a legitimate degree, the disbursements of the men of sound and disposing mind of only yesterday. Certainly the expenses of vast corporations for entertainment on the expense account are not negligible, but largely to enjoy their status family foundations must deal in benevolences and good works and are therefore not available to appraisal here. Expensive caprice may seem to be centered in the corporate identity of Neiman-Marcus of Dallas but it is still the individual Texan who does the spending. The theme is pregnant with contradictions and paradox.

In this confusion it would seem prudent to confine contemplation to the certifiable past rather than the speculative present and to take comfort from the fiduciary record of Gene Fowler whose aphorism about money on observation platforms of trains is one of the texts of this chapter. Fowler, who while on the staff of the *New York American* had already established a record as one of the bravura expense-account artists of his day, arrived in Los Angeles to work the Hollywood diggings in the middle twenties at a flat salary of $1000 a day. When met at the depot by a studio limousine with a suitable complement of flunkeys on the box, he pointedly ignored this conveyance and went to his hotel in a taxicab.

"I want to arrive in the same style I may depart," he said.

Distrusting the stability of the film industry on the basis of his initial dealings with its principal luminaries, Fowler demanded his pay at the end of each business day, a precaution against the possibility of the studio not being there next morning. Every afternoon an office functionary paid him $1000 in cash and most of it was gone before the next day dawned on Vine Street. In his years in films Fowler estimated that he had earned more than $1,000,000, none of which was around at the time of his death.

Walter Lord, an accredited commentator on the rich and their tribal rituals, inclines to the belief that the years of the ortolans came to an end with the loss of the *Titanic* where so many of the well-to-do of the world departed under auspices of significant decorum and gallantry. Their curtain call from the sloping sun deck, he maintains, was the final salute of a generation that knew how to spend money splendidly both in this world and on the threshold of the next.

In this context it would seem little short of churlish in a British politician of the time to announce that "paying twenty-two hundred dollars for a single suite for a five days' voyage is without any qualification utterly indefensible and morally wrong." It may be the merest casuistry to point out that, for the occupant of the suite, the trip was of longer duration than had been planned. In any event the passenger in question could have done better for himself had he wished, as did Emile Brandeis, an Omaha department store owner, who paid another $4350 for a private promenade deck.

Nowhere, it has been remarked, is moderation so debilitating and destructive of character as in the expenditure of money. The decision to spend excessively on the caprices of their choice is what lent the stature of greatness to most of the people who will be encountered in this book. It was they who validated the lost art of being rich.

Lucius Beebe
Virginia City 1966

Chapter One
Patroons and Parvenus

The Vanderbilts and the Goulds, Builders and Destroyers of Rail-roads . . . The Goulds Dearly Loved a Lawsuit . . . Vanderbilts Couldn't Resist a Nice Sixty-Room Chateau on Fifth Avenue . . . Much of the Loot from Erie Passed Through Gould Hands to the Midas Count de Castellane . . . Everything He Touched Turned to Gold . . . And then Disappeared. . . .

THE NEAREST THING to a royal family that has ever appeared on the American scene was not the three Barrymores who assumed the title from a play in which Ethel, John, and Lionel were starred, but the Vanderbilts. The parallel between the clan founded by the first emergent Commodore Cornelius Van Der Bilt can be drawn on any number of counts. Vanderbilts occupied for approximately three generations the very apex of social and tangible splendor reserved in other countries for regnant royalty. They seized dynastic succession from the palsied hands of other and previous social and financial monarchs who faltered in their exercise of power. When they took over the social domination of New York they took over, too, the perquisites and properties of royalty on a scale appropriate to hereditary and acquired power. The Mrs. Vanderbilt of the moment was undisputed queen of the nation's drawing rooms and ballrooms. From her predecessor on the throne she usurped the simplicity of being known merely as *the* Mrs. Vanderbilt. First names were superfluous, as are last names in the royal houses of Europe. And most of all, they lived and acted like royalty. Their palaces and summer palaces, their balls and routs and banquetings, their royal alliances and their vendettas, their armies of servitors, partisans, and sycophants, their love affairs, scandals, and shortcomings, all were the stuff of an imperial routine. To be socially accepted by the appropriate Vanderbilt of the moment was the equivalent of making one's bow at the Court of St. James's. There were even pretenders, mostly at safe remove, like Mrs. Potter Palmer who received on a raised dais in her Chicago palace in almost precisely the way the pretender to the throne of France maintained a court in exile in England.

From whatever angle you choose to regard them, the Vanderbilts had style. They showed Americans how to live, as nobody has done as a cohesive family group before or since. Like the royal houses of France or Portugal or Prussia or Roumania, they began as parvenus, but unlike many royal successions, they survived in high estate to become grandees and magnificoes. They were not much loved; they were widely feared and respected and they were envied on a scale to dwarf the human imagining. It was the envy of their inferiors, universal, consuming, explicit, and unabashed, that made them what they were.

For the most part, too, the members of this favored clan of acquisitive and ostentatious men and women cared little for public suffrage. The "public be damned" canard pinned on William Henry Vanderbilt by quoting him out of context was a commentary on the malicious yellow journalism of an irresponsible time, but, and in more decorous terms, it fairly represented their social and political philosophy. They looked after their own. The family was so well established as reasonable employers that during the railway troubles of 1877 a majority of New York Central employees refused to go on strike and were well rewarded for their loyalty, but the railroad management acted out of enlightened self-interest and not philanthropy. The Vanderbilts were feudal.

And, although they have, in their turn, vacated the high place they occupied in the American scheme of things, they have left their impress forever on the national awareness. When Wayne Andrews came to do his not-too-admiring story of the Vanderbilt family and all its works, he called it *The Vanderbilt Legend* and he was right. They were legendary people and the stuff of America's most enduring saga of wealth and wealthy ways.

Nor were the Vanderbilts regarded as a sort of royalty in their own country alone. When the Commodore, first of the line, made the grand tour of the Continent aboard his yacht *North Star,* the stupefying grandeur of this conveyance translated itself automatically in the Russian mind into a property of royalty (what else?), and the Grand Duke Constantine placed at his disposal transport and privileges at St. Petersburg that would, in the normal course of events, be accorded only a ruling family.

In London, where the haughtier aristocrats of Victoria's era turned up their noses at the Commodore as an *arriviste,* the *London Daily News* (not to be confused with the *Illustrated London News*) chilled the marrow of occupants of the House of Lords by seeing in the Vanderbilts the wave of the future. The Howards and the Percys, said the paper in a burst of unwonted republicanism, were on their way out and Englishmen of all ranks would do well to observe in the Commodore the image of the world's rulers in the almost immediate future. The word parvenu, the *News* declaimed, should be regarded not as derogation, but as a term of honor.

These were sentiments that, it may reasonably be supposed, did not find an audible echo in Buckingham Palace, but they showed which way the wind was blowing.

The first well-to-do people in the colonies and settlements that were presently to become the Unites States had very little money. This is not intended as a contrived paradox but a factual statement based on the circumstances that, until the rise of mercantile dynasties and hierarchies of banking and manufacture in the nineteenth century, most wealth was in tangibles: land, homesteads and mansions, livestock, clothes, jewels, carriages, slaves, and household furnishings. A very small proportion of the private resources of the nation's early years was in gold or silver, other than family plate, and almost none in banknotes, stocks, or other negotiable securities or paper.

A Virginia tidewater planter might be a man of towering wealth in the community yet handle at the most a few thousand pounds in gold in a year. Currency was in use among gentlemen almost exclusively for purposes of gambling and occasional travel away from home. Even foreign trade which secured for him the manufactures and produce of England and France, garments, cloth, wines and spirits, and articles of personal and household adornment from London and Paris were largely paid for through commission agents with the products of the plantation: flax, hemp, cotton, and tobacco. A city dweller in Boston or Philadelphia might have more occasion for the possession of currency but it was seldom, save in the case of professional bankers, a preponderant element of his resources.

Neither the tidewater planter nor the Yankee homesteader in Newburyport or Newport needs the sympathy of posterity for not keeping a checking account of the dimensions—a minimum of $25,000—once required by the Fifth Avenue Bank, New York's most conservative such institution, that maintained open fireplaces and roll-top desks long after other depositories had given their approval to glass and brick facades and tellers' windows without grilles.

They did well enough if you take for example Robert Carter, who was known from his regal ostentation as King Carter, of Westmoreland, Virginia. Carter owned more than 300,000 acres of the finest grazing land, in excess of 1000 slaves, a flourishing ironworks, and a flour mill, not to mention his stately residence, *Nomini Hall*, which had a white and gold ballroom and cellars of Madeira that were the envy of squires for a hundred miles in any direction. Carter was not only a plutocrat but, it is pleasant to recall, a scholar who studied law and music in his middle years, collected a splendid private library, and could match Latin tags with visiting divines and other gentlemen from London. Yet the records of King Carter's affairs suggest that, although he was reckoned one of the wealthiest colonials of his age, his actual cash transactions only infrequently exceeded 1000 pounds gold a year.

Liquid assets at the time we mention simply didn't have the appeal for the wealthy of vast resources of indigo, terrapin ponds, London small-clothes, fine libraries, and stables of blooded race horses. Even for the gambling which was so great a preoccupation with gentlemen in the South before the Revolution, and for that matter after, gold was not a necessity, and slaves, horses, real estate, and family mansions passed as currency at gaming tables where the stakes might well be factually ruinous to an unlucky player.

By the end of the eighteenth century cash resources of wealth were beginning to make themselves visible and felt, especially in New York, where the ancient patroon regime based on manorial lands along the Hudson was falling before an incursion of Yankee entrepreneurs, and in Boston where the China trade was forming the basis of immense mercantile fortunes, vestigial traces of which are still perceptible to this day in family trusts administered by generations of lawyers whose professions and the very accounts they oversee have been inherited since the days of clipper ships.

Mansions at Newburyport and in Louisburg Square maintained in aristocratic magnificence with portraits by Copley, pipes of the best Madeira, and coaches from the finest carriage makers of London required other mediums of exchange than those represented by the triangle trade in rum, Negroes, and molasses, and tradesmen in French brandy and Hudson Bay sables demanded settlement of their accounts annually in gold and silver.

On Beacon Hill arose a generation of magnificoes whose gestures of ostentation and splendid entertainment were the peer of those in many of the great houses of the English countryside, although more modest retinues of servants established a lower status rating in the colonies and was to continue to do so until on both sides of the Atlantic servants as a ponderable class ceased to exist at all.

Typical of the collective Medici of Beacon Street as the eighteenth century drew to a close and republican government was being reflected in unrepublican opulence was Thomas Handasyd Perkins, a crony of Massachusetts' splendid governor John Hancock, a fancier of the better things of life, and possessed of an endurance where bottles were concerned that would have enchanted a squire out of Fielding.

Perkins was in the habit of driving in state through Boston's narrow and muddy byways in a splendidly rocking coach with gilded coat armor on its panels and two footmen behind in dark blue liveries with white stockings, thus antedating by approximately a century the house livery of the New York Astors at the height of Mrs. Astor's social ascendancy. When Perkins rode abroad there were not only coachmen and footmen but equally handsomely uniformed outriders and a small mounted court of galloping exquisites, gentlemen in attendance on the private payroll of the great merchant.

Perkins' waistcoats of woven gold, crimson coats, and magnificent wigs were made to order by Old Burlington Gardens tradesmen who every year sent their representatives to solicit his custom and fit the finished accessories. His wonderful gardens of rare fruit trees and exotic shrubs were tended by a corps of imported gardeners whom the owner paid the unheard-of sum of $10,000 a year, an amount which in itself presupposes adequate liquid resources, and the whole pattern of life of Perkins and the merchant princes in the China trade whom he represented bespoke a style of commerce that had advanced a measurable degree from the simple barter of goods and services of the earlier days in the Old Colony.

In the light of the status that was to be established by subsequent conveyances and vehicles of locomotion, notably the steam yacht, the coach-and-four, the private Pullman Palace car, and, eventually and in lesser degree, the automobile, it is instructive to note that in the pre-industrial age a man's standing in the elegance sweepstakes was materially determined by his carriages. Keeping carriage-company was the first expression of the later American determination to keep up with or, preferably, to surpass the Joneses. Keeping one's own carriage in colonial New York was a notable evidence of secure finances and Maria de Peyster Spratt, whose husband loomed large in the ranks of the Common Council where he was president, drew attention to her worldly ways by being the first woman to own her own coach-and-four. The Van Rensselaers, Schermerhorns, Von Stades, and other patroons imported Dutch coaches, artifacts which, notably inferior to the later English importations, rolled through the Broad Way and the Bouwerie with a maximum of discomfort but reassuring solidity. In 1760 a young blood of the period, Levinius Clarkson, imported the first London-built cabriolet and attracted favorable comment by the handsome green liveries of his footmen. Mrs. James Beekman, whose family name was to be perpetuated in an ambitious uptown residential address two centuries later, owned a coach that established her social standing beyond all dispute. In Philadelphia, at the time it was occupied by General Howe and his British regiments, there were known to be more than 100 miscellaneous, privately owned carriages in town, a statistic of wealth the British didn't overlook, but only two of them were landaus, driven by Thomas Willing and William Peters. Sir William Howe commandeered for his headquarters during the investment of the city the Cadwalader mansion, but scorned the modest Cadwalader stables in favor of a sensationally handsome coach and pair belonging to Mrs. Israel Pemberton.

The trend toward mercantile fortunes rather than landed wealth patterned on that of the great landholdings of hereditary aristocrats in England had its origins in the seafaring fortunes centering in Boston, Salem, and Newburyport in the eighteenth century, most of which easily survived the American Revolution. By the beginning of the industrial age in the fourth decade of the nineteenth century, vast landholders were going into eclipse, although as late as 1838 a visitor to Stephen Van Rensselaer, last of the Hudson River patroons on a grand scale, estimated the magnate's annual income from rents and purely agricultural enterprises at more than $1,000,000. This was then such an exception to the trend of the times as to be widely remarked upon. The Van Rensselaers, moreover, participated in the status competition scarcely at all. They lived by the simple country standards of their forebears, kept early or country hours, inaugurated little ceremony in their entertaining, and, like their frugal counterparts on Beacon Hill in Boston, lived on the income of their income.

The new wealth of mercantile and industrial New York thought the Van Rensselaers very dull folk indeed.

The acquisition of personal wealth in colonial times and for fully three quarters of a century after the foundation of the Republic was a comparatively leisurely occupation whether it manifested itself in New England or in tidewater Virginia or in the Deep South where the Mississippi River traffic converged on New Orleans to produce a rich and aloof aristocracy of Creoles that went into decline but by no means disappeared with the Civil War. Making fortunes, building estates, rearing mansions, and establishing social status was an unhurried business spanning entire generations and continued to be so, roughly speaking, until the advent of the railroads, which made their appearance in appreciable force in the 1850s, and until the great industrial expansion in the North that was part of the economic pattern of the Civil War itself.

Ostentations of wealth until the emergence of a new class of rich American in the 1860s were private. Fantastic luxury might be the hallmark of the vast plantations of the Old Dominion and the Deep South, but even when the wealth of planters and cotton brokers went north to Saratoga Springs which was practically its only showcase away from home, southern money was never characterized by grandiose gestures of hospitality or entertainment. A southern gentleman's greatest extravagance was usually in the form of gambling, a preoccupation which might be indulged without let or hindrance either at home or at Saratoga but which occasioned small public remark other than to enter the realm of regional folk-lore. Again, gambling was private; it concerned nobody but its immediate participants and there were no newspaper paragraphers or society reporters to fill the wire services with accounts of spectacular losses or gains at whist, poker, or roulette.

Hospitality, too, was a private concern. The most magnificent entertainment imaginable in the private ballrooms of plantation or town house could hardly accommodate more than a few hundred persons at the most. Dinner parties, suppers, balls, and other organized routs were not acceptable in public premises such as hotels and restaurants until almost the turn of the century, a circumstance which limited the potential scope of spending and strictly inhibited its public record in newspapers or the periodical press.

Oceangoing steam yachts, vast stables of blooded race horses and thoroughbreds, mistresses of celebrity either tacitly or explicitly admitted, private garages with facilities for as many as 100 imported motorcars, privately chartered railroad trains and enormous country seats in Newport, in North Carolina, or on the peninsula south of San Francisco were all in the unforeseen future.

In general terms, ostentation arrived with the Civil War.

Nor did it wait for a cessation of hostilities to make itself known.

It is a matter of record so well known to students of the American social and economic scene as to constitute a cliché, that the Civil War, especially in the North, commanded nowhere near the total dedication at all levels to the war effort that was to characterize either of the world wars of the next century. Business was very much as usual in New York, Boston, and Chicago. Easy money made its by no means shrinking appearance in hotels, theaters, and restaurants, and the social awareness which made such ostentations unthinkable on the part of civilians in 1917 or 1941 simply didn't exist.

Ex post facto analysts have attempted to point an unsavory moral at civilians who in the Civil War years not only stayed well away from the battlefields but began the accumulation of great fortunes on the basis of war materiel, arms and explosives, railroad and ocean transport, horses, mules, blankets, saddles, and, above all, food for the Union armies. Jay Gould, August Belmont, and even the elder J. P. Morgan have been the targets of unfavorable comment for their accumulation of wartime fortunes, but the dis-approval of moralists didn't manifest itself until the Civil War gen-eration of what would later have been called profiteers were in their graves and beyond all censure.

No disgrace and only the envy of the less perspicacious and for-tunate attached to making money on either side in the Civil War. A man was a fool if he fought when he didn't have to. He was smart if he stayed safely at prudent remove from the shooting and made himself a tidy pile. That patriotism and moral fervor ran no higher in the Confederacy is evidenced by the circumstance that the holds of blockade runners which raced to Wilmington and Charleston from the loading ports of Bermuda and the Bahamas were filled with French dresses and parasols, champagne, vintage cognac, gentlemen's gloves, top hats, lace, perfumery, *foie gras,* and danc-ing slippers, and that cargoes of guns, ammunition, and other war matériel, even morphine and surgical instruments, were kept at a bare minimum. The Confederacy went to hell in style.

If evidence were needed to the effect that no social obloquy attached to civilian activity during the height of hostilities it may be found in the fact that 1864 saw a flurry of excitement every-where in the North occasioned by the opening of a new and greatly enlarged race track at Saratoga and that universal satisfaction rather than indignation greeted its inaugural. "William R. Travers, John Hunter, and Leonard Jerome, the men behind the project, were not the sort to jeopardise their substantial reputations by support-ing anything dubious or subversive of the general morale," wrote Richmond Barrett. "A public-spirited trio, they were proud of Sara-toga and trying their best to pull the place out of the doldrums."

Indignant commentators, attempting to judge the era according to the moral standards of a century later, are wasting their breath. The generation that was factually concerned couldn't have cared less.

Commodore Cornelius Vanderbilt was sixty-eight years old when he began to take a serious interest in the affairs of the New York & Harlem Railroad, an age that is not only in itself impressive, but worth remarking in light of the fact that retirement is today obligatory for presidents of the New York Central Railroad, the Harlem's successor, at the age of sixty-five. Under the terms of today's corporate requirements he would have been put out to pasture three years before he even cast an acquisitive eye on a railroad property. It is food for contemplation.

The time lag thus represented may have a personal explanation since, in the three decades that railroads had been in operation before the Commodore entered the lists, the silk-hatted and gold-headed cane-carrying railroad president was already emergent as one of the most enviable of business types. A source of the Commodore's distrust of the steam-train brigades, as they were then known, could have been the circumstance that in 1833 while riding the Camden & Amboy Railroad, a primeval streak of rust that was later to be gathered to the mighty Pennsylvania, he had been involved at firsthand in one of the first railroad accidents of record. He sustained fractured ribs and was otherwise barbarously handled when the carriage in which he was riding went into the ditch. That the railroads then occupied the role later assumed by the flying machine as an agency of wholesale slaughter of their patrons is suggested by the fact that all the other occupants of the carriage were killed outright.

It took the Commodore thirty years to overcome his distaste for accelerated surface travel, during which time railroads were born and died, went bankrupt or disappeared in great numbers, taking with them the investments of many men who risked their savings on a highly chancy enterprise. By 1862 many of the bugs that had troubled the operation of the first steam carriers had been ironed out. The effectiveness of rail transport was also being demonstrated in the conduct and logistics of the first war in which railroads played an important part. In the interim, the Commodore had acquired something better than $40,000,000 from his steamboat ventures while other men were losing comparable sums, in the aggregate, on land transportation. Vanderbilt's thirty-year reluctance to enter the field was one of the best of his many and conspicuously successful investments.

As long as the Vanderbilt dynasty lasted, which was approximately four generations before its wealth and prestige became hopelessly fragmented, its members illustrated in their every aspect of acquisitiveness and splendor the popular ideal of aristocracy. Few Vanderbilts were concerned with public affairs. Fewer were associated with virtuous causes. With the exception of Vanderbilt University and some trifling benevolences at Yale University, the family as a whole eschewed good works. Their concerns were with the making and subsequent spending of a spectacular family fortune, both of which they achieved with a panache of splendor and high-handedness without parallel in the record.

That the family fortune at the zenith of its intact magnitude of $200,000,000 at the death of William Henry Vanderbilt was not as great as the subsequent fortunes of Fords and Rockefellers is no derogation. The Vanderbilts with notable singleness of purpose spent their resources on themselves in spacious gestures of material satisfaction without recourse to the sanctimonious attitudes implicit in vast charities and in family foundations devoted to good works.

The scope of their indulgence embraced all the accepted agencies for the expenditure of substantial sums without hope of financial or spiritual increment. It expressed itself in lavish entertainments, fantasies of architecture in the form of palatial residences on Fifth Avenue, in Newport, Asheville, and other strategically located points of the landscape, in oceangoing steam yachts, private railroad cars to fill the New York Central coachyards, titled sons-in-law, art galleries, armies of domestics, pitched battles for social acceptance and domination, racing stables, 100-car garages, and matrimonial alliances with princely houses overseas.

When other and later magnificoes wanted schooling in spending money, they turned to Vanderbilts. Some of them, avid for postgraduate instruction, married Vanderbilts. This was as high as education could go.

᚛᚜ ᚛᚜ ᚛᚜

No family's collective genius for expressing itself in material possessions, neither that of the uninhibited generations of Vanderbilts nor the haunted inheritance of the McLeans, Walshes, and Beales, which found its apotheosis in the Hope Diamond, exceeded the talent of the heirs of Jay Gould for spending money. Whether they got their money's worth is a matter of opinion. Often enough, as in the case of Anna Gould's purchase of a husband in the person of Count Boni de Castellane, it seemed to qualified observers that Goulds were conditioned to buying a pig in a poke. On the other hand, there was so much Gould money around that it didn't make much difference. It was nearly endless and no Gould could be accused of keeping it out of circulation.

If there was any validity in the economic philosophy of the exiled Bradley-Martins that the well-to-do were obligated to spend freely in order to provide employment in hard times, the Goulds collectively and singly would seem to have justified themselves, in good times as well as bad.

Jay Gould, founder of the family fortunes, was without a doubt a charter member of the robber barons club and what Stewart Holbrook characterized as a "man of disaster." He made money out of other people's misfortunes and often as not the misfortunes were contrived by Gould himself so that he might salvage something from the debris and destruction which marked his going almost everywhere.

His associates in business, the extrovert Jim Fisk, sanctimonious Uncle Dan'l Drew, and the various members of President Grant's official family whom he hoodwinked and seduced, were clearly scoundrels. There was nothing of the empire builder, the pioneer industrialist, or bringer of order out of chaos about any of them. They lived by chaos and Jim Fisk, at least, died of it, riotously and in good time for the morning editions. Even in his own generation, which was conspicuously tolerant in such matters, Gould didn't bask in general acceptance or the regard of the community. Much of the time he was on the lam, hiding from mobs and sheriff's officers. During the last years of his life he lived on borrowed time, racked by pulmonary ailments, dyspepsia, and a variety of malaises which would have floored a less vital man early in the game. He was an insomniac as well, and the bodyguards at his rather modest Fifth Avenue home were accustomed to keep him company in the night watches while he strolled under the gas lamps, occasionally spitting blood into a fine cambric handkerchief and always planning new assaults, invasions, and forays where there was money to be snatched and looted.

Jay Gould was tireless in evil and his obituaries, when finally the old fellow with the scythe caught up with him, remarked that he was a man without a friend. Probably not true but at least symptomatic.

Gould in his lifetime took small pleasure from the vast sums of money which were attracted to his bank accounts and portfolios. His tastes were neither frivolous nor robust and a man who always traveled with a personal physician and a private chef skilled in the preparation of diet food had small inducement to the things that gave pleasure, say, to Diamond Jim Brady or the insatiably vital J. P. Morgan. It is notable that Morgan was one of the pallbearers at Gould's funeral.

The Gould heirs didn't begin to get in their licks at his fortune until later. Gould died in 1892 and it wasn't until 1896 that his family made its first bid for attention in the spendthrift sweepstakes by opening *Georgian Court,* the first of several Gould manorial residences, at Lakewood, New Jersey.

In terms of his contemporaries and peers and his own resources of wealth, the founder of the Gould dynasty lived in comparative simplicity and a minimum of ostentation. The Gould town house at the northeast corner of Fifth Avenue and Forty-seventh Street, a location which afforded the inmates a matchless vantage point from which to view the greatest of the many hotel fires of its time when the Windsor Hotel just across the street burned with the loss of many lives, was an understatement of modesty, as many New Yorkers can remember who knew it in the thirties as a shop stocked with Armenian rugs and hand-me-down light fixtures. It would not have served as gatekeeper's lodge to any of the lordly Vanderbilt mansions on the west side of Fifth Avenue a few blocks to the north. Certainly it was not one of the "haunts of iniquity" castigated by the Rev. De Witt Talmage whose notions of Babylonish excess were "men in high places smoking cigarets with their feet on Turkish divans." No. 579 Fifth Avenue was a no-nonsense Victorian home at a good address and assuredly no entry in the elegance sweepstakes of its era.

More in the millionaire manner was *Lyndhurst,* Gould's country seat at Irvington-on-Hudson with its 500 acres of meticulously landscaped grounds with lawns, rare shrubbery, carefully tended drives, and ornamental waters, all approached through massive gateways manned night and day by an army of private security guards. A masterpiece suggesting that the owner was an admirer of Horace Walpole's school of Gothic gloom crowned a grassy slope, with forty rooms behind crenelated towers, Gothic pointed windows, and a tall, ivy-grown belfry. The whole facade and atmosphere of *Lyndhurst* was one of Carpathian gloom and mystery, a setting for Dracula well suited to the owner's reputation in financial circles as a bird of ill omen.

Here amidst a comprehensive network of telephone extensions, burglar alarms, and other private communications systems were the conventional gatehouses, servants' quarters at some remove from the main structure, carriage houses, stables, a swimming pool and bowling alley, laundry, and yacht landing. Ponderous, built for doomsday, *Lyndhurst* was the solid and abiding tangible symbol of the dynasty of Goulds that its owner might establish to pass the Gould name to generations to come. Aside from the conventional amenities of comfort and stylized luxury, *Lyndhurst* embraced Jay Gould's one indulgence of expensive caprice, a magnificent system of greenhouses where he grew and experimented with the largest collection of rare and exotic orchids in the world. There were upwards of 8000 orchids imported "from beyond Trebizond" and 2000 azaleas, all tended and cherished by an army of educated gardeners supervised by Gould himself. Before the emergence of Nero Wolfe, Jay Gould was the world's most famous and certainly its richest orchid fancier.

Gould's other indulgence was a series of vessels ranging from the small steam pinnace aboard which it was for many years his custom to commute to downtown Manhattan, sometimes with Cyrus Field for company, to the extravagantly beautiful seagoing yacht *Atalanta* which very definitely was an entry in the elegance sweepstakes and was the peer in its every aspect of magnificence with its contemporaries: James Gordon Bennett's *Namouna*, J. P. Morgan's *Corsair*, and William Backhouse Astor's *Nourmahal*.

Atalanta cost $1000 a week to maintain, a truly staggering sum which might be represented by approximately a quarter of a million annually in today's depreciated currency. Guests were conveyed from the landing to *Atalanta's* gangway by cutters manned by ten oars uniformed in the Gould colors of white and blue and were piped over the side in naval style and ceremony. Oriental rugs, plush, rare boiseries, gold-mono-grammed velvets, costly draperies, and opulent furniture vied for the admiration of the beholder with a truly fine library, for Gould was a discerning reader, and a built-in upright piano in the music room. In the galley supervised by an English chief steward who had seen service with the Earl of Rosebery, French chefs labored over culinary masterpieces for Gould's guests while a specially gifted pastry cook from Vienna dedicated his entire time to the confection of the ladyfingers which were the sole delicacy permitted Gould himself by a rigid diet.

Because Jay Gould's own generation of archmillionaires, many of them as ruthless and rapacious as the debaucher of Erie but more sanctimonious of appearance, refused him admission to the New York Yacht Club, Gould founded his own squadron, the American Yacht Club, a stratagem for circumventing old-line aristocrats which was practiced with even more spectacular success when Gould and the other men of towering but recent wealth built their own opera house, the Metropolitan, which shortly put the older Academy of Music with all its stuffy attitudes of superiority out of business.

Perhaps, because Jay Gould was one of its general staff, a brief chronicle of this campaign which ended in one of the two or three most spectacular ambuscades in New York's social history may not be amiss here.

Until the year 1883 New York's upper-case musical circles had been contracted in a stoutly defended enclave represented by the production of grand opera at the old Academy of Music in Irving Place. Its boxes, entailed from generation to generation, were the Maginot Line of defense against the onslaughts of new money, and behind its red plush ramparts massed Livingstons, Barclays, Barlows, Beekmans, Schermerhorns, Schuylers, and Duers ranged themselves in hollow square under the joint command of Pierre Lorillard, August Belmont, and Robert L. Cutting. The premises of the Academy of Music permitted only eighteen really advantageous boxes and its structure precluded enlargement, an arrangement which perfectly suited its archaic patronage of breeding instead of money, and conservatism instead of ostentation. Even when William H. Vanderbilt offered $30,000 for occupancy of one of the momentarily available boxes, the hollow square was impervious to assault.

Inevitably the stratagem evolved by Jay Gould in the founding of the American Yacht Club suggested itself. Gould himself was involved to the great social advantage of his family in a group of insurgents which included such perfumed names as William Rockefeller, Darius Ogden Mills, George F. Baker, Collis P. Huntington, and whole shoals of Astors, Roosevelts, and Goelets who were enchanted to join an insurrection that promised once and for all to stamp out a snobbishness of senility in favor of a brave new snobbishness of solvency. Instead of the Academy of Music's parsimonious allowance of eighteen boxes, the new Metropolitan Opera was to have twice that number. The real estate on which it rose at Broadway from Thirty-ninth to Fortieth streets cost $600,000 and the auditorium itself $430,000, and when its boxes, ownership of which cost a tidy $60,000 each, were occupied on opening night, the occupants represented an aggregate wealth estimated by the newspapers of the land at $540,000,000. The circle of boxes was inevitably known as the "Diamond Horseshoe."

In every way the new opera had the advantage in fire power, reserves, terrain, and logistics over the ancient bluebloods of Astor Place and from the beginning the issue was never in doubt among informed observers. One of the few who did not see the handwriting on the wall was Mrs. Paran Stevens, wife of the "Prince of Hoteliers" who was proprietor of the Fifth Avenue Hotel and a notable aspirant for social honors via the cultural agency of music and good works. Mrs. Stevens owed her allegiance to the Academy but when, on October 22, 1883, the two rival temples of culture opened in the social battle of the century, Mrs. Stevens took the precaution of attending both premieres. In less than two seasons the Academy was humbled and went out of business.

Participation in the rout of the patroons and his association with the winners was of enormous social advantage to Jay Gould. His family found itself in the company of no fewer than five Vanderbilt box holders, and Whitneys, Goelets, Drexels, Rockefellers, Morgans, and Bakers in platoons, companies, and phalanxes. It was on the basis of their joint participation in the great victory at Broadway and Thirty-ninth that J. Pierpont Morgan assented, when the time came, to being a pallbearer for Jay Gould, a posthumous distinction, but one that was never discounted by surviving members of his family.

Jay Gould had six children, George Jay, a railroad president himself and director of a number of steam carriers who died in 1923; Helen Miller Gould, who became Mrs. Finley J. Shepard; Edwin, chairman of the board of the St. Louis Southwestern Railroad;

Howard, an expatriate who early in the game removed to England; Anna, who became successively the Countess de Castellane and Marchioness of Tallyrand; and Frank Jay, sportsman, turf enthusiast, Francophile, and finally proprietor of the Palais de la Méditerranée, the superb gambling resort at Cannes.

All the Goulds were present at their father's deathbed. It was one of the few moments that, for years to come, was to see them united in anything except the supreme family talent for vast expenditures.

The Gould men, notably George, Edwin, and Frank Jay, inherited in addition to what may vulgarly be described as a bundle a considerable degree of their father's executive competence and were railroad men of consequence and ability, but that is an aspect of their fortunes which is not the concern of this book. Some of the elder Gould's genius for chaos also descended upon George, who in the late nineties went to war with the all-powerful Pennsylvania Railroad and spent more than $12,000,000 securing an entry for the railroads of the Gould system into Pittsburgh. That the practical ill-will and malevolence of earlier railroading hadn't entirely disappeared from the Gould purview is suggested by the fact that during this encounter the Pennsylvania management ordered to be cut down every Western Union telegraph pole along thousands of miles of its right-of-way. Western Union was then a Gould property.

Some idea of the magnitude of the Gould estate, the management and administration of which was largely left to George Gould, may be gathered from the fact that, in addition to and over and above the private fortune of $82,000,000 largely in cash and in liquid assets left by Jay Gould, there were parcels of real estate in Louisiana which later brought in better than $12,000,000, while the control was vested in the Gould family of corporations capitalized for $350,000,000 with an additional $291,000,000 in bonds. The Gould empire of communications was in overwhelming measure in the form of railroads, with 8500 miles of main-line and secondary trackage, but there was also the

Western Union Telegraph Company as a minor source of revenue and authority.

In 1902, George Gould was heard to complain that his duties included the administration of business ventures employing 112,375 employees at a monthly payroll of $4,994,000, take or leave a few thousands for seasonal variations and business fluctuations from bonanza to borasca and back.

It was not the habit of the various members of the Gould family to take money as a serious matter, and sums running into tens of millions circulated from their private banking and investment accounts to those of the Gould corporations without serious question by any of the heirs or beneficiaries. George Gould seldom considered it necessary to apprise his brothers and sisters of any transaction involving less than $50,000,000 and he was sometimes absent-minded about these. No Gould, according to W. A. Powers, chronicler of their impetuous and gilded destinies, ever had any notion from year to year what he or she or the other members of the family might be worth collectively or severally. It was a state of chaos that could only have been understandable to Midas, King of Phrygia, and in 1912, doubtless because he was bored with the whole thing, George Gould in a whimsical moment burned all the family books and records. This casual pyrotechnic gesture disposed, for the moment anyway, of the headaches implicit in well over half a billion dollars' worth of corporate and private resources.

It was also a gesture entirely typical of the Goulds.

A certain amount of confusion was the by-product of this simplification of the family affairs, and sums of money that in other families would be felt worth keeping track of, disappeared for years at a time. George at one time advanced his brother Frank $3,000,000 from the family funds with which to modernize the International Great Northern Railroad in Texas, but no memorandum was made of the transaction and it didn't get into the record for nearly twenty years.

In a similarly vague manner peculiar to really rich millionaires, Helen Gould was never entirely sure how much she paid for rebuilding *Lyndhurst,* one of the family estates, at Irvington-on-Hudson and was mildly surprised when she learned that she had sunk better than $15,000,000 in its baronial acres. "I thought it was more than that," she is reported to have said when she saw the bill.

The conduct of the Gould railroads was of a piece with that of their personal fortunes, and the management of one carrier never knew until it was told from New York whether it was operating at a profit or showing a startling amount of red ink. Deficits in the revenues of one carrier such as Wabash were carried on the books of another, perhaps the Missouri Pacific, and properties showed huge losses or equally impressive profits at the whimsical caprice of whatever Gould might momentarily be interested in its conduct.

The collective Gould attitude toward money was that there was so much floating around that it was hardly worth while to keep track of it. Sums in the tens of millions disappeared from sight without explanation and might, or might not, turn up at some later date in the family's scatterbrained bookkeeping.

Now and then, as a family, they were united in common bonds of outrage as when Anna's brothers moved to cut off her seemingly illimitable expenses in the form of Boni de Castellane. In the interim they sued each other on the slightest provocation or none. They sued Goulds and they sued outsiders. Whole law offices were preoccupied for years on end with Gould litigation over fancied slights and imagined insults, and as late as the 1950s, when Gould resources were beginning to show signs of wear and tear, a group of Goulds still united in a ferocious assault upon a Hearst coated-paper periodical for no more than intimating that Frank Jay Gould had fun with his money.

ഐ·ഐ·ഐ

As has been remarked, Jay Gould and his family were not the most attractive of American millionaires in the nineteenth century. Socially the Goulds were unacceptable over a longer term of probation than most *arrivistes* and never did make the grade in the upper-case significance of the word Society. A crude, quarrelsome, shifty, and evasive family, they started from scratch and ended not far from it, but one quality which infected the other rich men of his era never was part of Jay himself: he was totally lacking in the sanctimonious overtones of religion and morality that drove J. P. Morgan to association in a big way with Anglican bishops and suggested that crusty old Commodore Vanderbilt, the lustiest pirate of them all, whine hymns on his deathbed.

Jay Gould, as somebody said of a later rascal, was scrupulously dishonest and made no pretense at anything else. His was a character complementary to that of his associate, Jim Fisk, whose happy motto for living was "Let each man carry out his own dead."

The Goulds being what they were, it was altogether appropriate that the most notorious titled marriage of an entire generation should be that of a Gould heiress to a sensationally flamboyant bounder who looted, rooked, pillaged, and sponged off his in-laws until he became the prototypal adventurous foreign nobleman preying on the fortunes of unsophisticated American millionaires. Boni de Castellane was the living caricature of what the American newspaper-reading public envisioned when they thought of a degenerate, titled, hand-kissing little foreign cad. His stature was diminutive; he reeked of perfume, engaged in duels of a strictly theatrical order, and snowed his naïve American victims with the manners and affectation of a *vieille noblesse* that was already an anachronism in his native France.

Anywhere but amidst the Goulds, Boni de Castellane was strictly for the birds. Anna Gould, a hard-eyed, grim-faced woman with a powerful urge to be a marchioness or better, thought him the answer to a maiden's prayer. They were a perfect match.

"My ancestors were in the habit of exercising their noble prerogative of coining money," was one of Boni's favorite boasts. Boni maintained the tradition with scrupulous devotion, using the Goulds as a private mint on such a grandiose scale as to bug the eyes of the beholders. As a social burglar he was of Jimmy Valentine dimensions.

Boniface, Count de Castellane, was born in 1867 in Provence and brought up in the manner of the French nobility of his day, that is to say as a cross between poet and a panhandler, at the ancient family seat, the Château de Rochecotte. He met Anna Gould in Paris at the salon of a common acquaintance in 1894 and at once determined to make a conquest of a woman whose family bore a reasonable resemblance to the United States Treasury. To this end he shortly turned up in New York, penniless, to be sure, but full of optimism.

A compatriot, Charles Raoul Duval, grubstaked him in his matrimonial venture much as a mining prospector might be grubstaked by a backer who, in the event of his striking it rich, would share the proceeds on a percentage basis. Duval underwrote Boni's expenses on a trip to Newport, and, on the basis of his title, manners, and unquestioned charm, De Castellane was soon moving in the wealthy circles affected by the Gould family. It shortly became a matter of widespread understanding, although the match was not officially announced, that he was betrothed to the Gould heiress.

De Castellane was already possessed of champagne tastes, and the lordly ways of the Goulds convinced him that a marriage with Anna would be no mistake.

To entertain his prospective brother-in-law in a style befitting the impending alliance between a Gould heiress and the haberdashery of old Chateau de Rochecotte, George Gould chartered a private train to take a party of invited guests to participate in a winter sports carnival at Quebec. We have seen how this was the period of the most splendid and ornate ascendancy of the private railroad car, and the entire train of chartered special equipment was the quintessential sublimation of its ostentatious elegance.

The train chartered by George Gould was one which had recently been among the more sensational exhibits at the World's Columbian Exposition at Chicago where it had been entered by the Pullman Palace Car-Building Company in competition with the almost equally effulgent display of the rival and hated car-building firm of Webster Wagner, a New York associate of the Vanderbilts who had ironically been killed in an accident aboard one of his own cars on the Vanderbilt-owned New York Central & Hudson River Railroad.

The Pullman cars were five in number, of similar external *décor,* designed to be used *en suite* as a self-sustaining unit and rented for $500 a day plus carrying charges, usually eighteen full first-class fares per car, of the carriers over whose lines they passed. There was a club car named *Marchena,* whose interior economy included a Mooresque barber shop whose Kochs patent chair reposed under a dome of many-colored glass; a diner, *La Rabida,* whose intricately carved boiseries were a tribute to the infinite capacity for detail of Pullman's famed Marquetry Room at Pullman, Illinois; a composite observation-sleeping car, *Isabella,* boasting a bathtub and vaulted ceiling with Gothic fretwork and named in honor of Columbus' royal patron; a sleeper, *America,* and a parlor car, *Countess,* a title that didn't come up to Anna's impending rank of marchioness, but whose heavy cut-velvet upholstery and fringes, all dazzling white, must have given pause to the maintenance department in an age well in advance of air conditioning.

This superb conveyance, fully staffed with chefs, butlers, footmen, valets, and lady's maids, ran on special schedule over the appropriate connecting railroads from New York to Canada as division superintendents and chief dispatchers at distant division points guided its glittering progress through the winter night. George Gould was one of the ranking railroad barons of the age and his guests were not the sort a friendly carrier liked to imagine as involved in anything resembling an accident.

Boni found the appointments eminently satisfactory. He was barbered in the Kochs patent barber chair and his mustaches waxed with appropriate solicitude. His private bedroom was furnished in bed linen brought for the occasion from Gould linen closets and supervised by a Gould housekeeper. In the matter of attire both for the guests and staff, all, too, was eminently *de rigueur.* Members of the party at the stroke of six retired to their staterooms to emerge for cocktails in full evening attire of white tie and tails; footmen were in formal court dress, knee breeches, silver-buckled pumps, ruffled shirts, and scarlet tailcoats heavy with gold bullion. A sommelier uncorked the wine and made the rounds of the tables in *La Rabida* in appropriate gold chain of office; the flat service was of silver gilt.

The menu on this junket to the frontiers of any appreciable social order has not come down to us, but it is safe to assume that it involved the classic elements of Fifth Avenue cuisine in 1895, caviar, canvas-back, Maryland terrapin, *foie gras,* pheasant Souvarov, and an ample supply of champagne in magnums. The footmen passed a light collation of broiled squab, quail on toast, *pommes Anna,* broiled Cotuit oysters, and more Krug's Private Cuvée before the guests retired.

It is evident that the appointments and conduct generally of the Goulds as represented by both *Georgian Court* and the interior *décor* of the car *Isabella* favorably impressed the Count de Castellane, for on their arrival at Quebec he formally asked Miss Gould's hand in marriage. "After High Mass at the Cathedral and still under the mystic influence of my Faith, I unveiled my inmost soul to Miss Anna Gould and asked her to become my wife." Her "unhesitating acceptance" of this proposal was the equivalent to Boni of a cashier's check running to nearly $12,000,000.

Anna Gould was nineteen when she became the Countess de Castellane in a ceremony performed by Archbishop Corrigan of New York in the severely handsome four-story George Gould residence at the northeast corner of Fifth Avenue at Sixty-seventh Street.

Boni, after a brief stay at the old Gould homestead at Irvington-on-Hudson, bore off his bride and presented her to the tenantry at Rochecotte where "she entered our world of traditions from a world absolutely destitute of them."

Boni's first purchase of magnitude represented a considerable amount of Union Pacific bonds and took the form of a yacht.

It was the noontide of oceangoing steam yachts of dimensions comparable to the Cunard and North German Lloyd liners that then plied the North Atlantic, and leaders in the sweepstakes for magnitude and costliness were Leonard Jerome's *Clarita,* William H. Aspinwall's *Firefly,* and James Gordon Bennett's weirdly named *Namouna* which carried a cow housed on its foredeck against the unlikely contingency of its owner's wanting milk. *Namouna* and cow were popularly reputed to set Bennett back better than $150,000 a year for crew and upkeep, and Anna and Boni thought they might be able to do the Commodore one better with *Valhalla* which was built to their order in England in 1897 and proved one of Boni's last tangible assets when it was seized by his creditors three years later.

Valhalla weighed 1,600 tons and required a crew of ninety and eight officers, not counting the owners' personal suites of valets, secretaries, tiring maids, and manicurists, and went far in living up to De Castellane's ambitions to outspend Commodore Bennett.

Once legally and factually in a position to spend the Gould millions, the floodgates of Boni's fancy began pouring foreign aid into the ateliers of the Rue de la Paix on a scale that occasioned nip-ups for joy among a wide variety of art and antique dealers, rug merchants, wine sellers, carriage builders, and purveyors of luxury merchandise and services generally. The diminutive mooch fancied himself, among other things, to be possessed of the most exquisite sensibilities where art, architecture, and decoration were concerned, and if the most expensive of everything in these fields was indeed the best, his good opinion would seem justified.

Word that the De Castellane carriage with its footmen and out-riders had turned in from Avenue de l'Opéra caused tradesmen everywhere in the Place Vendôme to comb their whiskers and assume poses of anticipation in the doorways of their shops.

In the Faubourg St.-Honoré, Giraud, the tapestry man, was the first considerable recipient of the blizzard of currency that had had its origins along the right-of-way of the Missouri Pacific Railroad and in carloadings on the Texas Pacific. Giraud was broker for some Gobelins from the collection of the Russian nobleman the Baron de Gunsburg, "marvelous creations in tones of blue and pink, bearing the royal arms of France, representing pastoral scenes depicted with delicious feeling and freshness and seeming to breathe the sensuous charm and artificial grace of the period to which they belonged."

If there was anything that aroused the collector in Boni, it was "sensuous charm and artificial grace," and without waiting to discuss anything as vulgar as price, he began pulling banknotes from his pocket and thrusting them on the bewildered tradesman "in such profusion that the floor was strewn with them." As an afterthought, he inquired how much the Gobelins cost and, on learning that the price was 250,000 francs, made up the sum on the spot.

Dealers in Gobelin tapestries were not used to doing business for cash on the barrelhead and "Giraud could find no words!" De Castellane later attested.

The tapestries were destined never to be hung in any De Castellane residence because Boni couldn't find a setting adequate to their beauty and they eventually passed into the hands of J. P. Morgan. By that time the price had risen to 1,500,000 francs.

From Giraud's, the De Castellane equipage was next observed outside Sedelmeyer's art gallery where Boni knew there was a rare bargain to be had: a Vandyke portrait of the Marquise de Spinola; and another 120,000 francs came out of the till of the Denver & Rio Grande Western Railroad. In due course, the Marquise, like the Gobelins, passed into the possession of the head of the House of Morgan.

At Samary's, Boni bought Rembrandt's "Man with a Fur Cap" for another 100,000 francs, a purchase which justified his judgment when it was eventually acquired by the Metropolitan Museum of Art on Fifth Avenue. In swift succession the De Castellane footmen carried out of their repositories a pair of celadon vases mounted by Gaffieri, an objet d'art known as "The Morrison Table" from Asher Wertheimer, and Reynolds' portrait of Judge Dunning and his sister from the same dealer. The De Castellane landau by this time was beginning to bear a marked resemblance to a furniture van.

Word of these doings was not slow to spread in Paris commercial circles and the appearance of a De Castellane carriage was the signal for an outpouring of frenzied tradesmen in frock coats and spade beards holding up Rembrandts on the sidewalk for his approval, waving diamond necklaces, and flapping costly rugs like Armenians at a boulevard café. Boni seldom disappointed them and shouted grandly to charge it as he rolled in a triumphant progress of spending through the streets.

One of his trophies, ransomed for a mere 80,000 francs from the vaults of Lord Rocksavage, was a wonderful carpet dating from the fourteenth century when it had disappeared from Lisbon Cathedral. It measured sixty feet in length and was ornamented with wreaths of acanthus on a rose-pink background interwoven with golden inscriptions. Later the same day he discovered at Jacques Seligman's a marvelous buhl clock that "it was impossible for me not to acquire," and at Stettiner's a dinner service of apple-green Sèvres. He was "weak as water" when beholding the famous Crescent cupboards at Hotchkiss' and offered 400,000 francs for, but did not get, the Crasse Fragonards which subsequently became the property of Henry Clay Frick.

> I likewise gathered a few tables inset with Sèvres plaques, rare Chinese cases from the Folques collection, a set of silver soup plates from the Demidoff collection, and a thousand and one similar trifles which combined to make my house one of the most wonderful museums in the world.

This was not the sort of thing to escape the attention of members of the Gould family back in New York. "My brothers-in-law, who neither knew nor cared anything about art, were actively hostile . . . but they troubled me not at all." It may have been this hostility that incited De Castellane to even greater heights of achievement in having fun with money and, when Anna, at the appropriate time, gave birth to a son and heir, he undertook to celebrate the occasion with a fete worthy of its importance and one which beyond all doubt would rock the disapproving Goulds on their heels.

He took counsel with his uncle, the Prince de Sagan, a monocled old party out of the pages of *La Vie Parisienne,* and together they called on the president of the Municipal Council of Paris with a request to be allowed to take over the *Tir aux Pigeons*, the ornate trapshooting pavilion in the Bois de Boulogne, for an evening's private entertainment.

Confronted with a project to use public property for "an illuminated ballet of the most beautiful description," this functionary was troubled, and asked what was its occasion and purpose?

"My uncle adjusted his famous monocle, and smiling an icy and mocking smile, addressed himself to the official.

"You want to know the object of this fete, sir? This fete is given simply for our amusement," and he repeated the words "for our amusement" several times in succession.

Thus put in his place by an aristocrat, the fellow was "amazed," but soon saw the reasonableness of the whole thing and even promised an escort of mounted Republican Guards on the eventful night.

In possession of the benediction of the municipality and practically unlimited credit at the banking firm of Morgan, Harjes & Cie., Boni and his uncle began demonstrating to what heights of fancy they might rise in the matter of a fete "for our amusement."

As a starter, 80,000 Venetian lamps were made expressly for the occasion at Murano and arranged in the trees of the Bois "where they glittered in a pale similitude of fruits and innumerable firefly lights outlined the walks and avenues." Fifteen kilometers of specially woven red carpet were commanded from Belloir, the upholsterer, and sixty footmen in scarlet court livery arranged along it supplemented at intervals by the magnificently uniformed members of the Republican Guard mounted and with drawn sabers. Eighty picked coryphees were to be mirrored in the waters of the lake while an orchestra of 200 musicians accompanied them and occasionally blew notes on hunting horns to suggest overtones of woodland rout. Three thousand guests were invited for the ballet and fireworks and Boni and the Prince de Sagan entertained 250 specially selected voluptuaries at dinner in a marquee decorated with 25,000 long-stemmed roses.

Observers were of the mind that it cost a pretty penny, probably $250,000 in Gould dividends.

On the big night there was a deluge of tropical rain which threatened to call off the entire affair and Boni's aides were in tears, but at the last moment the clouds cleared and the moon shone through on what was undoubtedly the most concentrated scene of splendor since Napoleonic times. To be sure, much of the rain that had fallen turned into steam which swirled in ghostly clouds among the celebrants, giving much the effect of 3000 people in elaborate evening dress who had somehow and mistakenly got trapped in a Turkish bath.

The fireworks were terrific; there was a Niagara of the best champagne. A Monsieur Camille Groult, who had amassed a formidable fortune manufacturing vermicelli for a firm of soup manufacturers, made a sensational entry in an open country cart from which he suddenly released twenty-five large white swans. The birds, terrified by the light and strains of Offenbach from the 200 picked musicians, flew wildly in all directions, scaring the hell out of the members of the corps de ballet who added piercing feminine screams to the already abundant bedlam.

All Paris agreed there had never been anything the like of Boni's fete, all, that is, except Anna de Castellane, who seemed to think it wasn't such a much and may well have been of the mind that, if they wanted to, the Goulds could do better at *Georgian Court.*

Far from discouraged, Boni went on to a resounding series of
fetes in which he played variations on the theme of footmen, fireworks, and ballet. Rochecotte proving too simple for his enlightened fancy, he purchased a chateau at Marais where he visualized
"glowing flower beds gilded by the setting sun, amongst which
wandered giant Nubians wearing plumed red turbans, holding jag-
uars or huge black panthers in leash—the whole scene silhouetted
against a changing background of evening sky." Again the house
liveries were troublesome—"scarlet would have desecrated
Marais"—so he evolved white coats embellished with Branden-
burgs, and pale-blue breeches, which, worn with powdered wigs,
transported Boni "back to the blue and silver days of the eighteenth century, when life was decorative and Courtesy and Refine-
ment walked hand in hand."

Alas, even royalty failed to live up to the artistic framework the
Gould money was able to provide, and when King Carlos of Portugal was Boni's guest for a shooting weekend and all the other guests
had been inspected to see if their tea gowns and dinner jackets har-
monized with the background, the King appeared wearing a bright
red, heavily quilted smoking jacket. Also, he was uncommonly fat.
"Flowers, gowns, liveries, all were ruined."

Despite Boni's distress, however, the evening was not ruined for
at least one of his guests, Mrs. Harry Lehr, who later recalled it in
her book, *King Lehr and the Gilded Age*, as an unmatched success.

"Boni had staged it superbly with an artistry that was worthy of
him," she wrote. "Never had their salons held a more distinguished
gathering of royalties, statesmen, beautiful women, the noblest
names in French society. Never had the music been more lovely,
the menu, the table decoration more perfectly chosen."

De Castellane's perfectionism made him at times miserable even
when others were taking acute pleasure in it.

In a way, this was the story of Boni's life as long as the Gould
money lasted; here he was possessed of vast resources and the
unquestioned taste for their proper expenditure, but he suffered

from a dearth of the right people to occupy the frames he provided. It was as though a scrupulous film director should create a truly magnificent throne-room setting for his principals and then discover that Central Casting was unable to supply the proper actors and attire for the crowd scenes.

Even a Russian imperial highness who visited *Marais* failed to live up to his billing. In order to produce a suitably atmospheric effect in the grand courtyard of *Marais,* Boni stationed a handsome, statuesque footman in a long red cloak who was to stand motionless in a strategic position with no function other than to furnish a spot of color.

"Who is the cardinal?" asked the Grand Duke.

Upon still another occasion when De Castellane was giving a *fête champêtre* at his chateau from which motorcars had been explicitly excluded to further the illusion of rusticity, an enormous white and red De Dion Bouton touring car arrived with machine-gun noises and a ghastly cloud of petrol vapor. From it, in the fearful and wonderful motoring garb of the era, dust coat, gauntlets, goggles, and peaked cap, and obviously no part of a peasant festival since he was smoking a Prince des Galles perfecto, there descended the Marquis de Périgord, a neighbor with whom Boni was hardly on speaking terms because of his crude nature.

Again, all was ruined.

Perhaps it was just as well that Boni remained unaware that the detestable Marquis de Périgord was shortly thereafter to become the second husband of Anna Gould and himself master of *Marais.*

The De Castellane entertainments, grand as they were, sometimes embraced contretemps which found their way into circulation in an unfavorable light even though Boni found them laughable. There was the supper party aboard *Valhalla* to which a number of Russian grand dukes had been asked and which the host, "knowing their passion for prolonged libations," had ordered terminated at midnight. In spite of this sensible precaution, when word got around that the bar was closing, Prince Orloff slipped on the deck and broke a leg. There was, too, the drag hunt given by the Count's father during which, and in violation of one of the strictest conventions of the hunt, the chase, without permission, galloped headlong across the celebrated lawns, flower beds, and ornamental waters of a neighbor, the Count Henri de Maille. The hunt swept past the old gentleman's lodge with blasts of the hunting horn in his direction and genial cries of greeting from De Castellane, *père,* who shouted "Good morning, good morning" at the Count, while his horse cleared the azaleas. Far from appreciating this bonhomie, the Count de Maille was so enraged as to bring on a fit of apoplexy from which he died within the hour.

De Castellane sent gardeners over to replace the turf.

In addition to his fiscal shortcomings and the constant insinuations of narrowminded people about his various marital infidelities, De Castellane was a source of annoyance to the Goulds for his propensity for getting into duels and other misunderstandings of a spectacular but frivolous nature. Duels as a recourse of personal satisfaction, however much they might be esteemed in France where hardly anybody was ever known to be hurt in such encounters, had long since been outmoded in the United States. While their vogue had lasted in America, largely to settle differences between journalists and politicians in the West and Deep South, duels had been a grim and often lethal business, and the powder-puff exchanges between Frenchmen who were invariably caricatured as attired in steeple-crowned hats and kissing each other effusively, were greeted with hilarity in the public prints in America.

The romantic cavalier in Boni naturally inclined to the code duello with its punctilious exchange of insults, seconds, and dainty rapier thrusts at dawn on the outskirts of the sleeping city.

When Boni's personal life was attacked by a newspaperman named Turot, who described him in a periodical called *Lanterne* as "an unwieldy person with little pig's eyes set in a wide expanse of pasty-hued face," De Castellane responded by sending him his card through the agency of seconds, one of whom was the Count de Dion, a famous motorcar manufacturer in the early days of French automobiling.

Turot and Boni faced each other on the Neuilly road by the banks of the Seine, and the challenger horrified onlookers when he threw off his opera cloak to be revealed in immaculate white lace shirt and white trousers where a prudent and experienced contestant in such affairs would have worn solid black to present a less eye-filling target. Boni's friend, Arthur Meyer, protested the indiscretion, but was ignored and Boni quickly vindicated himself by inflicting a scratch on his adversary's forearm.

"I was overwhelmed with compliments," recalled Boni in his autobiography, but his triumph was greeted with sneezes in the American press and the Goulds probably reflected that when anybody had undertaken the assassination of their father, which now and then happened, it hadn't been with a court sword.

As elected deputy from the town of Castellane, he was sometimes involved in the clouded but still violent political issues of the day and shortly found himself at odds with his cousin, the Count Orlowski, who had so far forgotten himself as to make rude remarks about the French Army.

Again there was the exchange of cards and seconds and, although Orlowski, whose second, Prince Galitzine, had come expressly from St. Petersburg for the affray, succeeded in passing his rapier through Boni's shirt sleeve, he came off second best and De Castellane received an ovation when he returned in triumph to the Travellers' Club that afternoon.

More catcalls greeted the news of the De Castellane victory when it reached New York, and Boni consoled himself by giving an elaborate Ball of Flowers at which Queen Isabella of Spain, who was enormously fat and wore an obvious blonde wig, was carried up the steps in a palanquin to avoid the possibility of apoplexy. Another guest who attracted special attention was an English woman, a Mrs. Moore, who carried a "tall white walking stick *à la mode de Louis Quinze,* on top of which a stuffed green parrot swayed to and fro."

It was about this time, too, that Boni absent-mindedly acquired a racing stable, one of whose members was a horse named Sleeping Car, and carried the De Castellane colors, mauve and green, to notable victories at Auteuil. But Boni shortly lost interest in horses. "I disliked the world of jockeys and trainers; politics and art alone touched my soul."

As time passed, Boni's fetes and his footmen, his fireworks and objects of art began to pale to insignificance compared to his real estate ventures. The French château of *Grignan* came into the market, an estate once occupied by Madame de Sévigné who was buried in the family mausoleum there beside a number of De Castellane forebears. It was a celebrated example of Mansard architecture and Boni purchased it with the idea of establishing a kind of seasonal academy of arts and sciences of the sort that an American millionaire some years later founded at Aspen, Colorado. When the bill for *Grignan* was presented, Boni was temporarily in arrears to a number of art dealers and couldn't come up with the money. *Grignan,* together with the down payment, returned to its previous owners. "I certainly never contemplated settling my accounts directly they were presented," said Boni in a huff.

Other creditors, learning that Boni had spent up to the temporary limit of his wife's fortune, which was held in trust, undertook to collect sums due for paintings, porcelains, and statuary "running to several millions" through American courts, an inconvenience which did nothing to raise the De Castellane stock with the Gould brothers, George, Howard, Frank, and Edwin.

Boni had once shown George Gould a set of four armchairs and a sofa upholstered in yellow tapestry treated with decorative parrots and flowers by Bérain which he had just purchased for 60,000 francs and George had shown a marked distrust of his brother-in-law's mentality ever since.

Now Boni created his masterpiece of extravagance. He purchased 7800 meters of land on the Avenue du Bois and set about building a town house whose palatial dimensions and appointments were to make *Marais* seem positively shabby. An incredibly costly marble staircase gave on a series of salons, ballrooms, and private apartments the like of which hadn't been seen since the time of the Bourbons. There was a private theater seating 600 where Boni purposed to produce grand opera, and his kitchens, cellars, and pantries had white marble floors while a cold-storage plant enabled the owner to keep food on hand for an impromptu dinner for 500 if the occasion arose. Boni's chef, Parrade, was one of the most distinguished practitioners of his special expertise of the age and, in Boni's own words, "was such an economical caterer that he was shortly able to retire on his perquisites with an income which today is as large as my own."

Boni excused the extravagance of white marble in the kitchen area by saying that the trains of the gowns of his female guests, whom he was accustomed to take on guided tours of the house, "swept over the marble floors with a sound almost exactly similar to waves breaking gently on the seashore."

There was a vast crystal chandelier in the wine cellar and masculine guests used to sit under it of an evening "toasting life in a magnum of Mouton-Rothschild '69, Château Lafite '75, and a jeroboam of Mumm."

In these surroundings, the three De Castellane boys, Boni, George, and Jay, were brought up, in Boni's own phrase, "absolutely unspoilt," although in the same breath he was pleased to describe their return from a romp in the park "when an imposing footman had thrown open the door of our palace, and, wrapped in their ermine coats, the boys traversed the long marble galleries looking, for all the world, like little kings."

But time, which had already some years previously run out on Boni's romantic concept of life, was running out, too, on the Goulds' collective patience. Whether or not there was justice in the charges of domestic infidelity aired at the divorce, Anna evidently felt when her husband's drafts against her bank account passed the $12,000,000 mark that, as Countess de Castellane, she had had it.

Although the concept in so many words would have inexpressibly shocked and alarmed De Castellane, he basically subscribed to the sentiments that some years later advocated "share the wealth." He felt that his most expansive gestures were good for the national economy, provided work for countless artisans such as dressmakers, upholsterers, florists, decorators, caterers, wine merchants, musicians, and even manufacturers of the fireworks to which he was devoted, and he was acutely aware of the social contract between patrons of great wealth and the workers who ministered to their extravagances. When he completed the rehabilitation of *Marais,* his first fete was not for well-placed friends and neighbors but for the stonemasons, joiners, glaziers, fitters, gardeners, and common laborers who had contributed their time and special talents to its restoration.

The identical sentiments to which Boni subscribed, when expressed by the Bradley-Martins in New York during a time of economic distress, led to their undoing and exile, but Boni didn't go on record in the newspapers only; he was truly grateful to those who made realities of his dreams and showed it in a manner from which the taint of patronage and condescension was altogether lacking.

The manner of a grand seigneur triumphed notably over the crude self-justification of the *arriviste.*

That Boni had made a bad bargain when he acquired a Gould for a wife became more and more apparent despite his inroads on her presumably foolproof fortune. His countess cared little for the things that delighted him and was resolutely unimpressed by his grandeurs of ancient title or modern circumstance. Like Althea, in Swinburne,

> Full of mine own soul, perfect of myself,
> Toward mine and me sufficient,

Anna was self-contained, hostile, and influenced by her equally hostile family, and it was only a question of time before she and Boni must come to the parting of the ways.

One afternoon, after an invigorating stroll in the park, Boni returned to find his enormous town house deserted alike of family and servants. Even the electricity had been shut off and the sole remaining member of his once immense domestic entourage, his sons' tutor, was reading by the light of a single candle.

Anna, once divested of the man who was certainly one of the most ornamental and expensive husbands of all time, married the Marquis de Périgord, the detested motorist of *Marais,* whose arrival had ruined the *fête champêtre,* and Boni became, like many a celebrity before him, a legend and a familiar figure of departed grandeur around the Paris boulevards.

And yet once again the irrepressible De Castellane feeling for the gallant gesture emerges through the mists of time, linking him with noble ancestors and his knowing way with fireworks and footmen's liveries.

One morning in the mid-twenties he awoke to a premonition that his own death was at hand and that, at last, time as well as fortune was taking French leave of this graying *boulevardier.* Calling his valet, the old man had himself attired in full evening dress, adjusted his ribbons, crosses, and honors, placed his court sword by his side, and lay down to meet his ancestors, formally, decorously, as a great gentleman should greet those who have gone on before him.

Only there was nothing wrong with him; the De Castellane heart continued to beat and Boni grew more and more impatient lying there to await a caller who never came. After a day of waiting, he got up, hung up his court sword, put the decorations back in the bureau, and rejoined old friends in the bar at the Ritz. It had been a most trying experience. Furthermore, everyone had taken leave of his manners. Even the Grim Reaper no longer kept his appointments on time.

An instructive coda to the Boni de Castellane legend was supplied at about the time the old roué was coming to the end of his career by the appearance as an undergraduate at Harvard College in 1923 of a nephew named Henri de Castellane. The young man's contemporaries knew all about his family and the Goulds and even if Henri de Castellane had been possessed of no personality of his own, he would have been something of a celebrity merely by association.

In connection with the brief but solvent visitation of young De Castellane in the grove of Harvard academe it may be worth noting that popular rumor supported the belief that his father, before enrolling him as an undergraduate, had inquired of President Lowell if an allowance of $25,000 a year would be sufficient to maintain the youth in keeping with his station in the student community. This, in an age when three-room bachelor apartments in Ridgley and Claverly Halls on Mt. Auburn Street, known as Harvard's "Gold Coast," rented for $100 a month and were an undergraduate status symbol comparable to maintenance of a Mercer two-seater, was generally thought to be ample.

Young M. de Castellane, however, was a playboy cut from much the same cloth as his wicked uncle and soon established himself in the undergraduate clubs that lined Mt. Auburn Street and Massachusetts Avenue as a junior cut-up with overtones, for the time and place, of authentic grandeur.

He was, for one thing, the best patron of the not inconsiderable assortment of bootleggers who did a thriving business within Seltzer squirt of Harvard Square, giving enormous open-house demonstrations of good will and hospitality that lacked his uncle's powdered footmen and fireworks but generally raised the level and standard of undergraduate entertainment practically to that of proof spirits. He admired, too, to provide stylish little picnics in the surrounding countryside or, even better, on the wide expanse of lawns and ornamental shrubbery that separated Charles River water from the highway in Cambridge. Since he asked guests at these *fêtes champêtres* please to dress for the occasion in morning coats and silk top hats, they attracted a certain amount of attention from passing motorists and occasionally caused severe dislocations of traffic. When the police arrived, they were almost invariably so charmed by their host and awed by the magnificence of the company that they readily consented to remain long enough to share a bottle or two of Bollinger and a water-cress sandwich.

Young M. de Castellane alarmed and delighted the mothers of debutantes by waltzing through French windows, glass and all, at coming-out parties at the Somerset Hotel in Boston and otherwise generally living up to the fondest of American notions of a dissolute member of the European nobility.

The radiant press accorded these opulent disorders on the far side of Charles River was understandably viewed with scant approval by Harvard's president, Abbott Lawrence Lowell, a brother of cigar-smoking Amy Lowell and a towering codfish aristocrat of severe mien. His distaste for De Castellane was in no way mitigated by the fact that there was a segment of newspaper readers of the lower order who got their information from the *Boston American* and the *Boston Telegram* who began regarding Henri de Castellane as titular head of the university and Dr. Lowell as a sort of impostor. The misapprehension was not diminished when De Castellane took to arriving at evening parties in Boston in an open barouche with footmen on the box and mounted outriders in military uniform with lances, recruited, of course, from the best undergraduate clubs, but open to misinterpretation by the uninformed.

When at last some particularly atrocious assault on the proprieties enabled Harvard to be shut of De Castellane, his expulsion took on aspects of an international incident. The press was able to report that the French embassy in Washington was in receipt of a telegram signed by the young milord demanding diplomatic intercession on his behalf. It never was quite clear who had sent the telegram.

To take his congee of Harvard, De Castellane rented every horse-cab still available in Greater Boston for an entourage which accompanied him in state down U.S. 1 the entire distance to Providence, where French steamships still docked for the Atlantic run. The cavalcade took three days to make it, and forethoughtful bootleggers had established oases at strategic points along the way.

Press photographers gave the pilgrimage adequate coverage while Dr. Lowell, in his offices at University Hall under the gaze of eminent departed divines, pondered fretfully on the meaning of life.

De Castellane's propensity for following in the well-shod footsteps of his dissolute uncle were given thoughtful attention by students of heredity and the theories of the Abbé Mendel.

Chapter Two

Golden Times,
Golden Gate

*Darius Ogden Mills Maintained His Own Personal Gold
Standard . . . A Mere $2,500,000 Could Get Lost in the Book-
keeping . . . Then, as Now, Californians Wanted Only the Best
of Everything . . . For Three Generations the Mills Family Got
Just That . . . Then There Were Senator Sharon's $2000 Window
Shades . . . James Ben Ali Haggin's Horses Lived En Prince . . .
So Did the Silver Kings of the Comstock Lode . . . Belle Kendall
Tossed $1000 Bills Out the Window . . . Quite Literally . . . W. C.
Fields Found a Way to Take It with You . . . Even Today the City
Dump in Hillsborough Grows Orchids. . . .*

A S LONG AS the crimson and golden glories of New York's
Metropolitan Opera survived at their original site on
Broadway, a Golden Horseshoe box bore on its door a
dull brass plate with the legend in script "Ogden Mills Estate."

It was a metaphorical link between California's Gold Rush days
of '49 and New York society of the tiara era, and it represented the
rise and decline of a transcontinental family of the most conservative sort of moneybags without mention of which no account of
American wealth would be complete.

Darius Ogden Mills had been born in North Salem, New York,
and by the time he was twenty-two was part owner of a respected

banking business in Buffalo. News of gold at Sutter's Fort brought him West, an authentic Argonaut but not of the feckless sort who arrived in California equipped with no more than a derringer and pair of pocket gold scales, still wearing the tile hat and frock coat of eastern usage. He had prudently laid in as great a supply of merchandisable articles as his cabin on shipboard could accommodate and readily found a market for them in San Francisco that was gladly paying $40 for Colt's patent revolvers and half that much for a bottle of genuine cognac.

Setting up as private banker, first at the Mother Lode town of Columbia, where his banking premises is preserved to this day as a monument to its times, and later as owner of the Gold Bank of Sacramento, Mills weathered all tides of tumult in the sixties in California and shortly emerged as head of the all-powerful Bank of California, richest and most important source of finance in the entire West.

D. O. Mills, although his multiple millions, in the beginning anyway, all derived from mining and milling, never himself owned mining stock if he could help it and never turned a shovelful of pay dirt. He dealt in gold dust and bullion, fairly, squarely, and to his immense profit. His realm of activity embraced the financing of other men who might go into the depths of the earth, but the frantic speculation in mining shares and Comstock properties that ruined so many men of the California sixties and seventies left him unscarred.

A frosty, prudent, controlled personality, his photographs even in youth depict him as typecast for the role of banker and he was listed in the San Francisco business directories unequivocally as "Capitalist."

Mills's properties for three generations were to include all sorts and conditions of tangibles and many of the prestige: symbols that were intangible as well: banks, railroads, vast resources of timber and water, ranches, newspapers, the Merganthaler Company, and eventually ambassadorships and memberships in the most exclusive and costly enclaves of formal society; and in 1860, D. O. Mills showed where his inclinations as a spender lay.

Seventeen miles south of San Francisco where the housing developments of Millbrae sprawl today, he purchased the 1500 acres that constituted the old Buri Buri Rancho, one of the original Spanish land grants in California that had for a time been known also as Rancho del Rey because it provided beef and garden stuff for the Spanish garrison at San Francisco's Presidio. It could accommodate 8000 cattle and 1000 horses, and now Darius Ogden Mills took it over as a dairy farm and began laying out fine gardens and rare trees from all over the world where once the *caballeros* had lounged in the shade and presumably played serenades on their guitars.

He also built a fine château, not as fine as William Ralston's, but one that was long to outlast *Belmont,* and named it *Millbrae.*

In addition to Mills's San Francisco and California banking connections, he was by now receiving an immense income from the mines of the Comstock Lode in Nevada, where the Bank of California's representative, William Sharon, had manipulated a complete monopoly of the Lode's mines, mills, and water rights, timber, banking, and transportation facilities. The coup by which they were consolidated into a tightly held private mint had not at first had Mills's unreserved blessing, but once it was factually accomplished he beamed approval on Sharon's high-handed financing when he discovered that his bank was not only milling all the ore of the biggest mines in Virginia City, but selling the mills and mines its own timber from the adjacent Sierra, floating the logs to its own sawmills on its own sluices, carrying the end product up to Virginia City on its own railway, selling Virginia City the water by which it lived and mined from its own costly and intricate waterworks, and banking every penny of money involved in all these interlocking transactions.

So gratified was Mills with his Nevada monopoly that he purchased from the car-building firm of Jackson & Sharp in Wilmington, Delaware, the first private car of any of the moguls on the Pacific Coast in which to ride in style over his incredibly profitable

Virginia & Truckee Railroad, the richest short line in the world. He didn't use it often, having no great fondness for the howling wilderness on Sun Mountain that was producing all this wealth, but his man Sharon, who was by now setting his cap for appointment as United States senator from Nevada, was glad to occupy it for him on frequent occasions of business and pleasure.

The brass plate on the box door at the Metropolitan could with perfect propriety have been fashioned either from Mother Lode gold or from Comstock silver, as the Mills fortunes had their origins in both.

Most of the other California millionaires of his time, James Flood, Jim Fair, Leland Stanford, Lloyd Tevis, John Mackay, Lucky Baldwin, and Charlie Crocker, were happy to make their permanent homes in San Francisco, occasionally commuting to London or Paris as their families might insist, but basically they regarded San Francisco as heaven and had no intention of going elsewhere until it was to their mausoleums in Woodlawn Cemetery.

But by the nineties, Mills felt that he had exhausted the possibilities of California so far as the extraction of large sums of money was concerned. He began divesting himself of West Coast holdings and putting down his roots in Wall Street. The Comstock, after long years in bonanza, was descending into borasca and Mills's eastern investments, notably the Merganthaler Linotype Company which he owned outright and the admirably managed Vanderbilt railroads in which he was a large stockholder, were occupying his attention. Some idea of the elder Mills's scale of operations may be derived from the circumstance that years later, when the Carson & Colorado Railroad, which had for a decade been gathering dust in his portfolio of Nevada properties, was in 1900 sold to the Southern Pacific Railroad for $2,500,000 cash, Darius O. was surprised to discover that he owned it.

His first out-of-pocket expense on arriving in New York was the block-long Madison Avenue mansion fronting on the rear of St. Patrick's Cathedral that had been built by former millionaire

Henry Villard of the Northern Pacific Railroad. But disaster had overtaken that carrier and Villard was living in humbler circumstances. The price tag on the house was $500,000.

When William Henry Vanderbilt decided, on behalf of his family, to sell stock in the Vanderbilt lines, namely the New York Central & Hudson River Railroad and the Lake Shore & Michigan Southern, Mills bought heavily in a pool with Drexel, Morgan & Company, Russell Sage, August Belmont, and J. P. Morgan & Company, and a substantial part of his Comstock profits were represented in the $18,500,000 so jointly raised. More specifically, he subscribed $500,000 in the projected Southern Pennsylvania Railroad with which the New York Central threatened the Pennsylvania's direct route from Harrisburg to Pittsburgh. Together with his old associates of San Francisco days, James Ben Ali Haggin and Senator George Hearst, as well as J. P. Morgan and Henry C. Frick, he invested heavily in the Cerro de Pasco copper mines. He was one of the original subscribers to the Metropolitan Opera when that august edifice was opened in 1883 but could hardly expect dividends on this investment save in social prestige.

These, for the most part, were investments that could reasonably be counted on to augment the profits taken eastward from the Bank of California. Not so the outstanding extravagance of the elder Mills in the form of a son-in-law.

Whitelaw Reid was a coldly arrogant aspirant for political honors of whom no warm, generous, or heartening gesture or trait of personality has ever been remembered, and even his official biographer, Royal Cortissoz, a member of the staff of the *New York Tribune* and a scholarly lackey of the first chop, was hard put to paint a portrait in tones of reasonable humanity.

A contemporary, unimpressed by the Reids' lavish entertaining in London which once achieved an all-time high with a fishmonger's bill for 500 pounds for a single month, described Whitelaw as "a vulgar, palatial fellow, scurrying toward Buckingham Palace as fast as his hands and knees could carry him."

The nearest approach to generosity of any sort or description ever attributed to Whitelaw Reid was his practice at his colossal country estate *Ophir Hall* at White Plains near Sing Sing prison of keeping a couple of old suits hanging to the side of the barn near the highway and in full sight of any wayfarer. "In that way," he explained, "I am sure never to be molested by any escaped convict whose first necessity is always a suit of clothes."

Reid had started life on the editorial staff of the *Cincinnati Gazette* where his reporting of the Civil War shortly saw him called as managing editor to Horace Greeley's *New York Tribune* of which from 1872 to 1905 he was editor-in-chief and eventually owner. His acquisition of the newspaper property, one of the most valuable in the country at the time, from Greeley was the result of Greeley's incurable optimism in the field of swindlers, bad investments, and hard-luck artists, and the constant presence at his elbow of Reid, well heeled and handy, whenever he ran out of cash. At the time of Greeley's death, New York's professional newspaper society was rocked by the story of Uncle Horace's last moments at Chappaqua which were attended by Reid and other dignitaries, as was the macabre custom of the age.

When it was apparent that the Grim Reaper was indisputably among those present, Reid was appointed spokesman to approach his bedside and take note of the great man's last words. Greeley, in a final moment of clarity, recognized Reid and muttered, "You son of a bitch, you stole my newspaper," and then lapsed into silence forever. Reid, solemn of aspect, rejoined the group at the end of the room. "What were his last words, Mr. Reid?" asked Tom Rooker, a faithful *Tribune* employee of thirty years' standing. "Give us his last message."

"His last words," Reid told him, "were 'I know that my redeemer liveth!'"

A glacial employer and stickler for the formalities, Whitelaw Reid also raised blooded sheep with which the grass was kept clipped in the English manner at *Ophir Hall* at White Plains. William

M. Houghton, a member of Ogden Reid's class at Yale, who was a member of the *Tribune* editorial staff for more than forty years, recalled that, in his youthful days as a reporter, staff members were often assigned to meet incoming cattle boats at South Street and escort their woolly cargoes through the streets and the length of the city to their baronial destination.

If by chance a shipment of Merinos was offloaded on Sunday, Reid's instructions to the city desk were that their herders, recruited from City Hall and West Side district assignments and usually Yale men, were to be attired in formal morning dress with cutaways and top hats when they went to the pier. The *Tribune* tolerated no departure from the sartorial amenities.

The marriage of Helen Rogers, who until then had been Mrs. Whitelaw Reid's social secretary, to Ogden Mills Reid was generally reported in London and New York, where the affairs of the Reids were a matter of close if not altogether approving scrutiny, to have been arranged by the elderly woman in the hope of keeping young Reid in line and, if possible, abating his fondness for the bottle and low associates from the editorial staff of the *Tribune*. Neither desired effect was even vaguely discernible at any time during their married lifetime, but the alliance served to occasion a schism of resounding proportions in the ranks of the Reid and Mills families where until now solidarity had reigned.

Mrs. Ogden Mills, who had been Ruth T. Livingston, a member of a notably manorial New York family with revolutionary antecedents and the best of connections everywhere, took a dim view of Helen Rogers whom she frankly characterized in her conversations as an upstart, adventurer, and *arriviste*. When the marriage was accomplished, over her dead body metaphorically, Mrs. Mills set about a poison pen campaign of letter writing that has few parallels in the annals of formal society. She wrote at length to an imposing number of friends in England, all of impeccable social position, urging them not to recognize Mrs. Reid and naming her grievances. Whereupon, although his father was at the time

American ambassador to the Court of St. James's, all invitations to visit the great houses of England and Scotland were addressed to Ogden Reid specifically and pointedly failed to mention his bride. Incensed, the Reids cut short their wedding trip so far as Great Britain was concerned and Mr. Reid forever dropped the middle name of Mills with which he had been christened.

Opportunist or not, Mrs. Whitelaw Reid, a Mills no longer, soon proved herself a woman of shrewd business sense and indomitable energy. One of Mrs. Whitelaw Reid's many good works had been to preserve from total extinction the *New York Tribune* which at one time, thanks to her husband's neglect of his once valuable property for greater affairs of state, had sunk to an all-time low of 12,000 circulation and was losing half a million dollars a year. Taking charge of the vagrant helm of this foundering ship with the title of vice president of the New York *Tribune*, Inc., Mrs. Reid accomplished what her detractors had said was impossible and in a few years the *Tribune* was again on a paying basis and tipping its hat on terms of old-accustomed equality with the other dailies on New York's Newspaper Row. Its merger under the Reid banner in the early twenties with James Gordon Bennett's *New York Herald* to form the *New York Herald Tribune* was one of the few substantially successful newspaper mergers in the record and the credit for its success belonged beyond dispute and in generous measure to Helen Reid.

In her lifetime it had been Mrs. Whitelaw Reid's occasional and usually whimsical boast that at no time when traveling abroad or in the United States was it necessary for her to sleep under a roof that wasn't her own. In New York City there was the Villard mansion on Madison Avenue, and, at White Plains, *Ophir Hall* and *Ophir Hall's* suburb, *Ophir Cottage,* a forty-room villa next door occupied by her son and daughter-in-law. There was *Millbrae* in Burlingame when she was in California, a camp at Paul Smith's in the Adirondacks, and *Flyaway,* a hunting lodge on Currituck Sound in North Carolina. There was a town house in Paris and during the term of

Whitelaw Reid's embassy to St. James's a mansion at Carlton House Terrace in London. When Mrs. Reid died in 1931 it was under the roof of the Cap Ferrat villa of her daughter, Lady John Ward.

A widow of imposing proportions, Mrs. Whitelaw Reid long survived her husband, living in outmoded but authentic state in the great mansion on Madison Avenue later shared by the Catholic Diocese of New York and the publishing firm of Random House. Shrewd, witty, and a cheerful old party, she reminded beholders of the late Queen Victoria, and her flowing widow's weeds and bonnet with veils perched high on her head heightened the illusion.

Although fairly well removed from the details of management of her properties and in the habit of sending for department heads when she wanted them, it was on one occasion her whim to ask the entire editorial staff, or at least such of it as could be spared for an evening and owned dinner suits, to dinner at Madison Avenue. The occasion was remembered with embarrassment for some time to come. Impious youths from the ranks of city side reporters, unaccustomed to butlered splendor, became alarmingly loaded and, when the plate was counted at the end of a tumultuous evening, the Reid steward reported that a substantial number of gold spoons and butter plates were missing. It was a gesture of hospitality that was not repeated.

Most of the widespread Reid real estate, taxed at its full valuation although a great national depression was then in progress, fell to Mrs. Ogden Reid to liquidate, a herculean task which she accomplished with the same brilliant business dispatch she had shown in revitalizing the affairs of the *Tribune*.

The Ogden Reids lived handsomely to the end of their generation in an exquisitely appointed town house on Eighty-fourth Street just off Fifth Avenue and at White Plains. As long as Ogden Reid was alive, too, the shooting box in North Carolina was maintained, but when they wintered at Palm Beach it was in a rented estate and the "vulgar and palatial" way of life of Mr. Reid's parents was no part of their scheme of things.

Socially, the Ogden Reids fairly early in the game gave up any great pretense of magnificence or even participation. Entertainment at Eighty-fourth Street or in the Ogden Mills Estate box at the Metropolitan was so often dominated by advertisers, prospective advertisers, business-office hucksters from the *Herald Tribune,* and other commercial associates as to resemble more an executive luncheon than a function of fashion. Anglican bishops in lawn lace and visiting milords with letters from Lady Ward found themselves overwhelmed, when the ladies had retired and the brandy was circulated, by arguments over circulation and advertising rates between Bernard Gimbel and Jack Straus of Macy's.

Often enough Ogden Reid was not even present at these dinners at Eighty-fourth Street, having become entangled with members of his city staff at Bleeck's speak-easy next door to the *Tribune,* and his place at the head of the table would be taken by Howard Davis, the paper's rotund, cigar-smoking business manager. Mrs. Reid's chef was a man of irreproachable culinary genius, but Mr. Reid often found sustenance for days on end in the olives from martini glasses and the free lunch provided at the end of the bar by hospitable Jack Bleeck.

That the pipeline stretching over the years and continents from Sun Mountain to New York was, by the depressed thirties, flowing fitfully was suggested to members of the *Tribune* staff who, in 1930 and '31 occasionally loaned Ogden Reid a little pocket money. Howard Davis once came to the rescue in the nick of time with $250 in back wages for the Reid butler just as that peerless personage was about to depart Eighty-fourth Street to take service where payday was a regular institution. The facade of affluence never really crumbled, however, and in a few years all was again well with the Reid exchequer.

There was a time when Ogden Reid's garages were reduced to a practically irreducible four Rolls-Royces. It had been the occasional habit of the publisher of the *Herald Tribune* on emerging from Bleeck's during the evening to enter the car handiest to the saloon's swinging door, a conveyance not always his. On opera nights when Fortieth Street was crowded with parked motors, all of them of superior make, it wasn't always possible for the Reid chauffeur to obtain a position directly in front of Bleeck's and, since all town cars looked very much alike at night, Mr. Reid sometimes popped himself into Robert Goelet's Packard or Mrs. S. Stanwood Menken's Isotta. This occasion for confusion was eventually overcome when Arthur Draper, for many years the publisher's confidential assistant, arranged to have all four Reid Rolls-Royces take up adjacent positions at the curb on Fortieth Street during the dinner lull in traffic, thus eliminating all possibility of contretemps since almost any car he might select on leaving the bar would be his own.

As editor and publisher of the *Herald Tribune,* Ogden Reid, on a basis of alcoholic bonhomie, enjoyed a measure of loyalty and devotion from his staff only infrequently encountered in a profession notorious for its criticism of its employers. A gentleman by every definition of the term, he tolerated no impertinences and his immense six feet three and magnificent head, almost completely bald, encouraged none. Usually he affected the four-button business suits and three-inch-tall stiff turnover collars of the Arrow Collar ads of 1904 when he was at Yale and turned up on opera nights in a vaguely dented silk hat and cigar-blown satin-faced evening overcoat. But his laugh was something to shake the rafters and sometimes alarmed passers-by as he issued from Bleeck's with Geoffrey Parsons, the chief editorial writer, or Wilbur Forrest, his executive editor, at closing hour to go across town to the Brook Club which never closed.

Ogden Reid would have been a match for the breed of men that inhabited the saloons of Virginia City whence his money came so far away and long ago. He could have matched Sun Mountain itself, but unhappily there is no record that he ever visited the Comstock or showed any least interest in where all the money came from.

Not so his cousin Ogden Mills, who had a very acute sense of obligation to the past and no little becoming sentiment.

Mills was of an inquiring mind and benevolent disposition. The faltering fortunes of the old Virginia & Truckee Railroad on which his grandfather had, metaphorically, ridden to wealth and over which so much of his own substance had been transported, engaged his attention and in 1933 he purchased the outstanding one third of its stock from the Sharon heirs and became sole owner of the romantic short line. He took pleasure in riding its ancient rails, now returning to the elemental earth that supported them and, until his untimely death four years later, paid its deficit of a reported $25,000 a year out of his own pocket.

Mills died suddenly with his affairs in some disorder and intimates were of the mind that, had he been warned or had any premonitions of mortality, he would have provided for its continued support and financing in his will. As it was, it reverted to his estate and into the hands of the harpies and rapacious janitors who eventually wrecked it.

Legends of the Reids once were thick as autumn leaves on Vallombrosa in New York publishing circles of the twenties and thirties. Ogden Reid was a name to which it was possible to attach all manner of anecdotes that would have been unthinkable in the case of sedate and self-satisfied Adolph Ochs of the *Times* or the unacceptable Thackreys of the once high-toned *New York Evening Post*. Reid's predisposition to the cup that cheers was well known and never denied by sanctimonious pretensions.

Once it was Ogden's whim to visit his shooting box in North Carolina and to accompany him on safari a group was arranged which included Arthur Draper and Wilbur Forrest, his ranking executive advisers, Geoffrey Parsons, and Howard Davis, all of whom spent frantic hours at Abercrombie & Fitch being outfitted with rubber waders, shooting jackets, and English shotguns of intricate and costly design. The expedition set out, of course, from Bleeck's with two of the Reid Rolls-Royces *en suite* after a delay of some hours because members of the party had become involved in conversation with Skipper Williams, the veteran ship's news reporter for the *Times* and a tall tower of mendacity whose anecdotes of Baron Munchausen dimensions, wing collar, and square Derby hat in which he met all incoming liners, were landmarks of the newspaper world.

Already off schedule by several hours, the entourage lost three entire days when it thoughtlessly called on John T. Custis, a descendant of the Father of His Country and widely known managing editor of the *Philadelphia Inquirer*. Custis took them all to his club in Rittenhouse Square and before you could have said Johnny Walker, three days had been added to the schedule.

From there a course was set for the ample duckponds of Dixie, but again the Fates intervened when it was thought inappropriate to pass through Washington without looking in on Ted Wallen, the *Herald Tribune's* Washington correspondent who, apprised of their arrival, had a bar set up in his office and convivial members of his staff assembled. The day was well spent when somebody said it might be a good thing to call on President Hoover at the White House as representatives of the only newspaper of consequence which in those dark days unequivocally supported him. Masking whatever misgivings he may have had, Mr. Hoover made them welcome and a cheery night was spent in the federal manse, although Geoffrey Parsons remembered that the entire party had to be supplied with pajamas at one in the morning and it was necessary to double up in the matter of beds.

Revived with Republican Bromo Seltzers, the cavalcade got under way again and in due course arrived at the Reid marshes teeming with mallard and red bills only to find the game warden busy posting a notice to the effect that the shooting season had ended.

Like many men to whom money, except in infrequent moments, had never presented a problem, Ogden Reid was vague about finances and his ignorance of accounting used to give Price Waterhouse, the *Tribune's* firm of accountants, the vapors. Once Howard Davis discovered him on hands and knees on the floor of his office, examining a vast expanse of trial balances which he had caused to be laid out on the carpet. Davis found fault with some of the entries.

"That five hundred thousand dollars in the second column shouldn't be in red," he said. "It's for replacement of equipment and maintenance, and that isn't a deficit entry."

"I told them to mark it up in red ink," remarked Reid on his knees. "It looks nicer to have some color instead of all those columns of black."

On another occasion a faithful veteran of the pressroom who had long been in the service of the paper had too much at the Type & Print speakeasy where the mechanical departments drank, fell down the cement steps of that cosy resort, and was dead on arrival at the emergency ward. He was stone broke at the time of his unfortunate demise and a collection was taken up among friends on the staff to assure his proper burial. The hat passer eventually got to Mr. Reid who was surprised at the touch.

"Didn't he have insurance enough to bury him?"

"No insurance, Mr. Reid, but he was an old and loyal employee of your father before you and we don't want him in Pauper's Field."

"Can't his relatives take care of him?"

"No family at all, Mr. Reid."

Ogden thought a moment and then came up with the obvious solution of the entire business.

"Well, then, let his estate look out for it!"

Ogden had never heard of anyone who didn't have an estate.

When, shortly after the conclusion of the second world war, Ogden Reid died and was buried from St. Thomas Church on Fifth Avenue, good times departed the New *York Herald Tribune,* perhaps forever.

Its management fell to two sons, Ogden Reid, Jr., and Whitelaw Reid, known respectively as "Brownie" and "Whitey." Its once brilliant staff was replaced, and in 1959 the property was acquired by John Hay Whitney, at the time American ambassador to the Court of St. James's and a man whose wealth easily permitted the acquisition of a far from profitable property.

With the disappearance into the surrounding anonymity of the sons of Ogden Reid, there ended to all intents the story of the Darius

Ogden Mills's multiple millions. Shirt sleeves to shirt sleeves had been accomplished with nice exactitude in three generations.

The foregoing précis of the dissipation and expenditure of a single California fortune from the days of mining precious metals has been rehearsed at some length, for one reason, because aspects of the Mills saga came to the personal attention of the author in the twenty-one years he was a member of the *Herald Tribune* editorial staff, and hence, by indirection, a beneficiary of the affairs of the Bank of California, and also because in its own special way the story of the Mills money is representative of the entire pattern of California wealth deriving from the nineteenth century.

When, in 1950, the writer resigned from the *Herald Tribune* and took his congee from the gallant company at the bar of Jack Bleeck's saloon to become publisher of *The Territorial Enterprise* in Virginia City, Nevada, he found himself at firsthand and in his own right part of the legend of western money and its ramifications everywhere. *The Territorial Enterprise,* apart from having been the agency of record and classic repository of the legend of the Comstock mines, had once belonged to John Mackay of the great bonanzas and later to Ogden Mills whose affairs have been chronicled at some length above. It had also, briefly and for reasons of political strategy, once belong to the remarkable Senator William Sharon.

Its bloodlines were inescapably those of the old West, the Far West, and the most solvent West of all.

The Territorial Enterprise had been involved in everything that transpired, not only as a mirror of its glory times in the economy and society of the Nevada-California complex of great wealth, but as an active agency in the affairs of the Bank of California, the recruitment of Nevada to the Union cause and in the Big Bonanza itself which had created millionaires by the score, caused San Francisco to rise in glory to the sun, and whose impact was still, at this long remove, felt in the fortunes of noble families in England and ancient dynasties of Italian scoundrels. My partner in ownership of the property and I were, vicariously at least, moving in very exalted echelons of history.

So much has been written of San Francisco in its early years, all of it in terms of wistful adulation and envious nostalgia, that it is hard for Americans elsewhere in the land to believe that its golden myths were indeed founded in fact and, as often as not, transcended the superlatives of their telling. It was a community to which wealth gravitated and toward which good fortune set its course.

At first the gold bullion of the Mother Lode, channeled through the strongboxes and counting rooms of Wells Fargo, had made Montgomery Street its entrepôt and point of embarkation to the states in the East. As the surface recoveries of the Mother Lode showed signs of exhaustion, since mining there was essentially superficial and only in a few instances, such as the deep diggings of Amador, penetrated more than a few feet below the surface, the Comstock Lode two mountain ranges away on the edge of the Nevada desert came into production on a scale to startle the entire world. By the time the deep mines of Virginia City had begun to slow down, other sources of revenue in fantastic quantities were in full operation to make San Francisco what seemed like a permanent and interminable bonanza in its own right. The Pacific Railroad and its ancillaries expanding north to Oregon and south and east to Texas and eventually New Orleans had its home offices in downtown San Francisco while its ruling magnificoes ruffled it on Nob Hill. Cattle ranching, sheep grazing, vineyards, water companies, land companies, agricultural projects, Pacific shipping lines, prophetic traces of heavy industry, and, most of all, great banks of issue continued to keep the Golden Gate a world capital of finance and golden in a strictly literal sense.

That such sudden, immense, and, in many cases, fairly easily acquired wealth should produce a race of nabobs and a tradition of magnificence beyond anything yet seen in America was a natural consequence of these concentrated evidences of good fortune. Openhandedness was a universal virtue. Civic pride esteemed a habit of splendor that would have been regarded with suspicion in Boston. San Francisco magnificoes lived like Roman proconsuls; the town mendicants lived like magnificoes elsewhere. It was the setting appointed by providence for the emergence of a race of spenders whose legend has become part of the great body of American folklore.

Part of the magic of San Francisco's glory years "Before the Fire" derives from the basic fact of gold itself. When practical jokers, thinking to laugh at the expense of gullible new arrivals, salted the unpaved streets along the Embarcadero with real gold dust to pull the leg of Johnny-come-latelies as they stepped from the gangplank of arriving ships, they were, all unwittingly, contributing their share to the legend of California the golden. The practical joke was certified fact by the time it got back to upstate New York or Newburyport, Massachusetts.

When Mike de Young, the legendary founder of the fortunes of today's *San Francisco Chronicle* threw his money on the bar when commanding one of Duncan Nichol's Pisco punches at the Bank Exchange, he did it in double eagles bearing the mint marks of Carson City or San Francisco itself, not in soiled shinplasters representing a distant and none too responsible government.

If it was openhanded John Mackay's whim to send to the Paris World's Fair of 1873 as a sample of the way the American West lived at table a flat service so heavy that it required twelve porters to unload it, it was fashioned by Shreve & Company, a firm still very much in business, from Comstock silver wrested from the deep shafts of Mackay's own Con Virginia and California mines.

As a footnote to San Francisco's reputation for opulence throughout the nineteenth century and well into the next, until the great fire of 1906 put an end to continuity with Nineveh and Tyre, in far-off Chicago special provisions were made at the railroad terminal of the Chicago & North Western Railroad for the reception of San Francisco millionaires as they stepped from the cars. There, in addition to the omnibuses of Parmelee Transfer and the public cab rank, was drawn up against the arrival of the *San Francisco Overland Limited* still a third contingent of wheeled transport. The forethoughtful management of Marshall Field & Company maintained a fleet of beautifully burnished hansom cabs with ingratiating cabbies on the box to transport eager California millionaires and their wives to the marts of trade even before they had registered at Potter Palmer's hotel.

Mr. Field and his partner, Levi Z. Leiter, let no grass grow under their congress gaiters.

It was no accident of chance that San Francisco's two best-remembered grandees of its golden era should, like its premiere absentee magnifico, D. O. Mills, date from the opening years of the money machine that was to function with such precision and for so long at the once humble Spanish mission at Yerba Buena.

The community's first and in many ways most effulgent Lorenzo was William Ralston, all-powerful cashier of Mills's Bank of California and the most clearsighted builder and visionary California was ever to know. His successor both to the mantle of regional Maecenus and the largest holder of tangible property, much of which had been evolved by Ralston, was Senator-to-be William Sharon, significantly enough the bank's representative at Virginia City on the Comstock Lode.

Other satraps of shipping and the steamcars, newspaper owners, beet-sugar magnates, stockbrokers to bonanza, tycoons of staging and the express business, barristers—for San Francisco was a potting shed for orchidaceous practitioners of law, and even men of letters were to follow in their footsteps, but the pattern of life in the San Francisco manner was established early by bankers. What the Egibi family were to Babylon and the several Rothschilds were to London, Paris, and Vienna, the Millses and Sharons and their collaterals, in-laws, and descendants were to the San Francisco legend. Posterity honors them today in Millbrae and the Mills Building, Mills College, the Sharon Building, the Sheraton Palace, Sharon Road, and the record of the liveliest lawsuits in the city's annals.

By 1871 San Francisco was so well supplied with millionaires that the popular relaxation of estimating fortunes on the comparative basis was in full swing among financial commentators and social appraisers. Under the delightful caption *"Mucho Dinero"* in that year, the *Morning Call* printed the following estimate of the resources of some of the town's first citizens:

- Leland Stanford (Central Pacific Railroad): $10,000,000
- James Phelan (Liquor and real estate): $2,500,000
- Michael Reese (Real estate and loans): $4,000,000
- Ben Holladay (Staging): $7,500,000
- Lloyd Tevis (Wells Fargo & Co.): $2,000,000
- D. O. Mills (Bank of California): $3,500,000
- James Ben Ali Haggin (Wells Fargo & Co.): $2,000,000
- Alvinza Hayward (Mother Lode gold): $3,000,000
- Henry Miller (Cattle): $2,500,000
- John Parrott (Real estate): $4,000,000
- W. C. Ralston (Bank of California): $1,500,000
- James Lick (Pianos, real estate): $3,000,000

If these figures seem, perhaps, trivial in comparison to twentieth-century fortunes where billions have supplanted millions in decimals if not in authority, it must be remembered, as elsewhere in this appraisal, that the money was hard gold currency and that in almost every case listed here, excepting William Ralston who died penniless and Ben Holladay who lost most of his millions with the same gusto he made them, all the owners of these sums vastly increased them in years to come. The Stanford fortune, for instance, by the time it had reached Leland Stanford Junior University was sufficient to stand a benefaction of between $25,000,000 and $35,000,000 without showing strain.

What is principally notable in this primeval listing is the total absence of the names of the Comstock millionaires who were, in only a decade, to be the most spectacular of all San Franciscans with the Midas touch—John Mackay, James G. Fair, William

O'Brien, Senator Sharon, and James Flood, and such collateral
eminentos as Senator George Hearst, Lucky Baldwin, and James
R. Keene who, like Darius O. Mills, went on to bigger things elsewhere. Also absent, because the Central Pacific Railroad had not
yet hit its stride, were Leland Stanford's partners, Charles Crocker,
Mark Hopkins, and Collis P. Huntington, all of whom became tall
towers of solvency in the years almost immediately following.

The men of the *Call's "Mucho Dinero"* in 1871 were only the
first crude pioneers in the realm of bank accounts with eight figures to the left of the decimal. Even so, it may be worth remarking that San Francisco was fairly well abreast of the rest of the
country in the elegance sweepstakes. Before Commodore Cornelius Vanderbilt had decided that railroads were probably here
to stay and shifted his interest from sidewheel steamers on Long
Island Sound to the New York Central, the wife of San Francisco's mayor William K. Garrison was pouring tea for her guests
from the first solid-gold tea set in the United States. Long before
Tiffany had a Fifth Avenue address, San Francisco's first jeweler, J.
W. Tucker, was advertising honest weight, solid silver one-pound
pocket watches "since no miner could be found who would carry
one that weighed less." When the future site of the Waldorf-As-
toria was given over to vacant lots and unused warehouses, the
Palace Hotel in San Francisco was serving titled foreigners champagne and oyster omelets for breakfast, and long before Ward
McAllister had been enrolled as instant Petronius in service as
Mrs. William Backhouse Astor's court chamberlain, his brother
Hall McAllister was a magistrate and arbiter of formal Society in
San Francisco and so secure in his status that he could afford to
appear in one of the impromptu charades beloved of that gen-
tle age impersonating Spring in his shirt sleeves, his magisterial
brows twined with artificial flowers.

Ward McAllister is remembered as a now archaic and faintly preposterous figure of fun; his brother, the Judge's memory is kept green
by a thoroughfare bounding one side of San Francisco's City Hall.

And it may be worth noting that, some years later when the *Call* which had assayed the community's ancestral men of *"Mucho Dinero"* was itself up for sale before a master in chancery, Delphin Delmas, representing the prospective purchaser, appeared in court flanked by five porters with $25,000 in gold coin in as many market baskets representing the down payment.

The town's primal Lorenzo was, of course, William Ralston, builder of the original Palace Hotel, benefactor of industry, architect of the fortunes (found to be somewhat faulty, alas) of the Bank of California, patron of husbandry, vineyards, and carpet factories, first citizen and civic front man and greeter without peer until the advent some decades later of Paul C. Smith, a brother magnifico who was also overtaken by misfortune and fell from comparably high estate.

Like so many other men of his social status, Henry Morrison Flagler, William Randolph Hearst, and practically all the Vanderbilts, Ralston was a builder. His masterpiece and showplace, his great estate at Belmont on the peninsula south of San Francisco and still the community's choicest residential real estate, is remembered with awe to this day. It possessed its own gas manufacturing plant, waterworks to activate its magnificent fountains, and an air-conditioning plant five full decades before the first such convenience was to be part of the St. Regis Hotel in New York. Better than $3,000,000 went into Belmont, the greater part of it into architectural splendors and landscaping, for Ralston was no great amateur of fine arts; its stables and its strain of blooded horses were a status symbol of the time comparable to a garage of Rolls-Royces and Bentleys at a later date with their attendant chauffeurs, mechanics, and maintenance plant.

Ralston's particular pride was his fine English-built stagecoach, aboard which he delighted to transport visiting notables from downtown San Francisco, there to dine them into comas on Lucullan fare and wines from a cellar said to have had no peer west of the Rothschilds. A superb horseman, it was his practice to take off from town just as the evening train of the San José Railroad was leaving the depot and pit his four matched bays against the more considerable horsepower of the locomotives *San José* and *San Mateo* as they snorted over the uneven right-of-way. As the Camino Real, where it approached Belmont, traversed the tracks at a grade crossing, the guests on the Ralston coach were almost invariably treated to a display of skilled brinkmanship when the rear wheels of the coach cleared the rails ahead of the locomotive pilot by the narrowest possible margin.

While the occupants of the coach were still congratulating themselves on being in one piece instead of fragmented along the ballast, one more sensation was in store for them. Urging his horses into a dead gallop, the driver headed them straight for a mighty portcullis which guarded the entrance to Belmont flanked by ponderous bronze and marble gateposts. In the nick of time, prompted by a forerunner of electronic controls, the gates flew open and stage, steeds, and guests bounded through.

The guests were ready for cocktails when they arrived.

Weekend guests at Belmont ranged from half a dozen to more than 200 according to Julia Cooley Altrocchi, the recognized chronicler of the spectacular San Franciscans. Dinners were a fabulous display of culinary virtuosity. There was dancing in the evening in the ballroom and on moonlit terraces, and a variety of stylish horse rigs were available for meditative twosomes and long drives in the gentle night air of an enchanted country. There were bowling and croquet, but no accounts survive of the more rugged relaxations customary among gentlemen of the day and place, draw poker and rondo coolo for fantastic stakes, and long sessions with the midnight decanter. Ralston's preoccupations, despite his origins in a lustier era on the Mississippi River, were those of cultivated domesticity, and in the General Grant era of strong whisky and stronger cigars, he appears in retrospect a gentle and well-bred aristocrat.

After Ralston's tragic death and the closing of the Bank of California on what was remembered afterward as San Francisco's Black Friday, his successors in the admiring gaze entered with complete gusto into an era of less private gentility and vastly more spectacular and publicized gestures of wealth and well-being. Its parallel many years later was to be noted by New York social historians and commentators on public mores in the emergence from the conservative cotillions of old-guard private entertaining to unabashed horray in public restaurants, hotel ballrooms, and the glittering precincts of the lobster palaces of Broadway and the Long Island turnpikes. San Francisco had few resorts of public ostentation, but those it had, have become the stuff of legend, "the cocktail route" of perfumed recollection.

When the Bank of California reopened its doors on a reorganized basis and good times returned, largely on the strength of new bonanzas on the Comstock and their attendant speculation in mining shares, it was apparent that the principal beneficiary of fiscal catastrophe had been a man who had played second fiddle to Ralston in his great days and now emerged to assume the mantle of his one-time patron. From the very beginning of William Sharon's career as a man of money, San Franciscans were genuinely happy to know that they had in their midst the proprietor of a residence where the satin draperies and lace curtains of each window cost "in excess of $2000," where the "richly garlanded" bedspreads were topped with mounds of pillows each in a $140 lace pillowcase, and a console mirror in the Senator's dressing room was worth $5000.

This set the style for Sharon's private life, and his public image, if anything, was even more sumptuously girded with magnificence.

෨ · ෨ · ෨

Much of the dazzling wealth that marked San Francisco in the closing years of the nineteenth century derived from the deep mines of the Comstock Lode 250 miles away across the High Sierra and underneath the howling wilderness of Virginia City, Nevada.

The wealthiest man in the West, John Mackay, had originally entered Virginia City virtually penniless in company with his future partner in the fabulous riches of the Big Bonanza, Jim Fair. Early in the Comstock excitements, the future archmillionaires came over the pass on foot from Washoe Valley and beheld Virginia sprawled below them in its noisy wickedness and primeval tumults. Mackay asked Fair if he had any money on him.

"Here's four bits; it's the only money I have in the world."

Borrowing it, Mackay raised his arm and sent the coin spinning into the Nevada sage far down the hillside.

"Whatever did you do that for, John?"

"So now we can arrive like gentlemen."

Ten years later Mackay was to give a dinner in honor of the visiting Duke of Sutherland in Virginia City's rococo International Hotel in which 1000 magnums of champagne were consumed by guests variously attired in evening dress and cowhide knee boots, and when Mackay died after the turn of the century his secretary was to tell the press that neither he nor his employer could estimate his fortune within $20,000,000.

Still a legend in San Francisco, a town that cherishes its golden memories as lovingly as an oenophile might cherish a cellar of ancestral Madeira, is the gilded folklore associated with Zeb Kendall who died a few years ago in Virginia City, whence at least one of his several substantial fortunes derived. Zeb, a powerfully muscled six-foot-three prospector at the Southern Mines, had first struck it rich in the Tonopah and Goldfield excitements of 1905, the last great gold rush in the continental United States, and had made a name for himself as equally powerful with a bottle and at any games of chance that were handy. At least six successive bonanzas each in excess of $1,000,000 passed through his hands and over the roulette and dice tables of a wide-open Nevada and at Tanforan and Bay Meadows race tracks outside San Francisco.

Comstock old-timers like to recall the time that Zeb, in his seventy-fifth year, was discovered by his wife Belle after a three-day absence from home magnificently in wine and in a non-stop poker game conducted by Honest Uncle Len Haffey in Virginia City's Delta Saloon.

In outrage, Belle leveled an accusing finger through the cigar smoke and demanded: "Zeb Kendall, at your age aren't you ashamed of yourself carrying on like this? Why, one of these days you'll just drop dead dealing poker with one hand and a glass of whisky in the other!"

"Can you imagine a pleasanter way to die, my dear?"

Back in 1910, Belle had extracted one of a recurrent series of promises of reform from Zeb at a time when, awash with profits from the Mizpah diggings at Tonopah, the Kendalls were occupying a suite in the St. Francis Hotel in San Francisco. All promises of reform to the contrary notwithstanding, Belle suspected the worst when she heard from Gus Boehl, the head barkeep, that Zeb and Wyatt Earp, an old friend, had last been seen looking over the day's entries at Bay Meadows.

Belle settled down to await the impending bankruptcy in her suite overlooking Union Square. Days passed while, disgruntled, she tapped a foot, and with each passing day her vexation increased. Geometrically.

At long last her errant spouse put in an appearance, unpressed, unshaved, and smelling powerfully of strong waters, and tossed a battered brief case on the bed.

Belle Kendall began unburdening her mind which had by this time acquired quite a freight of annoyance. At a pause for breath, Zeb tried to get in a placating word.

"My dear, in that brief case. . . ."

"I don't give a belch in a windstorm what's in that brief case," and with a sweeping gesture she scooped up the offending item and hurled it out the open window into Powell Street three floors down. As it fell it came open in a blizzard of what, even as they disappeared from sight, Belle was able to identify as banknotes of large denomination.

"Just one hundred ten thousand dollars even, my dear. There was a three-year-old named. . . ."

Belle in later years swore that three bellhops, an assistant manager, and an uncounted toll of loungers were trampled underfoot
as she tore through the lobby and beat her way into the crowd that,
understandably, had assembled to pick $1000 bills out of the air
and look upward, hopefully, to see if there were more.

A determined woman, Mrs. Kendall recovered all but $10,000.

"After that," Zeb recalled, "she at least used to listen to my story
before she began beating me around the ears."

ᴼᵞᴼ · ᴼᵞᴼ · ᴼᵞᴼ

A specially gifted member of the big spenders club in the California division centering in Hollywood was, improbably
enough, W. C. Fields, one of the most fascinating of curmud-
geons whose avarice was only matched by his hatred of relatives
and whose most enduring monument is the aphorism "A man who
would strike a little child cannot be all bad."

Fields became substantially wealthy in the films in a day before
income taxes were excessive and translated a large part of his assets
into cash on the theory that the security afforded by instant availability matched the inevitable erosion of inflation and the absence
of interest. In his last years his great preoccupation was seeing
to it that none of his money should, after his death, be available
to any relative of any degree of consanguinity whatsoever. These
were numerous, and, in Fields's book, only hovering in the background ready to pounce upon his estate the moment it was filed
for probate.

How to make his resources available to himself during his lifetime and yet not available to his heirs consumed his waking hours
and resources of crafty evasion. He at length came up with the
nearest thing yet devised for refuting the maxim that "you can't
take it with you."

In a widespread network of safe deposit boxes each rented under
an assumed name known to himself alone, Fields deposited sums

of money estimated at close to $1,000,000. As long as he lived he had only to produce the right key and remember the proper name to have access to cash resources of ample dimensions. When death took him their secret whereabouts would die with him together with the passwords required for access. Without clues to or evidence of their existence his heirs would be effectively thwarted.

"I once surprised him in a private moment when he was going over a card file of his secret bone yards of money," Gene Fowler wrote the author of this book in the last year of his life. "I caught only a few of the identifying marks to denote various cities, but I'd say there were at least thirty altogether, maybe more. He told me he had them in safe deposit boxes strategically located all over the United States and Canada and even one in Germany—in a Berlin bank. These, he confided gloatingly, were all kept under an assortment of names, none of them his own."

"When I asked him why in hell he kept money in Germany (for there was a war on at the moment) where he was unlikely ever to get it back, he fixed me with his Colonel Seller's gaze and replied without a nuance of mirth: 'Yeah? Well, suppose that little bastard Hitler just happens to win?'"

"I would not venture to suggest how much money he had hidden away, but know for certain that he deliberately and with malice against his heirs manholed a lot of loot. The late Gregory La Cava, film director and student of human nature, was perhaps closer to Fields than anyone after the death of Sam Hardy. He was in the best position to offer an educated guess on Fields's earning powers and his probable financial status.

"'The old sonofabitch,' he said to me a year or so after we had held *three* wakes for our friend, 'put away at least half a million where it will never be claimed or properly identified. I know that the known assets of his legally probated estate came to over eight hundred thousand dollars and it is possible that he had as much again where nobody but the government will ever get hold of it when the rent runs out on those strongboxes.'"

"In his halcyon days, W. C. began to live well. His suits cost him $300 a copy from the best Vine Street English pantsbuilder and were of fine cloth and cut, mostly the soft cashmere type of materials, never loud or of the Jimmy Walker-Damon Runyon style that Broadway used to think Edward VII would have liked.

"He ate well, mostly the Keen's Chop House type of food, although on one occasion he tried Italian cuisine. Never the French, so far as I know, and I was with him a great deal. He liked desserts, but only the ones that had brandy aboard; cherries jubilee, for example, and crêpes Suzette. On one occasion he visited the Hollywood Brown Derby while in the clutches of a monumental hangover. His doctors had limited him to one drink a day and he got around this as had Colonel William F. Cody in the long-ago Windsor Hotel days in Denver when Harry Tammen was bartender. Fields would order a fifth of gin, a fifth of vermouth, and a mixing glass the size of Strangler Lewis' neck. He would pour the fifth of gin into the glass, then add perhaps an eyedropper of vermouth, and there he had his one drink for the day.

"Anyway, on the day of his great hangover, he happened to mention his plight to the maître d'hôtel whose name was Milius or some such, who naively suggested an Alka-Seltzer.

"Mr. Fields became enraged by the prescription from a non-medical practitioner. 'Alka-Seltzer!' he said at the top of his Islamic prayer-caller's voice, 'Alka-Seltzer! Damn it all, the noise of its dissolving in the glass would kill me!'

"Fields was not a spendthrift in the usual sense of the term (like me, for example). He had two sides to his spending nature. When he was a host either in his home or at Chasen's, which was his second residence, he spared neither effort nor expense to do well by his guests. He entertained less and less in his last home in the Los Feliz district, mostly because of his dwindling health and interests. Before his small, shapely hands became unsure of their movements, he liked to serve a guest a plate of goodies from the buffet. Then, just as the newcomer reached for his full plate, W. C. would drop it. But he would retrieve it in mid-air, like an infielder digging one off the turf, and then give it, in sound condition, to the almost swooning guest.

"He used to give parties, for perhaps twenty at a time, and frowned upon gate crashers at these parties in his home. Curiously, too, he did not like drunks on his own premises. He believed that twelve was a better number than twenty and there were wines at all times and of all sorts, but W. C. himself was a fellow for the other stuff. If you became overserved he had a portable steam cabinet in which you might drain off the pores without leaving the party. He tried to leave this cabinet to me in his will, but I would have none of it and settled for the crooked pool cue that adorns the wall of what you call my caboose.

"Mr. Fields would never loan money. He said he didn't want to encroach on the sadistic rights of banks and loan agencies, but if he were sure no one was likely to find out that he had a kindly vein in the marble of his heart, he would *give* money in large sums to special friends. Believe it or not, he once tried to force $30,000 on me as a token of kindness and esteem. No dice.

"Mr. Fields also had occasion once (when paying off a secret agent who brought him in two bottles of Bols gin when he was in a drying-out home) to display a roll of bills as fat as one of the younger sequoias. When I urged him against display of this kind on the grounds that it might encourage some less affluent resident of Pasadena to call on him during his Nembutal hours, he snorted and said in his reedy voice:

" 'I am always feigning unconsciousness when I appear to be sleeping like some lovely, lousy child. I'll meet the brigand with my gun.' "

"This was an old .45 Frontier Model Colt's with which he shot at, but never hit, the sea gulls that regularly robbed his fishpond at Los Feliz.

" 'This is my getaway dough,' he said of the bank roll. He always seemed afraid that sometime, somehow, he would have to leave town as he indeed did in the old days and shouldn't be caught

without ready money. I was not with him when he died and sometimes wonder if he had that roll in the pocket of his big white
bathrobe, and if so, what honest person might have come upon it
and forgotten to mention it."

Fowler himself qualifies on a number of grounds for membership in the big spenders club of his generation, having gone
through more than $1,000,000, which is in the record as having
been paid him by the studios for which he worked, with nothing
more to show for it than the scars on his liver which, he was fond
of saying, looked like the face of a Heidelberg extra in *The Student
Prince.* The only thing he ever wanted badly, and neglected to buy
when he was in funds, was a Rolls-Royce.

"You haven't got an extra one you don't want?" he asked a
reporter who arrived to interview him in a Phantom III cabriolet.
Fowler always claimed his improbable address, 12323 Twenty-sec-
ond Helena Drive in Beverly Hills was really the combination to
W. C. Fields's safe.

In his time as a newspaper reporter in New York, Fowler was
widely celebrated as the most proficient expense-account artist in a
calling that boasted of its virtuosity in this highly specialized field.
Upon one occasion there was a project in discussion among the
higher executive echelons of the *New York American* that would
involve sending Fowler on a hurried assignment to London, and
the matter of expenses was advanced by Victor Watson, William
Randolph Hearst's special representative in the department of
finances. What did Fowler think would be required for a weekend
jaunt to London and back?

Fowler without hesitation named the sum of $1200. It was a
time when first-class fare and a single cabin on the *Aquitania* was
$275 with a considerable discount for round trip, and Mr. Watson
dropped his cigar at mention of the amount Fowler thought would
cover the bare essentials.

"It's a bargain, as you will see," explained the unruffled man of
headlines. "If I go to London it will mean I have to take my son out

of school and send him back to Denver. This will entail his expenses to Colorado and those incidental to getting him settled in college at Boulder. I'll have to cancel my own lease here in New York and probably have to pay more for whatever I can find when I return. My wife will have to move into a hotel, say the Plaza, while I am away, and you know what hotel apartments are nowadays. In addition to these basic costs I'll have to meet, I need some personal refurbishing. On a Cunard boat I'll have to dress for dinner every night and my old dinner jacket is far too seedy for Mr. Hearst's personal representative to be seen in. And in London, I'll need a top hat and morning dress. All English reporters wear formal attire on assignment. Then, there's...."

Watson hastily scribbled an order on the *American's* cashier for the $1200. "You've convinced me that this is the greatest bargain Mr. Hearst ever made," he reassured the author of *Timberline*. "Please be on your way before you convince me you need a valet for the assignment."

Fowler was present at a meeting between Hearst and Henry Ford where, over the after-dinner coffee, the conversation turned to money matters. Mr. Ford took a dim view of the current state of the stock market, prophetically as it turned out, and suddenly asked the master of San Simeon:

"Mr. Hearst, have you got any money?"

"I never have any money, Mr. Ford," replied Hearst, who had just purchased a Spanish monastery and was having it knocked down stone by stone and loaded in a freighter for reconstruction in California. "I always seem to have spent any money I have coming to me before I get it."

"That's no way to conduct your affairs," Ford said. "You ought to get yourself four or five hundred million dollars in cash. Tuck it away and forget about it. It'll come in handy sometime for a rainy day."

Arthur Brisbane, who moved in fairly rarefied circles and owned the Ritz Tower Hotel on New York's Park Avenue, once remarked of his boss that Mr. Hearst was the only man of his personal acquaintance who could get along on less than $10,000,000 pocket money a year. Hearst seldom had ready money in his pocket and often, by mid-evening on a night on the town in New York, would find himself without more than loose change and faced with giving a large supper party at some luxury restaurant. He once, in such a plight, stopped by the *American's* uptown circulation and classified ad office, a hole-in-the-wall on Columbus Circle, and asked the elderly custodian of the night shift if he could advance him, say, $5000 to tide him over the emergency. The day's total receipts came to only $400, which Hearst pocketed for cab fare with the courteous parting admonition to his vassal: "Would you mind, please, keeping five thousand dollars here at all times. Small bills, please."

It was a time of easygoing auditors in the Hearst organization and Damon Runyon, if he found himself out a few dollars at the end of the week that he couldn't account for, put it down to "going round and about." When Bugs Baer tried a similar expedient and charged the office with $15 for "going round and about like Damon Runyon" it was disallowed.

Fowler's most legendary assault upon the auditors of the *New York American* in his days as a reporter was the financing of an expedition to Moose Jaw in the Saskatchewan wilds of Canada in the early twenties to meet a party of lost aviators who had been downed in the arctic precincts of Hudson Bay and whose recovery was, for the moment at least, a matter of breathless interest to Mr. Hearst's readers. A high point on this safari, which was only undertaken after Fowler had purchased a full arctic explorer's outfit from Abercrombie & Fitch, was his conning a vice president of the Canadian Pacific Railway into lending him a private car, fully staffed and provisioned with potables for a six-week vigil in the wilderness, on the patently specious grounds that it would be good promotion for the railroad. In the light of later developments, it would have been better for the Canadian Pacific if all aviators had been strangled at birth.

Although he never stirred from the warm interior of the Pullman throughout his stay at Moose Jaw, Fowler regularly tabbed his employer for the full-time services of a dog-sled team and its proprietors and billed the Hearst organization, when one of the shaggy beasts succumbed to old age, for his value as "an emissary of mercy died in line of duty." He wrote a touching dispatch about the faithful and heroic dog to justify the $350 and, carried away by the pathos and grandeur of his theme, next week billed the *American* for an additional $350.

When the auditors complained that they had already paid the top going price for one Husky and what, please, was the additional charge, Fowler deposed that the deceased dog's mate was pining away from loneliness and broken heart and that only a replacement would prevent further and more costly deaths in the ranks. Since Fowler was known to enjoy Mr. Hearst's personal and particular favor, this expense was also honored and, as he departed Moose Jaw for home at the end of the assignment, the *American's* crack reporter appended a final item to his expenses: "To Marble Headstone for Sled Dog Died in Line of Duty: $100."

๑๖·๑๖·๑๖

Time was when Brookline, Massachusetts, was widely regarded by social historians, commentators, and statisticians as the most concentrated enclave of wealth in the United States. This was, to be sure, back in the Thomas W. Lawson age of Massachusetts finances and the claim hasn't been heard in recent years.

But even Brookline in its palmiest days of free-wheeling social and financial teem didn't have the greatest per capita concentration of Rolls-Royce and Bentley motorcars this side of West Brook Street, a police commissioner so polished and urbane as to have stepped directly from one of the flossier novels of the late E. Phillips Oppenheim, and half-million-dollar art robberies to add a panache of solid-gold chaos to an already well-advertised and very upper-case contest over the terms of a $12,000,000 will in one of California's two or three top-rank families.

All these enchantments are not exactly free for the asking in Hillsborough, California, where nothing at all is for free, but they are at least the conversational currency of the realm in a midst where police officers casually scuffle with the subjunctive mood and where Bing Crosby, when shopping for a *pied-à-terre,* rejects a forty-three-room residence (mansion, in the lexicon of the San Francisco press) because it is "too cozy."

San Francisco, to be sure, inclines to take Hillsborough in its stride, but intimations of its almost unearthly aloofness and implications of towering solvency began to penetrate the awareness of the outer world a short while back when, within a fortnight after the death of W. W. Crocker, titular head and patriarch of a family whose wealth reaches back to the pioneering days of the Pacific Railroad, his widow found herself on the receiving end of a suit contesting his $12,000,000 will at practically the identical moment when art in the form of Van Goghs and Renoirs and in terms of an estimated $500,000 was being looted from the fifty-three-room Crocker manse.

Nothing so delightful had happened to relieve the tedium of San Francisco's very tediously respectable top-drawer society since the golden era when Senator William Sharon was involved in spectacular adultery and the silver kings of the Comstock Lode were entertaining in the manner of Henry VIII and Cardinal Wolsey at the original Palace Hotel.

The will contest and its contingent fine arts burglary brought newspaper coverage from not only the usual city side reporters but the *Chronicle's* august society editor, Frances Moffett, who, putting a police card in her hat, drove down to the peninsula in person in an imported sports car to view firsthand the scene of the crime.

The investigation disclosed some aspects and properties of grandeur hitherto only suspected, but now validated, about life in ineffable Hillsborough. One was that the distance from the Crocker gatekeeper's lodge to the Crocker residence was a measured mile through a private park rivaled only by Blenheim Castle and in a part of the world a good deal more thickly populated than the country seat of the Dukes of Marlborough. It also revealed that the Crocker staff of domestics, both current and in the immediate enough past to be investigated by the FBI came to approximately forty maids, gardeners, chauffeurs, cooks, and house footmen, all supervised by a P. G. Wodehouse type of butler of Scotch ancestry named Graham with pronounced personal opinions about fine arts. "Van Gogh is not my favorite painter," he told the press. It also revealed that the household staff at *Sky Farm* on Redington Road was so numerous as in the ordinary course of things to be engaged in squads and platoons through the agency of the personnel department at the Crocker Bank in San Francisco. Other incidentals about life among the Crockers disclosed that the family silver, kept in a massive silver room or vault at *Sky Farm* was of such a dimension as to require the constant attention of a specially assigned domestic who did nothing but keep it polished, and that Mrs. Crocker was in the habit of sending her dry cleaning by air to Paris, a statistic translated by a local columnist into the figure of approximately $25 every time she had a frock cleaned.

This was a detail of life among the Crockers which, peculiarly enough, tended to endear them to the California public, if anything could be said to lend humanity to such chilly magnificence, because it established continuity with gold-rush times and San Francisco's early days about which the town is very sentimental indeed.

In '49 and the early 1850s some years before the first Charles Crocker, a hearty of immense vitality, was occupied laying the tracks of the Pacific Railroad, San Francisco enjoyed a labor shortage of acute proportions. Every able-bodied man had headed for the Mother Lode diggings and the few women who had come out from the East were not the washwoman type. The heathen Chinee had not yet been imported from Canton to become the universal laundryman and getting a ruffled shirt washed and starched was next to impossible. In this pass the pioneers hit on an ingenious solution, the forerunner of Mrs. Crocker's Paris dry cleaner. Since buying new shirts and sundries was cheaper than hiring a wash-woman at $100 a day, the Argonauts let their personal laundry accumulate for twelve months and then sent it out in a clipper ship bound for China where it could be washed and ironed for next to nothing. It came back a year later, and for some time it was an established California practice to send laundry across the Pacific and get it back next year. Mrs. Crocker's practice of sending her dry cleaning to Paris was clearly a bond with the ineffable past.

That the members of the Crocker family were not accustomed to being interrogated by the police was demonstrated in full sight of the San Francisco press corps by the arrival on the scene of Ann Coleman Woolworth in a jade-green Jaguar sports model. When asked by one of Hillsborough's positively Chesterfieldian police officers if she could contribute anything to the solution of the art robbery, "she adjusted her dark glasses, rolled up the car window, and roared off up the winding road." No duchess rejecting the over-tures of a crude Paris *flic* could have been more haughty.

The big art robbery at *Sky Farm* took place over a weekend and a gratifying all-star cast of performers assembled with practically the speed of light. Fingerprint experts, uniformed patrolmen, ranking police officials, and the FBI, because of the magnitude of the sum involved, converged upon the San Mateo County hillsides with a full complement of newspaper photographers and reporters. Seven police dogs, the full canine contingent at Hillsborough headquar-ters, combed the 100 wooded acres and the gardens of the Crocker demesne for traces, clues, and evidence. Russell Fisher, chief of police and so personable an officer that elderly matrons were reportedly considering art robberies of their own, posed amiably in Sherlock Holmes attitudes. He also posed with Zack, his opposite number in the canine detective corps. Zack posed with Sergeant Grant Mar-shall, an almost unendurably handsome member of the finest. Gra-ham, the butler, was agreeable to posing with a tray containing glasses and what turned out to be a bottle of California burgundy. "I'll fetch a bottle of Romanée Conti '55 if the label will show," he said affably.

All the setting lacked of a well-mannered English crime novel was an international art expert who, fortuitously enough, put in an appearance in the person of Robert Leylan, general manager in the United States for Christie's auction house in London, who was in town en route to the opening of an art museum in Los Angeles. San Francisco was agreeable to skimming the cream off his arrival and Mr. Leylan made everyone happy with the considered opinion that the value of the missing Van Goghs and Renoirs might easily top half a million dollars. This went far toward salving local pride, the more so since Mr. Leylan was delivering a $2,234,000 painting, Rembrandt's "Titus," to a culture-conscious Los Angeles Lorenzo who had bought it the week before in a splendor of headlines.

The variety and strictly eighteen-karat quality of these tailings from the Hillsborough diggings, far from being choice, selective samples are, as a matter of factual record, the merest run of the mill assays in a social and economic bonanza to rival the Comstock Lode in Nevada where many of Hillsborough's ancestral fortunes had their origins. As the choicest of all San Francisco residential suburbs, Hillsborough and its adjacent Burlingame, of which it is a sort of exalted suburb in itself, are a refreshing prospect for the historian or commentator who habitually inclines to a melancholy view of an ever increasingly egalitarian social scene.

Situated in the rolling hills to the west of the Camino Real approximately eighteen miles from downtown San Francisco, a Hillsborough address is the peer in the local status sweepstakes of maintaining nothing but imported motorcars in the garage and only male domestics in the front of the house. Its tax rolls glitter not only with the name of Crocker, but also with De Guigne, Cameron, De Young, Tobin, Moffett, Martin, and Miller, effulgent names in the mink dustcloth set, and with the veritable power structure of the financial community as well. There, on Floribunda Avenue, resides Charles de Young Thieriot, publisher of the venerable *San Francisco Chronicle;* there is the domicile address of Benjamin F. Biaggini, president of the all-powerful Southern Pacific

Railroad; there arrives the daily mail for Bing Crosby, owner of far-flung properties and enterprises, including a San Mateo bank.

Hillsborough is a township distinct from its parent Burlingame. Its first resident of great wealth and distinction was the late Colonel Daniel C. Jackling, founder of the Utah Copper Company and one of the truly towering magnificoes of the twentieth-century West. Jackling, whose estate was so vast and holdings so diversified that after his death it took auditors five years just to list and appraise them, already had a skyscraper apartment on the roof of the Mark Hotel in San Francisco that is now the world-famous Top-of-the-Mark Bar. When he undertook to build a country estate at Woodside, on the peninsula, adjacent to the newly formed township of Hillsborough, the corporate limits of the community were promptly enlarged to embrace the property of this princely taxpayer.

Some idea of the attitude of Colonel Jackling toward pocket money is reflected in the recollections of Schuyler Parsons of Palm Beach and Newport in the days when, as one of the foremost traders in art objects and an agent for well-to-do clients, he traveled on the occasions of his several patrons.

"In the late twenties," Parsons recalls, "Joe Widener asked me to go to San Francisco for him to look at four Chinese vases that were reportedly available at Gump's, the great art store there. The vases represented the four seasons and Widener said that if I liked the color I was to phone him and get his authorization for their purchase. I never saw anything finer in form, color, or contour, but Mr. Gump said he was holding them on twenty-four-hour option for a client. The client was Colonel Jackling, who wanted them for his new place on the peninsula south of San Francisco. The next day Colonel Jackling offered him $50,000 for the four and thereafter the phone wires were hot for three days and nights. On the fourth day I made my last bid in the sum of $105,000 for my client and it was then that the Colonel bid $110,000 and got the vases. The price would have stayed at $50,000 if two rich men hadn't started bidding against each other, one of them for a property he had never even seen."

"Amusingly enough, neither Mrs. Jackling nor Mrs. Widener knew of the transaction. Secrecy was enjoined on and maintained by all concerned lest the wives demand that the money be diverted to jewelry."

A notable Hillsborough eccentric was Mrs. Francis J. Carolan, a daughter of George Mortimer Pullman, who built an enormous country estate beyond her means to support. When, at one period in its affairs, the Pullman Company in Chicago was, as Mrs. Carolan felt, remiss in the matter of dividends, she waged active warfare against her father's corporation. When traveling on western railroads, her first gesture was to throw all sheets, linen, and fixtures that said Pullman on them into the aisle outside her stateroom, whereupon her maid refurnished the room with her personal bed linen and towels.

Today's reigning grandee, or one of them, is Christian de Guigne, a chemical-products magnate whose feudal château overlooks a wide vista from an appropriate hillside. The De Guignes are notable locally for, only three years ago, having added a private ballroom to their residence at an estimated cost of $75,000 for use at a single party. It was, beyond all peradventure, the last private ballroom that will ever be built in California.

In Hillsborough in the community's white elephant mansion known as *La Dolphine,* when he is not in Paris, London, or way points, dwells in state Hugh Chisholm, the only man ever to be born in the Plaza Hotel in New York with a published book of verse to his credit. The magnitude of *La Dolphine* is so considerable that neither Chisholm, who married Rosemarie Warburton, nor any of its last three owners has been able to furnish it. Noel Coward, on being shown its barren wonderments, called it "Vacant Hall."

Residential restrictions in Hillsborough forbid trade or the practice of any profession so that doctors and dentists with a Hillsborough clientele maintain offices in San Mateo, Hillsborough's commercial entrepôt and market town. Although it was generally felt that his occupation as author of best sellers might reasonably be

overlooked, Ernest Gann, author of *The High and the Mighty,* feared
that pounding a typewriter within city limits might lay him open to
legal prosecution and on this account rejected a good buy in Hillsborough real estate in favor of a less advantageous proposition in
Pebble Beach on Monterey peninsula. Samuel F. B. Morse, landed
proprietor and feudal overlord of Pebble Beach and its adjacent Del
Monte Lodge, takes a relaxed attitude toward men of letters.

As is true in Beverly Hills, a closely parallel enclave of privilege,
there are no sidewalks in Hillsborough. A car, preferably Rolls-
Royce or Bentley, is the only thinkable means of locomotion and
pedestrians, unless walking dogs, are automatically suspect, and
usually questioned by the police. Lord Kinross, the literary peer
of *Punch,* was only a few years ago a house guest who, in all innocence, undertook a brisk after-dinner constitutional on Hayne
Road. Before he had gone a block, he was apprehended and questioned by the occupants of a squad car. Thereafter, when inclined
to exercise, he borrowed a standard poodle from his host and was
immune to suspicion.

Police and fire protection in Hillsborough are legendary. So efficient are the local pompiers, seconded in the event of major conflagration by San Mateo and Burlingame departments, that fire insurance is the cheapest thing a householder can have. When the very
social Jackson Moffetts' Eucalyptus Drive home burned a few years
back, Mr. and Mrs. Moffett were alone in their upstairs bedroom,
since their domestics sleep in a converted stable, when flames cut
them off from the only stairway to safety. It was in the early hours
of the morning and Mrs. Moffett had sufficient presence of mind
to call the telephone central and give the details of their predica-
ment but, in understandable haste, hung up without saying who
she was or where the fire. In less than a minute, the operator had
traced the call, identified the address, called the fire departments
of both Hillsborough and Burlingame, and alerted two separate
hospitals to send ambulances, just in case. She then called back to
assure Mrs. Moffett that help was on the way and to suggest that,

if their position became untenable, they might resort to sheets tied together via the window. A good square knot, she insisted, nothing that would slip.

It is pleasant to be able to report that on the basis of prompt and unquestioning payment of their several adequate insurance policies, the Moffetts are established in a rebuilt residence with amenities of de luxe they lacked before the fire including not just the old-fashioned gold plumbing fixtures in their several bathrooms that everybody has in Hillsborough, but heavily gold-plated toilet handles and drainpipes as well.

Hillsborough police are celebrated not alone for the efficiency of the department in matters of basic protection but for their handsome persons and an urbanity that has to be experienced to be believed. When a San Francisco bank president inadvertently parked his Bentley Continental convertible in front of a hydrant while dining at the home of friends on Poett Road, the police officer who presented himself, cap in hand at the front door, addressed him by name and asked if he might have the keys with an eye to moving the car without interrupting the service of the meal.

On another occasion, when a Hillsborough stockbroker who had met with reverses had the bad taste to blow his brains out in the garage, the police charged with reporting the mishap submitted a list of eligible undertakers who they assured the family were reliable practitioners, and summoned the mortician of the widow's choice with a minimum of fuss. A Hillsborough piece of fire equipment then called, without bells, lights, or sirens, hosed down the garage, and retired after turning off the lights and leaving the keys in the kitchen.

Except in the Crocker mansion, servants, even in Hillsborough, are not so readily available that they are treated with anything but consideration. A case in point may well be the senior partner of one of the most patrician of all San Francisco law firms who doesn't drive a motorcar and is invariably driven on his social occasions by his wife. On the evening in question, the lady of the house happened to be in New York for a weekend at the Regency (where else?) and the host undertook to drive his guest home. They arrived at the barrister's well-maintained place at twenty minutes of eleven but the guest made no effort to leave the warmth and shelter of the car. Instead, he made small talk and kept consulting his watch. At just eleven he thanked his host for dinner and transport and presented himself at his own front door which opened and closed behind him as if on electronic controls.

A man not to be bothered with keys any more than with motorcars, he also employed a venerable and valued butler who, although given to retiring early, made a practice when his master dined out of getting up and dressed for his proper reception on the point of eleven. If the master of the house was early, he waited his man's convenience. Hillsborough to the hilt.

If further evidence of Hillsborough's perfumed way of life were needed, it might be found at the town's municipal dump, which is not only liberally spotted with empty caviar tins, *foie gras* firkins, and discarded magnums of Bollinger champagne, but also, quite literally, overgrown in spots with orchids. An estimated $5000 worth of these exotic blooms was recently discarded from the greenhouses of the Alfred Ducatos who, by happy coincidence, live on Floribunda Avenue. "They were getting out of hand," Mrs. Ducato explained, "so we decided to make a clean sweep and start all over again."

One of the distinctions of Hillsborough is that, whenever possible, it employs interior decorators, architects, and landscape designers who do business from either Rolls-Royce or Bentley cars, preferably the former. The decorator consistently awarded the fattest plums when a Hillsborough homesteader does a face-lifting job on the manse, although the De Guigne ballroom went to his dapper rival Tony Hail who only drives a Mercedes-Benz, is Clarence Slade. Slade, on his professional occasions, tools from his Jackson Square shop in San Francisco and parks under Hillsborough's most patrician porte-cocheres in a white Rolls-Royce shooting brake with wire wheels and a paneled body in natural wood. His fees run about 20 per cent above those of his competitors who merely arrive in Cadillacs, which on the peninsula are regarded as strictly for the help.

And, if additional testimony to Hillsborough's respectful attitude toward money in large emphatic bundles is in demand it may be found in that of Charles Clegg, a partner with the author in numerous skirmishes with belles lettres who maintains an opulent villa set amid three acres of gardenia trees on Vista Road. While walking his dog T-Bone unseen among the camellias near the next-door neighbor's, he chanced to overhear a colloquy between the neighbor's children who had agreed to entertain a visiting moppet with a childish charade involving Robin Hood.

"Good," exclaimed the untutored visitor, "we can steal from the rich and give to the poor."

"That isn't the way we play it in Hillsborough," he was admonished. "Here we steal from the poor and give to the rich."

Chapter Three
Pets of the Lobster Palaces

*Diamond Jim and the Big Eaters . . . Them as Has 'Em Wears
'Em . . . Meet Me at Delmonico's . . . Lillian Russell Rode a Golden
Bicycle and John Gates Bet a Million on Anything . . . The Music
Never Stopped at Rector's and a Case of Wine Per Person Was Par
at Dinner . . . Champagne Corks Were Collected in Laundry Baskets . . . Café Society Was Born at the Waldorf-Astoria . . . Hetty
Green's Son, Ned, Was a Reverse Chip Off the Old Block . . . He Collected Stamps, Mistresses, $10,000 Bills, a Limousine with a Toilet,
and a Jeweled Chamber Pot . . . Taxes on His Estate Were the Biggest Ever in Massachusetts. . . .*

W HEN THE PECULIAR manifestation known as café
society emerged upon the general awareness immediately after the repeal of prohibition to the delight of
Sunday supplement editors and the explicit disgust of social cave
dwellers encased in pearl dog collars from Park Avenue to Nob
Hill, the general impression was of something new under the sun.

Fun and games in public places, such as the Stork Club, "21," and
El Morocco, the availability of their participants to being photographed by the newly emergent technique of candid photography
and high emulsion speed film, and the taking over of social attitudes of elegance by professional exhibitionists, such as Brenda
Diana Duff Frazier, all were viewed with mingled emotions of

apprehension and pleasure. Everyone, however, agreed that there had never been anything like it before.

They couldn't have been more mistaken.

The New York café society of the 1930s had its antecedents and its bloodlines well established in a confraternity of playboys and self-publicists at the turn of the century which embraced in its personnel and activities almost every aspect of a Noel Coward first-night list on Broadway except its availability to photography. Lobster-palace society had its news-making names, its arbiters of elegances, its resorts of publicized fashion, its court jesters and heralds, its games, intrigues, and scandals in exactly the degree as these things were characteristic of the patrons of John Perona's El Morocco. They also had money, some of them in gratifyingly abundant quantities.

One other thing they possessed that somehow never attached to the glossy and expensive people who surrounded Cole Porter and sponged off Elsa Maxwell who, in turn, sponged off even better-heeled gullibles. The lobster-palace set entered into the historic record. So did the places they frequented and the attitudes they assumed. Bet-a-Million Gates, Diamond Jim Brady, Stanford White, James R. Keene, Lillian Russell, and, to a lesser degree, Manny Chappelle and George Kessler are assured of a fragrant immortality in the folklore of the land. So are Peacock Alley at the Waldorf-Astoria, Rector's, Shanley's, and Jack Dunstan's. That the people who comprised the lobster-palace set were largely vulgarians of the first chop, often barbarians with the manners and attire of Texas and Oklahoma and the accents of Ohio well upholstered in diamonds and claw-hammer coats, has faded from their collective recollection. They have become an enviable era, like the never-never land of San Francisco "Before the Fire." They radiated good times and good humor and they spent money, always the ultimate American attribute of status, like crazy. Them as has, wears 'em. Meet me at Rector's.

The greatest single contribution to expensive cheerfulness at the end of the nineteenth century was beyond all argument the

Waldorf-Astoria Hotel. America's costliest and most enviable pleasure dome was located at the corner of Fifth Avenue and Thirty-
fourth Street on the site that had previously been occupied by
the supreme ruler of New York society, *the* Mrs. Astor, who had
by 1894 removed further uptown. Lessor of the jointly operated
Waldorf and Astoria Hotels was George Boldt, a former Philadel-
phian with a loyal following recruited from the "fast" set of hard-
drinking, hard-betting, high-living bankers, stockbrokers, plung-
ers, horse owners, wine salesmen, and their hangers-on who shortly
made their established headquarters in the men's bar.

A not infrequent patron of this most exalted of all masculine
oases was the great J. Pierpont Morgan himself. Contemporary
sketch artists never failed to include the likeness of course, plebe-
ian Bet-a-Million Gates in their renditions of the scene. Usually
they also included bearded, silk-hatted James R. Keene, a professional hatchet man of the stock market who already had been
humiliatingly cleaned out by Jay Gould but had risen again from
the ashes of his fortune to be one of Morgan's most trusted captains among the bears and bulls. Henry C. Frick was a Waldorf regular as was Judge William H. Moore, an authentic highbinder who
had already established three powerful trusts in steel, matches, and
table biscuits and was about to move in on the Rock Island Railroad where he would leave that unhappy carrier a tangled chaos of
bankruptcy comparable to Erie when Gould had done his worst.

A frequent figure of speculative conversation was John W. Gates
who conned Judge Elbert H. Gary into participating in his wire
nail trust in the Waldorf bar while consummating even vaster
predatory ambuscades in an upstairs suite for which he paid Boldt
$20,000 a year and where greater privacy was assured. Here at least
one all-night game of baccarat terminated at breakfast-time only
after $1,000,000 had changed hands between Gates's guests. On
another occasion when a poker game was in progress with a $1000
limit on bets, Judge Gary sent word upstairs that he wanted to sit
in on the game. "Tell Judge Gary that this game is going to be so

high that it will be way over his head," was Gates's return message grandly carried by a bellboy.

The Waldorf's formal restaurants, under the direction of a suave diplomatist named Oscar Tschirky—Oscar of the Waldorf—all required full evening dress of their guests, an amenity of masculine elegance which, when it overflowed as it inevitably did to the men's bar, gave the premises the haughty atmosphere of a gentlemen's club on St. James Street or Pall Mall. Men of prominence whose wives were entertaining elsewhere in the hotel drifted into the men's bar and were sometimes retrieved with difficulty.

It was in this era perfumed with crisp banknotes that the Waldorf became the acknowledged center of ostentatious entertaining and dinner parties where the price per cover was as important a consideration as the vintage of the Madeira that was to accompany the terrapin. Here it was that the unfortunate Bradley-Martins en route to exile in foreign parts gave their terminal dinner party, "a delirium of wealth and an idyll of luxury and magnificence," as the *World* was pleased to call it. The price tag on the gay nineties version of The Last Supper was $116 per plate, a figure which firmly established the Bradley-Martins, even *in absentia,* as among the town's authentic magnificoes of the wine coolers.

Perhaps incited by contemplation of the Waldorf's celebrated creation, sweetbreads *financiers,* at least one of the big spenders of the period endeavored with conspicious success to raise this figure. Randolph Guggenheimer, president of the Municipal Council, one gelid February evening undertook to sluice and gentle forty political associates, mostly recruited from members in good standing of Tammany Hall, and told Oscar that the sky was the limit. Although cab horses were being felled in scores on the icy pavements of Fifth Avenue outside and the North River was frozen solid, Guggenheimer's guests shed their furs as they assembled for *apéritifs* in an arbor festooned with immense clusters of Hamburg grapes which inquiry disclosed had cost a cool $10 a bunch. In the private restaurant selected for the occasion it was again mid-summer beneath a flowering canopy of roses from Wadley & Smythe, the Fifth Avenue social florist. A pool twenty feet long in the center of the table was banked with rare orchids, American Beauty roses, and other costly blooms, although the host forewent the live swans which had recently participated in a similar sylvan scene at Sherry's but had seen fit to join the diners and emerged wet and flapping to share the *foie gras* and champagne with which they found themselves surrounded.

After the conventional canapés and oysters, Guggenheimer's guests went on to green turtle soup, broiled boned fresh shad which then still came from an unpolluted Delaware River, a columbine of larded fowl, and a crown roast of mountain sheep with marron purée. After a pause during which the participants refreshed themselves, as was the custom of the eating age, with sherbet delicately flavored with crème de menthe, they prepared for an all-out assault on canvasback duck, diamondback terrapin, and fresh asparagus, an almost unearthly rarity in those distant times, and gradually subsided in well-fed attitudes for a coda of fresh fruits, vanilla mousse, bonbons, walnuts, coffee, and cognac deriving from the revered Comet Year of 1811. If anyone present harbored doubts about the magnitude of the bounty in which they had participated, they were dispelled when word circulated that the bill for the evening was better than $10,000, or $250 a plate.

That would show the Bradley-Martins.

The two most publicized spenders of the age were Diamond Jim Brady, the gem-encrusted railroad equipment salesman, and John W. Gates, a barbed-wire promoter on the fringes of the steel trust whose willingness to wager incredible sums on the most trivial occasions of chance got him the name of Bet-a-Million. Both appreciated newspaper publicity, Brady with a shrewd eye to its commercial potential as a sales asset, and Gates with the parvenu's unabashed delight in the conspicuous consumption of news space in whatever context. Both were coarse, gross *arrivistes* who created a public image of insurmountable vulgarity, but they were top-notch newspaper copy and dearly beloved of city editors and a public clamorous for the details of their incautious spending.

James Buchanan Brady was a product of railroading when it was by far the most powerful American industry and the construction and operation of carriers the major preoccupation of the American people. Born into a typical Irish working-class family on New York's Lower West Side when it was predominantly an Irish community, young Jim's first job was as station agent and baggageman at the New York Central's suburban station at Spuyten Duyvil on the far shore of Harlem River at the northern tip of Manhattan Island.

Something about the boy, perhaps his determination to learn telegraphy as a steppingstone to better things, brought him to the attention of John Toucey, the celebrated and all-powerful general manager for the Vanderbilt family's immensely important New York Central & Hudson River Railroad. He became Toucey's chief clerk, a highly responsible position of confidential trust and delegated authority and one which, with his office in Grand Central Terminal, brought him into contact with such worldly men as Chauncey M. Depew, the railroad's urbane and affable president. Brady admired Depew as one of the town's best-dressed executives and a large part of his salary went to patronizing the same tailors, haberdashers, and hatters that enjoyed Depew's more consequential patronage. As a result the general manager's chief clerk soon acquired a reputation for sartorial splendor. His silk hats were the glossiest, his frock coats the most conservatively cut of any Central employee. His thirst for knowledge about the railroad business was as insatiable as his passion for clothes and soon he was able to supply, accurately and without hesitation, detailed figures and statistics essential to his employer: costs of engine repairs, the performance of brake rigging, the reliability of electrical equipment under given weather conditions. He was on bowing terms of acquaintance not only with all Vanderbilt employees of importance but with scores of other influential railroad executives with whom his duties brought him into contact.

Among the men of carloadings whom he encountered was Charles A. Moore, of the railroad supply house of Manning, Maxwell & Moore. Moore wanted a salesman with the right contacts to promote a new patent handsaw for cutting rails as they were being laid, a potential bonanza in an age when rails had to be cut to measure at the foundry and often shipped and reshipped over great distances for sizing. Fantastic savings in time, labor, and money were promised by a lightweight portable rail-sizing unit. With a proper salesman it would be sensational.

Moore borrowed Brady from his friend Toucey. It was a loan that was to have the most spectacular consequences. Brady's first thought was to draw an advance against his salary and order a wardrobe that should command respect wherever he called with his sales pitch. As a former chief clerk with absolute control of access to his principal, he knew the importance of appearances.

"If you're going to make money you have to look like money" was his basic philosophy. When he called on a potential customer Brady looked like a million dollars and deferential chief clerks bowed him to the head of the line of applicants. The rail sizer practically sold itself, but Brady, the super salesman of his age, followed it up with a pitch for a vast assortment of other equipment stocked or manufactured by his employer. He made a practice, before calling on a purchasing agent or general superintendent, of having a talk with the warehouse foreman, the dining-car manager, and the chief signal repairman. He knew what a railroad actually needed before he undertook to sell a bill of goods.

Overnight, Brady's commissions were fantastic. He perfected the newly emergent technique of expense-account entertaining. He took his out-of-town customers to mammoth dinners at the best restaurants: Sherry's, Delmonico's, the Waldorf, but most especially at Charles Rector's, on Broadway between Forty-third and Forty-fourth streets. Rector's was a favorite with highfliers from the West, railroad presidents, copper kings, masters of men, mills, and mines wherever huge fortunes were coming into being.

Stuffed with lobster Newburg and White Seal champagne and fetched by their host's lordly ways with stage favorites and head-waiters, railroad nabobs from Kansas City and Omaha placed equally opulent orders with Brady for brake rigging and draft gear, patent couplings and switch stands.

Brady basked in affluence and ordered his suits by the dozen. He also began to collect diamonds. In an age when the size of a man's diamond ring was an explicit statement of his credit rating, diamonds were nothing to be embarrassed about. Desk clerks in fashionable hotels and maîtres d'hôtel at luxury restaurants appraised a potential customer on the degree in which he glittered. After six, when they changed into evening dress, men of circumstance became dazzling. "Them as has 'em wears 'em," said Brady.

Although he never touched liquor himself, Brady blossomed into the most expansive wine buyer on Broadway, a provenance he gradually widened to include Manhattan Beach and Saratoga. In time he became celebrated for the fantastic consumption of orange juice which accompanied his formidable meals, and modern medicine would be quick to see a cause-and-effect relationship between the deluge of citrus juice and the later ailments which were to beset him.

Brady's diamond collection became so large that its owner was hard put to wear even a fraction of it at a given time. The better to diplay his assets, he had diamonds mounted in what was to become his most famous visual asset, the transportation set. This comprised large-size stones embedded in platinum in the shape of bicycles, automobiles, and locomotives, for shirt studs, Pullman-car vest studs, tank-car cuff links, and an airplane lapel button. Altogether the set contained 2637 diamonds and 21 rubies. It was valued at $87,315.

Nor should it be imagined that the diamond set was the extent of Brady's wearable assets. It was merely one of no fewer than thirty matched sets, largely identical as to their components but differing in the gem stones with which each was set. Sources close to Brady in his lifetime estimated that the value of his private collections

exceeded $2,000,000. A partial listing of his personal evening jew-
elry is, at the risk of being statistical, included here.

- Diamond Set $87,315.00
- Pearl Set $79,553.75
- Ruby Set $31,570.00
- Emerald Set $52,330.00
- Cat's-Eye Set $30,840.00
- Sapphire Set $36,700.00
- Marquise Diamond Set $38,257.50
- Racing Set $10,737.50
- Transportation Set
  (Jim had paid $105,000 for this) $13,557.50
- Trefoil Set $16,422.50
- Star Sapphire Set $21,815.00
- Black Opal Set $14,362.50
- Opal Set $9,664.00
- Turquoise Set $6,716.50
- Napoleon Set $8,815.00
- Initial "B" Set $6,737.50
- Colored Sapphire Set $5,312.50
- Garnet Set $5,210.00
- Sporting Set $6,080.00
- Topaz Set $3,173.25
- Abalone Pearl Set $3,834.00
- Amethyst Set $4,933.00
- Moonstone Set $1,886.00
- Coral Set $440.00
- U.S. Coin Set (Representing merely face value
  of coins—not their numismatic value) $809.60
- Sardonyx Set $1,095.00
- Amatrice Set $2,155.00
- Imperial Jade Set $1,157.00
- Thomsonite Set $757.00
- Plain White Set $209.00

The watch compartment of his dresser contained thirty-odd timepieces, some of them of such rare and costly workmanship as to be museum pieces and standing their owner as much as $2000 when they were acquired. One evening watch alone was appraised at $17,500 after Brady's death. The combined weight of Jim's diamond ring and his number-one scarf pin, each set with a single stone, was fifty-eight karats. More valuable by far was an emerald ring with a single cabochon stone weighing an amazing twenty-three karats which was matched by a scarf pin made of an equally fine emerald weighing seventeen karats, while a watch chain weighed in at eighty-three emerald karats. On evenings when it was his whim to appear in green, Brady probably was worth more on the hoof than at any time when only diamonds were indicated.

In addition to the jewelry which he counted as his own, Brady, by Parker Morrell's estimate, gave away to his lady and gentleman friends another $2,000,000 in trinkets including a $100,000 pearl necklace to Edna Macauley and dinner-party favors which averaged at more than $1000 each. After Brady's death his own collections were broken up by his estate as being unsuited to the tastes of any potential buyer and the stones reset so that today hundreds of women are wearing Diamond Jim Brady's once-prized ornaments without knowing it.

Other once-treasured possessions went equally as far afield. As recently as 1950 the Spanish mission dining-room suite from his New York town house valued at $20,000 by the decorator was a prize display in a saloon in Virginia City, Nevada.

Brady's possessions increased in what seemed to spectators to be geometric progression and multiplied so fast he was hard put to keep track of them. They included a racing stable, a fleet of primeval automobiles, a magnificent town house in upper Manhattan, suites at the Gilsey House for entertaining out-of-town buyers, suits by the hundreds, and, of course, the celebrated gold-plated bicycles on which he took the air in Central Park and which he bestowed on favorite companions male and female.

His patronage and approval meant fortunes to some improbable enterprises. Once when visiting Boston in the interest of selling $1,000,000 worth of new steel passenger cars to the Boston & Maine Railroad, he sampled the product of a modest local manufacturer of chocolates named Page & Shaw. "Best goddamned candy I ever ate," said Brady, demolishing a five-pound box of assorted chocolate creams, French bonbons, and glazed walnuts. He thereupon ordered the entire stock of Page & Shaw at S.S. Pierce, the grocer, to be sent with his card to various friends and business acquaintances. Pierce's candy department was reluctant to let all their after-dinner mints go to a single customer and disclosed that Page & Shaw was a very small operation and that they had to take care of regular customers on Commonwealth Avenue and Beacon Street. It was, in brief, merchandise in short supply.

"Hell," said Brady, "tell Mr. Page and Mr. Shaw to build a candy foundry with twice their capacity. Here's the money." With an advance of $150,000 to be taken out in trade, Page & Shaw were soon giving such old, established firms as Maillard's and Huyler's in New York a run for their money.

Brady's bicycles also came in case lots. Somewhere he had come across a former circus-performing cyclist whom he retained as his personal bicycle chauffeur. When it appeared that the Brady bicycle stable of a single machine wasn't enough to keep a full-time employee busy, he commanded his mahout, whose name was Dick Barton, to have Columbia, the ranking bicycle manufacturer of the period, build him a dozen. "And while they're at it, have 'em plated with gold and we'll mount some diamonds on the handlebars for class," he added.

Columbia, understandably, was glad to make a dozen custom wheels for so good a credit risk, but said they weren't in the jewelry business and why not try Tiffany? When Brady turned up at Tiffany with a dozen steel bicycle frames in an express wagon, Tiffany turned up its corporate nose at the assignment. The official purveyor of gold dinner services to Mrs. Astor and William C. Whitney felt it could ill afford to outshop gold bicycles which would invariably be ridden by Brady's play-actress friends, perhaps wearing bloomers. It would never do.

The rebuff only put Brady on his mettle. He found an electro-plate shop on John Street run by a man named William Mock who said he would be glad to plate the Brady transport, but it appeared there was no electroplating tank in existence designed for bicycle frames. At a cost of $600 Brady had him build one. When the twelve frames had been treated, Brady had the tank demolished. He wasn't going to have every Tom, Dick, and Harry in Central Park bragging that he rode a wheel just as glittering as Brady's.

While the cost of the run-of-the-mill Brady gold-plated bicy-cles is not, at this remove, available, no such reticence surrounds the extra-special model that he ordered to be more than ordinar-ily heavy with gold for Lillian Russell and on which she dutifully made her regular Sunday appearance for the photographers in Central Park in a white serge cycling suit topped with a Tyrolean hat. The Russell wheel, according to Parker Morrell, had mother-of-pearl handlebars, while the spokes of each wheel were encrusted with diamond chips, emeralds, rubies, sapphires, and other pre-cious stones mounted so as to catch the rays of the sun and make the rider's progress a miniature display of fireworks. Miss Russell kept the bicycle in a blue plush-lined morocco leather traveling case and it went on tour whenever she took to the road. Once, it arrived at Saratoga on a private car together with Brady's staff of thirty Chinese houseboys. It cost $10,000.

Brady's involvement with horse racing was brief but spectacular. Over the bar at the Waldorf a turf sport named Phil Dwyer had sold him for $10,000 two horses named Gold Heels and Major Daingerfield, the latter a product of James R. Keene's Kentucky stables and named for Keene's head trainer. For a brief time the Brady colors won an amazing series of races, but a tightening up of Jockey Club regulations of ownership and registry made it seem inadvisable to prolong the venture and the stable was dissolved.

To celebrate what to many men would have been a sad occasion, Brady gave a final dinner at the Holland House roof, which is still remembered with awe for its overtones of grandeur. Dominating the table was a life-size statue of Gold Heels garlanded in roses and so realistic that many guests undertook to pat it. The guests, seated at a horseshoe-shaped table, were fifty in number and the meal lasted from four o'clock Sunday afternoon until nine o'clock next morning when some of the participants had to go to work. More than 500 bottles of Mumm's were consumed, a creditable average of nearly a case to a person, considering there may have been, like the host himself, some non-drinkers present. The bill was $105,000 not counting tips to the staff but including the favors. These were brought in at midnight on velvet cushions as souvenirs of what seems in every way to have been a memorable occasion. Each gentleman received a diamond-studded stop watch and each lady a diamond-studded brooch of elaborate design and superb workmanship. The fifty mementos accounted for $60,000 of the total bill.

Although his adventures with money were conducted on the grand scale, it may well be that their memory will prove more transient than the legend of Diamond Jim at table, where his accomplishments must rank him with Henry VIII, Sam Ward, and some of the more notable Roman emperors.

Medical appraisal of a later generation would list Brady as a compulsive eater. He was a gourmand rather than a gourmet, but so heroic were his skirmishes with the roasts, entrees, and *pièces montées* as to elevate them to an actually epic dimension. Brady not only ate the full twelve-course dinner which was the conventional evening snack of the early decades of this century, he usually consumed three or four helpings of the more substantial dishes, beginning his repast with a gallon of chilled orange juice and finishing with the greater part of a five-pound box of the richest available chocolates. In between he might well consume six dozen Lynnhaven oysters, a saddle of mutton, half a dozen venison chops, a roasting chicken with caper sauce, a brace or so of mallard or canvasback ducks, partridge, or pheasant, and a twelve-egg soufflé. During this interlude of ingestion he drank no wine or liquor of any sort. It was a spectacle that unnerved some spectators while others gathered around the Brady table at Bustanoby's, Jack Dunstan's, or the Café Martin to cheer him on his progress through the cutlets and make side bets on whether or not he'd fall dead before dessert.

Brady's abstinence from liquor in no way inhibited his friends and guests who might well number a dozen of the prettiest girls from the Ziegfeld chorus line and the president of the Santa Fe Railroad. For them a bucket brigade of wine waiters was in attendance opening Mumm's, White Seal, and Irroy at such frequent intervals that their corks sounded like drumfire. At the end of the evening the management showed the host the corks as evidence of bona-fide consumption. Brady was happiest when they had to be brought to him in a laundry basket.

Upon one celebrated occasion, Brady was dining with Charles Rector and a group of convivial spirits that included Sam Shubert, Victor Herbert, Lillian Russell, and a number of other consequential stage names when some worldly member of the group apprised his host of a new culinary devising that was the talk of Paris called *filet de sole Marguery* as prepared from a secret recipe only at the Café Marguery.

The effect of this intelligence upon Brady was electric. If he valued his future patronage, he told Rector, he would be well advised to secure the secret of *sole Marguery* for his own kitchen and the sooner the better.

Rector's son, George, was next day withdrawn from Cornell where he was studying, given steamer fare to Paris, and told not to darken his parent's door until he could confect *sole Marguery* in all its glory and to pick up any other trade secrets he could in the course of his tour of espionage. Young Rector, under an assumed name, secured work as pot-walloper at Marguery's where he loitered near the fish chef whenever the secret sole was in process of creation. It required two months of fifteen-hour workdays before he was in possession of a working blueprint. Rector cabled his father and took the *Mauretania* for home.

"When I arrived in New York, Mr. Brady and my father were at the dock to meet me," George Rector recalled in later years. " 'Have you got the sauce?' shouted Brady while the vessel was still out in the North River. I assured him that I had, and immediately the ship docked, we went uptown and started making preparations for the dinner to be given that night."

"At exactly eight o'clock the same group of *bons vivants* sat down at one big table. There were, as I remember it, Sam Shubert, Dan Reid, Klaw and Erlanger, Marshall Field, Alfred Henry Lewis, Adolphus Busch, and Victor Herbert. It was midnight when I stepped out of the kitchen to receive the congratulations of the diners. I shall never forget Mr. Brady's tribute. He said: 'George, that sole was marvelous. I've had nine helpings and even right now, if you poured some of the sauce over a Turkish towel, I believe I could eat all of it.' "

ᘐᘗ·ᘐᘗ·ᘐᘗ

John W. Gates, the Illinois barbed-wire salesman who pyramided a $30-a-month salary selling wire to Texas cattlemen into a $50,000,000 fortune and the resounding name of Bet-a-Million, was an outstanding figure in the Waldorf-Astoria gallery of notables, if not its most urbane or cultivated. His personality provoked neither trust nor admiration. "The man cannot be entrusted with property," said J. P. Morgan when he excluded Gates from participation in United States Steel. "He's a brokendown gambler," sneered Andrew Carnegie. The aristocratic milords who ruled the English turf turned away in disgust from the boorish caperings with which he celebrated winning races against the best their own stables could provide. Richard Canfield tolerated him at his clubhouse at Saratoga because Gates could afford higher stakes than any of his other customers. George Boldt bore with him at the Waldorf on the grounds that he paid top rental, $20,000, for an upstairs suite of rooms which he used as a clubhouse and was a liberal tipper of the help.

Nobody really wanted much to do with Bet-a-Million Gates, but he entered the folklore of big money in the United States as a gambler whom no stakes ever feezed, a plunger who feared no odds.

A product of the emergent American economy of the nineteenth century, John Gates rode into affluence and public awareness on the revolution accomplished by barbed wire. As representative of a pioneer wire mill at De Kalb, Illinois, he demonstrated the effectiveness of the barbed wire that was for the first time being produced by machinery to doubtful Texans in the plazas of dusty cowtowns. The money he made in commissions he often doubled and quadrupled that night at poker, keno, or rondo coolo, for he was a born gambler and luck was with him all his life. He bought a $1500 partnership in a failing wire mill and soon had it paying him millions. By the time Schwab and Morgan were planning United States Steel his wire mills were important enough to be a factor in their considerations. But Morgan would not have an uncouth and all but illiterate drummer for a partner and bought him out rather than include him in his trust.

All his life Gates feared and hated Morgan. He called him "Liver-nose" but never seriously tangled with Jupiter after his first disastrous encounter. Morgan, who was sensitive about his nose, retaliated by seeing to it that Gates was refused admission to the Union League and also to the New York Yacht Club.

At the height of his fame as a big spender, and to surprise his wife, Gates bought the town house of George Boldt near the Waldorf for $300,000. With the residence came Boldt's personal valet, Francis, whom Gates instructed to furnish the premises.

Pausing only for a quick one at the Waldorf bar, Gates and Francis visited the Wildenstein Gallery in search of paintings for his downstairs rooms. They were shown a vast assortment in the taste of the time, largely battle scenes from the Napoleonic Wars, and all in massive gold frames.

"What do you think of them, Francis?" asked the master. "Are they the McCoy?"

"I believe them to be both authentic and of reputable genre," said Francis.

"Tell the fellow to pack them all up and send them over."

Gates's willingness to bet on everything and his insistence on the largest imaginable stakes were the basis of his celebrity, but the name Bet-a-Million derived from his reported winnings when his horse Royal Flush won the Steward's Cup at Goodwood, the most socially exclusive of England's several stately race tracks. Actually he pocketed only $600,000 because at the last moment the odds on the horse in the betting ring were sharply reduced, but the wire services variously named $1,000,000 and $2,000,000 as his profits and the name was created. It was at Goodwood after Royal Flush had come down the stretch that Gates's delirious shouts of triumph and waltzing with his wife on the clubhouse lawn embarrassed the English aristocracy.

Gates in his refulgent heyday provided the biggest single evening's play ever recorded at Richard Canfield's gaming rooms at Saratoga, a casino where the ordinary playing chips were yellow for $100 and special, jumbo-size brown chips of oval design for $1000 and where there was always $1,000,000 in the safe to provide against unforeseen contingencies. Gates had had a bad afternoon at the Saratoga track, having lost $30,000 to one bookmaker alone and another $20,000 in miscellaneous misadventures with chance. After dinner he rolled into Canfield's faro room looking for trouble.

The conventional limit at Canfield's was $500 on case cards and $1000 on doubles and after losing consistently for half an hour, Gates asked for the game to be removed to a small private parlor upstairs where, he felt, his luck might change. Here, by permission from the owner, the limit was raised to $2500 and $5000 but in spite of the change of venue, Gates still continued to lose.

By ten in the evening Gates was full of whisky but out around $150,000 and clamoring loudly for revenge. He wanted the limits raised to $5000 and $10,000, sums which made even hardened Saratoga players raise their eyebrows. Coe, Canfield's pit boss on the floor, replied that only on Canfield's personal order could he accommodate Gates, and the high roller sought out the owner in his office.

"Let me have five and ten limits," he begged. "It's the only chance I have to break even." Canfield later confided that he feared Gates would burst into tears if refused. "You may have it," he said.

In two hours Gates's luck did indeed change. He won back his $150,000 and before eight o'clock next morning was $150,000 ahead. It gave Saratoga something to talk about.

At the zenith of his celebrity as a plunger Gates enjoyed such notoriety in sporting circles that it was a mark of status to have lost money to him. In this respect he resembled John L. Sullivan in his glory years who, when on tour, offered large sums to any local contender who would stay in the ring with him for three rounds. Most of the hopefuls didn't even last one, but it was a form of social recognition to have been knocked out by the Boston Strong Boy and there was never any lack of contenders. In much the same way it was a mark of distinction, especially among local yokels, to have been trimmed by Bet-a-Million Gates.

Once when his private car, a well-known landmark of the era in the Southwest, was spotted at Kansas City, a local sport begged audience, saying that he represented a syndicate and might he have an opportunity of playing some game, any game, with Mr. Gates?

"You know I don't play for small sums," Gates warned him. "How much have you got to spend?"

The emissary produced a bank of $40,000.

Gates spun a $20 gold piece in the air. "Heads or tails, you call it."

The local sport lost, Gates pocketed the banknotes, and the loser reported his Waterloo to the syndicate. He became something of a local celebrity and drummers in the lobby of the Meuhlbach Hotel pointed him out as the man who had lost $40,000 to Bet-a-Million Gates in less than ten seconds.

Gates's son Charlie inherited his father's less admirable characteristics in ample abundance and while still in his teens was a notable devotee of the stuff that comes in bottles. After Gates's death he undertook to build a fantastic home outside Minneapolis at a cost of $4,000,000, by far the most costly that conservative community had ever contemplated, but he was inept in business and his directorates and large, inherited affairs bored him. Detectives were sometimes sent to discover his whereabouts when his presence was legally required at a board meeting. They had little difficulty, and Charlie would be retrieved from the nearest saloon and dried out at the Turkish bath of the Minneapolis Athletic Club.

In 1913 he boarded his private Pullman car, appropriately named *Bright Eyes,* for a rendezvous with his friend Buffalo Bill Cody at Cody, Wyoming. A single evening in the company of that accomplished drinker killed him. He died aboard *Bright Eyes* as his valet was administering restoratives the next morning.

"I didn't know he was a tenderfoot," Pahaska is reported to have remarked when apprised of the younger man's passing. "I never should have ordered those last six bottles."

The elder Gates and his wife had been among the first residents to move into the new and sumptuous Plaza Hotel in New York when it opened in 1908, taking a magnificent suite at an annual rental of $40,000 just down the corridor from Julius Walsh, the Royal Typewriter magnate. After Gates's death, his wife became one of the legendary "thirty-nine widows of the Plaza," a congeries of relics of great wealth who became an integral part of the hotel folklore of Manhattan. One of these select beldams for the last ten years of her life had her Rolls-Royce town car and its formally liveried chauffeur park outside the hotel every morning until precisely noon, at which time her maid would phone down to dismiss it for the day since Madam didn't contemplate going out. For the entire ten years Madam had been bedridden.

❧ · ❧ · ❧

Comparable in celebrity with Gates and Brady in the ranks of lobster-palace society were the two foremost champagne salesmen of the gilded age, George Kessler and Manny Chappelle, who represented Moët & Chandon and Mumm's, respectively. Attired in the top hats and tails of conventional fashion, they took their evening's circuit through Peacock Alley at the Waldorf and among the tables at Rector's, Bustanoby's, Shanley's, Martin's, the Holland House, Imperial, Savoy, and Delmonico's. Wherever they went, as they noted celebrities at play, they commanded the management to send over a bottle of their product with their business card. The ice buckets bore the name of the brand, being furnished by the dealer, the color of the foil on the neck identified the wine to the knowing, and being recognized by Chappelle or Kessler was in the nature of a public accolade. It showed that they thought your consumption of their product added to its prestige. It was only courteous for those signaled thus for honors to reciprocate by continuing to drink Mumm's or White Seal the rest of the evening. A form of elegant pump priming.

When, next day and on their more sober business occasions, Chappelle and Kessler retraced their steps of the evening before, the wine waiter at each establishment produced the corks from empty bottles as evidence of bona fides. They received a bonus of half a dollar for each quart cork, a dollar for magnums.

❧ · ❧ · ❧

One cold winter afternoon early in 1952, the mail clerk of the Chase National Bank of New York sent to the post office in a routine way 119 legal-length envelopes each containing a check. Their total came to better than $100,000,000 and they represented the final distribution of the fortune of Hetty Green, "the Witch of Wall Street," at whose approach even the usually fearless and arrogant J. P. Morgan had been known to dodge into doorways or cross to the other sidewalk.

A conservative estimate of Hetty's income in the year 1900 was $7,000,000, which in a day when the average American income was $490, put her well up in the financial brackets along with J. P. Morgan, Henry C. Frick, and Andrew Carnegie. Hetty didn't spend more than a few hundred dollars on herself, perhaps no more than the national average, but what she didn't toss to the winds was expertly dissipated for her at the rate of $3,000,000 a year for over half a century by her spectacularly odd six-foot-four-inch, wooden-legged, oversexed son "Colonel" Ned Green whose interests variously ran to stamp collecting, orchid culture, private railroad cars, teen-age girls, $1,000,000 yachts, and diamond-studded chamber pots. Equally well endowed with Hetty's money was her daughter, Sylvia Wilks, who maintained a $31,000,000 checking account which drew no interest and grievously worried the Chase National for fear she might show up one morning and demand the entire sum in cash.

Ned Green was assuredly one of the biggest spenders in the record but to what category of economic eccentrics to assign him for the purposes of this book presents something of a problem. For many years he preferred to be a resident and voter in Texas whence derived the purely honorific or political title of "Colonel." His most spectacular residence was maintained with its staff of 107 domestics on the payroll at South Dartmouth, Massachusetts, near New Bedford, where the fortune of his mother had had its origins in the nineteenth-century days of whaling. And he was one of the prize spendthrifts of the winter season year after year at Miami, where he signaled his arrival in town by presenting a $20 gold piece to each traffic policeman and repeated the donation the day he left for the North.

His wooden leg and various internal afflictions, some of which may have originated in his practice of drinking twenty Bromo Seltzers a day, inhibited him from the lobster-palace routs that distinguished Diamond Jim Brady and Bet-a-Million Gates, and formal society never even heard of him unless it was on occasions when the Goodyear blimp he liked to keep moored to a tree on his front lawn got loose and was pursued by its custodians over the neighbors' immaculately groomed Buzzards Bay estates. But his inordinate passion for diamonds and his relaxed attitude toward women most nearly suggest kinship to Diamond Jim. Unlike Brady, however, his tastes in the material amenities of life were deplorable. His notion of Lucullan fare included outsize hot dogs and his cellar, when it was appraised after his death by a New Bedford connoisseur, was described as "simply dreadful."

In her lifetime Hetty extracted from her son a promise not to marry without her consent, a vow he honored in the letter while finding satisfaction in the company of a long tally of mistresses starting in Texas where he was sent on errands concerning Hetty's railroad interests. When Hetty had been dead for less than a month Ned married his ranking mistress who had been living with him on and off for twenty-four years.

To celebrate his belated nuptials the Colonel cherished an ambition to order the world's largest private yacht, but the year was 1916 and the United States was at war. Unable to order a vessel to his own design, Green made inquiries about the availability of J. P. Morgan's *Corsair* and Vincent Astor's *Nourmahal*. Neither, alas, was for sale, and the anxious bridegroom was prevailed upon to accept a substitute. This took the form of a Great Lakes passenger boat named *United States* plying between Grand Haven, Michigan, and Milwaukee, which was available for an even $1,000,000. Green was, however, not entirely satisfied with its overall length of 225 feet, its five decks and 2054-ton displacement. He wanted the largest and costliest private yacht in the world and to achieve this the *United States* was sawed in half and forty feet of additional length inserted between the halves. When it was finished the ship did indeed have the best of everything and the most of some things. Each of its ten lifeboats, costing upward of $1200 each, was named for an American possession, *Alaska, Hawaii, Philippines,* and the like. *Alaska* was the largest, being thirty-five feet overall with a 130-horsepower engine. The main cabin was twenty-eight by thirty-two feet with Jacobean *décor* and an open fieldstone fireplace at one end. There were nine master suites, each with its own bath, and the entire interior was furnished by John Wanamaker. A staff captain, navigating captain, and a crew of seventy-one seamen were enlisted.

When it arrived at Buzzards Bay the *United States* ran into the first of several obstacles to its complete enjoyment by the owner and his invited guests. No coal fuel was available, due to wartime shortages, and it took 660 tons a year just to keep up pressure enough to activate the shower baths and fire lines. Shortly thereafter the *United States,* as a result of causes never precisely determined, sank at its mooring in sixteen feet of water. Colonel Green's pride took ten hours to sink and there were no casualties. A few weeks later its place was taken by a houseboat named *Day Dream* which cost a mere $90,000 and had sleeping accommodations for seventy.

Colonel Green admired to have adequate funds handy in the form of pocket money in case emergency should arise. Emergency arose on one of his frequent trips to Texas while he was breakfasting at the Adolphus Hotel in Dallas with Edward Harper, president of the Security National Bank. Just as the sausages were being served, a pallid and shaken emissary arrived to apprise the banker that there was a run on his institution and that additional funds were in urgent request.

Unwilling to see his guest inconvenienced, Green pulled out his wallet and counted out its contents, twenty $10,000 banknotes. This being insufficient for the emergency, Green sent a bellboy to his suite with instructions to fetch a battered Gladstone valise which was on the bed. It turned out to be almost entirely filled with $10,000 bills from which the Colonel counted out another thirty and handed them to Harper without requesting a receipt. Half a million dollars proved sufficient to stop the run and the bank was saved. Green sent the valise back to his apartment with instructions to the bellboy to put it in the closet where it would be safe.

The Colonel's preoccupation with diamonds, emeralds, and other precious stones was by no means a secret vice. A favorite diamond broker, H. S. Fischer of Philadelphia, in the role of court jeweler, traveled with Green wherever he went to appraise possible acquisitions. Between 1930 and 1936 Green bought $10,000,000 worth of jewelry, making his selections while double-parked outside a gem store on Miami's centrally located Flagler Street.

When tired of contemplating his collection, which included a diamond-encrusted chamber pot and an equally elegantly jeweled chastity belt, Green liked to solve jigsaw puzzles. Tiring of dime-store merchandise, he aspired to more sophisticated designs and in a single order purchased 150 pounds of puzzles from Milton Bradley of Springfield, Massachusetts. The cost was $456.

Although not attended by what could be described as the cream of Miami Beach society, Green's entertainments in Florida could hardly pass unnoticed. For a St. Patrick's Day celebration 300 couples were invited and ninety-five extra help called in to sluice them with vintage champagne. The florist's bill alone was $2200, and, as the merest incidental to the occasion, Green bought for $300,000 a Mississippi River show boat on whose stage a troupe of Irish players performed jigs and sang in County Mayo accents.

"It seemed to me," one guest later reported, "that all they played from eight in the evening until four the next morning was 'Killarney!'"

Now and then his mother's thrift and parsimonious ways would crop out in the Colonel, although not in the same dimension that had suggested that Hetty wear hand-me-down bonnets and live off soda biscuits bought in bulk. When the foreman of his estate told him that a tractor would save a lot of manual labor, Green, as a matter of economy, purchased two dozen of them.

"I checked on the price," Green explained, "and found that a single Caterpillar cost $3800. The dealer said that by the dozen they were only $2700 each. By buying twenty-four I saved $26,400."

In similar vein when apprised that fifty gallons of flat paint were needed for the outbuildings, the Colonel bought a carload for

$1.00 a can instead of the $2.00 retail price. The foreman never was able to figure what to do with the extra 3000 gallons on which his employer had made such a spectacular saving.

When Packard Motors introduced the straight-eight power plant, Colonel Green purchased the first one available from the leading Massachusetts dealer, who happened to be Alvin T. Fuller, later governor of the Commonwealth. The car had a special body fabricated by Nicholas Rommelflanger, a Boston designer, and a glass roof and inside toilet. The cost was $20,000.

Green's arrival in the staid old whaling town of New Bedford always attracted an audience. The New Haven Railroad brought him in aboard two private Pullmans and a baggage car. The domestics numbered thirty on such occasions, not counting a private medical corps of a resident physician and two trained nurses. Between Florida and Buzzards Bay, Green evidently felt the baggage car offered insecure protection for the jewels, currency, and stamp collection without which he never moved. His practice was to wrap up anywhere from $500,000 to $1,000,000 in currency, diamonds, and rare numismatic items in a shoe box and send it along by American Express. Once, after such a consignment had been forwarded, the express company chanced to learn of its contents and an army of private operatives was dispatched to retrieve the treasure and personally conduct it to its destination. They found it at New Bedford on the tailgate of a delivery truck whose driver was having a hamburg at a nearby diner.

When Green at last joined Hetty, his estate paid the largest single tax ever collected in Massachusetts. It came to $5,250,000 or, as the *Boston Herald* figured out, the equivalent of all other inheritance taxes paid to the state in 1938, reducing the taxes the following year by 30 per cent. Even from the far side of Jordan, the Colonel was still active among the biggest spenders of all.

ᏇᏇ·ᏇᏇ·ᏇᏇ

That the lobster-palace society of the early years of the century, as represented by the playboys of Rector's and the Waldorf, was the direct lineal antecedent of café society as it appeared in the twenties and thirties along Park Avenue is abundantly apparent to students of the American social scene. They even discern a symbol of its continuity in its departure from Peacock Alley at an older Waldorf to re-emerge in the Starlight Roof of a later hotel of the same glittering name.

During the long interregnum of what he was pleased to call "expensive cheerfulness" as William R. Hearst's *chef de protocole* in New York and entertainer in the grand manner for the Hearst organization, Henry Sell had ample opportunities for giving lavish parties whose bills were footed by somebody else. His dinner parties mounted with his imagination and the Hearst resources were among the most opulent in New York in the twenties when, it may be remembered, prohibition was around but little in evidence in Manhattan.

He liked to import entire orchards of apple trees from Vermont and have them set up again in the ballroom at Sherry's or the Ritz for the sake of their fragile and brief-lived blossoms. Anyone who has ever undertaken to uproot, pack, and ship over 400 miles of highway a blossoming Delicious or Winesap without its being deflowered of a single bloom can imagine the ingenuity involved in their handling.

He admired to pile sybaritic Pelion on voluptuary Ossa and then shatter the illusion of grandeur by some such device as having a screaming mob of gypsies rush upon his guests during a Lucullan banquet howling like dervishes and bamming tambourines to wake the dead. Or, after a course of sweetbreads *financiers sous cloche* have a course of hot dogs brought on by Italian vendors with parasoled hot-dog wagons. The gypsies became so much a hallmark of Sell's parties that they were, after a time, a regular fixture to climax his entertainments, making a chaotic entry just at midnight to demoralize the guests before they departed.

Sell believed in paying his gypsy entertainers in gold coin for good luck, a practice which came to an end after 1933 when sound money disappeared from circulation.

Students of the Sell technique believe his most bravura production was a dinner party aboard the French Line's *Ile de France* soon after it was placed in transatlantic service. Contemplating the long walk from the pierhead to the gangway down a gloomy length of dockside would, he feared, both weary and depress his guests. To overcome this hazard he imported from the Atlantic City boardwalk, at some expense, a fleet of rolling chairs complete with their attendants which took arrivals from their cars and taxis to the foot of the gangplank. To banish gloom during the passage gypsy fiddlers were assigned to walk beside each rolling chair and play exotic tunes. Lest guests should be overcome with fatigue and thirst and arrive in depleted shape at the shipside, Sherry's waiters with magnums of iced champagne, Dom Perignon 1921 at $75 a bottle bootleg prices, were stationed at strategic intervals of about twenty feet and the chairs stopped at each checkpoint. Guests arrived at the *Ile* in what witnesses described as mood radiant.

The main salon of the liner was hung in pink tarlatan, and pink and white trees, in blossom, of course, were strategically located hither and yon. "It was like a state banquet in hell," a survivor said afterward.

Sell also perfected the technique of having a number of guests of honor, say half those present, at any given occasion of rejoicing. He would tell every other arrival that, although the fact hadn't been advertised in the invitations, he was actually the guest of honor. It worked fine.

By the time the depression of the thirties arrived, a contingency that would have dampened the ardor of a less dedicated party giver, Sell was in fullest stride and, as a sideline to being editor of *Harper's Bazaar,* was moonlighting at an advertising agency of his own.

Although in a single morning's mail he received $2,000,000 worth of space cancellations, he saw no reason to stop being New York's most lavish host with somebody else's money. Two of his clients who were singing the blues, but fortissimo, were the newly opened Waldorf-Astoria, which had gone bankrupt twice before the first guest signed the register, and the Furness Withy Steamship Company, which operated the lavish Castle Harbor Hotel at Bermuda.

Waldorf bonds were in such low esteem that they were being traded in bundles and sheaves which nobody bothered to count for denominations. Sell remembers a period when there were by actual count more musicians in Jack Benny's orchestra playing the Starlight Roof than there were guests in the hotel including the Waldorf Towers. This was the moment Mrs. Lucius Boomer, wife of the general manager, took to buy a bushel basket of Waldorf Corporation bonds. She thought they would make nice wallpaper when hard times were over. Boomer flew into a passionate rage when he learned of the transaction and made the broker who had sold them refund his wife's $250, saying she'd been outrageously swindled.

Since bankruptcy among luxury resorts between 1930 and 1934 was only a matter of degree, even though a cheerful front had to be maintained, Sell's agency set itself up in business supplying shills for such places as the Waldorf, the Ritz, and Castle Harbor. He recruited platoons of good-looking boys and girls who owned evening clothes and could dance, to people what would otherwise have been completely vacant pleasure palaces in the hope of luring what little cash trade there was into joining the party.

He himself would make the rounds of his clients during the evening to be sure none of the shills was cheating by eating pork chops or veal paprika. It was in the contract that they had to eat only the most costly dishes on the menu, out-of-season strawberries Romanoff and pheasant *en casserole.* Anyone caught eating ham and eggs country style was stripped of his insignia and drummed out of the regiment.

Sell, a strict disciplinarian, made mental memoranda on the most promising epicures, young men who actually seemed to enjoy putting away three flaming desserts in succession and could drink three or four bottles of Krug's Private Cuvée without falling down on the dance floor. These paragons he marked for advancement and soon they were promoted to the highest echelon of shills who went for graduate instruction at Castle Harbor. This required an additional wardrobe of sports clothes and steamer attire for passage on the *Queen* and *Monarch of Bermuda* but somehow the most eager students made do. They had the time of their lives as Sell shepherded boatloads of hungry deadheads on the two-night shuttle. "Some of them never were the same afterward," he says. "When the lean years were over they had to go back to beef stew and weekends at Coney Island. It somehow warped their sense of values."

When numbers of identifiable former executives were selling apples on Madison Avenue corners, Sell was getting $25,000 and expenses, a princely living in those parlous times, for masterminding these luxurious charades. He even got so carried away with the spirit of the thing that he hired Theodore Titze, one of the two Theodores of the Ritz, away from the Madison where he was then in charge of the restaurant. Titze, an arrogant Prussian drillmaster type of maître d'hôtel who had great success with the very well-to-do whom he sometimes treated like dirt, was surprised to find himself walking backward in front of Sell's dressy freeloaders whose social rating was nil, but at least it was a living.

Furness Withy admitted that Henry Sell was the greatest single agency in keeping their show on the road for the dark years of the depression. Expensive cheerfulness paid off even when it was on the cuff.

Chapter Four
The Benevolent Blackmailer

Colonel William D'Alton Mann Looked Like a Patriarch and Was One of the Sights of Town . . . Behind His Saintly Whiskers There Lurked Larceny Incarnate . . . A Buccaneer of the Type Cases, the Best People Loaned Him Money So That Silence Was Literally Golden . . . Even J. P. Morgan Was Reasonable . . . Town Topics Was a Monument to a Merry Scoundrel . . .

ACADEMIC SCHOLARSHIP IS prone to trace the beginnings of the sensational annals of society back to classical antecedents and the scandalous odes of Catullus in Roman imperial times or the grossly libelous "pasquinades" of Aretino the Italian. Both of these legendary masters of invective named names and personal attributes that bring a blush to the cheek of readers centuries later and are legitimate candidates for the honor of being among the earliest practitioners of the calling of scandal columnist.

None brought the technique of scandal, and its by-product of blackmail, to the fine flower achieved at the turn of the twentieth century in New York and its allied social suburbs by a benevolent and patriarchally bearded old scoundrel named Colonel William D'Alton Mann. A legendary figure even today in Manhattan clubdom, during his lifetime he was a terror at whose name even such unlikely victims as the elder J. P. Morgan were known to turn pale and reach for their wallets.

Colonel Mann—the title was come by honestly in the big shooting of the sixties—was owner, editor, and publisher of a weekly magazine called *Town Topics*. He was also a member in irreproachable standing of such elevated gentlemen's clubs as the Lotus and Knickerbocker, and on the side he designed a compartmented type of railroad sleeping car known as the Mann Boudoir Car, some of which are in operation to this day on the railroads of Australia and New Zealand, tangible evidences of one of the most improbable alliances of all time of craftsmanship and rascality.

The years when *Town Topics* and Colonel Mann flourished, from the nineties through the first decade of the twentieth century, were ideally conditioned for the evolution of society blackmail. They were an age when the purity of womanhood, the sanctity of marriage, and the propriety of domestic relations occupied a top position in the general American consciousness if not in factual American practice. A breath of scandal could mean ruin to a well-born woman. Divorce was far less widely tolerated than it was to become, and while the double standard of personal morality generally extended freedom of a sort to men, impropriety of any publicized order meant a good deal of trouble no matter what the sex of the offender. Virtue in womanhood was invested with sanctimonious overtones and the vogue was the Gibson Girl, who could vanquish with a haughty stare of disbelief the advances of a cad.

Against a background of such almost unearthly rectitude, the practice of blackmail was so simple as to be irresistible, and the pickings so rich and derived from such affluent sources as to approach the dimensions of big business. American society at the end of the nineteenth century was largely if not predominantly populated with recent millionaires and their diamond-encrusted wives. Money made since Appomattox blew in cheerful blizzards down Fifth Avenue, in Newport, and in the only recently opened game preserves for the very rich in Florida. Just a handful of really good accounts, as they would be known in the lexicon of a later-day Madison Avenue, could keep a prudent blackmailer on Easy Street from one year to the next. Colonel Mann had scores of them.

Colonel Mann was one of the showpieces of turn-of-the-century New York and something to tell the home folks you had seen along with Diamond Jim Brady eating oysters at Rector's and the newly risen city blocks of Vanderbilt châteaux on upper Fifth Avenue. Professional New Yorkers liked to note the rakish air of his silk top hat, the jaunty set of his Old Testament whiskers, and the damn-your-eye gesture of defiance as he struck a kitchen lucifer to light his long Havanna puros. He specially liked to strike them ostentatiously on the red-stone front of the stately Fifth Avenue residence of Senator William Andrews Clark, the archboodler from copper-rich Montana, or the equally well-situated residence of Charles T. Yerkes, the traction king. These were successful and honored scoundrels, heirs to the great tradition of the robber barons of old, and Colonel William D'Alton Mann felt a kinship with them. He would have admired to be one of their company. In his modest way, he was.

The Colonel had performed distinguished service beside Custer at Gettysburg, which was later to save him from jail when his lawyer cited his record in the Union cause in a famous perjury suit. In 1891, he bought *Town Topics,* then a faltering and inconsequential weekly, from his brother. Its contents at the time fairly reeked of propriety and contained little but the bare listing of social events and approved lists of their participants handed out by the social secretaries of the fashionable world.

In no time flat Colonel Mann changed all that and *Town Topics,* although almost nobody was ever seen to buy or carry a copy, was one of the most widely read of American periodicals. Addicts of its spicy pages, especially if they occupied responsible brackets of finance or conservative society, carried it folded inside some chaster *feuilleton,* say *Collier's Weekly* or the venerable *Harper's.*

Colonel Mann set about making the reputation of his magazine so sensational that immunity from its attentions would come correspondingly high. A well-paid staff of literate and informed people edited the gossip and facts of the highest social circles collected by a network of agents ranging from telegraphers to house footmen. Disgruntled servants were an obvious source of domestic intelligence smuggled from mansions impervious to reporters. Colored servants, chambermaids from fashionable hotels, and backstairs servants in private houses got a fixed fee when they called at *Town Topics* with a detail of domestic infelicity: a kiss from the Colonel and a silver dollar. The scale for more responsible informers was never revealed, but the Colonel's subversion of butlers, grooms, valets, personal maids, coachmen, and cooks achieved such dimensions that society began to take measures for their detection or at least decontamination.

False leads were dropped in the course of dinner-party conversations and when their substance appeared next week in *Town Topics,* somebody's butler was at liberty. The most drastic defense measure was that incorporated in the Bar Harbor summer home of Mrs. Ann Archbold of the Standard Oil millions where the center of the dining-room table was motorized on guides to descend to the kitchen, located directly below the dining room, and return with the next course without the presence of domestics in the dining room. Although this device defeated Colonel Mann's operators, it wasn't proof against Mrs. Archbold's neighbor, Arthur Train, who made her career of social outrage the theme of one of his novels.

It is almost impossible at this remove and in the light of changing attitudes to evoke the terror which Colonel Mann wielded among the wealthy and gullible members of New York society and even more among those who attempted to force its portals.

"The most pernicious of all the nuisances that the Harry Lehr group set buzzing around their thoughtless heads was, of course, Colonel Mann's *Town Topics*" wrote Richmond Barrett in *Good Old Summer Days.* "Nobody who did not live in Newport when

Town Topics was at its virulent prime can have any idea of the sensation it created. Even today, an old Newporter has only to look at that black and white cover with the two pretty ladies whispering their eager secrets, and straightway his blood runs cold in his veins. . . . Nobody could be sure that the butler or personal maid wasn't a spy, that the charming but penniless young cousin wasn't selling his rich relatives down the river. To make confusion worse, *Town Topics* reporters weren't above spreading propaganda to the effect that some of the spiteful ladies in the inner circle were betraying the secrets of their deadliest rivals.

"Of course, Colonel Mann had no part in anonymous letters, but they fitted so well into his scheme of giving the people of Newport an attack of nerves that they would be willing to purchase immunity at any price no matter how large.

"It is obvious that *Town Topics* could not have wielded the power it did if all the paragraphs in it had been made up out of whole cloth."

Nor was society particularly reassured by the rumor circulated in the very highest circles of Newport and New York that Harry Lehr himself, clown to society and Mrs. Stuyvesant Fish's personal arbiter of elegances, was on the Mann payroll. An irresponsible moocher who admittedly lived off rich pickings wherever he found them, Lehr could have been an almost priceless inmate of the *Town Topics* stable.

One of Colonel Mann's most valued operators was Robert R. Rowe who in 1900 was chief night operator at Western Union in Newport. It was before the days of long lines telephones for common use and late in the evening men of society and affairs used to stop by to take advantage of night rates to send long wires of endearment to fiancées and mistresses or business instructions to financial associates. Rowe found these supposedly confidential messages interesting and shortly was sharing them with *Town Topics* for a substantial sum. In a short time Rowe was able to put together bits and pieces of Newport news into a cohesive pattern that made him better informed about the rich and important than the society correspondents for the New York papers. *Town Topics* constantly beat the *Herald* and *World* with news of impending engagements and, as often as not, announced prospective heirs before immediate relatives were informed.

When the Newport season ended and society began its southward progress toward the then unassailable battlements of Palm Beach, Rowe found himself technologically unemployed and Colonel Mann ran shy of copy. The Colonel spoke to George Gould, who then owned Western Union, about a deserving employee on his payroll whose health was frail and would greatly benefit from a season in the Florida sun. Rowe's emplacement as Western Union superintendent at Palm Beach was a great help, and members of the Gould family began getting a good press in *Town Topics*.

Once a breach had been effected in the social defenses of Florida, a great light seemed to dawn in the ready intelligence of Henry M. Flagler who found that while openly deploring the horrors of personal publicity, guests with names that made news in his hotels along the Gold Coast actually enjoyed appearing in *Town Topics*. A large ad for the Florida East Coast Railroad became a fixture in the magazine and its columns bristled with stirring accounts of the rich social tumults at the Royal Poinciana and other Flagler resorts. Flagler himself occasionally communicated with Colonel Mann, a circumstance which made him probably the richest gossip reporter in the world and an outstanding star on the *Town Topics* team.

Another member of the staff was Charlie Roper, a debauched and merry English remittance man who wrote graceful society verse which gave a tone of wit and elegance to the magazine's regular contents of clandestine fornication among the Four Hundred. Roper wrote best when stiff as a shirt front, and, instead of paying him, Colonel Mann established credit for him at Mouquin's, the Manhattan Hotel, Holland House, and other handy oases.

Still another contributor whose knowledge of formal society, of which he was conspicuously no part, was formidable in detail and accuracy was Harold Seton, a sidelines spectator of the great who lived until recently and collected the most voluminous iconography of rare society photographs of any known repository of such matters. Seton, a hypochondriac of multiple ailments, was still living in 1935 at the Drayton Hotel on East Thirty-ninth Street and in his *Town Topics* days had been such a fountainhead of accurate information about the well placed as to be Colonel Mann's right-hand man. Seton was a society fan in the sense that he took organized pretentiousness seriously and worshiped the half-world of Edna Wallace Hopper and Diamond Jim Brady the way a classic car enthusiast today venerates ancient Bugattis or a Rolls-Royce Silver Ghost with Park Ward basketwork for the body.

The weekly reports from this vast and heterogeneous network of informants arrived with efficient regularity at *Town Topics,* where it was assayed and processed by Colonel Mann's chief assistant, Theresa Dean, and his secretary, who was incredibly named Nevada Stoody. Miss Stoody wrote a regular column called "Lady Modish" while working for a $25 weekly salary but bettered her condition by four successive and increasingly remunerative marriages, the last of which gave her title as well, as the Princess de Braganza and Duchess of Oporto. Crude people who remembered her beginnings as transom peeper for *Town Topics* spoke of her as the "Duchess of Portholes."

With the passing of time, it became apparent to observers of the New York scene that *Town Topics'* best stories were the ones that never got printed. These were the truly dangerous stuff that was set in proof and then submitted to the principals concerned for their "correction of facts" before the edition was put to bed. There was nothing clandestine or furtive about Colonel Mann's submission of such editorial material. Clapping his top hat on his head and buttoning his frock coat in a military manner, he would set off at lunchtime for Delmonico's with a bundle of galley proofs under his arm and there set up shop as the world's most explicit and obvious blackmailer at a table reserved for him near the door by an obsequious management.

While waiting for potential victims—he liked to call them clients—to appear, the Colonel would order one of the light collations which became such an institution that curious out-of-towners sometimes tipped Delmonico's waiter captains highly to obtain vantage points to watch the proprietor of *Town Topics* consume six double Southdown mutton chops festooned with baked yams and studded with kidneys and slices of liver accompanied by two magnums of the best vintage champagne. As he downed these comestibles the Colonel would let out little, happy cries of "Woof, woof" to signify the dimension of his approval.

When a potential "client" put in an appearance with either his wife or a business associate, since few people took liberties with the proprieties at Delmonico's lunch hour, the Colonel would wait until he was well settled at table and a meal commanded, thus cutting off all possibility of strategic retreat, and then send a page or waiter over with the intelligence that an important business call had come through for him in the men's bar.

By happy chance Colonel Mann would also be in the men's bar supervising the opening of a double bottle of Mumm's Extra. Pleased surprise rippled his whiskers.

"Just the man I wanted to see," he would exclaim heartily. "I was just going out to lunch when this proof came up from the composing room and I wanted you to glance over it before the press run."

Erring husband or gilded youth overdrawn at Canfield's knew that the jig was up and was permitted to keep the blistering galley proof as evidence of the Colonel's good faith after the negotiation of a small loan. Colonel Mann's manner on such occasions was that of a benevolent family solicitor and he never pocketed $5000 in banknotes without buying the contributor a parting drink.

Nobody visibly resented paying blackmail to Colonel Mann and the writer's uncle, Ned Center, a Manhattan *viveur* and clubman of the period who occasionally pacified the old gentleman's appetite for money with offerings of $1000 bills, recalled that to be victimized by the publisher of *Town Topics* was a form of accolade and recognition as a *boulevardier* and fellow of fashion. Men who might not otherwise be able to do so, found themselves in the company of Astors, Vanderbilts, and Whitneys. To have been tapped by the Colonel for hush money was a distinction of which a gentleman sometimes bragged in the company, of course, of other members of the club.

Just who constituted membership in this organization it is difficult at this remove to ascertain. Ned Center cheerfully admitted that he had been a member and so had his cousin, Center Hitchcock, founder of the Brook Club. Obviously, from the record and from later indications in another Mann venture called *Fads and Fancies,* J. P. Morgan was a contributor as were Reginald Vanderbilt, then a gay young blade at Yale, Charles T. Yerkes, and probably Stanford White.

Undoubtedly, the capstone of Colonel William D'Alton Mann's long and industrious career of shaking down the rich was *Fads and Fancies of Representative Americans,* a volume of achievement and adulation which, even in an age that gladly paid top prices for flattery, must stand as a landmark of combined naïveté and opulence.

Excepting only the multivolume catalogue of William H. Vanderbilt's home and art collections, *Fads and Fancies* is also the most elaborately conceived puff sheet of all time, occupying a format which, quite aside from its calculated scarcity, makes it something of a collector's item. Printed in red and gold as well as conventional black letterpress on heavy vellum-type stock twenty-six by sixteen inches, each signed, numbered, and registered copy was bound in full green and gold morocco with end papers of heavy watered silk and top and sides of eighteen-karat gold leaf. The edition was limited, and its limit sworn in the frontmatter and signed by the printer, to one copy for each of its eighty-five subscribers, two for the Library of Congress, one for the New York Public Library, one for the library of *Town Topics,* one for the British Museum, "and no more." No. 76 of this compendium of costly properties is today in the collection of Everett De Golyer of Dallas and was made available to the author. No other single volume in the field is so rich a bonanza of folklore among the very wealthy and the very pretentious of its time.

The editorial consist of *Fads and Fancies* is a series of eighty-five personal biographical and character sketches written by the subscribers or, if total alphabetics, by qualified admirers. Each sketch is contained on either two or four pages together with a letterpress likeness of its principal framed in gold leaf and the whole typeset bordered in the wide margins of each page with the pictorial representation of the subject's appropriate properties—town houses, suburban villas, steam yachts, coaches, motorcars, racing thoroughbreds, stables, packs of hounds, blooded cattle, greenhouses, sailing vessels, art collections, wine cellars—business and political associates of equal or superior standing, and religious, educational, and charitable benefactions. A handful of the subjects in *Fads and Fancies* were crass enough to include photographic representations of the mines, mills, manufactories, and agencies of transport from which their elevation to the financial peerage derived. And although steam yachts and English drags are so frequent as to be commonplace, nobody included either the likeness of a mistress, a winning poker hand, or private railroad car. The last of these is not easily explained, as the private car was to the generation which sired *Fads and Fancies* the ultimate hallmark of success and gratification of elegance.

If the expensive format of *Fads and Fancies* must stand as a perpetual monument to Colonel Mann's industry in the painless pillage of the well-to-do, the names that adorn its roster are an equal tribute to the exalted levels at which he operated and in which he exacted tribute to his *Town Topics* enterprises, because, for the most part, these are no second-raters or small-town tycoons of mere bourgeois success stories, but the ranking names of the American social and political scene in the year 1905. They include President Theodore Roosevelt, John Pierpont Morgan, Colonel John Jacob Astor, Henry E. Huntington, James J. Hill, William K. Vanderbilt,

Charles M. Schwab, Grover Cleveland, Bishop Henry C. Potter, William Collins Whitney, Alfred G. Vanderbilt, Thomas Fortune Ryan, Clarence Mackay, and Senator Nelson W. Aldrich.

Here, obviously, is no gaggle of minor tributaries, but perhaps the most august assembly of captives to anyone's chariot since Tamburlaine harnessed the vanquished monarchs of Asia as his steeds. Neither J. P. Morgan, President Roosevelt, nor J. J. Hill, to select names at random, suggest themselves as the sort of people to submit quietly to petty blackmail, nor as candidates for anything but a con game of practically galactic dimensions. How then did Colonel Mann contrive their initiation into what can only be described as the most resounding club of suckers of all time?

The answers are various.

President Roosevelt indignantly denied that he had ever authorized his inclusion in *Fads and Fancies,* much less paid whatever the going price may have been for two or four of its money-perfumed pages. As a matter of fact it was a source of double irritation to the President in that it not only suggested the satisfaction of an inordinate personal vanity, but associated him by implication and in the expensive record with many of the "malefactors of great wealth" against whom he was politically allied. It later appeared that a Washington society woman had falsely represented to Colonel Mann that the President had authorized her to prepare his biography and its inclusion. Or so the Colonel said.

The New York Public Library at first refused to accept the copy Mann had reserved for its rare-book shelves, but there is one there today and it is cherished as one of the rarest jewels in the library's bibliographic crown.

J. P. Morgan in 1905 was sensitive to any references which coupled his name with that of Maxine Elliott, the actress, and although he later was to build a handsome playhouse in her name, he was definitely agreeable to loans without date or security to Mann on numerous occasions, and Miss Elliott's name did not appear in the columns of *Town Topics.* It is not difficult to imagine that, having thus established immunity with Colonel Mann, he might have been induced by a little further adroit pressure to reserve space for himself in *Fads and Fancies.*

Such a glorious start as that represented by the head of the House of Morgan makes it easy to envision Mann's subsequent success in soliciting the patronage of lesser financial luminaries and of Morgan's imagined peers who were not averse to being associated with the greatest of all figures in finance of his time. If the grim old lion of the Pacific Northwest, James J. Hill, were naturally averse to such frivolous ornamentation of his success as that represented by a puff sheet, his doubts could be allayed with the word that the hardest-headed banker of them all had led the way. By indirection, and directly too, Miss Maxine Elliott was perhaps the most spectacular asset in Colonel Mann's portfolio of peculiar properties.

The Colonel's luck with play actresses wasn't always so good. There was, for instance, the unfortunate affair of Lily Langtry, for whose personal occupancy Mann had built one of his boudoir cars as a token of esteem from Freddy Gebhard, a New York playboy and wine salesman whose infatuation with the Jersey Lily was the cause of some raising of eyebrows on both sides of the Atlantic. During the construction of *Lalee,* as this bedizened love barge was named, Gebhard had split many a bottle of Mumm's and Perrier-Jouet with the festive carbuilder and after the car was delivered, the Colonel found himself a repository of amorous confidences that it would simply have been silly not to use to advantage.

He approached the English actress, then at the height of her celebrity and powers, with the thought that $200,000 might be about the proper compensation for him not to run in *Town Topics* an interestingly written résumé of the playboy's reminiscences. Gebhard and the Langtry were both spectacular names in the supper-at-Delmonico's set and the feature would be a great circulation-getter. Two hundred thousand dollars would be just about right.

Langtry didn't take kindly to the suggestion and hastened to the law offices of Little Abe Hummel of the altogether remarkable criminal law firm of Howe & Hummel. Little Abe patted her hand in a fatherly manner and told her not to worry her pretty head. The next day he called on Colonel Mann at *Town Topics* and no mention was ever again made of the Gebhard reminiscences. Howe & Hummel had a dossier on Mann that would have sent him away for life and Little Abe, who was an impassioned admirer of everything connected with the stage, was fairly panting to pass its contents along to the district attorney for New York County. Lily Langtry never got a favorable paragraph in *Town Topics* to the end of her days and Mann was known to kick at cuspidors in a rage when her name was mentioned, but there was never any hint of scandal in the columns of his paper.

No record has come down the decades of what it cost to be included in the pages of *Fads and Fancies,* but it is a safe guess that it was neither more nor less than the traffic would bear. Court records later showed that Colonel Mann's profits from the excursion into biography had netted him $90,000 over and above a printer's bill for $60,000, making the gross cost of the book something like $1750 per subscriber. It is only reasonable, however, to suppose that the schedule of admission fees varied and that comparative nobodies such as Lewis Nixon and David Rowland Francis should pay what might be suitable to rub elbows editorially with William Collins Whitney and Grover Cleveland.

Fads and Fancies exists today among collectors and bibliophiles as an incredibly rich source book of the mores and folklore of aggressive capitalism and social ascendancy. True, a theme of honest simplicity of manner and of domestic fidelity which preferred the simple gratifications of home and family to the tinsel satisfactions of the great world runs recurrently through a large majority of the individual biographies. A gratifying number of men hitherto known as shrewd and even avaricious operators on Wall Street and midnight patrons of Bustanoby's private dining rooms were revealed as homebodies at heart who preferred roughing it in the gatekeeper's lodge to the solid-gold service plate and powdered footmen of the manor. Collie dogs rather than chorus girls appear as the constant companions of titans of finance, and the homely satisfactions of a good tramp in the woods triumph repeatedly over a box in the Diamond Horseshoe.

But there are glimpses of satin beneath the homespun, as when it is revealed that the great bronze doors of the Fifth Avenue mansion of Charles Tyson Yerkes, the traction king, had an outer plate of heavy-gauge platinum and that "the spoil from old Venetian palaces" with which Edward J. Berwind, the coal magnate, crowded his Bellevue Avenue cottage at Newport ran to about $15,000,000.

There is the Spartan example of James T. Woodward, president of the Hanover Bank of New York:

> Standing as straight as the proverbial pikestaff in the reception room of his city home (No. 7 East Fifty-sixth Street), Mr. Woodward said: "Give me four lines. I have no fads nor fancies." Thus did Cromwell against whom Mr. Woodward's ancestors fought, say to the artist: "Paint me as I am!"

Indeed, in Mr. Woodward, *Fads and Fancies* might find the finest expression of the proverbial heart of gold beating beneath a forbidding exterior:

> Yet, despite his positive and aggressive manner, Mr. Woodward is most amiable, loves his friends and is beloved by them. When he is talking most abruptly his twinkling eyes betray his humor. A master of finance on Wall Street, he finds enjoyment of being a master of hounds in Maryland. A member of the most exclusive clubs, he lives by preference a plain, unassuming life. Under a decisive manner . . . he has a warm and generous heart.

For the connoisseur of the world of money which flourished in the United States at the turn of the twentieth century, *Fads and Fancies* is a veritable bonanza of fascinations, representing long hours of almost sensuous delight that may be spent amidst the dense thickets of good works and wholesome, even homely relaxations attributed by men of substance to themselves.

Most of the contributors to Colonel Mann's anthology of representative success stories, J. P. Morgan, Henry M. Flagler, Charles M. Schwab, and Charles Tyson Yerkes among them, were satisfied with two pages in which to list the tally of their benefactions and to assert their noble sentiments toward society. Now and then a lifetime of sacrifice and renunciation such as that of Colonel John Jacob Astor or Perry Belmont required four pages, but alone among his peers Collis P. Huntington of the Pacific Railroad required eight pages of type and decorative pictures to attest his faith in human values and establish his authority in the realm of fine arts. "No sum of money could stand between him and the possession of a painting he coveted, but he knew, too, the value of a canvas, old or new, as well as any Old World dealer and no man ever got the better of Mr. Huntington in a bargain."

This Yankee prudence with money, which nobody who knew Huntington would care to deny, didn't, however, extend to his wife, Arabella, who once left a handbag containing eleven pearl necklaces worth $3,500,000 on a Fifth Avenue art dealer's desk in a moment of absent-mindedness.

Another entrant in *Fads and Fancies* whose presence in such profane associations might give pause to the peruser, was Bishop Henry C. Potter, head of the Protestant Episcopal Church in America and a servant of God to whom mere secular immortality might have appeared as frivolous. It is pleasant to speculate that Colonel Mann, in deference to the cloth, perhaps included the bishop at a specially reduced rate.

Colonel Mann's hatreds were both venomous and numerous, but none of them so deep rooted that it couldn't be overcome by the judicious application of a substantial sum of money.

He hated President Roosevelt for denying that he had authorized his biographical sketch in *Fads and Fancies*. He hated the daily press, which had no hesitation about cribbing his best society items from *Town Topics* and using them without credit while editorially posing in holier-than-thou attitudes about the Colonel's activities generally. He missed no opportunity to sink a harpoon under the tough Scotch hide of James Gordon Bennett, whose New *York Herald* was itself in no position to assume postures of unearthly morality but which frequently deplored *Town Topics* while basing its own news stories on Town *Topics* exclusives in the matter of engagements, impending divorces, and blessed events far in advance of their authorized release. He hated Joseph Pulitzer until Pulitzer's son married into the Vanderbilt family but then relented and even sent a reporter to the wedding.

Colonel Mann represented the first real encounter entrenched social position and vast wealth had with the possibilities of publicity and promotion. A little experience with the Colonel not only taught the well-to-do the perils of indiscretion but also gave them a taste for favorable publicity and flattery in the public prints that was shortly to elevate a good press to the same status among a man's possessions as yachts, racing stables, and collections of old masters.

Achieving a fair celebrity for his family in the daily and periodical press and laudatory profiles for himself in such puff sheets as *Fads and Fancies* soon became for a tycoon an approved and recognized way of spending money and one of the more agreeable aspects of being rich. Publicity shortly became as much a commodity in requisition along Fifth Avenue and Riverside Drive as real estate or vintage champagne and, like these tangibles and other luxury merchandise, it came in varying qualities and dimensions. Generally speaking, those who could afford the best got value received.

As a blackmailer and publicist Colonel Mann worked hard at his profession. He spent six hours a day, daily and Sunday, at *Town Topics* where a heavy ash walking stick was ostentatiously located handy to his editorial desk. Tuesday was make-up night, and in Rector's and Bustanoby's where playboys and the more worldly element of New York's society forgathered, significant glances passed between customers and bartenders when the fact was mentioned.

As a result of his industry and devotion to his calling, Colonel Mann lived and died moderately well off. He maintained a modest but sufficient town house on Seventy-second Street, a summer place at Lake George formally named Saunterer's Rest, which impious wits spoke of as "Saunterer's Roost," and made frequent trips to Europe at the appropriate seasons. When he died he owned several parcels of valuable New York real estate including the land on Forty-first Street west of Seventh Avenue where the *New York Herald Tribune* is located today. When his will was probated in 1920 it was found that he had left bequests to the then living members of his staff and assets of $500,000. There were also a number of outstanding debts for "loans" from various Goulds, Vanderbilts, and Morgans or their estates. Significantly, none of these was ever presented for collection from the Colonel's heirs.

Colonel Mann's significant contribution to the pattern of American substance and fashion was an understanding that publicity was a property of wealth, as available to purchase and possession as cottages at Newport or membership in the United States Senate and fully as satisfactory as either.

Chapter Five

Three Parties that Made Headlines

The Awful Seeley Dinner Was a Scandal... So Was the Great Brad-ley-Martin Ball at the Waldorf... The Bradley-Martins Had to Leave Town... So Did James Hazen Hyde Whose Admiration for Things French Wasn't Shared by the Stockholders in His Insurance Company... There Were Penalties Attached to the Grand Manner Even in the Golden Age....

By-product of the moneyed times of the *bon ton* along Fifth Avenue and on Murray Hill was the licentious revelry supposed to exist on both a large and private scale among the Four Hundred. Belshazzar's Feast, the Last Days of Pompeii (a favorite site for depravity in a generation that had yet to learn about Capri and Tiberius), and the events in Nero's gardens where Christian slaves furnished illumination comparable to the Welsbach gas mantle, were favored illusions from the best pulpits in Manhattan and then fashionable Brooklyn. Colonel Mann's *Town Topics* conveyed in asterisks the suggestion of perfumed love nests in mid-town hotels and a practically universal prevalence in private dining rooms at Sherry's and Bustanoby's of vast meat pies from whose inner economy dancing girls emerged at bachelor dinners.

At the other end of the scale the *Police Gazette* delighted a pool-room clientele from Bangor to San Diego with chronicles of high-life debauches specifically illustrated with wood engravings depicting the very things *Town Topics* only hinted at. In its pages everyone was in full evening dress and the men often wore monocles; silk hats served as ice buckets for cooling champagne and chorus girls in flesh tights did cakewalks on the table while wearing opera hats and whirling the canes of their escorts like drum majorettes at a Dallas football game. That the socially elect with whom the *Gazette* populated these Byzantine hoedowns turned out on close scrutiny to be named McGlory, O'Hoolihan, and Krausmeyer was of no consequence. They wore dress suits, didn't they?

Generally speaking, the moneyed aristocrats of the period were well along in years and fairly incapable of surviving a single evening's entertainment among the senators in *Quo Vadis*. Only a most elastic imagination was able to envision Mrs. William Backhouse Astor being ridden home at dawn in a wheelbarrow, or George Gould pursuing his guests at *Georgian Court* with champagne magnums in the manner of fire hoses. When entertainments among the elect diverged from the conventional, they were apt to be eccentric rather than of Dionysiac dimensions, as witness the widely advertised dinner party arranged at Mrs. Stuyvesant Fish's Newport villa by Harry Lehr, at which a monkey was guest of honor, and the "Horseback Dinner" arranged by C. K. G. Billings at Sherry's at which the guests ate in the saddle and combined at once the grotesque with the uncomfortable. To be sure, there was a testimonial at the Lotus Club in honor of Harrison Grey Fiske, editor of the *Dramatic Mirror*, at which all the guests were photographed with their brows encircled with wreathes of vine leaves, but their effect superposed above pince-nez eyeglasses, shawl-collar dinner jackets, and ample beards and mustaches suggested Bloomsbury rather than Petronius.

One thing many of the most innocuous entertainments had to recommend them to the attention of posterity: most of them, especially if given at one of the town's luxury restaurants or hotels, were both elaborate and costly; a few were of such sensationally expensive dimensions as to attract unfavorable attention in the public prints.

It was a time which saw the emergence of what later came to be known as café society, in which conservative ladies and gentlemen of impeccable character who hitherto had seldom dined in public save on massive occasions of civic or cultural circumstance, began appearing in ever-increasing numbers at resorts favored by well-to-do playboys, champagne salesmen, expense-account business executives with out-of-town customers, playwrights, newspaper-men, and the upper echelons of the musical-comedy stage and the race track. Resorts sprang up to accommodate the varying degrees of taste and reticence of these cosmopolites: the restaurants of the Waldorf and Fifth Avenue hotels, Sherry's, and Delmonico's for the ultraconservative; Rector's, Bustanoby's, Shanley's, and Wood-manston for gilded youth, wine salesmen, professional bridge play-ers, Texans, and the associates of Diamond Jim Brady.

Some of the lobster palaces boasted ballrooms; almost all had upstairs suites and private dining rooms whose symbol became a hot bird and cold bottle served by a graying waiter in sideburns who knocked discreetly before appearing with the Lynnhavens. It was the private dining rooms that lit up with pleasure the eyes of editors at *Town Topics,* the *Police Gazette,* and the newly emergent *American Weekly,* in which Morrill Goddard was suggesting to the readers of the Hearst papers the enchanting vistas of wickedness available to the upper classes. At the height of its vogue, 30,000,000 weekly readers of this repository of gilded folklore believed implic-itly that New York's social leaders went to bed in full evening dress, brushed their teeth in vintage champagne, married their daugh-ters without exception to shady French counts, and arrayed their poodle dogs in diamond tiaras. It was a cheerful image and one in which almost everybody took innocent pleasure.

As Hearst's Sunday editor, newly revised together with his com-plete staff from Joseph Pulitzer's *New York World,* Goddard, through the magazine pages of the *Journal* on which the *American Weekly* was a component, presented a panorama of high life that was cal-culated to confuse and even terrify its accredited participants, but it delighted readers in less exalted brackets and created a climate in which reality inevitably came in some degree to approximate what had originally been fiction. As another member of the Hearst staff, Arthur Brisbane, was fond of saying: "Repetition is reputation," and life among the *haut monde* of Newport and Manhattan, like an impressionable actor, came in a measure to live up to its billing. Butlers came to assume absurd and awkward positions of attention like drill sergeants on parade; dinners that had until now foundered participants with seven or eight courses and their appropriate wines, now found the benumbed aristocrats at table after four mortal hours of terrapin, canvasback, mousses and soufflés relieved by water ices between; eligible young ladies larded their most casual conversations with French illiteracies they imagined gave them elevated *ton,* and French maids until recently named Marie or Josephine all suddenly appeared to have been christened Fifine.

In another context, its own press forty years later demonstrably conditioned the public and private lives of Hollywood stars who might naturally have been otherwise inclined into a kaleidoscope of sports cars, swimming pool orgies, and marital infidelities. The dedicated student of American mores, not only in the lower and presumably impressionable ranks of society, but on Bellevue Ave-nue and Sutton Place South, will do well to study its image as pre-sented in the popular press, an image to which it found itself, often enough, conforming if only not to disappoint its public.

For it was publicity, whether of a decorous or irreverent order, and whether acceptable or embarrassing to its recipients, that shaped what Wilmarth Lewis has called "the nuances of snobbery, the discrimination and cultivation of which have been the major contributions of the Anglo-Saxon peoples to civilization."

On a fine May morning in 1893, President Grover Cleveland pushed an electric button and the flags of forty-seven nations broke out as one, to be whipped in a brisk wind off Lake Michigan. It was the start of the World's Columbian Exposition and it also launched Mrs. Potter Palmer, wife of Chicago's pioneer merchant prince and hotelkeeper, on a public career that was to last through a long and energetic lifetime. From then on, Mrs. Palmer was seldom out of the public prints, a circumstance well suited to her temperament. As chairman of the Board of Lady Managers of the Chicago fair, Mrs. Palmer would have had no considerable competition for public attention except for one other woman, separated from the millionairess by a wide gulf of both economics and social position. She was known as "Little Egypt," and she performed what was tactfully called a *Dance du Ventre* on the midway to the music of a Zulu band.

All hell promptly broke out over Little Egypt. Women's clubs protested the demoralizing influence of her, by the standards of the time, practically naked performance. A later generation would have thought her dressed for skiing at Sun Valley. Anthony Comstock, a professional snouter out of voluptuary attitudes who disapproved of almost everything including men's athletic supporters, made an issue of it. Under stress of great pressure from social purity groups, Mrs. Palmer, as the responsible official, was forced to suppress Little Egypt and her *Danse du Ventre,* but the accompanying publicity did nothing to enlarge the image of her worldliness or tolerance.

On the other hand, it made Little Egypt a national celebrity.

Although she would have been the first to deny it, and with gestures, Mrs. Potter Palmer might be considered personally to have pushed Little Egypt, nude except for a pair of black lace stockings and high-heeled slippers, onto a tabletop in a private room at Sherry's in New York four years later, as the central figure of what was always afterward to be remembered as "The Awful Seeley Dinner."

Nobody who lived in New York in the nineties is apt ever to forget it. Other explosions of high-proof folly, the Bradley-Martin ball, James Hazen Hyde's costume fete, scores of Mamie Fish's infantile caprices, achieved widespread celebrity without qualifying adjectives. Only the Seeley dinner will be remembered forever, with the crowning panache of the inseparable word, "Awful."

Herbert Barnum Seeley, a grandson of P. T. Barnum, who had inherited a large share of the showman's $4,000,000 estate, had for some time been a figure in the ranks of the bright young men of the town. He had departed from West Point without a commission after two years, and was a member of several of the best clubs, including the Larchmont Yacht Club and the Lotus. His brother, Clinton Seeley, was engaged to be married December 30, 1896, to Miss Florence Tuttle, one of Gotham's most eligible young ladies, and it was in anticipation of this happy event that Herbert Seeley undertook to give him an ushers' dinner on the night of December 19.

The natural choice of restaurants at this time was Delmonico's and it was here that the dinner was first scheduled to take place, but at the last minute the scene was shifted to Sherry's, where the party eventually took place in an upstairs suite. A pretty time the Seeleys had later, explaining exactly what happened during its progress.

The guests, of whom there were twenty, were mostly from the socially elect and numbered among them the Seeley family physician, included, no doubt, as was delicately remarked later, "in case anyone was overcome with indigestion or nervous shock."

After the exposing had got well under way and the customary denunciations of high life had commenced, the Reverend Dr. Charles H. Parkhurst declared from his pulpit that "the public should know just what went on at this dinner," and so far as the press and the police were concerned, a very substantial effort was made in this direction.

What actually took place was as follows: Captain George Chapman of the Tenderloin Squad, generally known as "Old Whiskers" Chapman, and famous for his eccentric practice of carrying an umbrella rather than a night stick, acting on a tip received earlier in the day and accompanied by Detectives Walters and Craddall, descended, Assyrian-like, upon the festivities shortly before midnight. "I had reason to believe," the Captain declared, "that there might be a display of immodest dancing at Mr. Seeley's party." As the raiding party entered Sherry's, displaying their badges in order to overcome any prejudice which might be aroused by their lack of evening attire, a doorman left his post and ran upstairs. "This to my mind was most suspicious," said Chapman.

The raiders marched boldly upstairs to the scene of activity, prepared to deal with any licentious revelry which might be in progress. They even spurned the pressing invitation extended by M. Flaurand, Sherry's genteel manager, to stop in the downstairs bar for a couple of quick ones. In their haste to discharge their duties, however, they mistook the door and burst valiantly into a dressing room reserved for the young ladies who were to sing and dance at intervals during the dinner. The screaming and uproar which ensued brought the dinner guests to the scene, and it was then that a Mr. Hamilton attempted the defenestration of Captain Chapman. "One of the gentlemen was so indignant that he was on the point of throwing the Captain out the window," said Mr. Sherry later. This project, however, was thwarted, and after the mutual exchange of insults distinctive of an encounter between citizens and the gendarmery, Captain Chapman withdrew his forces, convinced that his premature entry had rendered negligible the chances of detecting anyone engaged in immodest dancing.

This brief episode was the basis for the protracted clamor which followed, and if the Seeleys had been content to let it pass without further notice, the public would have been deprived of a great deal of edification, but they were not, and Monday morning Chief of Police Peter Conlin received a barrage of indignant protests over the conduct of his subordinate. The elder Seeley protested; the Seeley brothers protested; Mr. Sherry protested; Flaurand, Sherry's genteel manager, protested; Duchemin, the vaudeville agent who had staged the entertainment at dinner, protested; and the newspapers with all the enthusiasm of crusaders protested, denounced, and inveighed against the ungentlemanly intrusion of Captain Chapman and his attendant sleuths.

Outraged virtue and the defenders of civil liberty, not to mention the opponents of the administration, banded together to make a swift end of "Old Whiskers" Chapman. Chief Conlin promised a speedy trial and the execution of justice as soon as specific complaints were filed and signed. Things had come to a pretty pass when a gentleman, and a member of the Union League at that, couldn't give a private party in a private room without the gendarmes bouncing in and waving umbrellas at him.

The forces of morality and reform also took advantage of the occasion to denounce the degeneracy of the times and declare that the purple ways of high society could end in nothing good. Pompeii, it would appear, was at this period the classic example of license and depravity, for the Reverend A. H. Lewis likened "reports we have heard of a scene in this city to the most licentious periods of Pompeii," and continued to the effect that "when the police recently made a raid on Fifth Avenue, they lifted only a corner of the curtain that hides the prevalent iniquity. They gave us but a glimpse of what transpires in the highest circles."

For the further moral instruction of the public the papers carried column upon column of the more *recherché* details daily. The real sensation of the case was still to come to light, however.

During the trial of Captain Chapman before a police board, to which all the guests of the dinner had been summoned as witnesses, it was discovered that a dancer known as Little Egypt had been in the building during the raid, secreted in an upstairs room, and that she had performed to the satisfaction of everyone after the departure from the scene of Captain Chapman and his detectives. The exact nature of Little Egypt's entertainment has never to this day been discovered by students of Manhattan history, but that she participated in the first ballet in modern Gotham in which the Dance of the Seven Veils was enacted is the most nearly authenticated surmise.

This announcement with its attendant descriptions of Little Egypt attired, at least at the start of her performance, in "gauzy and diaphanous apparel," convinced the purer-minded element of the community that there was a great deal of agreeably dubious detail which had not yet been brought to light. Those in charge of Captain Chapman's trial at once dedicated themselves to remedying this oversight.

A theatrical agent named Phipps and a dancer, Annabelle Whitford, were promptly unearthed, or rather made a dramatic entry of their own accord, with a fine tale to the effect that Miss Whitford had been approached and offered the sum of $20 to appear at the performance in something less than the gauzy and diaphanous garments at first affected by Little Egypt.

Annabelle, it appeared, had scornfully rejected the offer and had told Papa. "Papa was very angry," she testified. "He swore terrible and wanted to go after Mr. Phipps," but as it was the scantiness of the offer rather than that of the costume suggested which had aroused Papa to a pitch of moral frenzy, he had finally been calmed and prevailed upon not to molest the vaudeville agent.

An interesting sidelight on the reluctant Annabelle's testimony was supplied by the discovery that at some time between the dinner and the trial, she and Captain Chapman had exchanged photographs. But the Captain was equal to the occasion and deposed as follows:

> I saw Miss Whitford in Chief Conlin's office when he was making his investigation. I told her I was proud to know a woman who was so guarded of her honor and that I would protect a woman's honor with my life if it were necessary. She gave her photograph to me as a token of her esteem on condition that I should give her mine, a gracious act which I reciprocated some days later.

Captain Chapman's trial dragged on interminably and the Seeleys found themselves achieving an almost international prominence. It seemed that everyone in New York was called as witness.

Miss Whitford had been assured that everyone would be so far gone in wine that they wouldn't notice what she wore or didn't wear. It was testified that gentlemen had made attempts to snatch at Little Egypt's ankles as she danced on the tabletop, that gentlemen had been free of the lady's dressing room on the night in question, that Phipps had approached other dancers with proposals of an interesting nature, that Sherry had attempted to lock his doors in the faces of the raiders.

Somehow in the midst of it all the Seeley-Tuttle nuptials were solemnly celebrated, and as disclosure upon disclosure was made, the grand jury handed down an indictment against Seeley, Phipps, and Theodore Rich on charges of "conspiring to induce the woman known as Little Egypt to commit the crime of indecent exposure." The trial was postponed upon various occasions and was finally lost track of in the manner of so many legal processes, but its threatened appearance could not have added to the peace of mind of the Seeley guests.

At last the charges against Captain Chapman were dismissed, but not before every shred of evidence in the case had been heard thrice over. It was really the participants in The Awful Seeley Dinner who were on trial.

Captain Chapman received a vote of thanks from the National League for the Promotion of Social Purity and another from the Woman's Purity Association. A bill was introduced into the legislature to compensate him for the expense of defending himself before the trial board, and he was generally lionized by the forces of morality and uplift.

As for Little Egypt, she was at once billed in an elaborate vaudeville performance at a salary in keeping with her generally admitted artistic abilities, and for years thereafter topped the bill of all houses as "Little Egypt, the star of The Awful Seeley Dinner."

If anything, after the echoes of The Awful Seeley Dinner had died away, were needed to call attention to New York's by now well-established legend of social debacle, it was the selection a few weeks later of the ballroom of the Waldorf as the setting for one of the two most celebrated balls in New York history, both of which, like that of the Duchess of Richmond on the eve of Waterloo, were a prelude to disaster and eventual exile for their principal instigators.

ᲘᲢᲝ·ᲘᲢᲝ·ᲘᲢᲝ

The Seeley dinner took place, as has been recounted, in the closing weeks of 1896. It was the merest curtain raiser to the Bradley-Martin ball of February 1897 which was to prove the most written about, denounced, defended, and generally dismayingly successful gesture of self-publicizing in the annals of Manhattan, at least until the advent of café society and Brenda Frazier more than three decades in the unforeseeable future.

It was not as though Mr. and Mrs. Bradley-Martin, well-heeled parvenus from Troy, New York, who moved to town and perpetuated "the slow growth of an imaginary hyphen" as an adjunct to social aspiration, didn't have warning well in advance of their downfall. For weeks before the appointed night, the public prints had been filled with the details of its extravagance "reluctantly released to the society departments of the New York dailies through the agency of Western Union messenger boys on bicycles." There were to be "five mirrors on the north side of the ballroom richly but not heavily garlanded in a curtain effect by mauve orchids and the feathery plemusa vine; garlands will be hung irregularly across the mirrors to loop onto the capitals of the columns separating the mirrors; the chandeliers on each column will be decorated with orchids and suspended from each chandelier will be a Rosalind-like pocket filled with Louis XVI roses and ferns. Roses will fall in showers over the balcony and will festoon the columns, not a space on the balcony, wall, or column that will not be festooned, banked, showered with bride, American beauty, and pink roses, or lilies-of-the-valley or orchids. The profusion of mauve orchids will stream carelessly to the floor, like the untied bonnet strings of a thoughtless child."

This was the merest sampling of the lyric gems that found their way to city and society desks throughout the lower city and, in large measure, were reprinted just as they came from the inspired hand of the Bradley-Martins' social secretary, who had evidently been a student of Swinburne.

Statistics vied with these impressive dithyrambs. There would be a grand total of between 5000 and 6000 orchids, each clump or cluster of which would be illuminated by a cunningly concealed electric bulb of candle power so subdued as not to damage the fragile blooms. The 22nd Regiment Band of fifty musicians would be one of several orchestras. Supper, to be served by waiters in royal livery with knee breeches and powdered wigs from midnight to 2:30, would include whole roast English suckling pig with the conventional trimmings. There would be an ample buffet available until the last guest left the premises. Mrs. Bradley-Martin had thoughtfully ordered 400 two-horse carriages from O'Toole the liveryman to obviate the inconvenience to her guests of keeping their own coachmen up until all hours.

Importunate letters were arriving from out-of-towners implicitly relegated to the status of social climbers by the Bradley-Martin secretary, asking to be invited to what was obviously going to be the most stately social occasion at least since Caligula married his horse in the Roman forum. Such intrusive tactics were resented by the Bradley-Martins as unworthy of serious consideration.

Inevitably, these sneak previews of beatification also drew an advance barrage of criticism and metaphorical dead cats. The country was suffering one of its recurrent depressions and, almost as voluminous as the out-of-town letters soliciting invitations, were more anonymous ones threatening red revolution in the streets, social upheaval of the most menacing sort on a widespread scale which would end with the entire capitalist system in the trash bin and the Bradley-Martins looped to the nearest lamp posts by their own feathery plemusa vines. More temperate voices from the pulpits and social workers suggested that the estimated $200,000 to be spent on the rout might be put to better use.

The Bradley-Martins had an answer to that one. The very ostentation they were sponsoring gave remunerative work to hundreds of dressmakers, florists, and other artisans involved. It was, on close inspection, nothing but a spread-the-wealth project of almost pure benevolence. A great many seamstresses, waiters, and flower growers wrote in to the newspapers championing this viewpoint and hailing the Bradley-Martins as selfless benefactors. One clergyman was so stirred by this aspect of the affair that he told his congregation in ringing tones: "The public be damned; let the Bradley-Martins spend their money as they please."

The Bradley-Martin ball was a public controversy of a major order, pre-empting politics and international affairs from the columns of the New York newspapers before the first fiddle sounded or the first errant forkful of terrapin Maryland landed on a boiled shirt. When the well-publicized night actually arrived, scores of police extras patrolled Fifth Avenue outside the Waldorf under the personal supervision of Theodore Roosevelt, Assistant Police Commissioner of New York City. Other scores of plain-dress detectives closely scrutinized the bidden guests as they arrived in the hope of detecting a sedan chair laden with dynamite or a known anarchist disguised as Henry VIII. None turned up and contrary to the doomsday voices of the Cassandras, the crowd that began assembling outside the hotel as early as seven o'clock, far from being ugly or threatening, was delighted with the whole occasion and cheered the appearance of especially spectacular arrivals.

Most of the guests came in closed carriages and their finery was only briefly visible as they scurried across the sidewalk under George Boldt's porte-cochere, but one participant, never identified in the papers, attired as a Sioux Indian chief in full-feathered headdress, was unable to find a carriage to accommodate his attire and arrived bolt upright and alone in the back seat of an open victoria. He rated a cheer from the onlookers and made a stately entry, bowing right and left with palm upraised and saying, "How!"

The only real casualty of the evening was the Metropolitan Opera, on the other side of town, whose performance of *Martha* played to a half-empty house with only gallery seats occupied, since regular box holders and lesser luminaries who would in the ordinary course of events have occupied the orchestra were all footing it to the Bradley-Martins done up as Mlle. Pompadour, George Washington, and Ninon de Lenclos.

Whatever dead cats of envy or recrimination might be thrown afterward, the Bradley-Martin ball did, in actual fact, attract the cream of New York society. Nobody who received an invitation for a moment considered missing what might be the onset of the revolution and certainly the most extravagant entertainment ever, until then, held outside a private home. Elaborate dinners were given in advance by Mrs. John Jacob Astor, Mrs. Ogden Mills, Mrs. Henry Sloane, and Mrs. Livingston Ludlow, all of whom, it may be presumed, did well by their guests with the then requisite ten courses including terrapin, canvasback, and *foie gras* even though, as advertised, there was to be roast English suckling pig at midnight when they could start eating all over again.

The costumes were almost incredibly elaborate; it was a time when society women and some men started planning months ahead what they were going to wear, thus anticipating thirty-odd years later the career of Mrs. S. Stanwood Menken who, every year, the morning after the annual Beaux Arts Ball, would start planning her next season's appearance.

Mrs. Oliver H. P. Belmont appeared attired as one of the more sartorially resplendent French queens of history; the reporter for the *World* never found out exactly which one. Harry Lehr, in a gorgeous Louis XV outfit shimmering with jewels borrowed for the occasion from Tiffany, dazzled all beholders. Schuyler Livingston Parsons wore the old Dutch costume of one of his own patroon ancestors. There were no fewer than three George Washingtons, each bitching the authenticity of the attire of the competition. Frederic de Peyster came as a Knight of Malta with red tights and shoes and a shirt of authentic mail surmounted by a white boat cloak. Mrs. T. J. Oakley Rhinelander was Marie Antoinette and Mrs. T. Suffern Tailer wore a Gainsborough gown "of great magnificence."

Mrs. Bradley-Martin herself went, somewhat prophetically, since she was shortly to take one-way passage for Scotland, as Mary

Stuart wearing what were variously estimated as $60,000 and $100,000 worth of diamonds. The conservative *Times* reported the lesser figure; the sensational and anti-Bradley-Martin *World,* the greater. By the time the affair was taking double truck spreads in the Sunday supplements a few weeks later, the figure had risen to $250,000. By then the Bradley-Martins were past caring.

The *World's* uncharitable attitude toward the whole affair was reflected in its next day's chronicle of the fete in which its reporter described Mrs. Bradley-Martin as

> a short, stout woman with cold blue eyes, a square, deter-mined face and a nose that looked as though it intended to tilt but stopped short. She wore a train twenty feet long, a crown on her brow, and $100,000 worth of diamonds on her stomacher, which looked like a waistcoat.

> It was perfectly astonishing how Mrs. Astor managed to find a place for so many jewels; they covered her like a cui-rass. She was gowned as a Venetian lady in a dark-blue vel-vet costume. It was laden with $200,000 worth of jewels.

> The supper, at which the guests behaved like children afraid of mussing their clothes, consisted largely of cham-pagne with a few things thrown in like bouillon, truffles, and duck. There was no stint in the champagne, like the usual stingy one quart to a person at most New York balls.

Everybody, even the *World,* admitted the superlative quality and unending quantity of the wine. It afterward proved to have been pur-chased the year previous by Mr. Bradley-Martin at a favorably-priced sale in London and shipped across the Atlantic where it occupied the entire hold of a small freighter. The management of the Waldorf, miffed at not serving its own champagne, charged $1.50 corkage on every bottle. Since Mumm and White Seal then sold for $3.50 at the table, the saving to the Bradley-Martins was not so much.

Revolution failed to materialize and at an early hour Assistant Commissioner Roosevelt left the scene, assured that anarchists or other antisocial intruders who had contrived an entry to the Waldorf ballroom were by now being humanized by the Bradley-Martin roast suckling pig and champagne. In any event, favored members of his police force were wiping their constabulary mustaches in the hotel kitchens and finding no fault at all with the supper or its subsequent buffet.

Even in the light of the inflammatory reportage of the *World* and other sensational New York papers, the ball appears in retrospect to have been decorous to the point of ennui. The reverend clergy took a disparaging look at the whole affair, however, and called upon a just heaven to avenge what it widely hailed as an affront to the Almighty in person.

"God pity the shivering, starving poor these days and send a cyclone of justice upon the ball of selfishness," proclaimed the occupant of a Brooklyn pulpit, impervious to the fact that the party was over with no manifestation of displeasure from heaven.

The Reverend Madison Peters, in a sermon on "The Use and Misuse of Wealth," said: "Sedition is born in the lap of luxury—so fell Rome, Thebes, Babylon, and Carthage." The cities of antiquity got quite a workout from other divines, with Rome the all-time favorite as a conspicuous consequence of depravity.

"The guests freely used cosmetics in making up for the ball," pondered *Truth* in London. "An estimate of the material so used ran to more than 500 pounds of rouge and *blanc de perle,* impalpable powder (a popular basic cosmetic), two and one half flour barrels, and powder puffs enough to make a bouquet ten feet high and six feet wide. The sermons that will be preached, the morals to be pointed, the tales to be adorned from the material here furnished would certainly fill eighty-three issues of the great *Sunday World."*

The *Herald* and the *Times* gave over most of their front pages to the ball and a reprint of the *Herald's* account was, of course, cabled at James Gordon Bennett's express order to the Paris edition where it aroused premature hopes in American exiles and unemployed

European royalty that at long last the United States was about to renounce democracy and become a monarchy.

> It seemed exactly like a stately court function in one of the capitals of Europe, even to the liveried lackey who stood at the foot of Mrs. Bradley-Martin's dais and announced every guest by name, character represented, and historical period in a loud tone.

Allowing for the transatlantic time lag, readers of the *London Daily Mail* were told over their morning kippers and tea:

> Mrs. Bradley-Martin, we have every reason to believe, is dressed at this very moment in a train of black velvet lined with cerise satin, and a petticoat, if it is not indiscreet to say so, of white satin embroidered with flowers and arabesques of silver.

The *London Chronicle* ponderously wrote:

> We congratulate New York society on its triumph. It has cut out Belshazzar's feast and Wardour Street and Mme. Tussaud's and the Bank of England. There is no doubt about that." Oscar Hammerstein burlesqued it at the Olympia with a skit called "The Bradley-Radley Ball.

Confronted with the printed evidence that August Belmont had appeared in a full suit of gold-inlaid steel armor from the collection of the Metropolitan Museum of Art worth $10,000 and that Mrs. Bradley-Martin, in addition to her disputed $60,000 or $100,000 diamonds, wore a massive ruby necklace that had belonged to Marie Antoinette and was valued at $75,000, the *London Chronicle* asked innocently: "Were all the costumes ticketed with the price?"

Regardless of the value of the various diamond, ruby, pearl, and emerald necklaces, bracelets, dog collars, and stomachers worn by their guests, the final bill for the Bradley-Martins' big evening came to $369,200 with the unforeseen result that the

New York City tax authorities immediately doubled the lawyer's tax assessment. In a magnificent huff at this churlish ingratitude for their benevolences, the Bradley-Martins removed themselves permanently to England and Scotland, pausing only long enough en route to the steamer to give a farewell dinner for eighty-six persons which cost $116.28 per plate. The *World,* still unreconciled, estimated that at least a dozen of the gentlemen present at this stylish Last Supper were worth more than $10,000,000, while twice that number were worth $5,000,000 and that among their ladies there were worn "enough diamond crowns to fit out all the crowned heads of Europe and have some left over for Asia and Africa."

The Bradley-Martin ball is remembered to this day with mixed emotions by social commentators and historians, but one aspect of New York journalism that emerged as a firmly fixed precept of the profession was, in reporting the extravagances of the upper crust, invariably to quote the price of everything. Hereafter, the price of the consommé at supper, the boutonniere in the best man's lapel, and the cost of cabs for the participants was a part of reporting anything even vaguely connected with the Four Hundred.

ෙ෴෴ • ෴෴ • ෴෴

The most significant aspect, at least for social historians, of the James Hazen Hyde ball of Tuesday, January 31, 1905, was not its voluptuousness, for it cost a mere $200,000, nor any indecorum, for its conduct was on a scale of unimpeachable propriety. What made it a benchmark in social history was that it was the first gold-plated romp to be extensively covered by the modern technique of photography. And while the photographs themselves depicted no thinkable departure from the most formal conduct, they were, nevertheless, instrumental in bringing about the eventual exile of the host almost exactly as the Bradley-Martins had been forced into exile back in 1897.

It was a very peculiar business indeed.

Until young Mr. Hyde took it into his head to give a ball on a theme of unabashed Francophilia, photography of these events had been conducted on a very abated scale and the candid camera of such practitioners as Jerome Zerbe, the yet unborn silver bromide *jongleur* of café society, was in the unforeseen future. Hosts often had photographers in to take still pictures of the setting for their more opulent sarabands. Table settings for dinners, the floral decorations for balls and weddings, were pictured as a matter of record, but not for publication in the periodical press if only because the halftone process was as yet imperfect, and until the middle nineties illustrated weeklies like *Leslie's* and *Harper's* relied almost exclusively on wood engravings made by staff technicians from photographic originals.

Guests, too, at galas, especially costume routs where their attire represented great outlays of effort and money, were privately photographed, usually at their costumer's or at home before setting out for the evening. Nobody before Mr. Hyde had ever conceived of complete photographic coverage of a party by professionals retained by the host and afforded every facility for the exercise of their professional expertise. It was to have resounding repercussions.

At the age of twenty-eight, James Hazen Hyde had inherited from his energetic father, Henry Baldwin Hyde, the control and absolute direction of the affairs of the far-flung Equitable Life Assurance Society of New York. With this position of authority vested in the title of first vice president, *honoris causa,* went directorates in no fewer than forty-six allied or subsidiary corporations or those doing business on a considerable scale with Equitable. Hyde had an enviable estate at Bay Shore, Long Island. He also owned a private Pullman car named *Bay Shore* whose home railroad was the lordly Union Pacific in Omaha. An ardent partisan of the Coaching Club, whose membership averaged a far more advanced age, Hyde maintained one of the best stables and some of the handsomest turnouts in Manhattan, a habit he was to follow, with necessary modifications, until his death.

At one time, it was his whim, following exalted examples in the British peerage and within the Coaching Club itself, to maintain a coaching service from the front of the Holland House, a resort of conservative fashion, to George Gould's incredible *Georgian Court* at Lakewood, New Jersey, a distance of seventy-eight miles. Halfway between the terminals, at New Brunswick, Hyde purchased a wayside inn which he had redecorated with commendable restraint as an old English coaching tavern where patrons of his service could lunch on Melton Mowbray pie, Stilton cheese, and Alsopp's draft lager before continuing their journey. The stockholders of Equitable, although they didn't know it at the time, picked up the tab for that one, too.

There was also, back in 1902, the dinner party Hyde had given in honor of the French ambassador to the United States. The check, in the sum of $12,600, had been paid by the Equitable stockholders and nobody had said a word. It wasn't that Hyde couldn't afford these things out of his own pocket—his salary as first vice president of a $400,000,000 corporation was a tax-free $100,000 a year—but he felt that Equitable ought to pick up the tab now and then. It was only good public relations.

A guest at one of the intimate supper parties that Hyde had given at *Bay Shore* remembered the details of the exquisite culinary hospitality, after which "ladies donned old postilion hats or bullfighters' bonnets and blew hunting horns while everybody did the cakewalk."

Above all, Hyde's interests lay in the direction of things French: French art, French literature, French fashions, French history, food, actresses, formal society—in a word, anything and everything that was French. While other college youths of his gilded generation at Harvard sought the rowdier delights of the Folies-Bergère and Maxim's where they could encounter such notables as the Grand Duke Cyril and James Gordon Bennett in their more relaxed moments, Hyde spent his time in art museums, among the châteaux of the Loire, or in airtight salons in fluent conversation with old ladies whose memories went back to the Empress Eugénie and the coaches of the Third Napoleon dashing up the ramp to the Paris Opéra.

He brought home memories of these delightful excursions into golden yesterdays with which to regale intimates at supper parties that were remembered by their participants long after the last souf-flé had been consumed and the last drop of Comet Year cognac inhaled from a balloon glass.

From these modest supper and theater parties it was no great elevation of Hyde's sights to a grand gala de luxe that would pop the eyes of his social peers and show the world how that sort of thing should be done. The theme, of course, was to be French, of a sufficiently dated period to make costumes mandatory, and an exponent of French *savoir-vivre* was at hand in the person of Mme. Gabrielle Rejane, a Parisian actress of mediocre talents but attractive personality who was playing in a French version of *Ma Cousine* at the Liberty Theater.

Hyde took thought with the management of Sherry's and the result was all that an imaginative young man and a stylish restaurateur could wish in terms of $200,000 of somebody else's money. For when the dust had settled and a New York attorney general named Charles Evans Hughes had sifted it with a fine mesh, it appeared that the stockholders of Equitable Life had been the real hosts and that Hyde was, in effect, only their impresario. This made a profound impression on the stockholders, most of whom inclined to be narrow-minded about the whole business.

The theme of Hyde's ball was, as Walter Lord remarked, almost inevitably the court of Louis XV, for which he had employed the fashionable architect Whitney Warren to convert Sherry's ballroom into a reasonable facsimile of a wing of the Palace of Versailles. As in the case of the fatal Bradley-Martin ball of only a few years previous, roses were present in almost overwhelming abundance. They formed barricades around the edge of the ballroom floor. Lattices, screens, arbors, trellises, canopies, arches, and blankets of roses were hung, festooned, draped, and emplaced wherever a blossom could be accommodated and some where it manifestly couldn't. Again, "cunningly concealed electrical lamps" peeped coyly through the encircling forest of roses. The hosts' preoccupation with flowers seemed to some to be positively psychopathic. It was an aspect of the evening which didn't bother Wadley & Smythe, the florists whose rose bill alone came to $28,500.

The guests, rising nobly to the occasion, for the most part were reluctant to let down their host or his architect and arrived in attire to match the florid opulence of the setting. Hyde, flanked by a niece whom he had hastily recruited to serve as the nominal guest of honor, wore his French beard, knee breeches with silver-buckled pumps, and the handsome dark-green evening tail coat of the Coaching Club with the various decorations with which a grateful French government had seen fit to invest him.

Startling everybody by her prompt appearance, since her reputation for tardiness was well established, Mamie Fish arrived riding herd on a contingent of sixty dinner guests—rendered docile to the point of subservience by twelve courses including quail in aspic and a *bombe Moscovite* eaten from the solid-gold Fish table service. They were to eat three more meals that evening. Mrs. George Gould, wearing all her diamonds and most of her pearls, but not all, since one of her minor necklaces worth a mere $150,000 was being restrung at Cartier's, impersonated Marie, Queen of France and wife of Louis XV, with a long train of green velvet lined with white satin and trimmed with gold and emeralds. The private detective whom George Gould retained to follow his wife whenever she wore more than $250,000 worth of anything, spent an uncomfortable night prowling the outer lobby in full evening dress amidst tide rips of courtiers dressed for another era and attended by shoals of small Nubian slaves. Major Creighton Webb, an individualist if ever there was one, refused point-blank to get himself rigged out as a bogus marquis and appeared in a Spanish bullfighter's outfit left over from another masquerade. Louis XV would have had a bullfighter or two around if he was any sort of king, was the way he put it.

Most pathetic of the guests because she had gone to inestimable trouble and expense for the occasion was Mrs. Clarence Mackay, wife of the Atlantic cable and telegraph tycoon whose mother-in-law had been Louise Hungerford who, until she married Bonanza Mackay of Virginia City, had taken in gentlemen's sewing and mending in the mining camps of the Mother Lode. Now, the second generation Mrs. Mackay had made up her mind to represent Adrienne Lecouvreur, an eighteenth-century actress, in her starring role of Phèdre, for which Mrs. Mackay was so burdened with watered silk, cut velvet, looped and ball-fringed like Pullman portieres, whalebone stays, and various heavy properties including a gold scepter, that she was unable to move more than a few steps at a time without sinking down from exhaustion. When she was able to move at all, two small Nubians in pink brocade court attire carried the ends of her sixteen-foot satin train.

The entertainment matched the elegance of Mrs. Mackay's costume but it, too, to the frivolous-minded, might have appeared attenuated, ponderous, and fatiguing. To begin with, there was an overture danced by eight debutantes and eight reluctantly recruited college youths in Pierrot suits who nervously performed a gavotte to the music of the Metropolitan Opera's only slightly overpowering forty-piece orchestra led by Nahan Franko. They were followed by something more professional when the entire corps de ballet from the Metropolitan went through the complex routine of an ensemble number that may or may not have had its origins in the court of the Louis of the evening. Their professional dexterity did nothing to comfort the amateurs who had preceded them.

At midnight there arrived on schedule the *pièce montée* of the evening in the person of Mme. Rejane herself, carried to the middle of the dance floor in a richly upholstered and historically correct sedan chair by four stalwart footmen. After a few well-chosen words of welcome from the host, Mme. Rejane stepped onto the rose-embowered stage and took part in an innocuous bedroom farce, specially written for the occasion, in words of one syllable so that everyone might understand, called "Entre Deux Portes." Some of the gentlemen, spelling it out with their lips, concluded that it meant "Between Two Doors."

After this was over, a corps of trumpeters led the by now slightly perspiring 350 guests to a lower floor where Whitney Warren transported them to a different wing of the same Palace of Versailles for supper. Before the service of the clear turtle soup, Mme. Rejane was again called into service to recite a short poem, also specially written for the occasion in easy French, hymning the enlightened joys of Franco-American amity and, presumably, a reduction of the tariff on articles of French import such as the White Seal 1898 champagne which was served immediately the applause had died down.

All who could make it, now made their stately way upstairs again to where there was dancing until three o'clock, when the staff of Sherry's had reset the tables on the lower floor and it was time for a second seating with this difference from the custom as it then obtained on ocean liners, that the occupants were the same ladies and gentlemen who had just gotten up from the first sitting. This made the third full meal since eight o'clock the previous evening for Mamie Fish's sixty veterans, who now faced *les médallions de foie gras en timbale à la genlée de Porto* and Pol Roger in magnums, like participants in a retreat from some gastronomic Moscow. Now they formed in hollow square to resist the combined assault of fresh troops of pastry chefs, flying squadrons of wine stewards, and artillery fire from flanking batteries of Veuve Clicquot and Mumm's Extra. Their heroism under this final attack was noted by everyone. Napoleon, it was felt, had he been there, would have handed out field marshal's batons right and left.

At length it was six o'clock and the battered troops, still in possession of their colors but showing traces of an arduous engagement, were making their adieus to their still radiant host.

"Don't you think it's time for a little breakfast?" suggested Mrs. Joseph Widener to Hyde.

"Coming up," or words to that effect, and Hyde snapped his fingers for a waiting maître d'hôtel. Everybody then sat down to New England fish cakes before staggering out into the cold Fifth Avenue dawn.

Last to leave, as the waiters were sweeping out the wilted roses and discarded handkerchiefs, fans, and odd gloves in the hope of finding a fugitive diamond from Mrs. Potter Palmer's tiara, were the five tired members of the photographic staff of Joseph Byron.

The photographs taken by the industrious Byrons between eight in the evening and six the next morning required the continuous activity of five cameramen and plate holders. The plates themselves, no fewer than 189 eleven-by-fourteen glass negatives, required an enormous outlay of physical exertion to be manhandled into a huge view camera and returned to their wooden compartmented carrying cases. As a concession to the wishes of their host and employer the Byrons were attired in formal evening dress topped by hooded gowns vaguely suggesting the witches in *Macbeth* unaccountably in tail coats and boiled shirts.

Among the finished prints were a stately solo of Mme. Rejane leaning regally on a long ribboned cane while a servitor in full court livery with white silk stockings emptied ash trays in the background. Hyde himself was photographed posed benignly beside the Countess de Rougemont, née Edith Clapp. In another group were Mrs. James A. Burden, Stanford White, Mrs. Sidney Smith, and James Henry "Silent" Smith, the ladies in full court turnout with powdered hair, fans and opera-length gloves, the gentlemen having settled for formal evening attire with Court of St. James's black silk knee breeches and silver-buckled pumps. There were several groups in which appeared, of all people, Edward H. Harriman, toughest railroad mogul of his time, looking embarrassed in hunting dress with knee pants and a pained expression.

Harriman, incidentally, was a director of Equitable and figured largely in the lurid scenes behind closed doors that were to be the consequence of the photographs in which he appeared; for through some agency of connivance or theft a number of the Byron photographs found their way into the hands of editors of Joseph Pulitzer's still rampaging and egalitarian *New York World.* Pulitzer himself, a blind sybarite with extravagant personal tastes of his own, viewed with alarm the gilded ways of high society until his son married a Vanderbilt, which brought the hitherto obstreperous *World* into line with practically the speed of light.

Not that the photographs reproduced by the now fairly reliable halftone process were in themselves incriminating. The whole business reflected rectitude to the verge of dullness, but there was considerable discussion in the accompanying letterpress of the cost of the Hyde ball. Was it, as rumored, really $200,000, and, if so, just who had paid the check? Newspaper readers somehow got the wrong impression that behind the entirely decorous facade of well-mannered boredom there had been scenes of riot and abandon. It was even rumored that the corps de ballet from the Metropolitan had performed a cancan in the advancing hours of the morning. The very notion of E. H. Harriman figuring in a setting of Roman riot and proconsular debauch was hilarious to businessmen who knew him and were privately of the opinion that it must have been necessary to drug him in order to assure his presence there at all.

Schism, however, raised its head inside the councils of Equitable Life itself. A dissident faction of the management there had long cast disapproving looks at Hyde's extravagant ways and especially at the publicity they garnered in the sensational press. Notoriety was the word they used, and here was a radiant example of it. Inevitably, newspaper headline writers made puns about "high life insurance," and public reaction wasn't good.

A faction in the inner councils of the company, which included E. H. Harriman, inclined to a charitable view of Hyde's perfumed escapades. Insurgents, led by Judge William Cohen, after toying with various stopgap compromises, flatly demanded Hyde's ouster and a complete reorganization of the company's internal economy. If Hyde were not replaced, they said plainly, they would ask for an investigation by grand jury and New York State officials. Breaches in Equitable's security arrangements leaked details of the controversy to the *World* and the schism became a full-blown public scandal, not without its overtones of comedy at a very elevated financial plane.

During one of the directors' meetings behind presumably closed doors, Harriman became so incensed as to be for some moments incoherent, during which time he was only able to utter the words, "Wow, wow, wow." Judge Cohen remarked blandly: "Mr. Harriman, that is an aspect of the matter which until now has escaped my attention."

Inevitably, politicians latched onto a heaven-sent opportunity for self-advancement in the specious name of the general interest. Charles Evans Hughes, then a rising lawyer with the highest imaginable aspirations, was retained by a legislative committee to give a thorough sifting of the evidence of interlocking interests, rebates, and reciprocal financial favors among the directors.

He discovered political corruption, nepotism, and a scandalous laxity of general business morality in the entire fabric of Equitable and, by implication, the other giant insurance companies of the land.

But by this time James Hazen Hyde was beyond caring. He had taken passage aboard *La Lorraine* of the French Line, denying to the last that he had any intention of living abroad, but it was nearly forty years before he returned and during that time he became one of the most celebrated of all fixtures in the colony of American expatriates in Paris.

Whatever moral, if any, may be drawn from the Bradley-Martin ball and James Hazen Hyde's fatal entertainment, it certainly is not one that paints New York society at the turn of the century as the new Babylon or another imperial Rome far gone in carnality and voluptuary riot. The Awful Seeley Dinner had confirmed a certain element of Americans preconditioned to the worst and hoping not to be disappointed in the belief that the upper classes lived not only in blizzards of extravagance but on a level of personal morality and licentiousness comparable to that of Petronius' *Satyricon* in its franker moments. The lamb potpie laden with emergent chorus-line beauties in diaphanous attire, or none at all, became the ultimate symbol of enviable sensuality and the pages of Mr. Hearst's *American Weekly,* under the management of Morrill Goddard, were gladdened with the image of a dress-suited playboy, often invested with monocle and opera hat for good measure, mounting a banquet table with a dripping champagne bottle in hand to pursue a nymph in the thicket of hothouse blooms which formed the centerpiece.

It was a gratifying image and sold incalculable numbers of Sunday papers, where it was a staple of bourgeois outrage as late as the 1920s, after which other rich disorders occupied its space. But neither the Bradley-Martins nor Mr. Hyde contributed to it in any appreciable degree. The participants in these revels were little more than overfed to stupefaction and, like Mrs. Clarence Mackay, overdressed into immobility.

Nor, in actual fact, were the Bradley-Martins or young Mr. Hyde "driven" into exile. The public couldn't have cared less, thus their flight must be attributed either to uncommonly thin-skinned timidity or an entire willingness to dramatize themselves as martyrs on an altar of Strasbourg *foie gras.* There is evidence that both the Bradley-Martins, who had a married daughter in England, and Hyde, who had frequently and articulately yearned for the good life of France where art was truly appreciated, had contemplated permanently removing themselves from the American scene before their own poor judgment hastened their departure. The pulpit denunciations and rolling eyes of the clergy meant little in their lives, still less the editorial ah-has of the *World* and the penny press generally. The by now well-established legend of Hyde and the Bradley-Martins as being "driven into exile by public opinion" is simply part of the great body of American social mythology. All concerned made exits of varying magnificence and theatricality and took passage more willingly than, say, Napoleon embarking for Elba.

The expense involved in the two celebrated fetes, $369,200 for the Bradley-Martin ball and $200,000 of the Equitable stockholders' for Hyde's guests, was indeed considerable and, translated into the dollar value of the 1960s which would multiply it by three or four times, fairly astronomical. As late as 1912 the George Jay Goulds spent the sum of $200,000, say $800,000 in today's depreciated currency, on a coming-out party for their daughter Marjory. As a comparative benchmark of extravagance, when Henry Ford II in 1959 gave a $100,000 ball at the Detroit Country Club for his daughter Charlotte, it was universally hailed as "the party of the century." Translated backward in terms of currency to the Bradley-Martin era, it would have been nothing more glamorous or remarkable than a $25,000 supper party peopled with the business associates of the host.

That hypocrisy or at least a singular divergence between preachment and practice was characteristic of most of the sensational newspaper publishers of the late nineteenth century and opening decades of the twentieth cannot be denied. Joseph Pulitzer, whose editorialists held up horrified hands in holier-than-thou attitudes about almost all the capers of the well-to-do including both Hyde and the Bradley-Martins, himself was given to grandiose gestures of phenomenal extravagance such as importing the New York Symphony Orchestra in its entirety to Bar Harbor to play for guests at a private dinner party and building a yacht deliberately calculated to be the equal of Morgan's giant *Corsair* and Vincent Astor's *Nourmahal*. While the *World* was chiding the idle rich of Murray Hill and Fifth Avenue on the Babylonish extravagance of their entertainments, the Society Grocery at Bar Harbor in a single shipment loaded $5600 worth of out-of-season strawberries and Scotch grouse aboard the *Liberty* where, if Pulitzer's guests tired of gastronomy, there was also a music room and a gymnasium comparing favorably in magnitude and equipment with that at the New York Athletic Club.

A notable inhabitant of glass houses himself, James Gordon Bennett in the columns of the *New York Herald* once denounced Saratoga Springs as "a seraglio of the prurient aristocracy" at a time when the major part of the *Herald's* revenue, and his own income as a result, derived from the advertising of parlor houses which at length got it barred from the mails.

Bennett's own personal reputation was such a scandal in his lifetime that he was justified in remarking: "American society largely consists of people who don't invite me to their parties."

Perhaps the most notorious of all stone shiers among the greenhouses was William Randolph Hearst who, in the early days of his political ambitions and before it was apparent that he couldn't get himself elected dog catcher on Bannerman's Island in the Hudson River, was a professional champion of the workingman and people's friend in editorial stances suggesting the barricades. His professions of egalitarianism and blood brotherhood with the working stiff continued long after he was paying $250,000 each for Cellini saltcellars and having Spanish monasteries knocked down and transported in their entirety to a California mountaintop.

In the case of Hearst, a large segment of the American public felt that the most accurate journalistic reflection of his personality was in the Sunday pages of the *American Weekly* where gentlemen wore silk hats to bed with heiresses and brushed their teeth with a light Moselle. Nor did the master of San Simeon command an altogether respectful hearing when he denounced society divorces and *bon-ton* lechery while conducting a marathon affair with Miss Marion Davies to whom he was demonstrably not married.

What the three parties herein listed had in common, aside from the extravagance of their financing, was not the degree of scandal which attached to them. That was a minor consideration. Their common denominator was their honesty. They were frankly and unabashedly engineered as private projects for the pleasure and amusement of their sponsors and their guests or for social advancement. None of them took refuge in the sanctimonious garb of charity; none was advertised to raise funds for dubious good works. A later generation would have taken to itself the social prestige that derived from these flamboyant charades while excusing their cost in the name of some public benevolence, but Seeley, Hyde, and the Bradley-Martins were more honest. They gave their parties on their own responsibility and for fun.

As Mrs. Jack Gardner was to say without qualification or excuse in similar circumstances: *"C'est mon plaisir."*

Chapter Six
Magnifico of Maxim's

James Gordon Bennett Was a Professional Expatriate... Libertine, Playboy, Publisher, and Millionaire, He Was a Perpetual Scandal on Two Continents... Also the Archetype of Crazy American and Gilded Cutup... He Bought Ciro's to Enjoy a Mutton Chop and Became a Paris Institution as Brandied as a Christmas Pudding... Only Harry Thaw's Marksmanship Prevented His Becoming a Permanent Part of the New York Sky Line....

IF EACH OF the other big spenders and magnificoes to whom space in varying degrees is accorded in this volume might be said to represent a type—Evalyn McLean, the lady bountiful, William C. Whitney, the grand seigneur on an epic scale, Diamond Jim Brady, the pet of the lobster palaces, and Colonel Mann, the roguish blackmailer—James Gordon Bennett the Younger, as he was known even after his forbidding sire had passed to his reward, was the great American expatriate and cutup of the Paris boulevards. The fact that in the years he functioned under the gas lamps of the *ville lumière* he was almost the only man to answer this description in no way invalidates it. One was enough.

Other Americans in the period between the Franco-Prussian War and 1914 might have had impact on the French awareness in other capacities; Myron Herrick as a personable and beloved diplomatist, Evander Berry Wall as the Edwardian dandy and beau ideal of sartorial splendor, Mrs. John Mackay as the ambitious social aspirant, James Hazen Hyde as the martyr in exile. These became known to newspaper readers in two continents in their several ornate and useful roles. None for a moment rivaled James Gordon Bennett in the magnitude of his excesses, his gestures of limitless opulence, and his disregard for the established conventions.

Bennett was unique. He was the first and prototypal "crazy American" and he was accepted on this basis in a society that comprised absentee Balkan monarchs, Russian grand dukes, expensive courtesans, monocled roués, Argentine archmillionaires, and a social aristocracy going back no farther than Napoleon I as an equal.

A playboy with $1,000,000 income a year after taxes, perhaps the equivalent of five times as much in today's currency, a libertine whose mere presence could cast doubt on the reputations of women of otherwise unassailable virtue, a voluptuary who remained as brandied and incandescent as a Christmas pudding for years on end, and, in addition to these qualifications for attention, proprietor and sole owner of two of the world's most successful daily newspapers, James Gordon Bennett was not a personality to pass unnoticed.

Had he chosen to remain a New Yorker as heir after his father's death to the responsibilities of ownership of the *New York Herald* he would have been a conspicuous personality.

Along the French Riviera of the nineties and in the gentlemen's clubs of Paris after the turn of the century, he found companionship worthy of his metal. Durable Russian grand dukes were handy who could take over the conduct of Maxim's for an evening as a *beau geste* and foot the bill in doing it. Younger sons of English lords, schooled in the horsemanship of long country ancestry, could keep up with his demented coaching. Amiable playboys of a dozen nationalities were on tap to participate in his expensive practical jokes, and the revenues from the *New York Herald* and the prestige of the *Paris Herald* excused everything.

James Gordon Bennett and pre-1914 Europe were made for each other.

James Gordon Bennett the Younger had been born in 1841 and after his mother's move to France spent half the year with her and the other half with his father amidst the tumults and dead cats which accompanied the elder man's progress in the professional and social worlds of mid-century New York. The Bennetts were not divorced; simply they lived apart, and a transatlantic mobility early came to be a notable characteristic of their eldest offspring.

His commuting existence as a very young and accordingly impressionable man did things for James Gordon Bennett that in the ordinary course of social and biological events wouldn't have happened until he was well on the way to maturity and perhaps his majority. Before he was fifteen he learned to speak French fluently, he was an experienced traveler in a world where transatlantic travel in itself lent a cachet of sophistication, he knew about hard liquor, and he had lost his innocence.

By the time the Civil War came along, young Bennett was a member in good standing of the New York Yacht Club and owner of a 160-ton sloop named for his Irish mother, *Henrietta*. This was offered and accepted by the Secretary of the Navy for service in protecting the Union seacoasts from Confederate raiders and assigned to patrol Long Island Sound with the owner, Third Lieutenant James Gordon Bennett, in command. Service on board *Henrietta* could not have been described as arduous or the hardships endured by the ship's company of a nature to try men's souls. Official business brought the sloop with remarkable frequency to anchor off the New York Yacht Club's own pier in the lower East River where servitors saw to its victualing with supplies that were certainly not the GI fare of the time. The commanding officer had a nice taste in cognacs, a predilection which was to characterize him for half a century to come, and *Henrietta's* mess more nearly resembled that of the Cunarders which were already attempting to lure passenger traffic away from the rascally Inman and other competition with sumptuous viands and well-stocked seagoing cellars.

With the end of hostilities Bennett the Younger, by now one of the acknowledged bloods of the New York sporting scene, added a new dimension to his activities in the form of coaching, a social and sporting activity among the aristocrats of London clubdom and hence calculated to appeal to the gilded elements of Manhattan's less inhibited upper crust.

Wild-eyed and shouting for way from the box, Bennett, who was usually brandied to his white top hat, appeared to most observers to be clinically disturbed when the reins were in his hands. Fears for his sanity were not allayed when it was reliably reported that at midnight on country highways he was given to tearing off all his clothes and driving at delirious speeds with only a cigar in his face, for all the world in a manner to invoke memories of Washington Irving's Sleepy Hollow horseman.

Bennett's celebrated confrontation with the membership of the Reading Room, a gentlemen's club of ancestral dignity at Newport, arose from his sponsorship of a British cavalry officer who, on a bet with Bennett himself, rode his saddle horse up the steps of the institution and into its library to the dismay and confusion of its elderly occupants. The board of governors, practically with the speed of light, informed Bennett that his guest card for the Englishman would no longer be honored and Bennett, in a completely predictable reaction, felt himself affronted.

The result of the fuss was another chapter in the familiar theme of the millionaire who buys a hotel in order to have the satisfaction of firing the manager.

Bennett retaliated against the stuffiness, as he was pleased to call it, of the Reading Room by purchasing an ample lot of ground directly across the way on Bellevue Avenue from his own house, and commissioned Stanford White to draw up blueprints for a new and extravagantly elegant club to be known as the Newport Casino. Everything about the gesture was done *en prince*. White was the most expensive and socially eligible architect in the business. The new club's locale was the most prominent in town and the scale on which it was conceived was calculated to make the modest premises of the Reading Room look shabby in comparison. The entire gesture was Bennett at his most expansive magnificence.

Decades after Bennett's exile and eventual death abroad, the Casino, by now the center of Newport's most stately communal sarabands, stood as a tangible memorial to a rich man's haughty whim. Bennett regarded it as a moral lesson to the Reading Room and retained stock in the Casino to his dying day, a last and final bond with his impetuous youth.

In 1868, the *New York Herald* passed into the hands of James Gordon Bennett, Jr., and a few months shy of his twenty-seventh anniversary the young man became sole heir and proprietor of one of the most valuable newspaper properties in the world. From that day forward, employment on the paper became synonymous in the profession with chattel servitude. In a buyer's market he was in a position to hire the best brains and most talented writers at a pittance and he never hesitated to let an underling know that not only was he not indispensable but that the staff would probably be the better for his departure from it.

Bennett in short order proved himself a fantastically successful practitioner of highly technical and exacting business. He anticipated William Randolph Hearst's "Gee Whiz" journalism by a quarter of a century and in a short time the *Herald* was not only the most talked of and lively paper in America but was making $750,000 a year net profit, a figure no other New York daily at the time could even distantly approach.

Bennett's newfound authority and its successful application in no way abated his youthful arrogance and, if anything, increased his already impressive consumption of whatever was handy in bottles, mostly the best French cognac. He was not so successful in dictating how things should be done outside his own office. Once when a fire broke out nearby while he was dining at Delmonico's,

Bennett, like all New Yorkers of his time a fire buff of the first chop, attended the conflagration with a bottle protruding from under the tails of his evening coat, shouting orders at the perspiring pipemen and generally making himself a nuisance. In the end an exasperated captain ordered a high-pressure hose turned on him and Bennett was removed unconscious and half drowned by subordinates who had accompanied him.

The next day, apprised of the magnitude of his folly and the scene he had created, he ordered a fine new rubber coat sent to every member of the New York Fire Department with his compliments, a gesture that did not pass unnoticed in an age when firemen had to buy their own uniforms. The bill was over $5000 and worth, Bennett later remarked, every cent of it. The *Herald* thereafter became the foremost champion of better wages and living conditions for the city's pompiers.

In 1876, Bennett decided that his foot-loose days and fancy-free nights might well be terminated in matrimony, and he became engaged to a Miss Caroline May, a Maryland beauty of irreproachable social position and amiable disposition who agreed to overlook the flaming lapses of the publisher's admittedly incandescent past in return for his promises of reform and domesticity.

New Year's Day of 1877 found Miss May, after the time-honored custom of the age, holding open house in her family's home in midtown Manhattan. The front drawing room was crowded with May family and friends in well-cut morning coats and Prince Alberts toasting the incoming year in a variety of potables passed on silver trays by impeccable house footmen superintended by a stylish English butler. Fragrant cigar smoke wreathed the gas fixtures and conversation was, perhaps, a little louder than was allowed by the proprieties at other times, but New Year's was still a special holiday in New York and, in deference to an old Dutch custom that had the sanction of long observance, even the most staid and respectable people took a glass more than was strictly advisable.

Young Mr. Bennett had been observing the old Dutch custom in a notable spirit of devotion when he drove up to the May mansion in a two-horse cutter, threw back the buffalo robes, and gave the reins to a waiting attendant. He made the front steps without immoderate difficulty and at once set out to be the life of the party.

Eyewitnesses to the disaster agreed when they compared notes next day that Bennett, while obviously in wine, still seemed in command of his senses. His voice was loud, his footwork complicated by a number of intricate steps, and he was reaching for drinks with more avidity than manners, but nobody had serious premonitions of catastrophe.

The events leading up to the episode that was to rock New York on its heels for days to come escaped attention, but suddenly it was apparent to those standing nearest the fireplace that the *Herald's* publisher had mistaken the purpose of that fixture for a plumbing facility and was extinguishing the flames in a most unconventional manner. There is another version of the Bennett legend which maintains that he committed the offense in the Mays' grand piano, but physical probability seems to rule out this exotic redaction and all reliable chronicles agree that it was the fireplace.

There was, one imagines, a moment of stunned silence. Ladies no longer at this advanced date pretended to faint, but a number of feminine fingers must have fluttered before well-bred faces, peek-a-boo fashion, as strong masculine hands seized upon the offender, and, as Richard O'Connor, Bennett's biographer, chastely put it, the Mays' New Year's party came to an abrupt end. Young Mr. Bennett found himself on the sidewalk where somebody called for his cutter and somebody else threw his overcoat and top hat after him. It was a scene which lingered in the collective memory of New York long after its factual witnesses had departed this world.

The events of the following day did nothing to abate the heady excitements of a truly gratifying scandal. At first Bennett was reluctant to try the temper of his favorite club, the Union. Obviously every private residence in New York was forever barred to him, but what would be the reaction of masculine New York and his peers in clubdom to his lapse? Bennett was greatly relieved when nobody at the bar of the Union Club or in its restaurant made reference to the deplorable episode. If he himself could carry it off with apparent non-chalance, his fellow club members were fully as urbane and worldly. True, a mannerless young man was observed to register exaggerated alarm as Bennett negotiated his way past a vast fireplace where logs were blazing in the front hallway, but Bennett paid him no mind. He lunched on a broiled Southdown mutton chop and half bottle of Pommery Brut and headed for the *Herald* office.

On the sidewalk outside the Union Club Bennett encountered young Frederick May, twenty-six-year-old brother of his affianced of the day before. Mr. May carried a horsewhip with which he forth-with had at the *Herald's* publisher, shouting the while that he was a cad and a bounder and that he had sullied the fair name and honor of the May family. Members of the club crowded to the wide win-dows and made bets on the outcome as the two men grappled and rolled in the snow. "Blood stained the snow from the sidewalk to the gutter," reported the *Sun* the next day, but the *Sun* was notably hostile to Bennett and may have been guilty of wishful thinking. Passers-by finally separated the two snarling antagonists and sped Bennett on his way downtown in a growler from the club cab rank.

At his office, where Bennett strictly forbade any mention of the recent hostilities in the morrow's paper, staffers surrounded him with encouraging bottles and decanters. After a little he began to feel that he, not May, was the affronted party. Only recourse to the code duello could satisfy the Bennett honor and, in the capacity of a second, May found himself waited on by Charles Longfellow, son of the good gray poet of Mt. Auburn Street, Cambridge, Mas-sachusetts, and Bennett's frequent companion in yacht races and other nautical excursions.

No duel of social consequence had been fought north of the Mason-Dixon line since Aaron Burr's fatal meeting with Ham-ilton at Weehawken. May and Bennett met two mornings later attended by the several seconds and surgeons at Slaughter's Gap, Maryland, a geographic detail which no contemporary accounts failed to mention.

On the given signal from a distance of twelve paces, May fired, as required by the code, but aiming his piece high in the air. Bennett followed with also purposely misdirected shot. Both men were good marksmen and could easily have done greater damage had they wished.

Before the year was out Bennett had departed from New York to assume the life of a well-upholstered exile, taking with him, as O'Connor remarks, the dubious satisfaction of having precipitated the last formal duel in the United States of which there is any credible record.

The Paris to which Bennett removed himself after the encounter at Slaughter's Gap was by no means the imperial metropolis and legendary *ville lumière* he had known when he alternated visits there with his mother with equal periods spent under his father's roof in New York. Chastened and humbled by the defeat of 1871 and the Prussian occupation, it lacked the excitements of urban conduct which Bennett considered the essential elements of life. Most of all, it lacked style. This was a situation which Bennett felt should be materially improved and an essay in upward mobility that he was eminently qualified to inaugurate.

As they had been from the beginning in New York, Bennett's horses and carriages in his first years in Paris were of a splendor to quicken the pulses of Parisians who remembered with pride and delight the turnouts maintained by Baron de Wimpferen for his imperial master, Napoleon III.

Beauty of design and fittings in Bennett's equipages were, however, secondary to the consideration of speed. When the automobile age dawned, his various Renaults and De Dion Boutons were purchased and maintained more with an eye to their potential kilometers per hour than the fine lining of the coachwork or the pattern of the West of England cloth that lined their tonneaus.

It must not be supposed that Gordon Bennett, merely by purchasing a town house in Paris and making his permanent residence
in France, became an accepted figure in the most exalted social circles. Such was by no means the case. His eccentricities, not infrequent boorishness, mercurial temper, and the occasion of his exile
all militated against his acceptance by conservative residents of
the Faubourg St.–Germain who had no welcome mat spread for a
voluptuary often so far in his cups that he couldn't find his way to
the men's room.

But a man, even a noisy American with close to $1,000,000
a year tax-free income and an expressed inclination to spend all
of it right now no more lacked for amusing company in Paris in
the eighties than he would today. Prince Danilo types material-
ized out of the woodwork at Maxim's; Carpathian noblemen,
profiteers off government contracts to build canals and railroads,
Transylvanian adventuresses, Balkan monarchs temporarily at liberty, musical-comedy stars, champagne salesmen, and the "grand
horizontals" described by Cornelia Otis Skinner, all converged
on the table of the crazy American when he was in a wine-buy-
ing mood and were solicitous for his health when overtaken by
outsize katzenjammers. Although not without titled hangers-on
from various aristocracies, mostly of shattered fortunes, Bennett's
associates were recruited from what a later generation of newspaper readers would come to know as café society. Probably they
were more amusing and intelligent than the real article. Certainly
they drank more, ate more, and laughed more appreciatively at
the master's droll ways.

The master's whims early set a pattern that closely followed the
couplet to the effect that

> Like many of the upper class
> He liked the sound of smashing glass.

His two favorite restaurants were Voisin and Maxim's although,
in later years and after it had become the greatest concentration

of American wealth east of the New York Stock Exchange, he patronized the Paris Ritz when Olivier, the monocled maître d'hôtel, thought it prudent to allow him on the premises. Olivier had a way with him that inhibited impertinences from anybody, no matter how big his bank roll, and an overripe newspaper publisher who might conceivably fall down in the middle of his restaurant and start chewing the carpet rated no special consideration. When Bennett was in a glass-smashing mood, Olivier, with the diplomacy of a Talleyrand, since the device would rid him of an unwelcome customer and at the same time fob him off on a rival, would suggest that the action was brisk that night at Maxim's, and Bennett would seek the Cambon exit from the hotel as being closer to the Madeleine.

Once arrived at the restaurant of his choice, Bennett would make his presence known by marching the length of the dining room and as he passed between the tables latching right and left onto the tablecloths so that the cloths, their *couverts,* food, flowers, crockery, glassware, and all, would be swept to noisy destruction in his wake. That the diners to whom he submitted this inconvenience might just have been served a dish of *quenelles de brochet Nantua* or a *contrefilet à la Clamart* that had taken the chef two hours to prepare was lost on the glassy-eyed publisher. At his command everything was quickly repaired, the places reset, a fresh covey of quail was popped into the oven and spilled wine replaced, almost invariably by a larger bottle of something more delectable than that which had been overturned. According to witnesses, few resented Bennett's outrageous conduct. Alert waiter captains whispered his identity to his victims and in time it became a sort of accolade to have had clear turtle soup spilled in one's lap by the publisher of the *New York Herald.* All cleaning bills in such cases were ordered to be sent to Bennett, but there were tuft hunters who preferred to take a spoiled dinner shirt home with them as evidence of participation in the authentic night life of Paris. It was a sort of status symbol long before Madison Avenue coined the phrase.

No estimate has been forthcoming of what such a *beau geste* might have cost Bennett in the hard-gold louis of the eighties and nineties, but in the light of Maxim's prices, for then, as now, it was one of the world's most costly restaurants, it couldn't have come cheap. Bennett simply held out a sheaf of banknotes and the management took what it thought proper. This could be on the liberal side.

Another of the publisher's amusements, when the mood was on him, was a military review of the staff of whatever establishment he favored with his patronage. The entire personnel would be lined up for inspection in soldier style, maîtres d'hôtel with their menus and wine cards rigidly under their arms, sauce cooks with long-handled spoons at present, wine stewards with corkscrews cocked. If the line were a long one and Bennett's vision more than usually clouded, participants in the drill from the extreme end of the line would run around back of the parade and be counted again, much as cutups in the class picture contrived to get photographed twice by a panoramic camera. A nice review of this sort at Voisin, according to O'Connor, paid for at 20 francs a head, could come close to $100 American gold. Ringers and shills hastily recruited from outside, friends of the kitchen staff, often shared in the publisher's bounty.

The founding by Bennett of the Paris edition of the *New York Herald,* a property that came in time and incorrectly to be known as the "Paris Herald," would not be accorded mention except on the basis that it was, in actual fact and over the years, much less of an investment than the gratification of a private whim. It only infrequently made money and then always to the surprise of its proprietor, and its continued publication was probably the most costly single indulgence of an extravagant nature.

The paper was an extension of Bennett's personality. That it had a commercial facade and undertook to bring in a certain amount of revenue doesn't alter the basic fact that it was as much an ornament and status symbol as his yacht, the *Lysistrata,* or the rose gardens at Beaulieu. He explained its founding and continuance on a variety of specious pretexts: he wanted to represent the American people in their proper frame of reference to European contemporaries, or he was concerned about Franco-American amity, or he maintained it as a convenience for his compatriots traveling abroad. All this was the merest evasion. The *Herald* in Paris enormously enlarged Bennett's importance in the community. It gave him status and stature throughout the Continent instead of merely in the limited society of cutups and moochers who were his normal associates. Politicians and statesmen were forced to reckon with the *Herald* and its publisher in their formulation of international policy. It raised James Gordon Bennett from the estate of a personality to that of a personage. It was a vanity that cost $100,000 a year.

In time the *Herald* came, in the American awareness at least, to be in the nature of an extension of American foreign policy and its proprietor of consular dignity with the American ambassador. Myron Herrick frequently remarked and only half humorously that he was sometimes at a loss whom to consult first when confronted with a problem of diplomacy, the State Department in Washington or the front office of the *Herald*.

Besides being an extension of Bennett's ferociously individualistic personality, the Paris edition of the *Herald* gratified some of his less attractive traits of character, most notably his use of wealth to make life miserable and uncertain for those unfortunate enough to find themselves in his service. Since the days of the galley slaves of the Phoenician tin traders it would be difficult to find an example of worse relations between personnel and management than were normal between Bennett and his serfs both in New York and in Paris.

It was Bennett's inherited belief that there was nothing within the range of human imagining that couldn't be bought for money and that conspicuously the cheapest of these was editorial and executive talent. He repeatedly and to their faces told members of his several staffs that so far from being indispensable to him, they could be replaced at lower salaries than he was now paying. The scale of pay on Bennett's papers being what it was, this was a question for the moot.

Absolute tyranny and ruthlessness attended repeated Waterloos and Little Big Horns where tales of managing editors demoted to the estate of washroom attendants and copy boys elevated to headship of foreign bureaus flew thick as autumn leaves on Vallombrosa.

Like all New York dailies when the author went to work there in 1929, the New *York Herald Tribune* still harbored a handful of old-time pensioners, relics from the days before the amalgamation of the *Herald* and the *Tribune* with pedigrees and grisly memories going back to the veritable days of James Gordon Bennett the Terrible. Bearded and quivering pantaloons for the most part, legionaries in the long and bloody circulation wars between Hearst, Pulitzer, Munsey, and the *Herald,* they were now content to last out their time in sinecures of obscure posts in libraries or on exchange desks. They ran to muttonchop whiskers and Inverness cloaks, and the bumfreezer tail coats that had been working press attire only a generation before, and occasionally they crept into Bleeck's saloon for a belt or two of rifle whisky and to offer their unsolicited opinions that the newspaper world had gone to hell in a handcart.

One of these who emphatically refused to subscribe to the mousy protective coloring of his contemporaries was Milton Snyder, who held down the post of exchange editor at the *Herald Tribune.* A venomous and profane old party with a wooden leg, he might well have been the original for Captain Trolley in Gene Fowler's *Salute to Yesterday.* Milton had for a time been Bennett's viceroy in London and had acquired his employer's habit of insult and affront in self-defense. As a young man he had also been assigned by Bennett to report on the first experimental beaming of messages on light waves by an Italian named Guglielmo Marconi. On Snyder's approving report, Bennett had commissioned Marconi for $5000 to establish communications for coverage of the American Cup races of 1899, a windfall that had come just as the inventor was running low on funds. In a way Milton Snyder was the father of wireless.

Snyder's appearance on marching days, particularly those commemorating the first world war, where he had lost his leg, was heralded by a seedy frock coat of Prince Albert design, festooned with medals, and a tile silk hat so dented and ruffled as to suggest that it, too, had been involved in the Battle of the Argonne. Brandishing a stout walking stick in the direction of impertinent copy boys, Milton hung his ancient hat on a peg and attacked a three-foot-high pile of exchanges as though they were a German machine-gun emplacement. His was the last top hat and morning dress to put in a regular appearance at the fifth floor, although the day of Mrs. Whitelaw Reid's funeral in the early thirties saw a blossoming of executive tail coats to have done credit to a convention of undertakers.

Edward Dean Sullivan, who had known Snyder, man and beast, for thirty years, swore his temper, vocabulary, and over-all facade of ferocious hostility were the factual reincarnation of the publisher of the *Herald.* He used to address him, in passing, as Mr. Bennett, which drove the old man to ungovernable fury. He once hurled his knobby walking cane at Sullivan's head, narrowly missing the *Herald Tribune's* most astute crime reporter and scoring a direct hit on Howard White's derby in society. It was a notable occasion.

The European scene which the Paris edition of the *Herald* was to mirror for a full quarter of a century before the debacle of 1914 was as rococo and florid as the pattern of life it suggested in the *Herald's* publisher.

It was, in its over-all continental aspects, an interlude of upholstered elegances which furnished a cut-velvet backdrop for so many of the novels of E. Phillips Oppenheim. Balkan monarchs incognito and absconding prime ministers in steeple-crowned silk hats of Frenchified design took passage on the *Blue Train* out of Paris and emerged in snowstorms of gold currency and purloined crown jewels in the roulette parlors of Monte Carlo. That favorite character of international intrigue without whom neither Phillips Oppenheim nor any Sunday editor in England or the United States could have made a living, Sir Basil Zaharoff, flitted on obscure missions of disaster aboard the *Simplon-Orient Express,* an indispensable merchant of death obligingly dressed for the part in benevolent whiskers, an Inverness traveling cloak, and an aura of Sunday-supplement inscrutability.

At Monte Carlo, too, there appeared among the *femmes fatales* in Theda Bara dresses and monocled army colonels attached to the staff of the unfortunate Alfred Redl in Vienna such American names that made news as Mrs. John Mackay, Jacob Schiff, Charles M. Schwab, and a rising young banker and promoter of railway stocks named Otto Kahn who was always in search of talent for his protectorate of wild animal life masquerading as the Metropolitan Opera in New York.

In England things were even better, at least until that benevolent monarch Edward VII contrived to eat himself to death on ortolans stuffed with other ortolans and the other components of eight-course dinners which he had served at his box at opera in Covent Garden so he wouldn't mind the singers so much. Here, as Frederic Morton put it in his epic chronicle of the Rothschild family, "joviality began to outrank genealogy." Gold bonanza kings from South Africa and diamond barons from the Kimberley diggings were flooding the Savoy Grill so that swans might swim among their guests at supper parties where Caruso and Nellie Melba furnished incidental entertainment. One Rothschild, scorning the new motorcars which were being perfected by the Honorable Charlie Rolls and the future Sir Henry Royce, preferred to drive his coach through the streets with a hitch of six diminutive zebras. An Indian prince, entrusting his young son to the hall porter at the Ritz Hotel for a day's outing at the zoo, tipped the unbelieving flunkey sufficiently to set him up for life with his own country inn at Cheltenham.

The year 1900 found the Commodore just as seafaring-minded as he had been thirty years earlier and somewhat more solvent. The *New York Herald* had prospered mightily during the Spanish War and Bennett was rolling in money. During the early years of his exile a modest 900-ton auxiliary steam and sailing yacht called *Namouna* had sufficed for his seagoing wants. Now with money burning a hole in his pocket and almost limitless vistas of future profits from his New York property floating in prospect, he commissioned a steam yacht that was to be the envy and wonder of the yachting world even in its royal echelons for years to come. *Lysistrata,* named "for a Greek lady reported to have been very beautiful and very fast," was built by the Dunbarton firm of Denny & Bros, for the then staggering sum of $625,000. Its various features bugged the eyes of yachting editors everywhere and provided Sunday feature material in the best "Gee Whiz" tradition of Bennett's detested rival, William Randolph Hearst.

On each of the three decks devoted to passenger accommodations the Commodore had an entire suite of bedroom, sitting room, and dressing room earmarked for his own exclusive use. No matter how full the other staterooms might be or what overflow of guests doubled up elsewhere, nobody but the owner slept in any of the three designated owner's big double beds. On a lower deck was a full Turkish bath complete with hot room, steam room, ice-cold showers, and rubbing tables where a round-the-clock masseur was on duty to help rid the master of the quantities of champagne, cognac, gin, arrack, tequila, Scotch, bourbon, and other assorted beverages which were his accustomed ration. Like the bedrooms, the hamam was exclusively for the use of the Commodore. He had no stomach for impertinent witticisms from his peers while sweating it out.

There was, too, a soft padded stall with special seagoing fittings for the ship's cow, an Alderney which, although Bennett had scant use for milk as a straight beverage, supplied to Commodore's table butter and the ingredients for his brandy milk punches at breakfast. An electric fan blew gentle breezes over the cow in tropical climes; the finest of all-wool blankets warmed it in arctic waters.

The well-upholstered cow was perhaps the most pampered such animal in the record unless it be her opposite number which had traveled in the baggage car of Jay Gould's private trains a decade or so earlier. When, for any reason, replacements in *Lysistrata's* milk barn were in order, crack reporters from the city staff of the *Herald* in Paris were requisitioned to scout the Mediterranean countryside for an Alderney with just the right butterfat content to match the Commodore's liking. Once located, the man of letters was commanded to stay posted on a likely wharf in some port where *Lysistrata* might be expected to show up. Sometimes he waited, cow in hand, for weeks.

For the more formally accredited members of *Lysistrata's* crew, life was no less unpredictable. For one thing, they all had to be cleanshaven. Because this was recognized as something of an imposition at the time, they received extra pay for shaving daily, much as house footmen of the period received $5.00 a week extra if they were required to powder their hair, to compensate for the perpetual trouble of washing it out when not on duty.

Not only were whiskers, except of course the Commodore's own mustaches, interdicted, so were all card games while at sea. Bennett considered long sessions belowdecks an affront to the elements and even did much of his drinking in the open air.

Guests aboard *Lysistrata* were subject to the Commodore's tyrannical whims in a degree which makes one wonder if the free grouse, plovers' eggs, and champagne were worth the price in inconvenience and indignity. No planned itinerary was ever available or even thinkable and the vessel stayed at sea for as long or brief a time as suited the owner's vagrant fancy. Sometimes he put off on protracted voyages with guests aboard who had only been invited for a cocktail or afternoon tea. Once at Amsterdam an entire musical-comedy company was hired to provide entertainment for what they imagined to be a brief interlude while the vessel was in port and only discovered when they had removed their costumes and make-up that they were out of sight of land. After the hysteria had abated, the mumpers mingled on terms of egalitarian camaraderie with the bogus dukes and down-at-the-heels duchesses who constituted the ship's regular sailing list and were returned to port next morning. Not only did the Commodore pay them handsomely for their fright but reimbursed the management of the theater for the money it had been forced to refund at the box office. Ned Center, a connoisseur of Bennett's capers, estimated that this particular floor show cost him in the neighborhood of $15,000, a considerable sum in the gold guilders of the era.

More serious were the consequences when three ladies of irreproachable social standing and propriety were virtually kidnapped for an overnight voyage when they explicitly had only been invited aboard for dinner. Two of them, Lady Lily Bagot and the Countess of Essex, were Americans who had married well in England and didn't appreciate Bennett's practical joke, which inconvenienced them personally and greatly embarrassed them when *Lysistrata* returned next morning to port at Villefranche and they were obliged to disembark still in evening dress.

Bennett's formal apologies were immediately required by the women's husbands and the Commodore, with memories of horse-whippings and duels in the not too distant past, hastily and abjectly complied. Concrete evidence of contrition was supplied in the form of a pearl necklace for the commoner and nice new diamond tiaras, hastily sent down from Cartier in Paris, for the peeresses.

Not all of Bennett's extravagant whims and caprices were either vulgar or malevolent, as O'Connor points out in appraising his services to gastronomy.

Although among the best-paying patrons of Maxim's, Foyot's, the Café de Paris, Voisin, and other top-notch Paris restaurants, the Commodore's tastes were not in the realm of transcendental gastronomy that was recommended by Brillat Savarin or justified by his income. Just as some epicures judge the status of a restaurant by the amount and pedigree of the Madeira in the terrapin à la Maryland or the proper decanting of its Vosne-Romanée '78, Bennett's benchmark of gustatory excellence was Southdown mutton chops. If this plain but succulent British dish met his exacting standards, a restaurateur was assured not only of the high regard of a notably generous patron but of favorable mention in both the Paris and New York editions of the *Herald*. Bennett's favor wasn't to be sneezed at. Chefs at the Bennett chateau came and went and their personal fortunes rose and fell on the excellence of the Southdown cutlets of well-aged mutton which came to the Commodore's place at table lovingly entwined around a well-grilled lamb's kidney.

A not inconsiderable anthology of Bennett anecdotes concerned almost wholly with his dedication to mutton chops could be the subject of a monograph if space permitted. Two examples will suffice here.

At Monte Carlo, on a hillside pleasantly overlooking the vista of almost repulsive wealth represented by the Casino, the Hotel de Paris, and the yacht harbor, was a small, home-owned restaurant which had engaged the favorable attention of the Commodore, as evidenced by his return there for luncheon day after day. Needless to say, it was not the view. The management had been apprised of its august patron's identity and his preferences at table were known in every de luxe kitchen in all Europe. The mutton chops were superb.

One day, in mood benevolent, Bennett arrived to find every advantageous table on the terrace occupied by a group of serious drinkers, and the eating patrons, even the regulars, had been assigned to tables inside the building. The drinkers had the Commodore's approval; indeed he would gladly have made one of them, but his mind was set on mutton chops and he wanted them at his regular place, outside, in the shade and commanding the view. It wasn't available. The waiter captain was desolated.

Seeking the owner, who was cowering behind the cashier's desk, Bennett came to the point. Was the restaurant for sale? The proprietor could name his price but the deal must be consummated as of right now. It was and Bennett bought it on the spot. Ned Center, who was in Monte Carlo at the time, heard the amount involved was $40,000.

Armed with the authority of possession, Bennett threw the serious drinkers out and sat down to his mutton chops which the chef, a fore-thoughtful man, had had on the fire against just such a contingency.

Bennett was grateful and, after his meal, expansive. As a tip he passed along the deed of sale to the waiter who had served him, telling him the place was his to have and to hold just as long as he reserved a place every day for James Gordon Bennett and the same chef broiled the mutton. As an afterthought, he asked the waiter's name.

It was Ciro, and that is how one of the world's most celebrated restaurants, Ciro's of Monte Carlo, came into being. Later, Ciro extended his activities to Paris and Biarritz. For a time there was even one in Hollywood but it was not affiliated with the great originals of Europe. The name entered the lexicon of de luxe gastronomy everywhere.

A second example of the Commodore's singleness of purpose where mutton chops were concerned became part of the record when the *New York Herald* moved uptown to new quarters in what is to this day known as Herald Square at the intersection of Sixth Avenue and Broadway. Fantastic sums of money were lavished on the structure itself for the design of which the newspaper had retained Stanford White of the formidable firm of McKim, Mead & White. Some idea of the munificence in which the project was conceived may derive from the circumstance that components of the bronze clock at the structure's apex were two bronze figures known to generations of New Yorkers as Ike and Mike emerged on the hour to smite a huge gong with bronze hammers alone cost $200,000. In the building itself, medieval Verona reappeared in a structure so beautiful in its time that it soon became a sight-seeing attraction for visitors to the city. For the top of Bennett's executive desk Tiffany executed a magnificent silver desk set in arabesques to have delighted a doge and solid enough to have advertised Prudential Life. It cost $14,000.

Such an extensive undertaking took several years to complete and, characteristically, Bennett lost interest in the whole affair and wasn't even present when the presses started to roll.

Four years afterward it was brought to the Commodore's attention that his architectural property in New York was assuming the proportions of a national monument, and Bennett decided to have a look for himself. It would afford him a notable opportunity, too, for discharging a number of editors and otherwise bringing chaos out of order. *Lysistrata* was in dry dock so the Commodore took passage aboard a Cunarder where he managed to destroy the morale of the entire ship's company in a period of eight days. He docked in the morning and decided to lunch at the Union Club before descending on the *Herald* offices and firing everybody.

Alas, the mutton chops arrived overcooked. Bennett threw the offending viands on the floor and sought the club manager with a demand that the entire kitchen staff be dismissed instanter. Also the maître d'hôtel, the steward, and all the waiters. Then, forgetting entirely the mission that had brought him 7000 miles across the winter Atlantic, he took one of the new auto-taxis over to the North River in search of a Europe-bound steamer that was sailing that afternoon. He found one, paid five full fares to occupy the captain's cabin, and sailed within the hour. By the time the ship had passed Ambrose he was discharging its crew wholesale.

He never even saw the $14,000 desk set.

Throughout his years of self-imposed exile, Bennett maintained a variety of estates, all of them fully staffed with domestics and ready for occupancy at any moment, although it might be a matter of record that their owner was then at the other end of the world. Long after he had renounced his American residence, he maintained his father's princely premises at Washington Heights, even though upper Manhattan was no longer open countryside and taxes were those of a populous metropolitan community. Although he never visited it, the Commodore kept this vast establishment in fullest operative condition in order that the families of favored executives at the *Herald* might play tennis on its well-maintained court.

In addition to the Washington Heights ancestral home, Bennett maintained his villa at Newport, the one from which he had directed the construction of the Casino just across the street, and a Fifth Avenue town house whose taxes alone would have given pause to a less-heedless inheritor of great wealth.

In the matter of upkeep of a multiplicity of potential seats in several countries, Bennett was no more than imitating J. P. Morgan, Sr., at whose Prince's Gate town house in London, the bed was turned down every evening of the year, current periodicals placed handy to the bedside for night reading, the light adjusted, and a glass of warm milk set on the bed table, even though it was known beyond all peradventure that the master was that night occupying his equally aloof residence on Murray Hill, Manhattan, several thousand miles away.

In Paris, Bennett maintained a magnificent apartment in the Etoile district where he entertained sumptuously, while at no great remove from the capital was a country seat at Versailles from which it was possible to organize coaching trips and shooting expeditions when he was in a suburban mood. There was also a shooting box in Scotland which he almost never visited but which supplied his several dinner tables, ashore and afloat, with Scotch grouse and plovers' eggs, the latter a delicacy he esteemed in equal measure with the mutton chops that had long been his gastronomic hallmark. Most lavish of his residences was that at Beaulieu on the Mediterranean.

It was at Beaulieu that the Commodore felt most at home and on whose upkeep he lavished the most care and money, and it was here that he entertained most sumptuously the ragtag of casting-agency marquises and road-company grandees who constituted his perpetual court of hangers-on de luxe. At Beaulieu a kitchen staff of four fully accredited chefs and innumerable pot-wallopers toiled day and night at a cost that could have supported a not inconsiderable restaurant on the grand boulevards even though it was a time when kitchen apprentices were paid the equivalent of $150 a year and found, and Scotch head gardeners managed entire platoons of undergardeners for a salary of $650.

Over the years and the decades the Commodore tossed away, most of it with little more to show for the gesture than a bad hangover, a sum in excess of $40,000,000, an estimate made possible on the basis of the earnings of the *New York Herald,* which, during all that time, was his sole source of income.

Sometimes, like mad Squire Mytton whom Edith Sitwell described in the *English Eccentrics* and whose progress through the countryside could quite literally be followed by discarded sheaves of banknotes which a dutiful tenantry retrieved and returned to him, Bennett actually had money to burn.

A young newspaperman stranded in Paris once waited on him in his apartment with the idea of asking for employment on the Paris *Herald.* During the interview he observed that the publisher was squirming in great discomfort, as if the adjustment of his clothing were troubling him, and at length Bennett drew from his rear trouser pocket an enormous wad of banknotes of large denominations which he irritably threw into the fire blazing on the hearth.

The young man in dismay leaped up and snatched the currency from the burning, smothered the flames, and handed the singed *mille-franc* notes back to their owner.

Bennett threw them back into the fire, where they were consumed. "That's where I wanted them in the first place," he growled.

Bennett's extravagances were seldom contaminated by gestures toward good works. When they were diverted to charitable endeavor they remained on a secular plane, showing that throughout a long life the Commodore was consistent in at least one aspect of his philosophy: he wanted nothing of religion or the church. On one occasion he contributed handsomely, in the amount of $100,000, to the allaying of suffering among the Irish peasantry. A similar sum went for the education of a distant relative so young he couldn't have personally advanced his cause with the Commodore. Bennett tossed a $100,000 bank draft in the infant's crib and never saw him again.

Mostly his largess was reserved for servitors whose good offices had contributed to his comfort, real or imagined. One night on the *Blue Train* between Paris and Monte Carlo he handed the *wag-on-lit* conductor, a functionary roughly corresponding to a Pullman porter in the United States and so available to tipping, a fee of 20,000 francs, the equivalent of $4000 American. Bennett's valet, a new man on the job and one devoted to his employer's interest, retrieved all but 1000 francs of the sum, which he felt to be about right in Bennett's mood of the moment, and the Commodore found the bills along with his watch and chain when he dressed for breakfast.

Bennett went into a towering rage, denounced the valet for impertinence, and promptly restored the sum to the conductor, who resigned from the *wagon-lit* and, true to type, opened a hotel of his own at Boulogne. The number of hotels, inns, taverns, and restaurants that should have been named The Commodore Bennett Arms staggers the imagination. Mostly they were named something approximating Hotel Marie et l'Universe.

Throughout the Commodore's long life and good times he resolutely rejected the, to him, bogus solaces of religion and placed his faith in the mystic power of owls. The source of this preoccupation with night birds or mouse eaters was never revealed, although it may well have been their association in classic times with unearthly wisdom. Whenever other folk were represented by coat armor, on their carriages, personal jewelry, domestic *décor*, and architecture, Bennett had owls engrossed, painted, carved, or otherwise emplaced. Enormous owls that blinked with eyes of electric lights were a feature, along with the massive bronze clock on the facade of the Herald Building in New York. When he eventually was buried at Passy, no cross but a pair of owls were on his headstone.

Only a freak of mischance prevented the Commodore from carrying his preoccupation with owls to the very gates of eternity. Like many of his generation, Bennett took more thought than would now be acceptable in anyone less a public personage than Sir Winston Churchill for his own funeral and final resting place. General Grant was well established over on Riverside Drive. At New Dorp,

Commodore Cornelius Vanderbilt, whose death had occurred the identical week of Bennett's disgrace at the May New Year's party, was entombed in a mausoleum of doomsday solidity where a time clock was punched by watchmen on a twenty-four-hour basis.

Bennett conceived of a mausoleum and personal memorial that would make his ghost envied by all the rich men the other side of Charon's barge. On his Washington Heights property, which would be cleared of its residences for the purpose, would rise 200 feet in stone the likeness of a mighty owl, 125 feet high on a 75-foot foundation. Nor would the occupant of this heraldry be buried at its base, as might appeal to anyone with less soaring imagination than the Commodore. The owl would be hollow. A stairway would lead to its two monstrous eyes, which would be observation decks looking out over the city, and suspended from the bird's head by chains in the center of the stairwell, Bennett's coffin would remain forever. The idea obviously dwarfed all other entombments of rich men and it had the added advantage of being proof against body snatchers. Nobody would be able to purloin the Commodore's remains and hold them for ransom as ghouls had done with A. T. Stewart, the department-store magnate.

Stanford White was commissioned from Paris to attend to the design of this splendid concept. A Massachusetts sculptor, Andrew O'Connor, was to execute the finished plan from glazed Vermont granite. Its details, subject to frequent reworking and correction, were the subject of a massive correspondence from Paris. The owl must be of ferocious aspect and glower at all comers, as if to perpetuate its tenant's habitual attitude of menace. There must be sufficient space between the pendant catafalque and the circular staircase entwining it so that irreverent viewers might not be able to set it in motion with umbrellas or walking sticks. Work must be expedited so that the Commodore might be able, as it were, to try it for size before assuming permanent occupancy.

Thus to be enshrined for the ages would cost the Commodore, on estimate, a cool $1,000,000. Bennett regarded it as a bargain.

Unhappily for the project, which would otherwise have lent a certain éclat to uptown Manhattan if it had been consummated, Stanford White was shot and killed in the roof restaurant of Madison Square Garden while the plan was in its formative stages. Bennett, as always, intensely superstitious, felt the auspices to be unfavorable and the project was abandoned.

When he died, as he himself foresaw he would, on his seventy-seventh birthday, a feat later rivaled by Evangeline Adams who foretold the precise hour of her taking off, he was buried at Passy under far less gaudy circumstances.

Chapter Seven

How You Traveled
Was Who You Were

Going Cunard Was a State of Grace . . . So Was Paying $25 Extra Fare on the Santa Fe's Refulgent De Luxe . . . An Aura of the Vanderbilts Surrounded Riding on the Twentieth Century Limited . . . In the Age of Elegance a Letter of Credit Could Work Wonders . . . Traveler's Checks Were Never Like This . . . Eventually All Roads Led to the Antlers Hotel . . . It, Too, Was a Way of Life. . . .

IN THE SPRING of 1965, Miss Jessica Mitford, a Californian and author of *The American Way of Death* and other social commentaries, took passage for London. Eschewing the leprosarium that masquerades as San Francisco International Airport, she boarded the Southern Pacific's *City of San Francisco* to Chicago where she changed to the New York Central's *Twentieth Century Limited*, arriving in New York to board the *United States* for the Atlantic passage. From London she wrote back to friends: "Isn't it wonderful to think that only eight days ago I was sitting in the Palace Garden Court having luncheon in San Francisco?"

In spurning the air lines in favor of surface travel, Miss Mitford was quite consciously reverting to a way of life at a time when how you traveled was who you were and before the advent of the airplane, which represents the total negation of style, luxury, or anything except getting there in a minimum of time and maximum of discomfort.

Travel, both within the limits of the United States and outside them, in the period that ended with the onset of the second world war and whether undertaken for business or pleasure, represented in most cases a very considerable investment of time, money, and planning, and the manner of one's going places was very much an index of one's social and economic station in life.

It was a world of very grand hotels indeed, of extra-fare limited trains and of steamships that entirely justified their conventional description in the literature of travel as "floating palaces." It afforded such amenities of luxury as entire private decks outside the de luxe suites of the *Titanic* which could be had for an extra $4300 for six days of occupancy. A favored patron of the aforementioned Palace Hotel in San Francisco might dine off its heavy gold flat service that had been fashioned for it when the hotel reopened after the fire of 1906 or he might command his sweetbreads *financiers* off its equivalent in the Plaza three thousand miles away in New York. Crossing the Great American Desert where the Mormons and overland gold seekers had perished miserably of hunger, thirst, and Indians only six decades earlier, he could sleep in a brass bed aboard the Atchison, Topeka & Santa Fe's crack, extra-fare flier appropriately named *De Luxe* and have at his disposal not only the conventional operative train crew but a corps of French chefs, expert waiters, a maître d'hôtel from Delmonico's, a barber, a librarian, a lady's maid, and a valet. Nor did these amenities come cheaply. The surcharge for riding aboard *De Luxe* from Chicago to Los Angeles in 1911 was $25 gold, perhaps the equivalent of five times that sum today, in addition, of course, to the basic railroad and Pullman fares.

The circumstances in which they traveled made a great deal of difference to the well-to-do when the infamies of mass transport of hundreds of passengers jammed into day-coach accommodations on a supersonic cartridge for delivery in London or Paris in a few hours was both unforeseen and unthinkable.

They crossed the Atlantic aboard the magnificent vessels of North German Lloyd, Hamburg American, Cunard, White Star, French Line, Red Star, and, for a time, Inman, at a time when twenty pieces of hold luggage were an absolute basic minimum for social survival and when even a gentleman required a wardrobe or innovation trunk in the corridor outside his stateroom to hold the four changes of clothes he was expected to make daily on an eight- or nine-day passage. They went with valets and maids, hatboxes and shoe trunks, jewel cases and, in some fastidious instances, their own personal bed linen. Invalids brought their own doctors and nurses, dog lovers traveled with mastiffs and St. Bernards. Occasional magnificoes or eccentrics brought their own barbers, and food faddists carried their special rations of sanitized lettuce leaves or graham nut bread. The transatlantic entourage of a well-placed man and woman might well number half a dozen persons, while there was no limit at all to the number of secretaries and couriers that could be kept usefully at hand.

Clarence Barron never traveled with fewer than three male secretaries. The Lloyd Hilton Smiths of Houston, upholstered with Humble Oil money aboard the French Line *Liberté* as recently as the 1950s, took their own automobiles with them for a tour of France, one for Mr. and Mrs. Smith, one for the children and their own entourage of nurses and governesses. People frequently made the westward passage on board the *Mauretania* or *Olympic* with vastly more luggage and motorcars than they had started out with. Many of the elite and doomed who took passage on the first and last voyage of the *Titanic* went well dressed for eternity with twenty trunks full of Paris frocks and evening dresses.

Travel within the boundaries of the continental United States was no less ponderous in its logistics. Trains in those days ran with baggage cars full of trunks and boxes that couldn't be accommodated in Pullman space, and the legendary railroad baggage smasher entered the national demonology amidst the debris of a thousand shattered Saratoga trunks and disemboweled Gladstone valises.

Traveling was a ritual, mannered, planned, orderly, and a matter of often massive logistics. Not the least of its details was that of money.

Transatlantic commuters aboard the *Berengaria,* the *Paris,* or *Rotterdam* in the 1920s became familiar with a personable and very stout French gentleman who traveled the sea lanes on his business occasions named Count La Riboissier. An affable and chatty member of the international set, the Count carried considerable sums of money about his person at all times and in all national currencies. He had, he disclosed to smoke-room acquaintances, about him whenever he was away from home the equivalent of $1000 each in pounds, francs, guilders, zloty, milreis, taler, yen, pesos, marks, pengö, drachmas, and the like, perhaps a total of $10,000 in all the currencies of the then traveled world. Invariably friends would ask why he exposed himself thus to possible robbery when traveler's checks were so much handier?

"It is this way," said Count La Riboissier. "I am, as you see, a fat man, nearly twenty stone on the hoof, and one day I am in a public café in Rio de Janeiro when a young lady acquaintance stops to give me good day. Chivalry is not dead. I leap to my feet and I break a leg in so doing. I have no appreciable money on me, so they throw me in the public pest house. You have never been in a charity hospital in Rio de Janeiro? A good thing. It is deplorable. So now wherever I am, I carry ample money of that country to be able to break a leg in ten languages. I am then a first-class street accident."

Few travelers took the extreme precautions devised by the Count La Riboissier. They carried letters of credit. In a day before American Express credit cards and traveler's checks, a letter of credit was a formidable document issued by one's home bank in the amount of a sum sequestered against it in Boston, New York, or Cleveland. This bedsheet-size document handsomely engrossed and sealed was presented at the bank's European correspondents, Morgan, Harjes & Cie., in Paris, Coutts or Baring Brothers in London, who advanced what the traveler might need in pounds or francs and wrote the amount on the back of the letter of credit. It was the only known way of financing travel.

Drawing against a letter of credit in the early 1920s was nothing to be undertaken lightly. It embraced ritual and punctilio, especially in London where transactions involving money were viewed with anything but levity.

The opening move was to dispatch either by hand or through the post a letter to, let us say, Baring Brothers' main office in the city acquainting the management with one's identity, references, family and financial background, and warning of one's impending arrival with the intention of drawing against a letter issued by the Old Colony Trust Company of Boston. It was wise to suggest a date for the rendezvous at least four or five days in the future in order to facilitate cable exchanges establishing the petitioner's bona fides. When by return post, almost never by anything as frivolous as the telephone, a convenient date had been set, protocol suggested alerting one's hall porter to the impending ceremony and requesting that he secure from the hotel's regular sources of livery an appropriate two-horse landau or victoria specifying that the coachman should be arrayed in somber attire suited to an occasion of financial gravity.

On the appointed morning the party of the first part arrayed himself as for a garden party at Buckingham Palace, braided-edge morning tail coat, black silk hat, umbrella, and wash gloves. Members of the hotel staff, if it was a family hotel like Brown's on Dover Street, assembled in small groups in the lobby to wish him well and friends waved handkerchiefs from upper windows. It was an occasion.

The reception at Baring's was no less so. A personage attired as would become the Lords of the Admiralty saluted and helped the arrival to alight from his carriage, while passers-by speculated on the possible identity of an obvious head of state. Within the hushed counting room where clerks on tall stools worked at vast ledgers, a receptionist in the somber garb of a custodian of royal properties inclined a courtly ear and led the way to the inner sanctum of one of the less august partners of the firm, where generations of his predecessors observed the occasion from the walls with the special disapproval reserved by bankers everywhere for persons withdrawing funds.

All mention of money was suspended while the welfare on one's family and the mercantile affairs of State Street Boston were inquired for, whereupon and only after these oriental courtesies it became apparent that any such momentous transaction couldn't be consummated on the moment. It would take until afternoon to secure the currency from the vaults, count it, and record the serial numbers of banknotes. First there would be lunch at the Travellers' Club, notable in the annals of London men's clubs as one where members spoke to each other in the bar, a revolutionary departure from tradition in the other leather-armchair bastions of masculinity on Pall Mall and St. James's streets. Colchester oysters, Melton Mowbray pie, a cold lobster, Stilton cheese, claret, Port, and cigars followed in the ritual of the businessman's luncheon, after which a state progress in reverse order to the bank was in order.

By this time the senior clerk would have finished with the heavy responsibilities of his office and the customer's money would be in hand. It might come to all of $100, gold, of course, after which, secure in the knowledge of a good day's work accomplished, the traveler returned to his hotel. It was a way of life.

Surface traffic across the Atlantic in the golden age of travel was also a ritual observance, hedged with convention and bulwarked in the stately amenities of going first class in the years when how you traveled was who you were.

Going Cunard as a friend of the company or an important personage with letters from Sir Ashley Sparks, the line's American manager, in the early twenties entailed almost as much inconvenience as it did prestige. The institution of cocktails served every night while at sea by the captain as is the practice today did not exist and the ultimate in social recognition was to be asked to sit at the captain's table, which had about it overtones of royalty. Captain's tables differed in their conduct at the whim of the master of the vessel. Cunard didn't select its captains on a basis of gregariousness or Chesterfieldian courtliness, although most senior sea dogs were fairly well indoctrinated by the time they reached this exalted rank in the social and financial status of the line's clientele.

It was possible to sail with a strict disciplinarian like Sir Arthur Rostron, who had been in command of the *Carpathia* at the time of the *Titanic* rescue, whose table was a tall tower of the maritime proprieties but small geniality, or a voyager of importance could be invited to sit with Sir James Charles, commodore of the Cunard Line and a legend of seagoing joviality and bonhomie.

Sir James's pennant flew from the masthead of the *Aquitania* and represented the ultimate cachet of nautical rank and dignity combined with voluptuary table practices which were a preview of Maxim's and the Café de Paris in an age when Americans were refugees from prohibition with an illimitable thirst for champagne washed down with Niagaras of gin, vodka, arrack, tequila, cognac, slivovitz, and bourbon, whatever was handy in the most substantial quantities.

Guests at Sir James's table lived by protocol. It was an age when the dinner jacket was not in universal acceptance among Englishmen as evening attire, and one's steward, on instructions from the bridge, laid out smoking or tails as the commodore might have decreed and left a note naming the dinner hour. You didn't dine at your convenience but the commodore's and on evenings of the Captain's Dinner full evening dress was required with decorations, which put Americans, unless they were of military background, at a disadvantage in the matter of crosses, ribbons, and miniatures.

Sir James's tastes at table were vaguely those of Emil Jannings playing Henry VIII. Stewards wheeled in carcasses of whole roasted oxen one night and the next evening small herds of grilled antelope surrounded a hilltop of Strasbourg *foie gras* surmounted with peacock fans. Electrically illuminated *pièces montées* representing the battle of Waterloo and other patriotic moments made an appearance while the ship's orchestra played Elgar. Chefs in two-foot-high hats emerged to make thrusts in tierce at turrets of Black Angus beef that towered above the arched eyebrows of the diners, and souffles the size of the chef's hats blossomed toward the end, like the final set pieces of a Paine's fireworks display on the Fourth of July. Throughout these flanking movements and skirmishes champagne circulated in jeroboams, Mumm's 1916, Irroy, and Perrier-Jouet, ditto.

Sir James Charles, a grandee of the sea lanes so portly and full of honors that his mess jackets required structural bracing in their internal economy to support the weight of his decorations, died in line of duty, at sea, almost literally leading an assault on a citadel of pastry moated with diamondback turtle stew *au Madeira.* When they took him ashore at Southampton it was necessary to open both wings of the *Aquitania's* half-ports to accommodate his going. It was the exit of a nobleman and a warrior.

Auctioning the ship's pools in the great days of the Atlantic runs, aboard such fast vessels as *Mauretania* and *Berengaria* and *Aquitania,* were memorable events both for the amounts of money involved and for the excitement which accompanied the bidding for twelve potential winning numbers each evening after dinner in the gentlemen's smoking room. The possible mileage for the next day's run, established every noon from the bridge, could be foretold with reasonable accuracy, give or take a few miles, by the ship's company and ten numbers were sold in its immediate range, the collective amount for which constituted the day's pool. If the estimated run was, say, 635 miles, the numbers sold were 630 through 639 which, when included with the high field and low field, covered all possible contingencies. If the engine room had trouble and the vessel stopped or slowed down, low field won. If, on orders from New York or Liverpool, it accelerated its speed, high field was the one to have.

The twelve possibilities were sold at open auction by some celebrity from the passenger list, usually a theatrical personality or someone well known in sporting circles who would lend the occasion an aura of distinction. Claude Grahame-White, the pioneer aviator, and a celebrated *viveur,* was a favorite in the role. So was Dudley Field Malone, the theatrical lawyer and barrister whose trade in Paris divorces for notables kept him constantly in transit. Perhaps the most celebrated of all pool auctioneers in the early 1920s was William A. Brady, the Broadway producer, father of Alice Brady and married to Grace George, a brilliant comedienne. An inflammable Celt with a bottomless capacity for liquor, Brady was also a student of parliamentary law and a witty orator, in short the ideal man to auction a ship's pool in those affluent and uninhibited days.

On occasion, when carried away by his own eloquence, not to mention ample potations as he labored, Brady would order wine for the entire smoke room out of his own pocket in order to beguile his audience into ever higher bidding. Daily pools well in excess of 1000 pounds, $5000 in those times, were not uncommon when Brady sold them and on one memorable occasion when his wife bid in what turned out to be the winning number, it seemed wise for her to spend the entire sum next evening on drinks for everybody to refute loudly voiced charges of collusion. A lot of drinks could be had for $5000 in those days.

Unabashed in their admiration for a spectacular pool auctioneer were the smoking-room stewards. Ten per cent was their conventional cut for holding the stakes.

As long as railroad travel remained the only thinkable agency of overland travel in the United States, the favored train of high rollers, big spenders, magnificoes, and great names generally was the New York Central's *Twentieth Century Limited* on the overnight run between New York and Chicago. No other train east of the Mississippi carried a prestige rating comparable to Trains No. 25 and 26 as they flashed between the country's two focal points of finance on the tightest possible schedule that roadbed and equipment could accommodate.

In its golden years the *Century* was all Pullman, extra fare, a mobile grand hotel peopled with names that made news and so much in demand for its speed, prestige, and luxury that it sometimes ran in as many as seven sections and so choicely regarded by its owning carrier that, in the years of steam motive power, relief engines with steam up and a crew aboard stood by all through the night at division points in case of motive power failure along the way. Delay of the *Century* was unthinkable both from the viewpoint of the importance of its passengers and from the fact that in its mail and express cars, millions of dollars in negotiable paper were carried on every run with interest mounting into hundreds of thousands of dollars while in transit.

Although the New York Central was not as celebrated for its cuisine as was that of Fred Harvey aboard the Santa Fe diners in the West, the dining cars on the *Century* were repositories of culinary splendors comparable to those of Delmonico's and Sherry's. In 1905, its $1.50 dinner included either terrapin Maryland or lobster Newburg as well as sirloin steak, long a favorite above tenderloin on the cars, and often pheasant and game birds in season. In 1919, the flower bill for the *Century's* dining cars alone came to $1000 a month and the dining-car department was expected to lose $2.00 for every $1.00 it took in. Two of the *Century's* dishes became famous as hallmarks of the train's gastronomic excellence, Maine lobster Newburg served on toasted corn bread and a particularly succulent brand of watermelon relish made in Cambridge, Massachusetts.

The departure of the *Century* every afternoon from Grand Central was ceremonious. Passengers, followed by porters with their luggage, walked to their sleeping cars down an originally Vanderbilt maroon and later imperial crimson carpet lined with potted palms. They paused at the gate to surrender their transportation to conductors and Pullman officials while a train secretary took the name of every passenger, both for future records and in case messages were received during the night. Newspaper reporters regularly covered the train's departure with cameramen in tow just as they covered the sailings of Atlantic liners from their North River berths.

A passenger on the first run westbound in June 1902 was Bet-a-Million Gates, who told reporters when they met the cars at Chicago: "This train will make New York a suburb of Chicago." He was so delighted with the service and equipment that he turned right around and rode the eastbound section to New York that afternoon. There he diplomatically told the press: "The *Century* will make Chicago a suburb of New York."

A sampling of the *Century* over the years would turn up J. P. Morgan the Elder, Nellie Melba, Jim Keene, Enrico Caruso, Andrew W. Mellon, John Barrymore, Joseph Conrad, Ganna Walska, and Henry Ford. A British member of the House of Lords called it "my gentlemen's club when I am in the United States." It was a train which, merely to have ridden, conferred a cachet of elegance and distinction.

One aspect of high life and the presence of big money that never was associated with the *Century* was the professional gambler who in other years had ridden the name trains of the land and was so conspicuous in the legend of transatlantic steamer travel. The New York Central, regarding the *Century* as its best showcase and most glittering advertisement, went to any lengths to discourage professionals from riding its club and buffet cars. No introductions between strangers were ever made by members of the train crew and, if known gamblers were spotted attempting to get up a card game, their prospects were bluntly told by the conductor that they were in bad and perhaps expensive company. Speculators on what the railroad considered a respectable scale, such as Bet-a-Million Gates, James R. Keene and other big time market operators, were, of course, the backbone of the *Century's* patronage, but card sharps were not encouraged.

Some idea of the progressive increase in the cost of railroad travel in the more than fifty years of the *Twentieth Century Limited* may be gathered from a comparison of the charges for single bedroom space over the years. In 1910, when the train was seven years old, the rail fare between New York and Chicago was $19.75, while the Pullman charge was $14. In 1930, the fare was $32.70, the bedroom was $18. In 1965 the rail fare was $67.38, the room space was $23.54.

Other prestigious trains on continental runs were the Santa Fe's *Chief* and *Super Chief* between Los Angeles and Chicago, both extra fare, all Pullman, and studded with names from the higher echelons of business, the professions, and Hollywood. In Frederic Wakeman's best seller of the 1940s, *The Hucksters,* both trains were depicted as rolling love-nests filled with Sunset Boulevard infidelities, high-pressure business, and low-boiling-point amorousness:

> The *Super Chief* plunged forward and rocked sideways into the night, a long twisting aluminum pot, boiling with the noises people made to impress, to distress, to flatter, to seduce, or simply pass time away. . . . The *Super Chief* pulled into Albuquerque and Vic went out with Kay to stroll and stretch. He amused himself by buying Indian trinkets for the children. . . . The *Super Chief,* deaf, dumb and blind to the travelers who paid its way, rushed relentlessly toward Hollywood, alive with motion, pushed and prodded by the old railroad watch, time.

Now and then, of course, although it was the fastest of all long-distance runs and its competition, the *Broadway Limited,* on the Pennsylvania, met its schedule minute for minute down the years, the *Century* was too slow for the urgent necessities of well-placed travelers. Doctors and surgeons were often hurried to the bedside of important patients by special trains on cardings faster than the carriers cared to contemplate. Captains of finance commanded specials such as that which brought J. J. Hill East over his own lines at the time of his epic battle with Harriman for control of Northern Pacific.

One strong-willed woman was Dorothy McCormick, wife of Chicago's Cyrus McCormick III. In the days when the crack trains of both the Central and the Pennsylvania were on twenty-hour schedules between New York and the Loop, Mrs. McCormick had placed at her disposal a special consisting of a private hotel car, a coach for the train crew, and a baggage car to act as stabilizer over the Pennsylvania to make the run in seventeen hours and at a cost of well over $5000. The trainmen got down from the cars at Chicago's Union Station visibly shaken. Not so Mrs. McCormick, who had burned up the right-of-way for the express purpose of attending a meeting of Christian Scientists.

Inevitably, when the knowing world traveler in the years before the first world war wearied of the Negresco at Nice, the magnificent Hôtel de Paris at Monte Carlo, and even the superb appointments of the Savoy in London where the first patron to purchase a bottle of wine when the hotel opened in the eighties had been an American, he turned to the American West. Almost as inevitably, he sooner or later arrived, Gladstone bag and Louis Vuiton baggage, at the Antlers Hotel at Colorado Springs, a vicinage so favored by nature and geography as to be a health resort of the first magnitude, and so favored by English visitors and by wealthy Americans with English ways that it was locally known as "Little Lunnon."

Colorado Springs, destined in time to become the greatest concentration of money and fashion in the Rocky Mountain region, started life as a company town on the main line of General William Jackson Palmer's narrow-gauge Denver & Rio Grande Railroad, an operation so diminutive and precarious that high winds sometimes blew the little engines and cars from the tracks. It turned out to be the most stylish and successful company town anywhere excepting only Florida, where it had spectacular competition from Henry M. Flagler's company towns at Palm Beach, Miami, and way points.

The Antlers, in like manner, was a company hotel just as were the Royal Poinciana and Ponce de León some 2000 miles to the east, and it deserves the attention of the student of wealthy ways in the United States because it was to become the paradigm, or model, without reference to which nobody would put up a de luxe resort of any sort, anywhere, until the coming of the motor court many years later.

It was a landmark, beloved and institutional, and when, in 1964, it finally closed its doors forever, there were Coloradans and others, too, who felt it was an old friend gone away.

The first Antlers had been built when the Rio Grande, "the baby railroad" of Colorado tradition, was new to its spectacular right-of-way in the shadow of Pikes Peak. It had burned down on October 1, 1898, and was already so well established in Colorado legend and so necessary to the community's economy that the fire took on overtones of public disaster. What Notre Dame was to Paris and Westminster Abbey to London, the Antlers was to The Springs, a status symbol of the best of everything that a perfectionist management could incorporate into it. General Palmer, in England at the time, didn't hesitate for a moment, but by return cable assured his worried townsfolk that there would be a new Antlers, almost instanter and with a minimum of delay.

The original Antlers had burned at an auspicious time. The greater part by far of Colorado Springs' economy derived from the mines of Cripple Creek just over the looming shoulder of Pikes Peak and in 1898 the output at Cripple was $13,500,000 in hard gold bullion, a considerable sum of money at the time and most of it earmarked for marble statuary, crystal chandeliers, rare oriental rugs, vintage port, and blooded horses variously in the mansions and stables of The Springs' elect. One of the prime beneficiaries of Cripple's bounty was to be the new Antlers on which General Palmer promised no less than half a million dollars to be lavished in terms of Italian Renaissance architecture, English wallpaper, Gobelin tapestries, and Flemish oak-beamed smoking rooms. It was a time when stonemasons and bricklayers working a ten-hour day achieved take-home pay of $25 weekly and half a million dollars bought quite a lot of stonemasonry.

Spencer Penrose's $3,000,000 Broadmoor, when it opened in 1918, didn't, dollar for dollar, represent more grandeur than the Antlers when it was completed for half a million in 1901.

When it was finished, the Antlers lived up to everybody's

expectations. Its two tall towers, illuminated by night, might have dominated an Italian pastoral. Designed by Frederick J. Sterner, a Denver architect of fair repute and numerous triumphs, it had red tile roofs, acres of them; loggias in Venetian red, scores of them; Florentine balconies of ornamental iron, sixty of them; and green-and-white striped awnings at every window in the house, which gave it a jaunty air in summer. At the western facade a graceful Roman stairway of noble dimensions led to formal gardens giving immediately on the Rio Grande's passenger station, so close that there was no necessity to take a cab.

The interior lived up to its exterior billing. French windows with enormous expanses of glass gave onto the terraces and verandas beloved of the time for lounging in the sun and rocking-chair therapy. There was an East India sunroom, a magnificently mirrored and crystaled main restaurant with Spanish leather armchairs at every place, an ivory and cerise ballroom, Louis XIV parlors, and not one but two heavily wainscoted smoking rooms. There was also, records Marshall Sprague, the Antlers' historian, a bicycle stable with an attendant on twenty-four-hour duty.

All this grandeur was under the management of an excitable and gratifyingly stately Frenchman named Henri Marucchi whom General Palmer had ravished directly from the Casino at Monte Carlo and who lived up to what a Frenchman was supposed to be by kissing women's hands and wearing morning tail coats almost to his ankles.

The assistant manager was William S. Dunning who had helped open Denver's resounding Brown Palace only a few years before and knew Colorado society, its divorces, amorous habits, and the brands of champagne it preferred for breakfast like a well-thumbed book. The maître d'hôtel was also French, a M. Berget from the Bristol in Paris who was so familiar with royalty and the great world of the boulevards that merely to be recognized by him was an accolade. The French *chef de cuisine,* Marcel Renault, presided over his immaculate culinary empire from a raised dais halfway between the ranges and the *garde manger* who did the desserts and salads, and Sprague recalls that when he thundered a command for *"Three hunnert turbots soufflé à l'Admiral,"* the kitchen staff manned their stations with the precision of soldiers going into action. The Antlers became famous for Renault's fillet of halibut Dugléré, *tournedos Rachel,* and broiled quail on toast. There was also a baked Alaska, a specialty of the house that achieved a truly enviable celebrity. An agent from the Palmer House in Chicago arrived in town on the Rock Island and was detected trying to smuggle some of the baked Alaska off the premises for analysis in a rubber pocket built into the tails of his evening coat. Renault grandly gave him the working recipe and challenged Potter Palmer, a veritable impostor, to duplicate his baked Alaska.

An era of splendor dawned for The Springs on the basis of the fame of the Antlers and its presence as a sort of certification of elegance. Verner Z. Reed, a bright young exquisite who had made a $1,000,000 commission in a single day by selling a Cripple Creek mining property, celebrated at the Antlers with limitless Cazanove Special Cuvée 1893 and place cards "of ivory bristol board embellished in real gold leaf."

Potential schism ended in gallantry when General Palmer entertained the veterans of his Civil War cavalry regiment at a grand reunion, paying their carfare from all over the country and putting them up in baronial elegance on their arrival. Horse soldiers of the outfit had almost succeeded in capturing Jefferson Davis after the fall of the Confederacy, and at the inevitable grand banquet a contemporary wartime poster offering $300,000 bounty for the capture of the discomfited statesman was part of the *décor.*

Quick to take umbrage at this was Davis' daughter, now, as Mrs. Joel A. Hayes, a pillar of Springs' society, who denounced the General as a cad of the first chop. Palmer, who had never lost an engagement in the wars, quickly capitulated and ordered the offending poster down.

Less controversial political moments were part of the Antlers' record. In 1901, when the hotel was just getting into its stride,

Theodore Roosevelt came out to participate in the celebration honoring the Centennial State's twenty-fifth anniversary as part of the Union. In 1908, William Howard Taft stopped by during his preliminaries to running for President on the Republican ticket. Great excitement reigned in 1920 when, at a speech made at the Antlers, Senator Warren G. Harding publicly repudiated the League of Nations in his assault upon the battlements leading to supreme office.

The Antlers, because of its reputation for costliness and social chic combined, was a mecca for sports and high rollers of the early motorcar era. It was not unusual to see three or four of Spec Penrose's seven identical canary-yellow Lozier touring cars out front at one time. Clarence Carpenter, the Detroit radiator magnate, bought a maroon Cadillac every season just to keep up his record as a fellow who did things right even though the mileage on the previous model was microscopic. Charlie MacNeill, who had made his first pile at Cripple Creek and now rode to and from New York in his private Pullman which was spotted under his apartment windows at the hotel, drove grandly up and down Pikes Peak Avenue with its eight traffic lanes in a $12,500 Rochet-Schneider brougham with his chauffeur, Thomashefsky, in livery on the box. Some of the townsfolk had trouble remembering which was the chauffeur and which the car, but took great pride in the combination. Chester Alan Arthur, son of the former President and, like his noble side-whiskered father a *viveur* of florid gestures, spurned the internal combustion motor and drove his two-wheeled gig with two equally fine horses hitched tandem long after it was evident that the automobile was here to stay.

Big doings were the scene in the Antlers bar. Here it was that Carpenter, on descending from his Cadillac of the moment, would command a ten-cent beer and pay for it with a crisp $1000 bill peeled from a thick wad in the pocket of his sports jacket. Everybody enjoyed the confusion of getting change.

In 1915, Emily Post, by this time established on an international basis as the ultimate arbiter in etiquette, manners, and their allied amenities of social conduct, stopped at the hotel and reported her stay in a best seller, *By Motor to the Golden Gate.* "It is a big, splendidly kept hotel," she wrote, "with its broad white hallways, wide verandas, and sunny terraces." Later on, perhaps having just witnessed the arrival, in tandem, of Chester A. Arthur, Jr., or possibly fashionably dressed Verner Reed, she described a typical Antlers patron: "He plays all games recklessly; he drives a powerful motorcar, and he is flirting outrageously with one of the prettiest women imaginable, whose invalid husband seems to care very little how much attention she accepts from her ardent admirer." This, in 1915, was fully as racy and daring as Spec Penrose's yellow Loziers.

Of all the great moments of the Antlers many, perhaps the one most warmly remembered by old-time Springs' residents was New Year's eve of 1909 when a gale of wind had blown down the sides of Pikes Peak so strenuously that the power company's lines were down and the electric lights, never an altogether reliable quantity at that time, were not expected to go on in time for the New Year's ball. It was a time, however, when automobiles, seeing no future in electricity, were still and reliably lit on their precarious nocturnal occasions by carbide lamps. The hotel's garage man, who by now had replaced the bicycle attendant, had an inspiration. With the enthusiastic permission of their owners, he detached the carbide headlamps from every car on his premises, Charlie MacNeill's unpronounceable Rochet-Schneider, Verner Reed's Pope Hartford tourer, all seven of Spec Penrose's Loziers, and Dr. Gerald Webb's air-cooled Franklin, and placed them, lit, at strategic intervals around the ballroom. The effect was stunning and, happily, the hotel wasn't burned to the ground as it might well have been.

To light the guests through the front door, the management borrowed a big, old-style locomotive headlight, fit to serve as a kennel for St. Bernards, from the Rio Grande Railroad shops. It played effulgently on the finery of The Springs' Four Hundred as they arrived for the gala. It even played brightly on the hotel's stately doorman, Frank Loper, a courtly colored man in plum livery with gold shoulder boards you could have carved bread on. Loper had been a slave in Richmond before Jefferson Davis' daughter, now Mrs. Hayes, had brought him with her to The Springs in the eighties.

Chapter Eight

How to Move Stylishly

In the Beginning There Were Horses . . . For an Investment of $20,000 You Could Drive up Fifth Avenue in Elegance . . . Twenty Carriages in the Stable Was Par . . . The Private Palace Car Was the Status Symbol De Luxe . . . It Teemed with English Butlers, French Chefs, and Gold Plumbing . . . Palm Beach Was a Trailer Camp of Sorts . . . Then Came the Motor Age . . . Bugatti Royales and Rolls-Royce Town Carriages . . . Vanderbilts Built 100-Car Garages. . . .

"I PREFER THE KIND of heathenism that wallows in filth and disgusts the beholder," thundered the Reverend De Witt Talmage, a headline-hunting New York divine of the nineties, in his celebrated sermon on "Lepers in High Life," "rather than the heathenism which covers up his putrefaction with camel's-hair shawls and point lace, and rides in a three-thousand-dollar turnout with a liveried driver ahead and a rosetted flunkey behind."

A good many of the Reverend Talmage's congregation, which was not a fashionable one, at the huge Brooklyn Tabernacle which held 5000 people, probably felt that $3000 was a considerable sum for any vehicle of personal transport, but it didn't even approximate the cost of a coach-and-four, a rig that was fairly numerous on Fifth Avenue until driven to cover by the advent of the gasoline buggy.

At approximately the same time the Reverend Talmage was denouncing camel's-hair shawls as ostentations of voluptuousness,

Harper's Weekly, "The Journal of Civilization," was saying editorially: "There is no reason why coaching should not become one of the popular amusements of New Yorkers, for a good drag can be procured, and the horses necessary to draw it and the whole establishment supported through a season for a trifle over $20,000."

While it may reasonably be supposed that the suggestion that everybody should have one in the coach-and-four department was written with tongue in cheek, well-to-do Americans had perhaps less hesitation about lavish investments of horses and their equipages than they were later to have, on a grand scale at least, in the matter of expensive motorcars. A horse was an animate thing and somehow the odium of extravagance attached less to a living property than to a mere mechanical arrangement of tubes and carburetors whose functions nobody really understood. No matter what investment of money they might represent, nobody denounced even the most extravagantly maintained horse rigs as "rich men's toys," as they did with the first motorcars.

Neither the Reverend Talmage nor the other seedy divines who loudly asserted that hell-fire and damnation rode the carriages of the rich of their era were without bias. Taking the air, whether it was from the haughty vantage point of Mrs. August Belmont's *demie-daumont* with its outriders or plain citizens in one-horse curricles, was done to best advantage on Sunday morning, and empty pews that should have been filled with devout parishioners attested the dimension of the menace. Horses in the nineties were much the instruments of godlessness that golf was later to become.

Almost as wide a gulf separated the world of carriage horses from trotters and race horses as that which divided pleasure yachts from racing vessels. Howling swells like Commodore Vanderbilt, Robert Bonner, and William R. Travers thought nothing of paying $30,000 for a trotter certified by Daniel Mace, New York's foremost arbiter of equine elegance. The vehicles that complemented these favored beasts were the least expensive, usually a two-wheeled sulky valued at a few hundred dollars at most. Carriages of fashion reversed the economic scheme of things, for here a brougham or barouche from a London carriage builder might stand the owner ten times the value of the horses that drew it.

The number of carriages maintained by fashionable persons varied somewhat with the circumstances of climate and season, but a well-furnished Newport stable in the days of the resort's greatest grandeur might number between twenty and thirty. Certainly, the days when keeping a gig represented respectability and social acceptability were long in the past. The John Drexels boasted twenty-six different carriages while Mrs. Stuyvesant Fish and the Pembroke Joneses approximated the same count. Requirements for a minimal availability of transport included light phaetons for morning driving with silk-fringed white canopy tops in summer, a single-horse victoria with one servant on the box for shopping and informal calls, a more formal victoria with two horses and two men on the box for afternoon drives along the ocean, a gig if the master of the household was moved to take the air alone, shooting brakes for hounds and picnics, and, for occasions of great state, a *grande daumont de visite* with grooms riding the near horses and two footmen in full family livery on the step behind. The color scheme of family house footmen's livery was, of course, carried over to coachmen, grooms, and mounted footmen so that the Vanderbilt maroon, Mrs. Astor's bottle-green, and Mrs. Hermann Oelrichs' deep tan with red piping identified the turnouts to the knowing and announced their occupants to the world as clearly as the coat armor engrossed on the carriage doors. Silver-finished harnesses and carriage fittings were approximately the equivalent hallmarks of status in their time, as gold-washed plumbing fixtures were at a slightly later period.

The sums of money, astronomical as they were, which were lavished on stables and carriages in the era before the motorcar were often matched by their owners' genuine love of horses which found expression in ostentation tempered by pride and affection. The great horror of horse lovers everywhere, fire, was in large measure abated in the carriage houses of Newport, Saratoga, and Tuxedo Park because the owners could afford fireproof construction. When William C. Whitney built one of the most magnificent of all stables at Westbury, Long Island, with sixty-eight stalls at a cost of $2,000,000, immediate access to outside was available to every stall, sometimes via several exits, and grooms were told in no uncertain terms that their safety was a minor consideration in the event of fire compared with that of the horses. On this 530-acre estate, Whitney's son, Harry Payne Whitney, raised some of America's greatest thoroughbreds, conditioning them on his private race track and playing polo on his private polo grounds.

At Newport, Oliver Hazard Perry Belmont liked to live under the same roof with his beautifully groomed and much loved horses, so the ground floor of his palatial estate, *Belcourt,* was designed by architect Richard Hunt, to accommodate the stables, the upstairs Belmont's own living quarters. The Belmont horses changed their bedding as often as their owner changed his clothes and at night slept on pure Irish linen sheets with the Belmont coat armor hand-embroidered in the corners. In the main salon of *Belcourt,* amidst priceless objects of art and antiquity there stood the stuffed remains of two specially loved steeds from whom their owner could not bear to be parted even in death.

At Alfred Gwynne Vanderbilt's Newport stable the name of each occupant was inscribed on a gold plate fastened above the entrance to his stall and twenty types of carriages, each with its appropriate harness trimmed in sterling silver, were maintained in mint condition and handy for instant use.

Although hardly to be mentioned in the same breath with the perfumed names of Belmont and Jerome, Jim Fisk's turnout, when he took the air in Central Park, was perhaps the most spectacular of all. Other aspirants for envy drove four-in-hands; Fisk drove a six-in-hand with black and white horses in heavily gold-washed harnesses. Two Negro grooms rode the lead horses attired in white livery while two white footmen brought up on the rear step in black livery. The interior was upholstered in cloth of gold and the whole effect was very satisfactory.

In San Francisco the James Ben Ali Haggin stables on Nob Hill were a showplace of the city on a par in celebrity with the Emperor Norton and the Palace Hotel, and here an elaborate after-theater supper was served to a gathering of great distinction only a few hours before the earthquake that helped destroy the city in 1906. A full staff of waiters and domestics was cleaning up the debris when the first shock was felt and the horses were all led to safety before fire reduced the structure to some of San Francisco's "damndest finest ruins."

At Menlo Park south of San Francisco the stables at *Sherwood Hall,* the fantastic country seat of millionaire Milton Latham, were as baronial as the residence of the nabob himself. Here harnesses depended from solid-silver brackets shaped like horses' heads and the gas lighting fixtures were fashioned from the same metal from the deep mines of the Comstock Lode at Virginia City.

Testimony to the solid construction of the stables and carriage houses of the wealthy still exist today on Murray Hill in New York, on the slopes of Beacon Hill in Boston, and Chicago's Gold Coast in the form of structures remodeled as expensive and desirable apartments long after the town houses they served have been razed to make way for skyscrapers.

The only other tangible reminders of the horse and carriage age to survive into the era of the universal motorcar are, curiously enough, the uniforms of doormen, still known as carriage starters, in fashionable hotels. Here the frogged greatcoats, cockaded top hats, and, often enough, yellow-topped jack boots of an older time are a pleasant archaism from a world where the great Dr. Johnson asserted that a nice ride in the country in a coach-and-four was the end of human happiness and the sum of all good things.

With the triumph of the motorcar and the disappearance of horses and carriages as agencies of transport, the horse reverted to his original status as a conspicuous property of wealth in the racing stables of such families as the Whitneys and Ryans where the enormous sums expended on their maintenance are sometimes in part compensated by the substantial amounts of money won in prizes or the betting of their owners.

Stories of the peculiar financial caprices of the Ryan family are almost limitless and include the sale to Barry Ryan in the mid-1920s of a promising young colt at the Saratoga sales for several thousand dollars by Mrs. Payne Whitney. No payment was made at the time, a matter over which Mrs. Whitney lost no sleep. That fall at Hot Springs, Ryan waited on her at her apartment and she in her mind's eye envisioned the payment of the debt, but, instead, with the courtesy of perfect assurance, Ryan told her that he was momentarily on the shy side for money and could he have an extension of credit? He then returned to New York, not aboard anything as Spartan as a private car, but an entire private train which he had chartered over the Chesapeake & Ohio.

Barry Ryan, when friends or relatives got married, invariably gave the same wedding present—twenty-four handsomely carved paper cutters. Ryan also wrote mildly acceptable verse under the pen name of Barry Vail, although largely it wasn't acceptable enough for professional sale to the magazines, so he commissioned a well-known vanity press in Boston to publish a slim volume at his expense for distribution to friends. When the press run was completed and the publisher notified him that his books were ready, he sent a privately chartered plane from New York to Boston, at a reported cost of $900, to fly the edition down to him. On another occasion he was discovered to have built a small fire on one of the fairways at Piping Rock over which he was frugally heating a tin of Campbell's tomato soup. Didn't like the soup at the clubhouse, he explained.

Alone among agencies for human transport, the lowly bicycle never seems to have achieved standing in the ranks of luxury properties. Except in the case of Diamond Jim Brady's gold-and-diamond presentation model for Lillian Russell, the details of which are elsewhere contained in this volume, its investment with any degree of costliness seems to have been a sleeveless errand. Only excessive vulgarity could contrive a bicycle that was out of the range of any youth in the land and the extras available to its adornment, and perfection seldom cost more than three or four dollars at the height of the bicycle craze.

Mention has been made of James Gordon Bennett's brief encounter with the bicycle as an agency of exercise and at the same time locomotion from one drink to the next. The only recorded case of a cyclist who was able to invest wheeling with a degree of splendor seems to have been that of Dr. S. Weir Mitchell of Philadelphia and Bar Harbor fame. When taking the air on the country roads around Mt. Desert on his New Departure Special, Dr. Mitchell was trailed at a suitable distance by a bicycle groom in full footman's livery including a cockaded top hat, yellow top boots, and tail coat of the Mitchell family color.

At a somewhat later period, during the second world war, when gasoline was rationed, Miss Julia Berwind of Newport took the air on a sort of adult tricycle which her otherwise unemployed chauffeur brought around to the front door when she wanted to take a ride down Bellevue Avenue.

ᐧᐧᐧ

For approximately five decades, or roughly the period between 1890 and the second world war, no status symbol in the lexicon of wealth glittered more refulgently than the private railroad car. No property was more explicit evidence of having arrived both socially and financially, since its occupancy breathed of privilege and aloofness and its resources of luxury were almost limitless. When all else had been achieved—a château on Fifth Avenue, English butlers, fleets of Rolls-Royce town cars, powdered footmen, a box in the Diamond Horseshoe, gold plate at table and old masters on the walls, there remained a crowning cachet of elegance, the capstone of material success. It was a sleek, dark-green private hotel car outshopped to one's own specification by Pullman and attached to the rear of the great name trains of the period when its owner wished to travel. It was absolute tops.

The first private cars were built for railroaders of presidential rank and their immediate subordinates, general managers, division superintendents, and operating vice presidents, but by the late eighties their vogue had spread to men of means who were merely directors or large stockholders in railroads, and soon they were a necessary property for men of exalted financial status who had no railroad connections at all.

Men of means everywhere began commissioning splendid hotel cars from Pullman or one of the several competing carbuilders in existence until Pullman achieved an absolute monopoly in the field in the late nineties. In California, Darius Ogden Mills, silver-whiskered old moneybags of the Mother Lode and Montgomery Street, ordered the first private car in the region from Harlan & Hollingsworth of Wilmington, Delaware. The tab was a modest $25,000. A few years later, in the Middle West, Adolphus Busch commissioned the first *Adolphus* from Pullman with chilled beer piped under pressure into its every apartment and stateroom. Silver senator William Sharon of Nevada owned a beauty; so did copper senator William Andrews Clark of Montana. For $50,000 Pullman in the late eighties outshopped *Katharyne* to the order of coal baron R. C. Kerens. E. H. Talbot, editor of *Railway Age,* had Pullman build him *Railway Age,* and mining millionaire James Ben Ali Haggin of San Francisco and Kentucky became owner of *Salvator,* which had a gold dinner service and a chef ravished from Foyot's in Paris. Newspaper publisher John McLean of Cincinnati came by the car *Ohio,* and Harry Oliver, pioneer ironmaster in the Mesabi region, rode comfortably in *Tyrone,* named by the sentimental Irishman for the county of his birth in the old country. Charles M. Schwab was at various times owner of two *Lorettos,* the second even more magnificent than the first.

For five full decades the order books at Pullman and to an only slightly lesser degree at American Car & Foundry were a roster of the great names and powerful personalities of American industry, society, and politics.

The cost of private cars rose with the passing years. In the early seventies $25,000 was considered ample and all California was gratified, vicariously, when Mrs. Leland Stanford paid that amount for *Stanford* as a birthday present for her husband. By the turn of the century the going price had about doubled, although Charles M. Schwab paid a reported $100,000 for the first *Loretto,* the most elaborate and ornate ever seen at that time. By 1915, the general run of private cars from Pullman was $75,000 and in the late twenties Joseph Widener, William R. Reynolds, and Thomas Fortune Ryan were signing checks for $300,000. Perhaps the top price of the era, which incidentally was the final flowering of the private railway car, was $350,000, reportedly paid by Mrs. James P. Donahue to American Car & Foundry for *Japauldon,* named for her late husband.

For these substantial sums private car owners could point to a considerable variety of conveniences and luxurious appointments, all of them contained of necessity within the clearances and dimensions decreed by the specifications of the Association of American Railroads. Beyond these basic functional properties, the imagination and financial resources of the owner took over. English butlers and French chefs were often supplemented by valets and personal maids and secretaries. The mother-of-pearl call buttons in Mrs. Schwab's stateroom on *Loretto II* suggested the availability of seven servants. Gold dinner services were often indicated, and as mentioned elsewhere, Mrs. E. T. Stotesbury pointed to her gold-plated plumbing fixtures as a genuine economy: "Saves so much polishing, you know." The first air conditioning on any railroad car was an innovation on Major Max Fleischmann's *Edgewood.* Jewel safes, wine bins, and other capacious repositories for food and valuables came in all dimensions. Aboard *Lalee,* Lily Langtry was happy to announce there was a food locker capable of holding an entire stag. Adelina Patti aboard her appropriately named *Adelina Patti* had a sunken marble bathtub which, when the car was finally dismantled, turned out to be painted metal. Fritzi Scheff, another thrush, had a bathtub neither sunken nor allegedly marble, but the water splashed so that she could only take a bath when her train paused for twenty minutes or more. Sometimes this was at three in the morning, an inconvenient hour.

Jay Gould had ulcers of the stomach and when he traveled on *Atalanta* with a private physician in attendance and a chef specially trained in the preparation of the ladyfingers which were one of his staples of diet, the Gould cow, whose butterfat content was just suited to the financier's requirements, rode in a private baggage car up ahead. When J. P. Morgan, who never owned a car of his own, voyaged afar he rented as many private cars as his party might need and had a baggage car fitted with racks for carrying his own stock of champagnes, Rhine wines, and Madeiras. When the Goulds traveled as a family there might be as many as four Gould cars with a special engine traveling as an extra; Jay aboard *Atalanta,* Helen Gould on her own car, *Stranrear,* George Gould on his *Dixie,* and guests and miscellaneous retainers on still another Gould car, *Convoy.*

When Cissy Patterson, publisher of the *Washington Times-Herald,* had *Ranger* in commission, her butler carried with him seven complete and different sets of slip covers for every piece of furniture in the car. Mrs. Patterson liked variety and they were changed every day in the week. She was also devoted to flowers, and florists along the right-of-way were alerted in advance by telegraph and had wagonloads of fresh blooms at strategic stopping places. The flower bill on occasion came to $300 a week.

The private car on the Great Northern Railroad of Louis Hill, son of the Empire Builder and an ardent motorist in the early days of gasoline, contained a garage at one end available by a ramp and sleeping space for a chauffeur and a mechanic. The staff on August Belmont's *Mineola* was uniformed by Wetzel, at the time the most expensive men's tailor in the United States, and a number of private cars including George M. Pullman's own *Monitor* and Arthur E.

Stillwell's No. 100 on the Kansas City, Pittsburgh & Gulf, boasted parlor organs for music either sacred or profane.

The Stillwell car later came into the possession of Bet-a-Million Gates and it was aboard this car and as a result of a wager on a raindrop's progress down a window pane with James R. Keene that, according to one school of thought, he derived his nickname.

Henry Ford distrusted the safety of Pullman Standard construction and *Fair Lane* was so heavily trussed and reinforced with steel that it had to be routed to avoid all but the most massive trestles on carrier railroads.

Perhaps the most sybaritic devising of all was designed and built by Pullman as part of the architectural economy of *Errant,* the 100-ton car of Charlie Clark, son of Senator William A. Clark. At the touch of a lever a partition beside the master stateroom's double bed dissolved to reveal it in convenient juxtaposition with the equally capacious bed in the adjacent guest stateroom.

Henry C. Frick's *Westmoreland* had such sentimental attachments for its owner that, by the terms of Frick's will, it was eventually destroyed rather than allowed to fall into improper hands or be downgraded to the estate of shooting camp or roadside diner as is the fate of many once-proud private cars. The Pennsylvania's presidential car in which the Prince of Wales journeyed to Washington to call on Calvin Coolidge is a maintenance-of-way dormitory.

Although their massive dimensions, if not their expense, inhibited ownership of private railway cars on the scale that many Americans have maintained carriages and automobiles, many fanciers have had two or more in their lifetime and a taste for private varnish can also be inherited. In his brief but meteoric rise to fortune Jay Gould himself owned at least five cars while the number of official cars on railroads controlled by him was almost beyond counting. Commodore Vanderbilt owned two, *Vanderbilt* and *Duchess,* August Belmont II owned two, *Mineolas* and *Oriental.* Schwab, as noted above, ordered two *Lorettos* in succession. Bruce Dodson, a Kansas City insurance tycoon, in much the same manner was proprietor of two *Helmas,* named for Mrs. Dodson. Dodson's car was comfortable but only vaguely regal of interior *décor,* but the owner was fanatic in his concern for the upkeep of draft gear, trucks, and brake rigging so that the running parts of his cars, usually neglected by other owners save for the essentials of maintenance, gleamed like a Tiffany window display. Twice a year *Helma* was deadheaded from Kansas City to the Pullman shops in Chicago to have its trucks taken down and reassembled, a gesture which would approximate that of a Rolls-Royce owner sending his car back to Crewe in England for every grease job. In Dodson's case the routine checkup cost approximately $2000.

Probably the ranking families of private-car clubmen have been the interlocking dynasties of the Vanderbilts and the Whitneys. From the time of the Commodore, down to the thirties when Vanderbilts were in retreat from the affairs of the New York Central they had so long dominated, there was no Vanderbilt or Vanderbilt in-law of consequence but maintained his own private varnish and traveled in it in the style becoming the greatest name in American transportation.

The first two generations of Vanderbilts, the Commodore and William Henry, owed their allegiance to the firm of Webster Wagner whose sleepers and other palace cars enjoyed a monopoly on the Vanderbilt roads, the Harlem, New York Central, and connecting lines in Michigan on the through run to Chicago. Wagner supplied the Vanderbilt private varnish and a Vanderbilt in-law, Dr. William Seward Webb, who had married Eliza Osgood Vanderbilt, was president of the Wagner Palace Car Building Company. In addition to the Wagner-inspired loyalty of the two founders of the dynasty, Cornelius Vanderbilt II, Frederick William Vanderbilt, William H. Vanderbilt's widow, George Washington Vanderbilt, William Kissam Vanderbilt, and H. McKown Twombly, another in-law, all at one time or another were owners of Wagner products.

Among the more celebrated Vanderbilt private Pullmans were Frederick Vanderbilt's *Vashta,* William K's *Idlehour,* and Alfred

Gwynne Vanderbilt's *Wayfarer* which in 1908 achieved the shady distinction of being named by his wife in divorce proceedings as the rolling love nest in which her husband had misconducted himself with the wife of a Latin American diplomatist assigned to Washington. *Idlehour* also achieved a minor notoriety when, in 1905, a Hearst feature writer listed it among the follies of the rich for having cost $50,000. This, it may be noted, was some years before Hearst himself began collecting Cellini wine cups at $250,000 a pair and building San Simeon out of other people's used palaces and castles.

The Whitney family joined the private-car club when William C. Whitney, founder of the dynasty, acquired his first varnish, *Pilgrim,* from the Wagner works in the year 1894, and in the years immediately following it appeared regularly on the train sheets of the Florida East Coast and connecting carriers bound for Palm Beach at the right seasons. In 1902, William C. ordered a second car, *Wanderer,* from Pullman, and *Pilgrim* was retired. In 1896, William C's son, Harry Payne Whitney, had married Gertrude Vanderbilt, daughter of the second Cornelius, and eventually inherited *Wanderer* as part of his father's substantial estate. *Wanderer* was rebuilt and modernized by Pullman in 1913, and in 1931, Harry Payne ordered *Wanderer II*, one of the last private cars to be outshopped by the master carbuilder during the then crescent depression.

Payne Whitney, a first cousin and the father of John Hay Whitney, had meantime maintained the family tradition of elegance by giving the Pullman-built *Adios* as a present to his wife, Helen, the daughter of John Hay, and the car was eventually inherited by John Hay Whitney when the air age caught up with it and the car was lost in the shuffle of the vast Whitney properties and estates.

To make the cycle complete, Pullman, in 1930, accepted a check for $275,000 from Harry Payne Bingham, a cousin, for *Pawnee.*

Top-ranking players in the days of the theatrical road, and opera and concert stars, no less than business tycoons, had a high regard for the status attaching to private cars and often they were written into their tour contracts. Lily Langtry had her own car, *Lalee,* the gift of playboy Freddy Gebhard. Its affairs when she was on tour were administered by Beverly, a butler of almost unearthly perfection whose top hat and lofty mien were in no way abated for the cow towns of Colorado and California.

Incontestably, the most elaborate long-distance private-car safari was that arranged for his family and suite of domestics by Dr. William S. Webb of the Wagner Company in 1889 for the round trip between New York and San Francisco. To this end, Dr. Webb, who was in fact a surgeon of some practical experience, assembled an entire private train of four palace cars serviced by no fewer than twenty retainers not counting train crews and conducted with all the safeguards of a military convoy passing through hostile territory.

Ahead next to the engine there was a combination baggage and sleeping car with accommodations for the Webb servants and the trunks of the entire party. Here, too, was a complete armory of rifles and small arms and a surgical dispensary capable of dealing with the casualties and even fatalities that might be expected in encounters with hostiles while crossing the plains, a bath, a smoking room with a Chickering piano, and a liberal wine cellar whose key was retained by Dr. Webb.

Following this came the buffet car, No. 60 of the Lake Shore & Michigan Southern, a Vanderbilt road, and the private hotel car, *Mariquita,* which had been remodeled as a nursery car for the three Webb children, two nursemaids, and Mrs. Webb's personal maid. Finally came Dr. Webb's own car, *Ellsmere,* with master staterooms for the head of the family and four masculine guests. All told there were two chefs and eight porters, as well as the personal domestics of the Webbs, and conductors, brakemen, and head-end crew provided by the railroads involved.

An elaborate system of alarm gongs connected all four cars and beyond Kansas City, which Dr. Webb evidently felt was the limit of any dependable social order, there was a military guard of two riflemen under command of a retired army colonel, and Pinkertons with Winchesters rode the platforms at night.

Even in 1889 carrier railroads required a minimum of eighteen full first-class fares for every private car which, together with the rental of special locomotives, Pinkertons, commissary, and servicing over 6000 miles going and coming with extensive side trips in Colorado and Wyoming, must have come to what may be loosely termed a pretty penny.

Probably the best-publicized private train ever scheduled in the United States was the *Coyote Special* mounted by the Santa Fe Railroad from Los Angeles to Chicago at the behest of Death Valley Scotty, a desert rat and eccentric whose source of wealth was never fully explained although the wealth itself was incontestable. The special put Scotty in Dearborn Station in forty-five and three quarter hours, which was practically the speed of light in 1905, and cost him $5500, a fantastic bargain in terms of the newspaper space devoted to the event which dominated the press of the entire nation for three days and made Scotty a public character for the rest of his life.

Generally speaking and for all the exalted and presumably "fast" company in which it moved, the private railway car was a property of unimpeachable respectability. The wicked diversions of high life might flourish in Park Avenue penthouses or the cottages of the United States Hotel at Saratoga or around the swimming pools and cabanas of Hollywood, but with the exceptions of the Alfred G. Vanderbilt divorce and Lily Langtry's perfumed boudoir, the breath of scandal almost never blew through its mahogany corridors and rosewood salons. Poker games for high stakes and bourbon whisky were the ultimate in private-car dissoluteness.

Sometimes the habit of magnificence is transmitted from authentic grandees to their retainers, as witness Clifford, houseboy, chauffeur, and valet to John Barriger, president of the Pittsburgh & Lake Erie Railroad. When Barriger traveled aboard the presidential private car, Cliff headed the staff of colored cooks and waiters and, in his master's absence, dispensed hospitality in the manner of a proconsul. Once, passing through Chicago's La Salle Depot, a friend of Barriger's saw P & L E Car No. 99 spotted on the private-car track and paused to pay his respects before boarding the *Century* on an adjacent track. Barriger was ashore at the time and Cliff did the honors. The friend didn't want a drink, he didn't even have time for Cliff to fix him a cup of coffee, he declined cigars. Finally, in desperation, Cliff rose to truly ambitious heights of hospitality.

"Have something, do," he urged. "Mr. Barriger will be mighty vexed with me if you don't go away with something to remember him by. Take something, please! Take a case of whisky!"

Like everything else, the cost of private railroad cars has soared with the passing years and the long vanished days of the nineteenth century when a nice palace car could be had for $25,000 or $50,000 are now only a matter of history. No Pullmans have been built to the order of private individual owners since 1941, but a number of business cars for ranking railroad executives have been constructed on a cost-plus basis for the presidents of the Santa Fe, Northern Pacific, and Southern Pacific railroads. The last of these, *Sunset*, built when the aristocratic Donald J. Russell was president of the carrier, is reported to have cost the Southern Pacific the staggering sum of $550,000, although the amount is microscopic in view of the dividends paid by the Espee during Mr. Russell's tenure of office.

The costs of maintaining, servicing, and hauling private cars have, with the exception of labor, remained far more static than those of their construction. By edict of the Interstate Commerce Commission the cost of hauling a private car in passenger service is a flat sixteen first-class fares for the distance traveled west of the Mississippi, eighteen east of the river. This comes to approximately $1.00 a mile in the West and $1.10 in the East. Parking on a private-car track at terminal or way station is conventionally at a flat rate of $50 a day, although this is raised to $75 a day at New Orleans during Mardi Gras and at Louisville for the Kentucky Derby. The fee includes water connections, sanitation, steam in winter and for the heating of domestic water, electricity for light and whatever appliances may be used, air pressure for the distribution of water throughout the car from its own tanks, and a telephone jack connecting with the depot switchboard. Ice is usually included as a gesture of magnanimity by the renting carrier.

Dining-car cooks in private-car service have been found to possess culinary repertories somewhat inhibited by the limited menus available on public diners in the declining state of the railroad's fortunes. The wife of a member of the private-car club once in recent times suggested to the cook that it might be a pleasant change from Yankee pot roast and Southern fried chicken if there were a suggestion of French cuisine in the menu. The cook assured her affably that he was well versed in French cooking. That night dinner consisted of French bread, French lamb chops, French fried potatoes, French peas, salad with French dressing, and French pastry.

Nowadays, when people generally are less familiar with railroading than they were only a few years back and many of a new generation have never even ridden a train, the private railroad car awakens small response or none where once it engendered awe and admiration.

☙·☙·☙

As a simon-pure property of affluence and social position, the automobile enjoyed the briefest of all mobile seasons in the sun. The horse, technologically outmoded, lingered on in racing stables and show rings long after he had disappeared from the awareness of most people. The private railroad car never, from first to last, was downgraded by common availability or middle-class patronage. Pullman never advertised a family model and no equivalent of Ford or Volkswagen ever rode the rails of the nation. The private palace car was the least compromised of all status symbols.

The esteem in which the motorcar was held as a property of privilege was the shortest of any comparable possession or artifact, for almost as soon as it was taken up in the favor of Newport and Long Island, it lapsed into popular availability with low-priced family models spreading egalitarian chaos on highways that had briefly been dominated by the touring cars, limousines, and roadsters of the well-to-do. The improvement and simplification of automobiles generally, as well as their availability in modestly-priced models, downgraded them with the quality. As long as its conduct and maintenance were a mystery requiring the professional services of a chauffeur and mechanic, an arrangement which lingered on in England long after it had disappeared from general circulation in the United States, an automobile was a distinguished mode of personal transport. A few gentlemen amateurs undertook, daringly, to pilot their own Winton Sixes and Pope Toledos, but they were almost always, in the primeval days of motoring, accompanied by a chauffeur or mechanic, often both, whose duty it was to take over when motor failure or tire trouble set in, which was early and frequently.

William K. Vanderbilt, an early-day automobile pioneer and enthusiast who often drove himself and widely promoted the sport of racing, maintained garages at his Long Island residence for 100 cars. He also employed twenty chauffeurs and repairmen.

Woodrow Wilson, a man who was more often wrong about more things than most men who get to be President of the United States, as head man at Princeton foresaw the automobile as an agency of incitement to socialism and radical violence. "Nothing has spread socialistic feeling in this country more than the use of the automobile," he proclaimed. "To the countryman they are a picture of arrogance of wealth with all its independence and carelessness." As usual, Wilson couldn't have been more wrong. Within a few years of his remark the motorcar was to become the universal property of democracy and the triumphant symbol of an egalitarian economy in which the working stiff without two cars in his garage is in the minority. The countrymen whom Wilson envisioned in terms of revolutionary outrage were the first large class of Americans to take to the highways in low-priced cars in universal availability.

In seeming contradiction of his own democratic principles, Wilson, as President, rode in the world's most expensive and enviable of

It was when questioned about the cost of maintenance of his seagoing yacht Corsair that the elder J.P. Morgan uttered his celebrated aphorism: "Nobody who has to ask what a yacht costs has any business owning one."

Great society weddings such as that shown here of Florence Vanderbilt to Hamilton McKown Twombly at St. Bartholomew's Church represented what Mr. Dooley used to call "solid gilt-edge bonds of matrimony." The bride's father (right) was the first American to acquire a fortune in excess of $200,000,000, and Florence proved to be the last surviving grandchild of old Commodore Vanderbilt and one of the most august matriarchs of New York Society.

That it was possible to ride on horseback into the more exalted realms of society and the big spenders is suggested by the arrival of the Havermeyers' drag with its full complement of footmen and guests for lunch at Claremont Inn overlooking the Hudson River. *Harper's Weekly* estimated that the basic cost of such a turnout was $20,000 and, tongue in cheek, suggested that everybody should have one.

1895, Museum of the City of New York, Byron Collection, 93.1.1.18307

Conservative New Yorkers sneered when C.K.G. Billings gave
a horseback dinner at Sherry's where the guests dined in the saddle
at an estimated cost of $250 a cover.

1903, Museum of the City of New York, Byron Collection, 93.1.1.18339

The turnout of grooms, kept in their place by helmeted policemen outside a
Vanderbilt wedding, suggested no servant problem in the year 1905.

1895, Museum of the City of New York, Byron Collection, 93.1.1.18329

The supreme moment at the Patriarchs Ball at the new uptown Metropolitan Opera House when Elisha Dyer, Jr., cotillion leader and acknowledged *arbiter elegantarium* of New York society, led Sir Roger de Coverly.

One of the two or three most swaggering magnificoes of an era of gilded
grandees, the senior August Belmont was an American representative
of the banking Rothschilds. The intelligence that his wine bill alone ran in
excess of $20,000 a month reportedly hastened the end of his
parsimonious neighbor, James Lenox.

In the golden noontide of its fortunes, the United States Hotel at Saratoga was the enviable summer resport of pleasure-loving William Henry Venderbilt as it had been with his father, the Commodore. From the Civil War years until after the First World War, its broad verandas and stately vistas of public apartments at one time or another saw every person of social and financial consequence in the American record. Only full evening dress was tolerated in its ballroom, and Evander Berry Wall was once asked to leave for appearing in a short dinner jacket. Here W.H. Vanderbilt is shown on the United States' mile-long porch surrounded by race-track touts and tipsters and giving the days' orders to his betting commissioners.

Scene of San Francisco's stateliest sarabands in the silver seventies and aureate eighties was the Palace Hotel, a swaggering edifice that represented the community's highest social and communal aspirations and was built with no expense spared by banker William Ralston with money from the deep mines beneath Virginia City in the Nevada hills. Here lived and gloried in decorous extravagances the railroad rajahs, the silver kings, and the nabobs of steamships, stock market, and land speculation. For two entire generations, the Palace was the focus of the activities of the well-placed of the Western World, and most of the face cards of its era at one time or another signed its register. Destroyed in the fire of 1906, it was rebuilt and the name survives to this day in the Sheraton Palace.

Jim Fisk, a partner with Jay Gould in the ill-fated corner on gold
and later in the scandalous looting of the Erie Railroad, in many
ways has been felt by subsequent historians to typify the low
estate of public morality in the years of President Grant. Fisk
gave the age an image of gross voluptuousness and chaotic
carnival. His champagne suppers, his mistresses, horses, brass
bands, and public hurrah and the gratification of every caprice
characterized many of the newly rich profiteers of the age.

Jubliee Jim Fisk, who typified public misconduct in the era immediately after
the Civil War, was at length shot on the grand stairway of the Grand Central
Hotel (above) by Ned Stokes, a rival for the favors of showgirl Josie Mansfield,
shown below participating in a sleighing party on Broadway
in the approved manner of the time.

Gambling at Canfield's at Saratoga was such an accepted part of the social scene that in 1889 *Leslie's Weekly* had no hesitation in running a sketch of it. The figure in the immediate foreground with the flowered waistcoat is Evander Berry Wall, King of the Dudes and ranking arbiter of men's fashions.

In the Waldorf-Astoria Hotel's Peacock Alley, a parade of fashion and wealth could be viewed by the curious. Largely, at the time of evening depicted here, the fashion was masculine and its top-hatted participants were bound for the hostelry's celebrated bar where Jim Keene, Bet-a-Million Gates, Elbridge Gerry, and sometimes the great J.P. Morgan himself plotted financial coups that would rock the stock market next day.

In a time when a late supper of a cold bottle and a hot bird was an essential of high life at one of New York's top-level resorts, Delmonico's, Sherry's, and the Waldorf-Astoria were the starred places to be seen. Flashier cutups and what would be later known as café society favored Rector's, Shanley's, Bustanoby's, the Holland House, and the Astor Hotel, all of them esteemed lobster palaces along the Gay White Way. One and all of these gilded traps had to await the final curtain at the Metropolitan Opera, whose patrons contributed the hard core and select inner circles of the really big spenders admired of waiter captains everywhere.

The man of a certain financial and social status as of the year 1913, when how
you traveled was who you were, largely went places aboard a private car such
as Charles M. Schwab's second *Loretto* whose observation salon is shown here.
Loretto stood the ironmaster $150,000, but twenty years later it was possible to
spend $350,000 for such a conveyance.

Pullman Standard

Mme. Gabrielle Rejane brought bad luck to youthful James Hazen Hyde when
she appeared in period attire as a French courtier
at his ill-starred costume ball at Sherry's.

1905, Museum of the City of New York, Byron Collection, 93.1.1.9413

The Hope Diamond brought bad luck to all whose paths it
crossed during a long history of misfortune. Evalyn Walsh
McLean pretended to take no stock in its evil mystique,
but after her death no purchaser could be found for the
stone and it was presented by Harry Winston to the
Smithsonian Institution where it reposes today not far from
the McLeans' Friendship where it glittered at the most lavish
entertainments ever seen in Washington.

The National Museum of Natural History, National Gem Collection
© 2008 Smithsonian Institution

all cars, a Rolls-Royce, the only imported motor to have been driven by any occupant of the White House. It was, however, the gift of well-meaning admirers who wanted their idol to have nothing but the best. No American car then or later was in a class with Rolls-Royce.

In its brief heyday as a plaything of the rich, the motor enjoyed the unabashed approval of the ostentatiously well heeled. When Mrs. Oliver Hazard Perry Belmont had her French De Dion Bouton car shipped to Newport in 1897 at the comparatively modest price of $1500, automobiles were known in society slang as "bubbles." Obviously they weren't here to stay and one might as well have fun while they lasted. America's first sports-car meeting or, as they would come to be known in time, *concours d'élégance,* was held on Mrs. Belmont's lawn in 1899 and an obstacle race was run through a course spotted with dummy nursemaids and traffic police. A roadster driven by Tessie Oelrichs (make unspecified) and freighted with a ribboned bower filled with stuffed doves threw a wheel as it rounded the conservatory, the first automobile accident of social consequence in the United States and precursor of the automobile as an agency of aristocratic fatalities which was eventually to shame the guillotine.

Things were better all 'round in this, as it were, Early Ordovician age of internal combustion. Mrs. Stuyvesant Fish, attempting to master the conduct of an electric whose only control, a steering lever, perplexed her sadly, contrived to run over a colored gentleman, not once, but three times. The car kept reversing itself and then going forward every time the unfortunate fellow got to his feet. When the occupant finally managed to drive it head-on into a gate post and emerged, never again to drive a car, her victim had departed. There were no thoughts of legal redress or damages, although one hesitates to think of the suits that would have been filed in a later age of shyster lawyers, ambulance chasers, and fantastically inflated awards by witless juries.

From the very beginning imported motorcars were the ranking properties of status among the American well-to-do. They were to remain so long after Detroit and its allied automotive suburbs were turning out cars numbered in the millions every year. Mercedes, Darracq, Fiat, Rolls-Royce, Renault, and Napier early cornered the expensive American market, although in a few years they were to be crowded by American-made Pierce-Arrows, Loziers, Packards, Peerlesses, Stevens-Duryeas, Pope Hartfords, and Welch as long as American makers produced quality cars only for a limited quality market. A Welch touring car of 1907 cost $5500, a very considerable sum of money at the time. In 1908, a Stevens-Duryea tourer, strictly a quality six-cylinder built-to-order car, cost $3500. By 1914, the celebrated Stutz Bearcat two-seater was selling for a mere $2000 and the market was crowded with now-forgotten gasoline buggies for well under $1000. A few highly individualistic cars, what a later generation would characterize as "personalized," such as Mercer, Duesenberg, Locomobile, Marmon, Cord, and Pierce-Arrow, clung tenaciously to the quality market until comparatively recent years, but the prestige automobile in the United States after the second world war almost invariably came to mean Bentley, Mercedes-Benz, Jaguar, or Rolls-Royce.

It seems improbable that any name artifact or commercial service has ever been absorbed into the folklore of wealth and the superior attitudes of the wealthy to a degree achieved by Rolls-Royce which simply advertises itself as "the Finest Car in the World," a superlative with much evidence to justify its use. Ritz among hotels, although the word has become generic in the language and is used without capitals as a connotation of luxury, Tiffany in the world of jewelry and adornment, Cunard as the pinnacle of ocean transport and matchless standard of service, Delmonico as a hallmark of culinary perfection, Corona among cigars, Colt and Winchester in the world of firearms, Revillon for the opulence of furs, Huntley & Palmer biscuits, Dom Perignon champagne, Peal boots, Poole suits, or Santa Fe and Harvey in railroading—none of those has quite the connotations of unchallenged and universally acknowledged excellence implicit in the name Rolls-Royce.

It may very well be that from the point of view of engineering, other cars enjoy higher regard among knowledgeable experts. Ken Purdy, dean of automobile writers and savants in the field, believes that from every aspect of technical excellence Mercedes-Benz out-ranks Rolls-Royce, although this is a viewpoint to which he has subscribed only in recent years.

Rolls-Royce was not, of course, without competition in the $30,000 and up car market that ended with the chaos of 1929. Ettore Bugatti, a perfectionist whose name is among the immortals of automotive legend, once deliberately undertook to manufacture a car which would outprice Rolls-Royce and whose chassis alone, when finished at the factory, sold for $30,000 in the comparatively hard currency of the twenties.

The Bugatti Royale was inspired, according to Ken W. Purdy, accredited historian of this remarkable make of car, by the patron-izing attitude of an English woman seated next to Bugatti at a luncheon party who remarked: "Of course, M. Bugatti, everyone knows you make the finest racing cars in the world, but for a genu-inely elegant town carriage, one still has to go to Rolls-Royce."

M. Bugatti's reply, if any coherent one was made, is not in the record, but that afternoon found him at the drafting table in his private office designing the largest, most luxurious, and most costly factory model in the history of the world. It was, says Purdy, to put to shame not only Rolls-Royce, but every other pretentious motor-car that enjoyed international celebrity in the year 1927—Daimler, Minerva, Hispano–Suiza, Mercedes–Benz, Bentley, Isotta–Fra-schini, Cunningham, and Duesenberg.

La Royale, as he called this end product of a spendthrift's dream, had a wheel base of fourteen feet, two inches, a straight eight engine of 784 cubic inches capacity—more than twice that of the contemporary Cadillac—and every working part in the entire vehicle was to be machined to zero tolerance, that is to say, not even a thousandth of an inch in any moving component. As remarked above, the chassis was to cost $30,000 at the factory and Bugatti ordered his shop foreman to run up twenty-five of them forthwith.

No detail of elegance, convenience, or mechanical perfection was overlooked. There were four horn buttons, one at every spoke of the steering wheel, the 220-pound crankshaft machined from a solid forging ran in nine individually water-cooled bearings, and the bonnet dimensions from windshield to radiator measured just seven feet. With each car, on which its builder estimated a purchaser would have to spend another absolute minimum of $10,000 for a body, bringing the initial cost to $40,000, went a lifetime guarantee of free service and overhauling and a radiator ornament in the form of an ivory white elephant.

The depression, which came along in the fall of 1929, put something of a crimp in the world market for $40,000 stock model cars and only seven Royales were ever actually outshopped. Bugatti himself kept No. 1; No. 2 went to King Alfonso of Spain, a great *aficionado* of Bugattis, and himself a racing driver of note; and No. 3 was acquired by King Carol of Rumania who had a $22,500 armored body built on it at the behest of his mistress Madame Lupescu, who wanted to take no chances on the life of her meal ticket. One of the seven Royales survives to this day in the collection of D. Cameron Peck of Chicago who at one point in his career owned more than 250 fine automobiles.

The Bugatti estate retained Le Patron's own car, and a well-to-do American once offered to purchase it at any price the owners might care to set. *"Le Patron est mort"* was the reply of his son Roland. *"La voiture est morte aussi."*

Other makes of cars could approach Bugatti but not surpass it in costliness. James. J. Walker, mayor of New York in the thirties, had a $20,000 Duesenberg town car, reportedly the gift of an admirer, A. C. Blumenthal. It had yellow basketwork for its body and the mayor liked to use it when attending Board of Estimate meetings to discuss civic matters of pith and moment. "Keep your motor running, I won't be long," he told the chauffeur. After moments

among the financial audits he would take a farewell of his col-
leagues. "Keep your hands to the plow, dear friends!" he would tell
them in leaving.

The only comparable equivalent in elegance to owning Rolls-
Royces in the American lexicon of upward mobility was, in his
lifetime, to have purchased one's old masters from Lord Joseph
Duveen, the significance of which never circulated outside a circle
of the most eclectic and solvent of collectors and dealers in fine
arts. Only a few hundred persons at the outside were aware that
such a person as Lord Duveen existed at all. Rolls-Royce has significance to millions who have never set foot inside one.

In the six decades that Rolls-Royce has been produced, first at
Derby, later at Crewe, and briefly in Springfield, Massachusetts,
a number of explanations have been advanced for the mystique
which surrounds it as is associated with almost no other end product of human devising. One is its comparative scarcity. Figures are
not available over its entire life span, but in the first fifty years of
its existence only 25,000 cars were outshopped altogether, a figure
which assumes perspective when viewed in the light of the production of 30,000 cars in Detroit in a single week of March 1965.

Another is Rolls-Royce's imperviousness to change and uncompromising refusal to downgrade its product from the plateau of
absolute excellence it achieved in the lifetimes of the two men whose
names it bears, the Honorable Charles Rolls and Sir Henry Royce.
Its radiator shell, bonnet outline, and Spirit of Ecstasy mascot on
the radiator cap are essentially what they were half a century ago.

Rolls-Royce, although the firm has made a determined effort
since the mid-1950s to abate "chauffeurs and baronial halls" in the
car's collective image, has remained over the years and the decades
primarily a car for heads of state, towering social grandees, and
the upper-bracket one-thousandth of one per cent of the very rich
of the world. In 1958, the New York advertising firm of Ogilvy,
Benson & Mather was commissioned to "show Rolls-Royce in the
context of American life," presumably being driven to cookouts

by housewives in curl papers, and while the concept did indeed dramatically increase the sale of Rolls-Royces and Bentleys in the United States, it did absolutely nothing to abate the almost unearthly splendor of their associations.

Long after other of the world's car manufacturers assumed that all but a microscopic fraction of their products would be owner-driven, Rolls-Royce both factually and by implication assumed that owners of its cars would have limitless resources of servants both to drive and maintain their automobiles. The management adopted a very high tone with its patrons and a handbook of comparatively recent years directed the unfailing manual lubrication of thirty points in the mechanism to be greased every 500 miles, eighty-four points at every 1000 miles, and twenty-nine at every 2000 miles, not to mention routine overhauling and adjustments, checking of filters, tappets, and spark plugs, and the periodical removal of wheels for greasing. This sort of thing presupposed Rolls-Royce ownership by people for whom the servant problem simply didn't exist and the assumption was flattering to those who not only drove their own cars but emptied the ash trays as well.

Rolls-Royce found itself elevated far above the estate of a merely elegant and well-appointed agency of personal transport into an article of faith and a way of life itself.

The first Rolls-Royce, a ten-horsepower, two-door saloon of 1905, sold for $1080. Today it is possible to purchase them in a price range from $16,800 to $26,000 with conventional fittings and the standard amenities of de luxe transport. As with private Pullmans, the sums that can be expended on special effects and interior *décor* are almost without limit. They run from jeweled traveling clocks on the dashboard to individually controlled air conditioning, sun roofs, built-in bars, and telephonic communication between passengers and driver. In the late twenties a dealer in rare period furnishings saw no reason his Rolls-Royce, a Phantom I brougham model with carriage work by Clark of Wolverhampton, shouldn't be as luxuriously furnished as his home, and upholstered the interior with Aubusson needlework tapestry, the cost of the fabric alone coming to $3000 in a time of gold currency. Mrs. Hamilton McK. Twombly's favorite limousine contained a gold and emerald built-in vanity by Cartier valued at $10,000. Solid-silver drinking tools, Abercrombie & Fitch picnic baskets, and Baccarat glasses in the bar are a commonplace. Gold-plated motors in the James Bond tradition were never a matter of record but gold-washed radiator shells and mascots have been executed, one such job by Mappin & Webb, the London gold and silversmiths, coming to $4000 in weight of metal alone.

The most expensive car ever seen in California and one which, in world comparatives, ranked in costliness with both Andrew Mellon's $40,000 car built exclusively of products of the Mellon enterprises and Sir Bernard Docker's $35,000 gold-plated Daimler, was shown at the Pebble Beach *concours d'élégance* at Del Monte Lodge in 1961. It was a Phantom V model Rolls-Royce owned by Martin Martyn of Beverly Hills which had cost its owner $54,000. The body was designed by Osmond Francis Rivers, a celebrated craftsman who had for many years been chief body designer for the house of Hooper and architect of many of the cars used by the British royal family. The two-tone black and beige body was fabricated by the Paris firm of Henri Chapron, one of the last great bespoke body builders still in business. It required more than a year to build, and to supervise the work three trips to the Continent were made by Rivers and four from the United States by Mrs. Martyn. A working bar was furnished with drinking tools from Van Cleef & Arpels and glasses and decanters by Baccarat. There was an air-conditioned humidor for cigars, three-length radio reception controllable from each seat, individual armrests, and a locked compartment for the owner's binoculars and parasol on race days. "It has an English soul and a French body," said Mrs. Martyn, dusting its already immaculate bonnet surface with a small dustcloth sewn of matched mink skins. Unknown at the time to the owners was the fact that before they took delivery on the car in Paris, the workmen who had labored over it had had a private christening party of their own and sent the car into the world wreathed with roses and formally christened with champagne. Some of the workers had wept to see it leave their shop.

Perhaps the most radiant of all chapters in the saga of social Rolls-Royce in the upper-case sense of social concerns Mr. Hamilton McKown Twombly whose death in 1952 at the age of ninety-eight put a final period, according to Cleveland Amory, to Newport's era of elegance. Mrs. Twombly's memory is still green in the upper brackets of the New York Four Hundred for her determined effort in 1935 to attend the Hollywood wedding of her grandson to Florabelle Fairbanks, a niece of Douglas Fairbanks.

Already in her eighties, Mrs. Twombly was forbidden to fly. The family private Pullman car had long since been discarded and Mrs. Twombly wouldn't even toy with the idea of renting one from the New York Central, let alone ride in a public train. Driving the entire 3000 miles from Newport to the church was the only solution, but it, too, was fraught with grave perils and the ever-present dangers of the Great Plains and other accidents of violence in the howling wilderness west of St. Louis. The James boys, she understood, were no longer in operating condition but who knew about others, the Daltons, for instance? And there was always the chance of hostile Indians. If they recognized her she would be held for ransom, a most inconvenient possibility.

Finally a solution presented itself. For 3000 miles going west and an equal distance coming back, the last grandchild of Commodore Cornelius Vanderbilt dressed as her personal maid, rode in the front seat next the chauffeur in one of the Twombly Rolls-Royces while for an equal time and distance Mrs. Twombly's maid dressed as Mrs. Twombly, rode in lonely state in the back seat.

It was a triumph of ingenuity and determination still mentioned with pride in Park Avenue as a gesture the Commodore himself would have applauded.

Like all Vanderbilts, Mrs. Twombly rode in sometimes seedy but inevitably grand Rolls-Royces which she kept *en suite* at *Florham,* her incredible estate near Convent, New Jersey, to match her mood and attire of the moment. John Mason Brown recalls being present at one Sunday morning when, returning from church, Mrs. Twombly was holding court, receiving her guests in the foyer under the sculptured likenesses of twelve Roman Caesars. "She stepped out of her violet Rolls-Royce," recalls Brown, "and swept inside wearing a violet hat, violet gloves, and carrying a bunch of violets. It was unforgettable. I even remember where I was standing. It was inviolate, too—right underneath Caligula."

Rolls-Royce has often in the long history of its triumphs enabled owners to penetrate precincts of inner fastness where their other qualifications were ineffective. A borrowed or hired Rolls-Royce has secured many a parvenu's toehold on the precarious edge of social or financial recognition, but seldom has it been used, as it were, in reverse to procure admission of irreproachable social status and the most exalted professional rank into the good graces of a sensationally truculent *arriviste* as it was in the case of the terrible-tempered Dr. Albert C. Barnes of Philadelphia.

Barnes, who became in his own lifetime a legend of mingled horror and hilarity among Main Line Philadelphians, was the most snubbed of all Philadelphia parvenus of modern times, which is, in itself, perhaps a distinction. He had made a fortune in a patent nostrum called Argyrol, a medicament for sore throats which made him enormously rich. The astuteness which had led him to Argyrol also suggested that he buy up vast resources of fine arts in fields as yet undiscovered by conservative collectors, and the Barnes Collection on the Main Line houses to this day formidable resources of Modiglianis, Cezannes, and Renoirs. (He bought something like seventy paintings by a French unknown named Soutine for $3000 which the delighted artist blew on a taxi ride not, unhappily, in a Rolls-Royce, from Paris to the Riviera.)

But it required more than a few million dollars' worth of fine arts to secure the recognition of fortunes which had reposed in the Girard Bank in some cases for four or five generations. Philadelphia's Social Register remained a closed book to Dr. Barnes, whose rage and indignation knew no bounds but was most effectively expressed by allowing nobody at all to see his admittedly superlative paintings.

Well-recommended art authorities were brusquely turned away from Dr. Barnes's implacable door. Internationally accredited connoisseurs made no dent. Tentative approaches by Philadelphians of the most exalted status were met with abuse couched in water-closet terms. Inevitably, the art critics raised a suspicion of the authenticity of masterpieces they were not allowed to view or appraise, and Barnes hit the proverbial roof. A feud of the utmost vindictiveness involving lawsuits, letters to the editor, and the physical ejection of importunate art lovers followed in which an elderly Rittenhouse Square grandee, whose name alone opened doors in the most palatial precincts in Europe, was thrown physically down the Barnes front steps.

All unwittingly there arrived amidst this barrage of insults and metaphorical dead cats the determined person of Mary Garden on concert tour accompanied by her impresario, Merle Armitage. After a concert, it being Miss Garden's whim to see the Cezannes, they drove together to the Barnes museum-residence and were bluntly refused admission. A few months later, in town again on a similar mission, Miss Garden called on a day when the Barnes Collection was advertised to be open to the public and sent in her card to the doctor. It came back scrawled "Please go away!"

Nothing daunted, and finding the impervious hauteur of the Argyrol king something of a challenge, Miss Garden, on a still later occasion, undertook to breach the battlements accompanied by her friend Mrs. William Kissam Vanderbilt. It was her optimistic notion that where Cadwaladers and Biddies might have no influence, the ranking member of the Vanderbilt family might make some sort of impression. Happily they drove out from the singer's hotel in a Vanderbilt Rolls-Royce town car with two men in Vanderbilt maroon on the box, an equipage to combat social barriers comparable to a tank in trench warfare.

Taking no chances on physical assault by the collector, whose reputation for a low emotional boiling point had by now grown in the telling, Miss Garden and Mrs. Vanderbilt sent their cards to the front door by the footman, while themselves prudently remaining in the protection of the rear seat.

As it chanced, the doctor himself answered the door. His face purpled with rage as he tore the calling cards into fragments and seemed about to commit physical assault on the terrified flunkey when his eye lit on the Rolls-Royce spotted at the curb. In an instant the terrible visage was all smiles and urbane contentment succeeded grim wrath as it was wont to do of an afternoon in Squire Western as soon as he had consumed his first bottle of Port and his daughter began playing on the harpsichord.

Dr. Barnes would be honored personally to escort Miss Garden and Mrs. Vanderbilt through his museum and point out the highlights of his collection if in return he might be allowed to inspect the Vanderbilt car and perhaps drive it around the block. An hour's guided tour of the hitherto inaccessible Soutines and Modiglianis was followed by a ride to the Bellevue-Stratford during which the doctor shrewdly cross-questioned Mrs. Vanderbilt about the car's self-lubricating system and the firing order of its cylinders, matters about which, more or less understandably, the owner knew little or nothing.

Immediately after the thaw, however, the Barnes chill reasserted itself. Returned in Mrs. Vanderbilt's car to his stronghold, Dr. Barnes, according to Merle Armitage, forthwith sat down and wrote a three-page letter to Inskip in New York, taking the dealer to task in no uncertain terms for selling so superb a car to so ignorant a woman!

The Vanderbilt maroon which dominated the family's successive fleets of Rolls-Royces was, of course, directly inherited from the color of the family's house footmen and other liveried servants and the color that identified their carriages and horse rigs in the days before motoring. Its ramifications extended far beyond the world of formal society, for the Vanderbilt maroon of the family cars and carriages dictated that a matching maroon carpet be laid across the sidewalk of each of the several Vanderbilt mansions on upper Fifth Avenue to the curbside whenever an occupant arrived or departed. When the passenger department of the Vanderbilt-owned New York Central Railroad was casting around for some matchless panache of elegance to distinguish its crack *Twentieth Century Limited* and at the same time be one up on the Pennsylvania's competing *Broadway Limited,* it came up with the idea of a Vanderbilt maroon carpet to be laid for the train's departure every afternoon from Grand Central. Thus the identifying cachet of family elegance was made to serve the ends of commerce, an alliance to which Vanderbilts have never been averse in any generation.

The climactic example of the owner-driven Rolls-Royce came seven years after the campaign was first launched to make "the Finest Car in the World" a property of the masses, and must have been viewed with mixed emotions of frustration and gratification by Rolls-Royce itself. Returning, soon after the new year of 1965 from the funeral of Sir Winston Churchill, in itself enough to give the event a cachet of resounding privilege, the sixty-four-year-old Duke of Gloucester, an uncle of Queen Elizabeth and eighth in line for the British throne, managed to drive his Rolls-Royce into a ditch in the township of Eaton Socon about fifty miles north of London.

It had long been the Duke's practice, said the head of his household, Major Simon Bland, to have his chauffeur drive him to state and official functions and for the elderly nobleman to take the wheel himself on the way home. As a result of failing to make a turn, the ducal car went into the ditch, hospitalizing the Duchess with a broken arm and concussion, breaking the arm of the Duke's valet, and severely shaking up the chauffeur. The Duke himself was discharged from the local emergency ward with a badly skinned nose but no more severe injuries.

The mishap landed on the front pages of the press of the world in a fine farrago of strawberry leaves and coronets, bandages and arnica, and may well prove to have been the most distinguished owner-driven event in the long history of Rolls-Royce. It flattered both aspects of the Rolls-Royce saga, involving as it did an owner-driven car in which the owner-driver was heir to a title that has thrown a long shadow in English annals since the times of the Plantagenets.

The press of the world was at pains to follow the Duchess of Gloucester's fortunes in the hospital at Bedford, and every day bulletins, none of them failing to mention the ducal Rolls-Royce, apprised the newspaper readers on two continents of the progress of her recovery. On February 8, 1965, a United Press dispatch recorded that she had been discharged from her suite at Bedford and had gone home. In the family's spare Rolls-Royce. The accident Rolls-Royce was still undergoing repairs.

The high interior construction of Rolls-Royce by most body-makers and especially for heads of state and magnificoes of finance was, of course, largely predicated on the wearing of high silk hats by their occupants and retained as a vestigial heritage from the past into an age when silk hats were less universal than they once had been. In *Portugal and Madeira* Sacheverell Sitwell recalls an anecdote in point. "The writer remembers meeting a certain Indian potentate at a luncheon party. The host said to him: 'May I ask why you commanded your new fleet of Rolls-Royces built with such high roofs?' The maharaja replied, 'Oh! I don't know. I might want to wear an aigrette.'"

It is difficult, even to the dedicated student of motoring history and legend, to determine where the facts of Rolls-Royce and its excellence end and where folklore begins to assert itself. An extensive and, it may be remarked parenthetically, expensive bibliography of Rolls-Royce exists in all engineering libraries. Both in England and the United States, True Believers foregather in confraternities such as the Rolls-Royce Owners Club to hymn their veneration of a car that has long since transcended its utilitarian aspects to become an enshrined *mystique* and way of life itself. The Rolls-Royce owners in the United States publish their own coated-paper house organ, *The Flying Lady,* in whose columns used treasures in the field of Phantom II tourers and 20/25 Cockshoots sports sedans are advertised for sale to applicants presenting proper credentials certifying their ability and intention to give the car a good home. There are also available Rolls-Royce sets of evening studs for wear by *aficionados* with platinum outlines of the Rolls-Royce radiator and headlights set with rubies.

Used Rolls-Royces command uncommonly high prices in comparison to their American opposite numbers, asking prices of $12,000 and $14,000 being frequent for a "one-owner car." A car that has had but one owner, if possible from the British peerage, is more highly esteemed than one which has passed through several possibly dissolute and irresponsibly conducted garages.

In the United States wealthy enclaves of Rolls-Royce exist in special density on Long Island, in Maryland, eastern Pennsylvania and, above all, in California. In these localities owners foregather to show their properties and restorations in *concours d'élégance* where no other car except Bentleys are permitted.

Rolls-Royce devotees are both fanatic and articulate and, more even than religious groups, make trouble for newspaper editors in whose pages solecisms of Rolls-Royce lore have been detected. When the film *Lawrence of Arabia* was shown in San Francisco, drama critics were showered with abuse for reviewing the performances of the actors instead of the Rolls-Royces which figured in several scenes of desert combat. To forestall such complaints one San Francisco paper, the *Chronicle,* several years later when *The Yellow Rolls-Royce* was screened, ran two reviews of the premiere, one by its accredited drama critic appraising the actors, the other by its automobile editor devoted to the car for which the film was named.

Other expensive imported motorcars have made a not too lasting impression on the American awareness of the better things of life. Minerva, Hispano-Suiza, and Isotta-Fraschini, some of them ranging in price delivered in New York from coach builders of England and the Continent up to $25,000 and $30,000 in a time of hard currency, all had their rather limited day mostly on Madison and Park avenues and Sunset Boulevard.

The Hispano-Suiza in particular enjoyed a short-lived but truly fabulous reputation on both sides of the Atlantic as a by-product of Michael Arlen's equally fantastic best seller, *The Green Hat:*

> Open as a yacht, it wore a shining bonnet; and flying over the crest of the great bonnet, as though in proud flight over the scores of phantom horses, was that silver stork by which the gentle may be pleased to know that they have just escaped death beneath the wheels of a Hispano-Suiza car, as supplied to his most Catholic Majesty.

The reference was, of course, to the so-called Alfonso XIII model named for the King of Spain and often driven by that dapper monarch in his years at Cannes, Nice, and Monte Carlo.

A favorite, seemingly, of men of letters, the Hispano lent the cachet of its name to a romantic French novel of high life called *L'homme à l'Hispano* (The Man in the Hispano-Suiza) by Pierre Frondaie.

A common denominator of all these cars of *Grande Marque* were the severe-faced chauffeurs, the jeweled traveling clocks and vanities, the mink lap robes, the cut-glass decanters in retractable cabinets, and the beautiful West of England cloth upholstery. Many of them represented an investment of $30,000 on the hoof, as it were, with ceilings painted by celebrated muralists, Upmann Specials in the humidors, and London Docks cognac imported by 21 Brands at $60 a bottle in the folding bars.

None of them, however, it is safe to say, rated the salute in passing that must be accorded Joshua Cosden, of oil fame, who insisted that, on the richly ornate woodwork of the dashboard of his Park Ward Rolls-Royce convertible, all the operational switches be identified in raised gold letters in Old English type.

Infrequently encountered, too, is such selfless devotion to the *esprit* of Rolls-Royce as that of Reginald Stocking II, a California youth who, in order to support his ownership of a classic town car, makes it available as a sort of one-man car-hire service in which he operates in full English livery with the express provision that

patrons do not ask him to drink or dine with them while on duty.
A perfectionist, like many of The Faithful, Stocking one summer
attended the school maintained at Crewe by Rolls-Royce for the
training of chauffeurs. His presence raised the problem of the propriety of a gentleman lunching at the mechanics' mess, a problem
of protocol that was resolved when he was asked to patronize the
executive dining room. "Two wines every day," he told friends, "one
of them a very passable claret."

As of the year 1966 the future of Rolls-Royce was felt by thoughtful amateurs of the mystique of "the Finest Car in the World" to
be clouded. Discarding the highly successful Clouds I, II, and III,
the firm came up for its 1966 model with a Silver Shadow that so
widely departed from the established image of Rolls-Royce as to
occasion anguish and outrage among The Faithful to whom tradition and splendor are as important components of the Rolls legend
as its engineering.

In the Silver Shadow the venerated Rolls-Royce profile has been
notably ensmalled. A so-called "monocoque body" embraces an
approach to the dimensions of a compact car and the hitherto invi-
olable bonnet and radiator grille have been watered almost out of
existence. Critics see in its engineering an effort to adapt to the
narrow roads and limited clearances of England on the one hand
and at the same time maintain the luxury standards that justify a
steeply upped price of $20,000 in the United States.

"Trying to please both markets, Rolls-Royce has fallen between
two stools," says one widely respected automotive editor. "American purchasers of Rolls-Royce want a car twenty feet long and
eight feet high for that sort of money and a radiator grille measured not in square feet but in acres. Gas consumption and that
sort of economy mean nothing to Americans in the Rolls bracket
who want the massive image of a traditional luxury car. This is one
thing the Shadow hasn't got and it may well be that Rolls-Royce
has cut its own throat by attempting a compromise between English and American requirements."

If, as one disgruntled American critic remarked of the new Silver Shadow, "he'd have to buy two, one for each foot," Rolls-Royce still produces the seven-passenger Phantom V for Texans and heads of state. It sells for approximately $34,000 and has two air conditioning systems, one for the owner and one for the separately compartmented driver.

Chapter Nine

Good Times in the Money Mountains

Noblest Roamer of Them All and the Most Expensive, Too, Was St. George Gore ... He Also Invented the Economy of Expensive Scarcity ... Molly Brown's Husband Used Banknotes to Start His Fires ... Colorado Springs Was an Enclave of Splendid Ways ... Ethel Carlton Took Caviar When She Felt Depressed ... Spencer Penrose Wanted to Live in a Hotel So He Built the Broadmoor ... Memorandum for Tomorrow: Try Not to Spend More than $1,000,000. ...

THE WORD MAGNIFÍCO has been frequently but by no means miscellaneously used in this book to suggest men of great estate, spaciousness of gestures, and splendid ways generally. Its intention has been to connote the grand seigneur, not merely the rich man, and the number of well-to-do Americans who have also been qualified for the role of grand seigneur is indeed a limited one.

Beyond all argument, the elder J. P. Morgan was a magnifico. The grand manner became him in every aspect of his personality so that he was known, behind his back to be sure, as Jupiter, and the world of finance was so in awe of his authority that he was able to control, if not prevent, panics and by his mere presence prevent catastrophe from becoming universal.

So was William Collins Whitney indisputably a magnifico, at some remove to be sure from the elder Morgan, but one who indulged the sybaritic taste of an authentic Corinthian as no American has ever done since. Mediocrity in Whitney was unthinkable. So, too, was James Gordon Bennett in his erratic and well-brandied manner, a grandee, the author of innumerable *beaux gestes* that in lesser men would have been mere evidences of solvent bad manners. In San Francisco it would have been possible to nominate James Ben Ali Haggin to the club.

It would be unthinkable to attach the status of magnifico to Diamond Jim Brady or Bet-a-Million Gates, Horace Tabor or Whitelaw Reid, who, although they moved in snowstorms of $1000 bills and lived on a scale that was often baronial, never transcended the spiritual status of the parvenu who strove constantly for effect and strained to achieve the image he envied.

If Spencer Penrose hadn't been, both congenitally and in his own right of achievement, a magnifico, which he pre-eminently was, the power of myth and legend in the Rocky Mountain region would presently have elevated him to that estate. For Colorado is, if any continental region of the United States may be selected for this eminence, a land of enchantment where folk heroes are of Paul Bunyan dimensions and regional mythology only emerges briefly into the realm of certifiable fact from mist-enshrouded parks and high passes of the Shining Mountains.

Everything about the Colorado legend is outsize, the primeval exploits of the Mountain Men and the Long Hunters in the days of the fur trade, the capacity for Taos lightning and killing Indians of Dick Wootton, the infallibility of that arch-frontiersman Jim Bridger, the craft and guile of Otto Mears, "Pathfinder of the San Juan," and the later voracity and tumults of the inheritors, the wealth of Tom Walsh and the Camp Bird Mine, the disdainful aloofness of Senator Edward O. Wolcott, and the Midas touch of Colonel Daniel C. Jackling.

Nobody in the Colorado legend did anything by halves and if he had had the bad judgment momentarily to cut a corner of expansiveness or even fractionally to shade a gesture of splendor, the custodians of Rocky Mountain folk legend, be they Gene Fowler, the *Denver Post,* David Lavender, or Marshall Sprague, would have hastened to conceal the lapse. Even the comparatively trivial episode of Julian Street at Cripple Creek, in reality no more than a footnote to the joyously low moral tone of Colorado mining towns in general, has been expanded into a dimensions of national anecdotal currency on a par with what the governor of North Carolina said to the governor of South Carolina.

Like participation in the *chansons de geste* or the Arthurian legend, candidacy for Colorado's regional hall of fame was a matter of timing. Jim Bridger, Dick Wootton, that great hunter Sir St. George Gore, Buffalo Bill Cody who spent most of his time in Colorado and is buried there, Haw Tabor, Baby Doe, General William Jackson Palmer, all had time and to spare. Players of some of the best parts, however, Albert Carlton, the Unsinkable Molly Brown, Fred Bonfils and Harry Tammen, Colonel Daniel C. Jackling, the Count James Pourtales, Charlie Tutt, and Spencer Penrose just got in under the wire variously represented by the federal income tax in 1914, prohibition, and the mining of precious metals, the last of which came to an end in the second world war.

As it was in so many parts of the world in the nineteenth century, the pattern of splendid gestures was conformed fairly early in the game by an Englishman and it remained for Sir St. George Gore to set the style for lordly safaris which was followed, albeit in diminished dimension, by every notable who came after him including the much more widely publicized hunting expedition of the Grand Duke Alexis. Sir St. George remains the only private individual to have offered his services to the United States Government to raise an army for the extermination of the Sioux on a cost-plus contract basis, and his name today is part of western geography in Gore Canyon, the Gore Mountains, and Gore Pass.

Sir St. George first swam into the consciousness of the old West in 1853 when he appeared in St. Louis with unlimited letters of credit on the London firm of Baring Brothers. His dealings were direct and unequivocal; he wanted a lot of the best of everything, he wanted it right now, and he paid gold on the barrelhead without any argument. St. Louis at once took off its coonskin cap and stood at attention.

Sir St. George, whose private purse derived from almost the entire rents from the Irish counties of Sligo and Donegal, spent $500,000 on a single hunting expedition and the impact of his advent on the frontier can be measured if you multiply that sum by between five and ten times to approximate its equivalent in today's currency. He wanted to hunt buffalo and everything else that moved on western plain or mountain, and he secured as the head of his safari the best obtainable talent in the person of Jim Bridger. Second in command was also a top-notcher, Henri Châtillon, one time *voyageur* for the American Fur Company. It may be speculated that if Louis Sherry and Mme. Nellie Melba had been available he would have taken them along to prepare the terrapin Maryland and provide music at dinner.

The Gore safari was in the grand manner when it outfitted at St. Louis and it terminated, as we shall see, in the most expensive gesture of patrician contempt for expenses in the western record. His initial purchase from the wagonmakers of Missouri included twenty-odd bright-red-painted two-horse wagons known as Red River carts and in great demand among hunters and trappers in the Rocky Mountain region for their durability which compared favorably with later arrivals in the form of Studebaker wagons and Abbot Downing Company's now legendary Concord coach. There were also four six-mule rigs, two heavy-duty oxcarts, and a Beverly wagon for the use of Gore himself. No fewer than 112 horses, nine span of oxen, three milk cows, thirty-six greyhounds, and a pack of fourteen giant staghounds out of Ireland completed the entourage. The forty-one members of its personnel included expert gunsmiths for the maintenance of the Gore arsenal, a specialist in tying dry flies, and an official astronomer with a six-inch-lens telescope.

When the expedition hit the trail at the beginning of each day it must have presented an impressive sight. First came the British milord attired in the fearful and wonderful costume of the time, yellow side whiskers, deerstalker fore-and-aft cap of the sort later associated with Sherlock Holmes, pleated Norfolk hunting jacket with bellows pockets for dead birds, ammunition, and perhaps sandwiches, corduroy breeches, and linen gaiters over stout hunting boots.

Following the viceregal charette was Gore's mobile arsenal, a wheeled gunsmithy and wardroom containing the seventy-five rifled weapons and numerous shotguns and small arms considered necessary to the specialized business of exterminating wildlife on a wholesale scale and under the terms of a sort of protocol which dictated a Hawken's over-and-under two-barreled single-hammer .56 caliber breech loader for buffalo when shooting from a stand and a shorter over-all length, or carbine-size, Sharp's rifle when firing mounted. A British huntsman who used the incorrect weapon of precision in Gore's generation to burn powder under given circumstances was as gauche and inept a fellow as the commanded dinner guest at Windsor Castle who chose the wrong cutlery from the array provided at his place to dissect a ptarmigan. It was the first intimations the Great Plains had had of this sort of ritualistic observance of established conventions, and the sweating porters and wagoneers were amazed. That Sir St. George dressed formally for dinner along the margins of the North Platte is not established. That he did indeed maintain a head table where precedence was strictly observed, is.

Each evening when the wagon master and a council of guides had determined upon a campsite, Gore's personal shelter was wheeled into place and made habitable. This consisted of a ten-by-fourteen green-and-white-striped tent over a vast wagon box of similar proportions. At the appointed hour, four stout fellows in buckskin manned crank machines at the four corners of the wagon, and through the agency of cunning machinery, elevated the canvas top which "lifted into view" and provided shelter for a full-size brass bedstead, cast-iron washstand, and marble-topped commode.

At dinner only the members of the party of flag ranks, which meant Châtillon and Bridger, dined at head table. Gore ate well and drank well, the latter sparingly by frontier standards, and the sole flaw in his facade, in the eyes of his retainers, was that he favored wine over spirits. A bottle of Larose and glass of Comet Year cognac sufficed where his followers, had they possessed his resources, would have been barrel-house full each evening on St. Louis trading rum and sleeping happily in the sagebrush by sundown.

Bridger was fascinated by the baronet, both as a man and as a specimen, and addressed him always as "Mr. Gore," the frontier equivalent of "Sire" in moments of informality with royalty. After dinner Gore read aloud to Bridger from Shakespeare and other recognized classics, not in any patronizing way but because the veteran of a thousand hairbreadth 'scapes himself was genuinely moved and excited by Henry before Harfleur or the Moor's encounters with the Infidel.

One likes to linger over the patriarchal scene as, with the ardors of the day's pursuits behind them, the two friends foregather beside the campfire where the master of Manor Gore, by the light of a patent reading lamp, impersonates first Bluff Prince Hal and then a scheming Richard to an antiphonal chorus of prairie wolves howling in the darkened background. It is a continental moment.

As a huntsman Sir St. George left something to be desired but made up in sheer volume of carnage what he lacked in finesse. He never deigned to load his own weapon, which made it difficult for gun-bearers to keep up with him when giving mounted chase to buffalo or antelope, but in firing from a stand, where as many as seven loaders were kept busy as the game was driven past, he did carnage to have commanded the respect of Buffalo Bill and other contract hunters of a later generation.

Although an indifferent horseman, he excited the admiration of his retainers by a truly British devotion to his own special mount, a Kentucky thoroughbred named Steel Trap whom, when rations were short or the beast was off his feed, he fed hot mash from his own hands. The cold-blooded huntsman, who could devastate the surrounding prairie of all life as far as his beaters could range, would be saddened by the death of a pack animal in his service. The *voyageurs* had never encountered anything like him.

For two full summers this imperial entourage ranged the hunting grounds of western Colorado, Utah, and southwestern Wyoming, camping on all four sides of Pikes Peak and wintering at Fort Laramie, a stronghold not to be confused with today's Laramie, Wyoming, but somewhat to the north of the main line of the Union Pacific and the Overland trail. The second summer, the party followed the course of the Bighorn north into the great buffalo fastness of the Yellowstone and wintered the seasonal snowfall on the Tongue a few miles from today's Miles City, Montana.

When, in 1856, Gore had had his fill of shooting and had lost his guide and companion Jim Bridger, who had been requisitioned by the Army for an expedition against the Mormons, the huntsman arrived at Fort Union determined to terminate his long safari and set a course for home. Here it was that he had occasion to indulge the *beau geste* which, if he were remembered for nothing else, would make his name immortal in the annals of the old West.

At Fort Union he offered to sell his entire equipment, valued conservatively at $50,000 even after years on the road, for a nominal sum and in exchange for a pair of flatboats aboard which to float his numerous trophies 2200 miles downriver to civilization at St. Louis. A commandant at Fort Union, a shortsighted churl named George Culbertson, undertook to fleece the hardy baronet. His offer for the equipment was niggardly; his estimate for building the boats ruinous.

He reckoned without the temper of his opponent.

On the headland across the river from the fort, Sir St. George Gore built a bonfire, the costliest yet seen anywhere on the far side of the rolling Mississippi. Into it went all the expensive equipment that had weathered two full years of arduous service on plain and mountain. Feeding the flames were the Red River carts, the vast ox wains, the saddlery and harnesses for more than 100 horses, the lordly masters tent, the brass bedstead, and the marble-topped commode. While the watchers at Fort Union gaped, the fire consumed all and every artifact that Gore and his immediate suite were incapable of carrying off in their personal luggage. The next morning, as the ashes cooled, the baronet personally groped among the embers and threw into the river every piece of metal fitting that might not have been reduced to ashes.

He then set his face for Ireland and was never again seen on the buffalo grounds. It was a Wagnerian exit.

It would be unrealistic to suggest that Sir St. George Gore set a pattern for future hunting safaris on the Great Plains as long as the superlative attraction of the buffalo lasted. The most widely publicized successor to the Irish baronet was the Grand Duke Alexis of Russia who, in the winter of 1873 and with benefit of full press coverage, the United States Cavalry, and the indomitable Buffalo Bill Cody, hunted briefly along the North Platte. By the Grand Duke's time the Pacific Railroad was in operation and his party rode aboard the Palace Cars to a suitable point of disembarkation where the horse soldiers took over. That Buffalo Bill was in charge of the party gave it the fullest possible measure of theatrical presentation, but it lacked the wild grandeur of the Gore anabasis and already, as a by-product of the railroad, the frontier was headed for oblivion. The field equipment of the magnetic telegraph, the daily communications from the State Department, ice for the ducal champagne, all contributed to divest the occasion of the spontaneity and freedom that had characterized the spacious magnificence of an earlier Jamshid. And, of course, the Grand Duke burned no bonfire of defiance in full sight of the commandant of Fort Union.

When private parties of State Street bankers out of Boston got down off the steamcars at North Platte in the mid-seventies and went off to rough it in well-appointed campsites determined in advance attired in tightly buttoned frock coats and well-brushed silk hats, the tradition of the Long Hunters on the Great Plains was reduced to the merest transparent parody. The correspondent for the *Boston Evening Transcript* might hymn the wonderments of sleeping beneath the stars but there was no Irish baronet in his dispatches feeding Steel Trap hot mash out of his own hands. Times had changed.

ᛟᛜ·ᛟᛜ·ᛟᛜ

The most durable and enduring figure of Colorado legend in the nineteenth century, and indeed the only one to be the central figure of a full-dress biographical motion picture where he was impersonated by Edward G. Robinson, was an unlikely Argonaut to the Rocky Mountain diggings from the rock-ribbed state of Vermont named Horace A. W. Tabor. So much has been written about Tabor's romance with another man's wife, his eventual marriage to Baby Doe, including an operatic score that was first sung, appropriately enough, at Central City, Colorado, only a few years back, and the tragic denouncement of this ill-starred alliance, that no useful purpose could be served here by its recapitulation.

Tabor's extravagances of conduct and money are, however, worthy of brief investigation because, for one thing, they are a perpetual source of delight to Coloradans and constitute an almost flawless paradigm of opulent vulgarity. Nothing in the record compares with Tabor's ostentations of solid-gold grossness which make the raucous rejoicings of Bet-a-Million Gates at the race track and the porcine gruntings of Diamond Jim Brady engorging oysters and orange juice the mannered elegances of exquisite breeding in comparison.

Part of the fascination of the Tabor legend is its reassuring message that good fortune, at least as long as precious metals in the old West continued to be its tangible evidences, could and often did select the most undeserving objects for its favor. Beyond the talents of an average journeyman stonecutter in his native Vermont and an undistinguished postmaster in the Colorado diggings, H. A. W. Tabor had little or nothing to recommend him to the attention, let alone the envy, of his fellow citizens. Yet fortune smiled

on him with beaming effulgence, showering down on him wealth
beyond the expectations of any but the most audacious dreamers
and, in the end, only withdrew her favors in the face of the most
persistent effrontery and bad judgment with which a rich man was
ever endowed.

Tabor was the living embodiment of the maxim that any fool
could become a millionaire but that it takes a genius to remain one.
He was no genius.

Coming West in the Pikes Peak rash of 1859, Tabor, with his first
wife, Augusta, a woman of forbidding mien and strict moral principles, worked various diggings without success and at length settled down to keeping a small store dealing in miner's supplies and
acting as postmaster at Oro City.

Presently there came to the little shop with its inventory of pick-
axes, giant powder, and mule shoes, two not very bright German
shoemakers named George Hook and August Rische beseeching
credit or a grubstake to take them on their way. Tabor was busy
playing draw poker with three of Oro City's more prominent
clubmen and *boulevardiers* and absent-mindedly told the suppli-
ants their credit was good for $17 and no more, to take what they
needed and be off. Tabor was too busy to superintend their selection of necessities from his stock and failed to notice that, when
they left, there also went along a full gallon of the proof spirits of
Bourbon County, Kentucky. It wasn't in the bill, but no matter; it
was the best investment Horace Tabor ever made.

The day was hot and, within a mile of camp, Rische and Hook
were moved to sit down in the shade of a handy tree and try the
contents of the jug. Lubrication stirred them to unwonted activity
and, without moving from the shade, they started digging into the
hillside. Had they dug a few feet removed in any direction, they
would have struck nothing but country rock. As it was and with
a minimum of effort, for the outcropping surfaced almost to the
top of the ground, they came upon silver ore of sensational rich-
ness. When it was properly monumented and staked, they hurried

to town to file their claim to what was shortly to become the Little Pittsburgh Mine. Without turning a hand, H. A. W. Tabor was on the way to becoming the richest man in Colorado.

∞◦∞·∞·∞

Although the carbonate fortunes of Colorado's bonanza years endowed many women with the means to live expensively, as witness Mrs. Spencer Penrose, Mrs. Crawford Hill, and the matchless lady spendthrift of them all, Evalyn Walsh McLean, none lived higher on the hog while she remained in funds and only Evalyn McLean achieved the national celebrity of Margaret Tobin Brown, who entered the mythology of money as "the Unsinkable Mrs. Brown," heroine of the *Titanic*.

The wife of a diamond-in-the-rough type miner named James J. Brown, the Unsinkable Mrs. Brown had her origins across the railroad tracks and never made it at the grade crossing so far as Denver's formal society was concerned, a circumstance that brackets her with Cleveland's Mrs. James Corrigan who enjoyed social success and acceptance everywhere except at home. Like Laura Corrigan, Mrs. Brown gained entree to foreign circles where no prejudice was entertained against American gaucheries if they were sufficiently underwritten with hard cash, but the Sacred Thirty-six over which towered the emerald tiara of Mrs. Crawford Hill refused to be impressed by Molly Brown's exploits even after her elevation to the status of heroine. Formal dinners at the Country Club never knew her presence.

The legend of the Unsinkable Molly Brown has been one to confuse historians because of a penchant for picturesque mendacity on the part of its principal figure. The truth wasn't in her when fabrication suited her ends, which was most of the time, and the resulting fabric of conflicting facts has confused even so meticulous a chronicler of Colorado's golden years as Gene Fowler. Although her married name was Mrs. James J. Brown, she became less and less closely associated with her pipe-smoking husband's Irish brogue as she removed further and further from Leadville, so that in London she had no hesitation about claiming to be the spouse of multimillionaire Leadville Johnny, who in fact was John F. Campion, principal owner of the Little Johnny Mine where Jim Brown was employed.

Then, too, there was the first of the many legends about Molly Brown's ascendant fortunes. As first circulated, it was to the effect that Jim Brown had struck it rich early in their Leadville days, sold out for $250,000 spot cash, and after a night of celebration been carried home the worse for wear by kind friends to the Brown manse, which at the time was a two-room miner's cottage on Fryer Hill. Before they left, the night being cold, his companions thoughtfully built a good hot fire in the stove where Jim had but a moment before stashed his newfound fortune in banknotes.

"Never mind, darling," Jim is supposed to have told his wife the next morning, "there's plenty more where that came from."

That afternoon he is supposed to have brought in the Little Johnny, one of Leadville's greatest bonanzas.

Critics have since pointed out that most transactions at the time and place were in gold and that Irish Jim Brown's mentality was of the sort that would have recoiled from paper currency with gestures. On the other hand, nobody could have carried $250,000 in double eagles, provided that was the amount actually involved.

In any event, the record attests the fact that Jim Brown was, in the late eighties, employed as one of the superintendents at the Little Johnny and a very good miner indeed. In the liberal manner of the age, the Little Johnny's principal owner, John Campion, whom Molly was to claim as her husband from sufficient remove, gave Brown an eighth share in the property which was then in full production, an equity amounting to perhaps $2,000,000, which was a good deal of money in the Denver eighties. In its own dimension it was enough to allow Molly to travel extensively and to lie even more extensively about her resources, so that by the time the reporters and feature writers got through with it, Molly was the lady Croesus of California Gulch.

The Browns couldn't wait to shake the dust of Leadville from their stout brogans and assume the ways of city folk in Denver where they bought a residence of the sort spoken of at the time as a mansion at 1340 Pennsylvania Street, whose parapet was ornamented with four carved stone lions that were shortly to become landmarks in the Queen City of the Plains.

Armed with no more than a million or two, but determined to spend without stint to achieve her ends, Molly Brown began her prolonged assault on what proved to be the impervious portals of Denver's upper crust. She called, all unintroduced, on members of Mrs. Crawford Hill's set, who never seemed to be at home. Still without introduction, she sent invitations to lavish buffets, dinners, and supper parties which were also studiously ignored so that the neighboring children had to be asked in to consume oceans of chicken à la king, quail in aspic, and ornamental ices. She wrote letters to the newspapers to call attention to herself, which society editors were happy to print with grammar and orthography intact, and in no time at all the future Unsinkable Mrs. Brown had made herself so impossible that even the kinder-hearted members of Denver society, who might eventually have eased her into its outer fringes, recoiled from her name as from a witticism in bad taste.

Mrs. Brown's notion of fashionable attire may conservatively be described as bizarre and her taste in expensive and preposterous fur coats was so celebrated that members peering at her progress from behind the brownstone-framed windows of the impeccable Denver Club shouted with mirth and brought others hurrying from the bar with the cry of "Here comes Colorado's unique fur-bearing animal!"

The domestic existence of Molly and Jim Brown bore a startling resemblance to that of Maggie and Jiggs in the cartoon funnies of an only slightly later age devised by George McManus. Molly, like her counterpart in the Sunday supplements, longed for grandeur and associations with the *bon ton*. Down-to-earth Jim, the hard-rock miner, was the prototype of Jiggs who hankered for Dinty Moore's corned beef and the boys in the back room at the corner saloon.

When Mrs. Brown, by now known as "the Impossible" Mrs. Brown, planned gala fetes in their mansion and, attired in what downgraded *couturiers* assured her was the height of fashion, awaited in her ballroom the guests that never came, Jim Brown foregathered in the furnace room with boon companions and a case of whisky, not to reappear until the coast was clear.

Ravenous for publicity and recognition, Mrs. Brown seems to have been uncommonly naïve, even for a girl from the far side of the Leadville tracks. She had her photograph taken against studio backdrops in a variety of attires and artistic poses, looking coyly at stuffed birds or wielding the long cane with jeweled hilt which she somehow associated with a dictator of fashion, and mailed them to society editors with affidavits to the effect that they were casual snapshots exposed at splendid routs attended by Denver's Four Hundred at the Brown manse on Pennsylvania Street.

Add to these adverse circumstances the fact that Molly Brown undeniably looked like the public concept of an Irish washwoman and even more closely resembled the type as years went by, and it is understandable that even the occasional down-at-the-heel foreign adventurers of title who prospected Denver were unavailable to her charms.

The unhappy truth was that Molly was totally lacking in any of the sensibilities that might have entitled her to being taken seriously in a formal order of things. When she learned that Mrs. Crawford Hill, whom she regarded as the greatest single obstacle to her social pretensions, was about to be presented at the Court of St. James's, she waited on the American ambassador with demands that she too was eligible for the accolade of royalty, and it was with difficulty that the embassy was cleared of her presence. It had been simpler for an earlier American minister to reject a parallel claim on his offices by Eilley Orrum, the Washoe seeress and first of the Comstock millionaires from Nevada, when she wished to take tea with Queen Victoria. Eilley had been divorced and was automatically removed from the Queen's acceptability.

Entree to the Court of St. James's was less difficult for other Colorado heiresses, however, and Evalyn Walsh McLean, whose fortune was several hundred times that of Molly Brown's, had no difficulty, in the Calvin Coolidge regime of having distant friends accorded that honor. When Mrs. Edward F. Hutton wanted to be presented at the same Court with her daughter, Barbara, the then ambassador Alanson Houghton pointed out that because of the great pressure under which his office was laboring, it was quite impossible for more than one member of a family to secure the favor.

Mrs. James B. Duke offered Evalyn $1000 to her $10 that she couldn't get the matter fixed, and Evalyn was delighted to pocket her winnings after a phone call to Silent Cal at the White House.

But, although the most optimistic necromancer would have been hard put to see it, Molly Brown's finest hour was at hand when, in 1912, she decided to abandon Denver as a bad job and tour in foreign parts where her superior person and her still abundant dollars would be appreciated.

Fate decreed that she should take passage home, after a tour of the less exclusive European spas and *plages,* aboard the Royal Mail Ship *Titanic,* bound out of Southampton on her maiden voyage. Jim Brown was not along, having packed his Gladstone valise and headed for parts unknown when he returned one day to the House of Lions to find that his wife, in a moment of mistaken hospitality, had turned his grounds over to an encampment of Cheyenne Indians who had pitched tepees on the lawn and were sleeping in the Fritschle electric automobile in the coach house.

Like many phases in the lives of the great, Mrs. Brown's first days out of Southampton on the ill-fated luxury liner are clouded and, aside from the fact that she carried a Colt's automatic pistol in her muff and let it be known that she was a Girl of the old West who could take care of herself in any company, she seems to have attracted little attention. The bridge games of Major Archie Butt, the dinners ordered by Colonel John Jacob Astor, the merest conversational pleasantries of knightly old Isidor Straus, all somehow survived in retrospect to be incorporated into that classic of disaster, Walter Lord's A *Night to Remember.* But not Mrs. James J. Brown. She was just one more queer old American woman, reputedly wealthy, who wore eccentric fur coats and would eventually have to be dissuaded from performing in the Ship's Concert the last night out.

Late on the *Titanic's* last evening afloat, Mrs. Brown was moved to take a quick turn around the deck before retiring to her cabin and appeared muffled against the cold in the following inventory of garments: a suit of woolen unmentionables, a pair of heavy walking bloomers that she had purchased in Switzerland and which fastened at the knee with elastics, two woolen petticoats, a walking dress of Scotch cashmere, heavy woven golf stockings, a pair of sensible flat-heeled shoes, knitted mittens, and a $4000 Russian sable muff in which reposed her automatic pistol. Over this ensemble she chose to wear a $60,000 chinchilla evening cape.

If, as Gene Fowler later was to remark, anyone ever was dressed to meet an iceberg it was Molly Brown.

The details of the *Titanic's* last doomed hours are not the concern of this chronicle save in that, as the luxury ship and so many of her celebrated sailing list plunged to the bottom of the Atlantic, Molly Brown found herself in No. 6 lifeboat with twenty-eight survivors, all but two of them women, many of them crazed with fear that the *Titanic's* suction would carry them with her under the waves.

"I'll row," said Mrs. Brown, who was already starting to assume the "unsinkable" role she would play to the hilt beginning the next morning. "I haven't for years—but I learned when I was a child on the banks of the Mississippi. I bet I still can."

Shortly after this it was apparent that many of the women and children in No. 6 had come away without appropriate garments and were suffering intensely from the bitterly cold night air that followed in the wake of the fatal iceberg. Off came the sable cape to be wrapped around a shivering coal trimmer who had come away from the stokehold in nothing but a pair of trousers. Soon afterward the expensive tweed walking dress went to cover a whimpering woman in the bows and the formidable woolen petticoats were wrapped around ill-clad children, while Mrs. Brown, increasingly a figure of terror as her garments were peeled from her ample person, swore mighty Leadville blasphemies at able-bodied survivors who were reluctant to man the oars.

"Row, you sons of bitches," she thundered at the cowering occupants of No. 6, "row or I'll let daylight into you," and she brandished the Colt's with fine disregard for the fact that no daylight was available at the moment.

The Unsinkable Mrs. Brown achieved immortality standing in the back of a lifeboat in the midnight North Atlantic attired in her underwear while brandishing a pistol and using language that would have been offensive in Leadville.

Next morning when the *Titanic's* survivors were safe aboard the *Carpathia,* Mrs. Brown appointed herself a one woman USO, nursing the shaken survivors in the *Carpathia's* saloon that had been turned into an emergency ward, comforting the distraught, and raising a purse of $7000 for women who found themselves widows with none to meet them at the pierhead in New York. A robust and profane angel of mercy, she was veritably a heroine of a disaster that shocked the world.

It was when the reporters swarmed aboard the *Carpathia* at New York that Molly became unsinkable.

"I had typical Brown luck," she told representatives of the Fourth Estate, "I'm unsinkable."

It would be pleasant to record that, having achieved a genuine celebrity in the nation's press, whose emissaries besieged her for months thereafter as a Sunday editor's dream, Molly Brown grew more responsible, but the reverse, alas, is true.

It was now that she assumed the role of the wife of Leadville Johnny, Colorado Croesus, and an heiress of limitless resources. She took to fancy resorts where she had no authentic friends and paraded the lobbies of expensive hotels at Palm Beach, Newport, and New York, in attire that was increasingly exotic. She showered money on servants, demanded the best of everything, and lived up to the role of fabulously wealthy widow in all but fact.

When in Denver she preferred staying at the Brown Palace Hotel to her home, the House of Lions, and let it be known that she and not Henry C. Brown was the true owner of this eye-popping hostel. She let the society editors know that she was about to become a member of the British peerage, but nothing came of it. She redecorated the House of Lions as her concept of a bower of the muses and gave recitations, readings, and levees which were attended by few but shameless hangers-on who came to sponge and sneer. On these occasions she was attended by a diminutive Negro whom she had attired as a Nubian slave in silk sash, turban, and flowing trousers, with shoes turned up like the noses of the Four Hundred. She uncovered a former dramatic coach of Sarah Bernhardt whom she hired for a startling fee to cram her for the role of L'Aiglon and mounted a full-dress presentation of this classic in Paris with herself in the Bernhardt role. It was accounted by the critics a greater catastrophe than the *Titanic*.

And everywhere she went she personified the essence of corn that she came to believe was the aristocratic mien when she was a miner's bride in Leadville. A tall duchess's cane like that carried by Madame Du Barry became her hallmark and with it she poled her way through the lobbies of de luxe hotels and opera houses in London, Paris, and Nice. In the evening this shepherdess's crook was adorned with fresh flowers to match her dresses. She became an international eccentric, one of the sights to see at the Royal Poinciana in Palm Beach or on the boat deck of the *Mauretania* where she perhaps longed for another disaster comparable to the *Titanic*.

Her final gesture was as spacious and, alas, as spurious as the many that had preceded it; she offered to redeem the $14,000 mortgage on the Matchless Mine in Leadville, where a colorful contemporary, Baby Doe Tabor, by now as mad as a Macbeth witch, was living in destitution that was to end in death.

But the Unsinkable Mrs. Brown had no $14,000. In 1922, Jim Brown had died intestate with the result that what remained of the once ample estate was besieged by fortune hunters and impostors. Molly's claim to great wealth had attracted many claimants.

She died ten years after her Jim, a dowdy inmate of a single room in a New York women's club hotel where she frightened occupants of the elevators with her Du Barry cane and muttered snatches from Racine and other classic French dramatists.

Accused in her lifetime of being profligate with money, the Unsinkable Mrs. Brown had been fond of laying her spendthrift ways to a generosity that was as big as all outdoors. "I have a heart like a ham," she used to say. History has returned the verdict that simple, ambitious, homely, strident, boastful, generous Molly Brown not only had a heart that was big as a ham; she was ham all over.

❦ · ❦ · ❦

Although not a Coloradan but a Clevelander, Mrs. Laura Corrigan was similar to the Unsinkable Mrs. Brown on so many points that it may perhaps be as well to rehearse some of the more significant aspects of her finance and extravagance here as at any more appropriate point in this gently guided trip through the world's affluent precincts.

Up to a point, Laura Corrigan was Molly Brown all over again, only in a Midwestern setting. Pushy, preposterous, and repulsed, a reject and cull of the social *faubourgs* of Cleveland and New York, she was as celebrated for her malapropisms and preposterous pretensions as ever Molly Brown had been in the days when she poled her way through the resort hotel lobbies of Cannes and Nice with a jeweled shepherd's crook while telling all who would listen that she was the veritable Queen of the Rocky Mountain Elect.

Born Laura Mae Whitrock in 1895, very much a contemporary of Molly Brown, Mrs. Corrigan was the daughter of a Waupaca, Wisconsin, journeyman carpenter and handyman. She went to

Chicago and worked as a waitress until she contrived to marry the house physician at the socially irreproachable Blackstone Hotel, her first step up the social ladder which she was to climb with such resolution despite the catcalls and sneezes of rude spectators.

As the wife of Dr. Duncan MacMartin, she contrived to scrape up a number of acceptable acquaintances among the Blackstone's patrons, a number of them Clevelanders, among whom was James Corrigan, an ironmaster who was one of the two founders of the great Corrigan-McKinney Steel Co. A quiet divorce from Dr. MacMartin was arranged, but her subsequent marriage to Corrigan could scarcely pass unnoticed when he gave her as a wedding present, as has been noted by Cleveland Amory, a $16,500 Rolls-Royce town car with footman and chauffeur on the box who had formerly been in service to George Gould. Mr. Amory assigns their domestic pedigree to Jay Gould which may be in minor error since Jay Gould died in 1892 and had no motorcars. George is a more likely candidate and would be equally gratifying to Mrs. Corrigan.

Even the Rolls-Royce complete with Gould footman, Jay's or George's, was unable to pass the massive portals of Cleveland's Shaker Heights formal society. Cleveland did not cotton to Mrs. Corrigan's background and as concrete evidence of his special disapproval, Corrigan's father died and left his holdings in Corrigan-McKinney only to his son in trust, to be administered by Laura's archenemy, Price McKinney. Undismayed, Laura Corrigan contrived to purchase the pivotal holdings of a third partner which gave James Corrigan control of the corporation just before he conveniently dropped dead in the Cleveland Athletic Club.

Laura Corrigan was now in the authentic big money. In relatively taxless 1927, $800,000 a year went a long way and it took her as fast as passage could be booked via the Cunard Line to London, Paris, and other outposts where American money, far from being suspect because it was new, was welcomed for, as Damon Runyon said, the pleasure it seemed to incline to buy.

Almost before you could say "Room service" Mrs. Corrigan had collected around her a docile zoo of dukes, marquises, counts, barons, and other only slightly shopworn coronets and was firmly emplaced in public and commercial esteem for her extravagances, as a sort of forerunner of Lady Bernard Docker of later gold-plated Daimler fame. Her gestures, such as buying out at one fell swoop the entire delicatessen department of Fortnum & Mason to be sent to her apartment for a light collation, didn't escape public attention and in short order Laura Corrigan was one of the institutional American expatriates along with Berry Wall and James Hazen Hyde. She provided what was generally considered at the time to be the most generous free meal ticket for downgraded entries in Burke's Peerage this side of James Gordon Bennett.

She remained in France doing war work which achieved her government recognition and ended up practically on the status of Ann Morgan as a professional friend of France. Her decorations hadn't cost more than an aggregate of $6,000,000, mostly in the form of wine and food fed into the right faces, and she ended her public days in a blaze of glory as bright as any Christmas pudding served to deserving prime ministers and out-of-work dukes.

She organized the greatest safari ever mounted by a white woman in Africa which was at such notable odds with that of her contemporary, Mrs. E. T. Stotesbury, who organized a $500,000 hunting expedition in order to kill sufficient alligator skins to make herself a suite of traveling bags and hatboxes, that Laura achieved the praise of humanitarians and animal lovers as well as unprecedented newspaper lineage. "For pure comfort amid tropical rigors," wrote Cleveland Amory, "Laura Corrigan organized a safari that has never been equaled. She took with her, in three airplanes, a newspaperman, a photographer, two maids, two secretaries, a doctor, a nurse, two cooks, three waiters, a hairdresser, a manicurist, and a dressmaker. She scoured the Dark Continent for fourteen animals of varying degrees of rarity. These she did not shoot but captured them alive and, with infinite tact, sent them, along with $5000 for their food, to the Cleveland Zoo."

Since the long hunting of Sir St. George Gore in the Shining Mountains of another time there has never been anything in the elegance sweepstakes quite comparable to the African safari of Laura Corrigan. One likes to think of her at dinnertime, her retinue around her dressed for the evening in the best British tradition of the jungle, the chef busy with *les quenelles de brocheton Nantua* and *contrefilet à la Clamart,* the waiters icing martinis, and the photographer as busy as ever was Jerome Zerbe at a night of gala at El Morocco, while in the tropical night distant drums announce the advent of a great female potentate, a matriarch and her retinue from a far country called Cleveland, a veritable queen in her own right, which is just what Laura Corrigan had wanted to be all along.

ᑯᕯᐧᑯᕯᐧᑯᕯ

The peer, or perhaps peeress would be more appropriate, of The Unsinkable Molly Brown and later Mrs. James Corrigan in the ostentatious vulgarity sweepstakes in Paris at the turn of the century was a Mrs. Kate Moore, the source of whose American wealth was clouded but the magnitude of which was beyond doubting. An ambitious hostess, she even rivaled James Gordon Bennett as a collector of bogus titles and shopworn aristocrats who crowded her hospitable board in menacing numbers and drank her champagne in Niagaras. It was her practice each year to subscribe to no fewer than thirty grand-tier boxes every night for the duration of the Italian opera season at the Châtelet which she filled with ornate but questionable dukes and deposed Carpathian monarchs who had been gentled for the evening with superb food and wine. On one occasion, so great was her fame as the most formidable of climbers, that she managed to get Edward VII as a dinner guest at Biarritz. The monarch was amused at her gaucheries and pretensions and remarked, not unkindly, that she should have lived in the age of Louis XIV. "There were kings all over the place then," he told her. When she died, Mrs. Moore left generous bequests to those who had assisted her in her campaigns against continental society, and a boulevard wit remarked, "Mrs. Moore departed from life as she would from the Ritz, handing out tips to everyone."

๑โ๑ · ๑โ๑ · ๑โ๑

Although he visited San Francisco at only the most infrequent intervals and, at the time of his death at the age of seventy-four in 1939, hadn't seen the Golden Gate in a decade, Spencer Penrose maintained active membership in the Pacific Union, the town's most exclusive and expensive gentlemen's club on the top of Nob Hill, as long as he lived. Asked why he remained a member of a club he never used, Penrose's reply was characteristic.

"My God, man!" he said in astonished tones, "I might want a drink out there!"

The idea of drinking in a public premises, although he was at the time sole owner of Colorado Springs' Broadmoor Hotel, the Rocky Mountain region's most dazzling resort, never occurred to him. That he might not want a drink at any place, any time, was equally unthinkable. Therefore, it was only prudent to maintain membership and with it the availability of bourbon whisky at strategically located clubs around the landscape.

His home base for such activities was, of course, the Broadmoor where, when prohibition loomed ominously on the horizon, he caused to be built the biggest private cellars west of the Mississippi. It is probable that the only ones on the other side of the river that could rival them were those of Secretary of the Treasury Andrew W. Mellon in Pittsburgh. Mellon was richer than Penrose, and besides, he was owner of Old Overholt Distillers.

Spencer Penrose, perhaps the most conspicuous of all Colorado's long and gorgeous tally of swashbuckling grandees, began life as a black sheep, the youngest son of eminently well-placed Philadelphia parents, the sort of youth who, in an English family of comparable consequence, having missed the title, passed up the Army, and rejected the cloth, ended up a pucka sahib in the tea gardens of Darjeeling or a prospector in the Rand.

He was born at an impeccable address, 1331 Spruce Street, November 2, 1865. His father was Philadelphia's most popular obstetrician and his mother a celebrated beauty. Most Penroses married either Drexels or Biddies and as a result were related to everybody of importance along the Main Line and in the Gerard Bank. Spec, as he was known from earliest boyhood, graduated from Harvard in '86, the only thinkable background for a man who was, almost immediately, to become a legend of fist-fighting, self-assertive masculinity in the tough mining towns of the old West. He was also broke, comparatively speaking, when he hit Colorado, a necessary ingredient in any saga of genteel rags to rowdy riches.

When he started West, his older brother by four years, Boise Penrose, who was destined to make something of a name for himself too in Pennsylvania politics, warned him: "Don't take on anybody bigger than you are." It was advice wasted.

Spec Penrose already had a friend well established in Colorado. His name was Charlie Tutt and in 1892 as the first aureate echoes of Cripple Creek began reverberating on the world's mining exchanges, Tutt urged his Philadelphia neighbor to come on out, big doings were in prospect. Tutt had also written letters telling about the wonderful country, the splendid saloons and big bar at the Antlers, the remarkable beauty of the Colorado girls, and the polo balls, all of which presupposed the sort of frontier society that would welcome a handsome young man of irreproachable person and antecedents, even if momentarily on the shorts.

Penrose was not the sort to make anything but a grand entrance. Tutt put him up at the Cheyenne Mountain Country Club and the first evening he beat up a polo player and tossed him through a French window, glass and all. It was an episode that set the tone for the rest of his life as Colorado's number-one cutup, showpiece, magnifico, and public benefactor. Lesser personages might indulge in fisticuffs and attract no attention; it was not a docile age. A

Philadelphia Penrose and Harvard man could only be challenged by equals and in the precincts of Colorado Springs in the nineties, a polo player was about as equal as they came.

Thinking to cool his ardors, Tutt placed Penrose in charge of his affairs at nearby Cripple Creek, the principle asset of which was the C.O.D. Mine which Tutt had prospected the year previous. Penrose made a personal assay of Cripple Creek, a howling wilderness and suburb of hell whose Myers Avenue was the widest-open red-light district anywhere outside Butte, Montana, and whose three booming railroads were daily rolling up the hill with palace cars filled with additional girls, madams, hard-rock miners, anarchists, three-card monte men, tippers of the keno goose, whisky salesmen, confidence-game artists, eastern capitalists, newspaper reporters, and real-estate speculators.

Penrose liked what he saw. The town liked Penrose, too, especially the girls of all classes and categories from Myers Avenue to mine superintendents' wives. The only criticism anybody had was of Spec's clothes. He wore beautifully tailored riding breeches and English boots that cost $100 a pair. Apprised that the community considered him a dude in some respects, Penrose at once sent East for a suit of evening tails and a half-dozen opera hats and started dressing for dinner. There were a few catcalls at first but most of the roughnecks who took exception to his attire were out of the hospital as good as new in two or three weeks.

Cripple Creek was something new under the sun that shone refulgently on the mining camps of the old West. The cast of characters had been fairly standardized at Alder Gulch, Virginia City, Austin, Eureka, and Treasure Hill and had included sourdough prospectors and primeval saloonkeepers, madams and their girls, a Wells Fargo route agent, and an appropriate number of professional gamblers, and sometimes a frontier newspaperman. In time, if it turned out to be a proven diggings, the original discoverers, the sourdoughs who monumented the first claims, were bought out by big money from San Francisco or the East. Incompetence, gambling, drink, and lead poisoning robbed them of their small holdings and, in any event, they would have been forced out later if not sooner because, as the mines went deeper into hard rock and the superficial deposits were exhausted, money and machinery were needed for the operation of the deeper diggings. The discoverers didn't have this sort of thing; outside capitalists did and brought with them as well the intelligence and know-how to build a railroad. The transition from tent and shack town to metropolis complete with a railroad depot, international hotel, gas-lit barrooms of great opulence with reclining nudes and crystal drinking tools, and, like as not, an opera house, took very few years. It took place almost overnight if the mines found real bonanza as they did at Goldfield, Nevada, and Cripple Creek.

Cripple Creek's something new was a tight-knit cadre of young easterners who by every American standard could be called gentlemen. Most of them were, like Spec Penrose and Charlie Tutt, younger sons of well-to-do families in Boston, Philadelphia, and New York. They had college educations from Ivy League academies such as Harvard, Princeton, Yale, and Columbia. They wore city clothes with assurance and they were tougher than they looked.

One of these well-connected young men was Albert E. Carlton who was to become the acknowledged kingpin of Cripple Creek in its palmiest days and later a magnate of more than local importance when he purchased the faltering Colorado Midland Railroad. His wife Ethel and Spec Penrose's widow Julie were, as long as they lived, the ranking dowagers of Colorado Springs, which meant the ordained social rulers of the Rocky Mountain West. There was Horace Devereaux, a Princeton boy whose expertise on the polo field was legendary. While this might not at first sight seem an asset among the smelters and deep diggings, it made him very much a figure at The Springs, where the Cripple Creek industrial complex was owned and where its dominant personalities made their homes. The Cheyenne Mountain stage was for a time driven by Harry Leonard, improbably a graduate of St. Mark's School at Southborough, Massachusetts, and Columbia. Harvard men in wing collars, pin-stripe suits, and bowler hats were a dime a dozen at the Topic Dance Hall and the long bar off the lobby of the Palace Hotel, a premises which lent éclat to one of Cripple's recurrent conflagrations when its boilers blew up and added explosion to the already gathering holocaust.

These dashing ornaments of Cripple Creek, Verner Reed, Harry Blackmer, Harry Leonard, Bert Carlton, Charles MacNeill, and Spencer Penrose, all of them born on the right side of the tracks, were to remain there all their lives and leave fortunes in their aggregate coming to more than $200,000,000. What set them apart from the Silver Kings of the Comstock, the bearded old builders of the Pacific Railroad, and the later copper nabobs of Butte and Helena was that they had been born to wealth and, in coming to Cripple Creek, merely sought more of it. They had the tastes and habit of people accustomed to fine homes, rare wines, evening attire, and polo for relaxation, which set them apart from, say, the Big Four of the Southern Pacific and their California contemporary magnates, most of whom had never encountered a house footman before they were in their own right millionaires and who, as a result, approached the amenities of life with inept gestures and reticences.

The litmus-paper test for separating the self-made millionaires of the American West from the inheritors who improved their already elevated social and economic status seems to have been their footing with God. Collis P. Huntington spoke frequently of God and at all times assumed attitudes of public piety. He had the facts of Promontory Point and the Gold Spike ceremony rearranged in a painting to show him conspicuously in communion with a clergyman. Spec Penrose gave God little time and when, after his death his widow joined the Catholic Church and majored in good works, it was commonly remarked that she was in some measure trying to atone for his lack of spirituality.

As if awaiting Spec Penrose's entrance, Cripple Creek began the most sensational booming of any gold camp in the old West. Its grand production of high-grade gold over the sixty-one years that it remained in bonanza has been estimated by Marshall Sprague, the official historian of the region, at $432,974,848. This was, of course, peanuts compared to the Witwatersrand in South Africa which has supplied more than half the world's gold supply to date in the sum of $9,714,900,000. In the late 1930s after Cripple was hopelessly in borasca, its total was surpassed by both Kirkland Lake and the Porcupine Diggings in Ontario and by the Hearst Home-stake Mine in South Dakota, the last of these a single operation. But at the turn of the century when it was consistently producing as much as $17,000,000 in gold ore a year, there was nothing comparable to Cripple. The Comstock Lode in Virginia City, Nevada, 1000 miles and four mountain ranges and three deserts away, was, of course, a silver camp with only an incidental yield of gold.

The C.O.D., in common with every other gopher hole in Cripple Creek, yielded handsome profits to its owners, but early in the game Penrose and Tutt became convinced that the real profits in mining were to be made from milling, not digging, the ore. Mining was a speculation. Milling was a relatively stabilized commercial operation. Together with Charles M. MacNeill, a brilliant mill designer, the partners built mills at Colorado City. In only a few years the Tutt-Penrose mills were handling more than three quarters of Cripple's low-grade ore at fabulous profits and at thirty-eight Penrose was rich enough to retire.

The intervening years had not been without episode. When he first hit Cripple Creek in '92 Spec had wired his by now well-established brother Boise, back in Philadelphia, asking for a grubstake of $10,000 to invest in Tutt's C.O.D. Boise had sent him $150 carfare and instructions to come home and stop making a fool of himself. Spec cheerfully invested the $150 in the C.O.D. and a few years later sent his patronizing older brother a cashier's draft for $10,000. It was the interest on his investment, he explained casually.

But even though he was a millionaire ten times over, Penrose was still under forty and full of beans. He dreamed of real money. He felt he had the Midas touch and events justified this suspicion.

An employee at the Tutt-Penrose mills named Daniel C. Jackling had a crazy notion that a process could be perfected for the profitable milling of low-grade copper ore which was available in almost limitless abundance, whole mountains of it, no further away than Utah. Until now big copper operators like the Guggenheims had refused to handle anything but almost pure copper, wasting so much in their skimming of the cream that their very tailings promised incalculable wealth if the means for treating them on a vast scale were perfected. Jackling claimed he could, given a pilot mill and a few hundred thousand dollars, evolve such a process. That he was correct in his surmise is suggested by the statistic that after his death many years later in California, it required five full years at their adding machines for the auditors even to estimate the Jackling fortune.

Penrose and Tutt put up $500,000 for Jackling's experimental mill and incorporated it as the Utah Copper Company. Overnight the entire copper-producing industry was revolutionized and the price of low-grade ore on the mine dumps of Bingham and Garfield tripled in value. Utah Copper had taken the precaution of buying up several million tons of low-grade ore bodies including some of the Guggenheims' discarded tailings. When Charlie Tutt felt he was crowding his luck and decided to unload, Spec Penrose bought his holdings in Utah Copper, making him the majority stockholder. When his profits from copper were averaging $200,000 a month, Penrose was still ploughing them back into Utah Copper for more ore bodies, more open pit mines, more mills, and more railroads to haul his wealth around. As the merest sidelines and with the loose cash that assembled from time to time on his bureautop, Spec revitalized three declining gold mines in Cripple Creek to a point where they were again operating in wildest bonanza. He created the beet-sugar industry in western Kansas and he built the Broadmoor Hotel, the last of which never made a dime in his lifetime if only because good-natured Penrose allowed it to be turned into a nest of thieves, moochers, spongers, and incompetent pensioners.

Chefs left the Broadmoor at regular intervals to start restaurants of their own on stolen steaks and embezzled lamb chops.

In the 1920s Penrose negotiated the sale of Utah Copper to the Kennecott Copper Company. He emerged from the lists with approximately $40,000,000 in profits despite the fact that along the way he had lost what most men would consider substantial fortunes in such ventures as real estate in the city of Penrose, just north of Florence, Colorado, and Alaska gold stocks. It cost him $500,000 to have a town named after him and he never gave it a thought. On one of his ranches he experimented with burning the range grass annually until one spring the fire got out of hand and burned up most of El Paso County. Penrose paid for the county and told his foreman to be more careful in future.

Penrose's greatest monument of all was the Broadmoor Hotel, which stands today, making money for a change, at the foot of Cheyenne Mountain, one of the extravagantly operated resort hotels of the world. It is difficult to run down the well-established Colorado legend that Penrose built and placed the Broadmoor in operation as a gesture of retaliation for being rebuked by the management of the Antlers when he rode his saddle horse up the front steps and into the bar. There are several redactions of the saga including one to the effect that the bartender gave the horse a mickey finn and another that it wasn't the hoof marks on the deep pile carpet that grieved the management, but Spec's inconsiderate habit of shooting drinks out of the hands of customers at the far end of the bar.

Whatever his motivation, he did indeed build the Broadmoor. And he built it at some expense to the competition, too, since he took with him from the Antlers the hotel's manager and its *chef de cuisine*. General Palmer had made Billy Dunning manager of The Springs' most opulent resort in 1901 and Dunning had hired a high-strung Italian prima donna named Louis Stratta to run the very extensive kitchens. This was at a time when the Antlers advertised that it could, on short notice, prepare and serve any recognized dish of any national cuisine from any part of the civilized globe. Besides his saucepan lore, Stratta appealed to Spec Penrose's sense of magnificence; his favorite occupation was shooting wild-life on the Great Plains adjacent to Colorado Springs from a 1913 Pierce-Arrow touring car. This he accomplished by sitting on the back of the driver's seat and steering with his feet, which left his hands free to decimate the ranks of coyotes, antelopes, and prairie chickens with shotgun and rifle.

Such virtuosity, Penrose felt, must be the identifying hallmark of a chef of Escoffier dimensions, although subsequent investigation disclosed that Stratta encountered serious difficulty cooking a dish of ham and eggs. He brought with him an *élan* that Penrose admired, and Dunning came along at double the salary he had been getting from General Palmer.

The Broadmoor opened in 1918 at a cost to Penrose of better than $3,000,000 although, because the owner never stopped improving it, the investment was to become much more with the passing of time.

In its *décor* Spec indulged his wildest flights of fancy and caprices of grandeur. When it first opened there was a vast riding academy adjacent to the hotel with half a hundred for-hire horses who didn't rent very well but whom Penrose kept on the payroll because he admired to dress much of the time in riding clothes and the horses validated his appearing in stock collars and tweed breeches. He admired to have exotic animal life in the ornamental waters around the hotel and started out with seals. The seals found that the water was too cold for their liking and it was much more fun to flap around the hotel's stately red-plush lobby where the guests encouraged them in the notion that they were welcome. The seals were given the heave-ho and flamingos installed in their place with instructions to stand knee-deep in the water and look ornamental. The flamingos shortly discovered that there was food being served at tables on the adjacent terraces and verandas and joined the party, scaring hell out of dowagers over whose shoulders a long, scrawny neck would appear to snatch grilled sardines or whatever off their plate.

The flamingos joined the seals in outer darkness. So, too, did the horses; their stable was replaced by a monster skating rink with ice in July, and their place was taken by seven identical canary-yellow Lozier touring cars which Penrose and his wife shared on a super his-and-hers basis. In 1902, Penrose had married a pretty, well-endowed widow named Julie MacMillan whom he had met at a dance at the El Paso Club. Unwilling to propose in the manner sanctioned by tradition, he had followed her on a different liner to Nice and installed himself at a beach pavilion adjacent to the one he knew she would occupy. On her appearance he made no mention of tender emotions but in a businesslike way pulled a letter from his pocket. It was from his father in which Dr. Penrose said he approved of Mrs. MacMillan's antecedents and that if Spec married her, they should have his blessing and approval.

They remained married and enviably happy for thirty-three years. Julie Penrose was a perfect complement for her husband. She enjoyed fine clothes, grand hotel suites, numerous motorcars, big parties, and lots of the best of everything to eat and drink.

Penrose nursed nickels but thought nothing of losing great sums if they were lost stylishly and with éclat. Years before the first deep freeze was placed on the market, he built a vast and complicated mechanical icebox which, when they were in season and available in carload lots, he filled to the roof with the best Georgia watermelons. In mid-January following, he gave a watermelon party for 300 guests at which he figured every slice of melon as it came to the table cost him $9.85. He bought the Mt. Manitou incline railway because he admired to have picnics on the eminence it served, and at night there was always a pad and pencil at his bedside for jotting down fugitive notions that occurred to him in the midnight hours. One such message to himself, when it was retrieved in the morning, read: "Build concrete dam at Rosemont; don't spend more than a million on it! Dammit!"

Prohibition, when it came along to vex rich and poor alike, brought out the best in Penrose. Apprised that the time would shortly be at hand when it might not even be possible to get a drink at his strategically located clubs in New York, San Francisco, and Denver, he set methodically about abating the sufferings of himself and his friends for at least their lifetimes. Penrose had aroused admiration in his undergraduate days at Harvard by drinking a gallon of beer in just thirty-four seconds, and with this as a minimal standard of consumption, he undertook to provide for at least fifty years of legal deprivation without leaving Colorado Springs.

Liquor of all sorts started converging on the Broadmoor in freight-car lots where it was unloaded from the tracks of General Palmer's Rio Grande Railroad with armed guards in attendance. Two carloads of whisky came from his New York apartment. Two more came from the cellars of the Penrose sugar plantation in Hawaii. Something like 1000 cases of vintage champagne were rounded up from Charles & Company in New York, most of it, sad to relate, destined to perish in its bottles in the years before explorers penetrated to that part of the Broadmoor cellars. The entire bar stock of miscellaneous spirits and cordials was purchased from the Brown Palace in Denver. Another shipment of several thousand cases came from Philadelphia where Spec had inherited a magnificent collection of Ports, Madeiras, and cognacs from his brother Richard. All this hoard of potables was secreted in a vast labyrinth of cellars under the lakes and ornamental waters of the Broadmoor. Vaults, time locks, and round-the-clock watchmen guarded it so effectively that during the thirteen calamitous years that prohibition afflicted the land there was no record of any important theft or disappearance.

Much of the wine, unhappily, went bad from age and mistreatment that could have been avoided by an intelligent program of recorking and consumption as the wine achieved dubious longevity, but Julie Penrose, rational in all other matters, completely refused to have anything changed that had been instituted during her husband's lifetime. The corks, she said, had been bought by Spec and he ought to have known about corks. The will said nothing about recorking wine and nothing that could be kept static was going to be changed from the way Spec left it.

Housekeepers found the realization of this ideal difficult in their administration of rooms at the Broadmoor. Beds and other furniture both in public rooms and in private apartments were to stay just where they had been in Penrose's lifetime. Replacement of carpets that Spec had bought was forbidden. Servants that Spec had hired couldn't be discharged on any grounds short of arson.

On one occasion during the second world war, a close friend of the family got up courage to tell Julie Penrose that a ranking member of the culinary hierarchy was stealing her blind. The food at the Broadmoor, never Lucullan, was becoming a scandal because the embezzler was sending all the hotel's allowance of steaks and chops down the street to a Springs restaurant of which he was the principal owner. Here there was a sign in the kitchen: "Push Filet Mignon," while Broadmoor patrons couldn't get bacon with their morning eggs. Julie wasn't even cross. She not only believed her friend but said she'd known it all the time. "But Spec had hired the chef and he could have his job just as long as he didn't steal the carpet out of the front lobby."

Penrose was, like all personages of imperial dimension, a builder at heart. Long after the Broadmoor was completed, he maintained a full-time crew of 300 artisans, carpenters, carpet layers, glaziers, and construction men on the payroll just in case he had the whim in the middle of the night to build something.

One of these whims was to move his private zoo, another regal property, from its original location next door to the hotel to its present site, halfway up the side of Cheyenne Mountain. The whim was implemented by the fact that easy access to the cages had resulted in a monkey's biting a child, for which Penrose had to pay $8000 damages. He almost at once saw the advantages of relocating the zoo with properly protected dens for the immates.

Spec could be grand when large sums of money were involved and as irritable over a four-bit overcharge as Hetty Green. Once in

Peking in the early 1930s Julie had conned him into a shop specializing in rare art objects and antiquities where the proprietor had given them a full hour's sales pitch in an effort to unload a $15,000 item of Ming statuary. Julie was all ears while Penrose, an indifferent listener under such circumstances, buffed his nails and wondered where the next drink was coming from. When, exhausted by his own eloquence, the dealer at length lapsed into silence, Penrose reached for his hat. "Send along a dozen of those," he ordered from the doorway.

On another occasion Penrose attended a directors' meeting of Utah Copper carrying in his hand an inconsequential copper plumbing fixture. Millions of dollars were voted for plant replacement, loans in similar sums authorized from banks; Penrose gave the matters his bored attention. When the meeting had adjourned he buttonholed Charlie Tutt and shook the faucet under his nose. "Look at that goddamned sprinkler," he snarled. "The man at General Hardware charged me eighty-five cents for it. On the way down the street I saw the same thing at Cash Merc, for forty-five cents. I'm going back and throw it through the goddamned window at General Hardware."

Long after Spec Penrose's death, Mrs. Penrose continued the grand manner to which she had accustomed herself in his lifetime. She maintained her magnificent apartment at the Broadmoor, which was occupied after her death by her friend Ethel Carlton, but she wanted somewhere to have small dinners away from the hotel. In 1956, she built a sort of Petit Trianon near the Cooking Club which she called "The Shack" and which cost her, out of pocket, $178,000. She used it two or three times a year. She also, at a cost of $3000, built a little hanging bridge across the adjacent ravine so that guests going from The Shack to the Cooking Club could save walking less than 300 feet.

"It would have been better for all concerned had they been made to walk," says Marshall Sprague. "The bridge made you dizzy if you'd had a drink."

The Cooking Club was one of Spencer Penrose's solid-gold hobbies where his memory is perpetuated in an atmosphere of bonhomie to this day. It cost in the neighborhood of half a million dollars and in it is incorporated every known device for the preparation of the most exotic dishes. Ranges, grills, broilers, salamanders, ovens, iceboxes, and deep-freeze compartments are arranged in a multiplicity to bemuse the cookout experts at Abercrombie & Fitch. Here Penrose delighted to don a chefs apron and tall hat and regale groups of friends with fillets as thick as the armor plate on battle cruisers cooked in a special sauce and washed down by vintage clarets and Burgundies that stood him $25 a bottle wholesale. Unlike many amateur chefs, Penrose was an accomplished and skillful student of gastronomy, an expert with grilled steaks to rank with Samuel F. B. Morse, his opposite number as feudal overlord of Pebble Beach, California.

After Spencer Penrose had joined the perfumed shades whose origins had been approved of Rittenhouse Square and the Pennsylvania Railroad, Julie Penrose lent continuity to her husband's grand manner and added something of her own. On one occasion she had been dining with friends aboard a private car in the Colorado Springs railroad yards before being driven back to her apartment at the Broadmoor at an advanced hour. Over eighty at the time and frail, though indomitable, Mrs. Penrose by some accident of mischance contrived to tumble into the bathtub of her well-appointed dressing room.

"I wasn't hurt," she later deposed, "only startled, but I couldn't seem to get out of the tub. It was so late I hated to ring for Annie, my maid; she's so old, you know. So I just turned on the warm water and spent the night. It was entirely comfortable and I think good for a head cold I felt coming on. Annie helped me out in the morning when she came on duty, but I'm afraid it spoiled a nice new evening frock. It had just come from Worth in Paris."

And while contemplating the relics of Colorado's authentic magnificoes, we may well pause in brief salute to Mrs. Albert E.

Carlton when her Colorado Springs estate was appropriated by the federal government as an adjunct of the Air Force Academy. Ethel had experienced some difficulty in persuading her husband to so much as look at the place when she finished building it in 1931. When at length she conned him into moving in, it was just in time. He died the next evening.

In any event, the federal government paid Ethel Carlton only $125,000 for a property she had thought of in terms of three times as much. The news reached her from Merrill Shoup, her lawyer, by wireless when she was aboard the *United States* in mid-Atlantic, en route to Paris with Ralph Giddings, another heir to vast Colorado Springs resources.

"Ethel was brokenhearted," Giddings later told friends. "She at once sent for the chief dining room steward and ordered a double magnum of Krug's Private Cuvée and a five-pound-tin of fresh Beluga caviar which stood her about $200 and both of which we consumed then and there. She felt better right away."

A quarter of a century after Penrose's death, the Broadmoor Hotel is not only his most impressive tangible memorial, but a repository of the grand manner with which he admired to do everything. As part of El Pomar Foundation, the trust set up by Penrose to administer his benevolences, it has to make money and can no longer be regarded as the mere expensive whim of a free-spending rich man. Its value has grown from the initial $3,000,000 named when it was built to a point where the management regards the mention of $20,000,000 as a frivolous understatement, but its facade is the character of the man who built it.

In the hotel park are thirty-six live plains buffalo and two longhorn steers, wild, rangy animals whose bloodlines antedate the universal shorthorn of the present century and whose ancestors shared with the buffalo the limitless horizons of the old West. You can step 100 feet from the Turkish bath and purchase from an accredited breeder a $5000 Hereford bull or a twelfth-century Chinese Buddha for $4500 from Sarkisian's shop. Or Abercrombie & Fitch will sell you a $500 bamboo fly rod which can be tested through Abercrombie's open window in the hotel lake. The hotel swan dietician feeds 300 pounds of balanced swan ration every month to the hotel's four white and two black swans. The steward buys turkey in thirty-ton lots and fish is flown in weekly from Marseilles for the bouillabaisse on the Friday menu.

It is a concept in hospitality conducted along generous lines.

A profound sentimentalist, Penrose was a firm believer in keeping things the way they had always been, on the theory that they were apt to be better this way than they would be if changed. Once, in the 1930s, he stopped briefly in Philadelphia to see a friend and visit his birthplace at 1331 Spruce Street. It had not been occupied for years and not a piece of furniture had been moved in over half a century. An ancient butler met the master at the door as though he had only left that morning. A venerable cook appeared to get her orders for dinner. Penrose had kept it that way as a sort of family shrine, a memorial to his youth impervious to the hostile winds of change in a mutable world.

Even from the afterworld, Penrose exercised the baronial hospitality which had characterized his lifetime. A provision in his will set aside $10,000 whose income is to be spent annually on a Spencer Penrose cocktail party at the El Paso Club.

His more conventional bequests came to $125,000,000. It was the largest sum ever filed for probate in the Rocky Mountain region, a circumstance that Penrose would have liked.

Chapter Ten
The Men

Masculine Elegances of Attire . . . Every Man a Berry Wall . . . The Tiffany of Love Stores . . . Patrons Wore Evening Dress to Visit the Everleigh Sisters . . . The Cow Collectors and Amateurs of the Close Shave . . . Also, the Women . . . How to Be Well Dressed on $200,000 a year . . . The Big, Economy-Size Pearl Necklaces. . . .

IN THE REALM of masculine attire and adornment, a very considerable latitude must be invoked in reporting both the cost and dimensions of men's wardrobes and their accessories if for no other reason than that aspirants for honors in the sartorial sweepstakes have always been, in large measure, well traveled and that the same article of clothing may well run a considerable range of price, depending on where it is purchased. Less fluctuation obtains in the field of men's jewelry for the obvious reason that gold, platinum, and precious stones, if not skilled labor, tend to approximate the same value whether purchased in Paris, New York, London, or Hong Kong.

In the case of men's bespoke garments, however, the price range is a considerable one and has been for most of the years that are the general purview of this inquiry. To take as a standard of comparison a conventional men's three-piece business suit comprising jacket, trousers, and waistcoat of an acceptable material—sharkskin, hard-finished worsted cheviot, or flannel—in the middle sixties of the current century the price tag at Earl Benham, a highly esteemed New York custom tailor, is $300. The same suit for Henry Poole & Company of Cork Street, Burlington Gardens, London, carries a price tag of approximately $175, while a nearly identical garment from the firm of Fenwick of Hong Kong will stand the customer only $65. For purposes of simplification we will suppose the customer orders the garments from London and Hong Kong *in situ* and wears them then and there, thus obviating import taxes.

The material in all cases will be identical since bespoke tailors the world over procure their suitings from the same British sources, the great woolen merchants of the English Midlands and the equally esteemed weavers of choice fabrics in Scotland. There are almost no other sources of men's luxury cloth if you except the brief rash of Italian silk suitings which found such favor with American gangster types that they never made an appreciable impression on the market.

In London and in New York the workmanship in each case will be identical, painstaking, expert handcraft performed by an ancient guild whose numbers are shrinking alarmingly in a mechanized world of cheapness and shoddy. The product from Hong Kong will be as skillfully cut and designed as the other two, since Fenwick or any other Hong Kong bespoke tailor will undertake to duplicate any suit you wish them to use for a model, but the findings, that is to say the stuff inside the pockets, the thread with which the garments are sewn and the buttons attached, the lining, unless you specify a high-grade silk at a small extra charge, and the coarse materials used to stiffen shoulders and lapels will be of quality inferior to that used by reputable men's tailors in New York and London.

The same scale of prices with somewhat less variation in quality will obtain in general in the field of custom haberdashery. A pleated dress dinner shirt made to order by, say, Sulka of New York, Paris, or San Francisco at a cost of $30 will cost about a fifth of this amount at Fenwick of Hong Kong in the Hong Kong Hilton Hotel. The workmanship in this particular field is almost as good in one place as another since findings have no part in the manufacture of shirts, pajamas, and similar garments. The difference in cost is the price of skilled labor, about ten cents an hour in Hong Kong to $5.00 an hour in San Francisco.

When it comes to men's jewelry, it will cost the purchaser, with only the slightest variation due to taxes and the currency differential, much the same anywhere in the world. A $1000 gold cigaret case will cost the same from Cartier in Paris, Shreve in San Francisco, or Mappin & Webb in Burlington Arcade, London. If he buys the same case from Van Cleef & Arpels of Paris or New York, the world's most celebrated emerald brokers, it may well cost him a markup up to 25 per cent over what he would pay Tiffany on Fifth Avenue or Strongi'tharm, the Queen's inciser and a famous goldsmith on Dover Street, London. Van Cleef & Arpels pride themselves on being more expensive than anyone in the field and enjoy a snob trade on this basis.

The foregoing prelude to a discussion of men's attire is included with an eye to suggesting in some degree the variations of price which are available depending on the time and the place.

In 1935, when the author was a man-about-Manhattan columnist on the staff of the *New York Herald Tribune,* he was inspired to prepare for his syndicate an estimate of what a well-attired New York gentleman would be worth on the hoof after six o'clock in the evening and came up with the following median appraisal:

- Evening dress tail-coat suit — $325.00
- Evening linen, shirt, pique waistcoat, etc. — $50.00
- Dress dancing pumps — $25.00
- Silk or opera hat — $30.00
- Dropped mink-lined evening greatcoat — $2500.00
- Gloves — $6.00
- Muffler — $20.00
- Diamond-and-platinum dress pocket watch and chain — $1500.00
- Cuff and shirt studs without jewels — $350.00

- ▪ Gold garters $150.00
- ▪ Silk socks and men's underwear $20.00
  Total   **$4976.00**

That a man on the hoof should assay out at such a figure at the time excited some discussion and was widely reprinted in the popular press, it being an article of general belief that only women as a sex spent sums in this bracket on their own adornment and shelter against the elements.

Yet thirty years later this estimate could easily be doubled all down the line; the price quoted the author for an evening tail coat in 1965 being $600 and a mink-lined evening coat from Revillon being well in advance of double the $2500 quoted above, which was the price paid for such a garment in 1935 with the skins by Revillon and shell and tailoring by MacDonald Heath, a ranking men's tailor of the time with premises in the Squibb Building on Fifth Avenue.

But although the sums a man of means may spend on his personal attire and adornment are by no means inconsiderable, they are inhibited by a specific ceiling in one category beyond which they cannot aspire, where the sky is the limit for women.

This is the men's jewelry department, where unless one is a maharaja or other potentate entitled to royal regalia, there are well-defined limitations on what one may spend and wear within the rather narrow boundaries of accepted masculine good taste. By common usage, for example, a gentleman may only wear one ring, preferably a plain gold signet ring, at a time. He may not wear precious gems on his hands except in the form of cabochon stones such as cat-eyes, emeralds, or sapphires, and then only in the plainest of platinum settings. There is almost no place that a gentleman may wear diamonds unless it is in microscopic size as elements of a platinum watch chain. About the most conspicuous jewelry available today to a man envious of the opinions of his peers in polite society is a solid-gold Rolex chronometer wrist watch with solid-gold mesh bracelet which retails everywhere for

$1100. A top-notch gold signet ring with incised coat armor can hardly come to more than $250, most of it workmanship, and gold garters, which are optional in any event, seldom top this sum.

Not an absolute necessity in the inventory of a gentleman's evening jewelry, but still an accessory prized by many *viveurs,* is a *fouet* for champagne which is usually carried on the far end of a watch chain and whose purpose is to eliminate the carbonated effect from wine into which it has been incorporated with such trouble by the vintner. It consists of a slender gold tube from which retractable spines emerge in a whisk-broom effect, each spine with a jeweled end which, when briskly agitated in the glass, can effectively reduce the best and most costly champagne to a flat white wine comparable to a low-grade Chablis. In many European restaurants a wooden *fouet* is provided by the management, but fastidious drinkers used to be able to procure them from Cartier in New York for about $200 in plain red gold, $350 with tiny rubies. They were, and are, specially favored by sufferers from stomach ulcers who are allowed low-proof beverages but forbidden all sparkling drinks.

Time was when diamonds were not interdicted even for gentlemen of fastidious habit, let alone river gamblers, saloonkeepers, and salesmen of railroad supplies. A diamond shirt stud centered in the bosom of a boiled dress shirt knew no limit to the size with which it could be worn with propriety and pride of ownership in the years after the Civil War. The same was true of finger rings, tie pins, and other jeweled accessories of masculine fashion which found their ultimate expression in the railroad set of studs worn by Diamond Jim Brady to the envy of all, race-track touts and members of the Union League alike.

There was a time at the turn of the century, give or take a decade in either direction when, just as women went to Paris for their clothes, American men of means had their clothes made to order by one of the great firms of bespoke tailors of London, Henry Poole & Company, Gieves, or Kilgour, Stansbury & French, or one of the other world-famous gentlemen's purveyors of Savile Row and Sackville

Street, whence the center of pants and tail coats had recently removed from Vigo Street. Benjamin Disraeli, better known as the Earl of Beacons-field, who was both prime minister and, in his younger days, a novelist, created as a central figure in one of his novels a "Mr. Vigo," generally thought to be the great Henry Poole himself, and the only tailor in history who was acceptable in the most exalted circles of English society. It is worth noting that this acceptance was achieved, not on the strength of his commercial product, but on the basis of his fine horses and carriages, a sure recommendation in nineteenth-century London. "The most beautiful horses I remember," wrote the Duke of Portland in his memoirs, "were those of Mr. Poole, the Savile Row Tailor."

To Poole for their morning coats cut bias and their hunting attire, went such American magnificoes as J. P. Morgan, Sr., William Collins Whitney, Center Hitchcock, Chauncey M. Depew, William K. Vanderbilt, Judge Thomas Mellon, Henry C. Frick, and, above all, Evander Berry Wall, King of the Dudes. The author's uncle, the late Edward C. Center of Château de Monrepos, Celettes, Loire at Cher, and one of the best-dressed men of the New York nineties, was of the often expressed opinion that unless you were attired by Poole you were the sartorial peer of Happy Hooligan.

In those days Americans, even of J. P. Morgan estate, didn't just walk into Henry Poole's salesrooms and order suits unannounced. They came with introductions or they were not received at all. Poole's archives show that in 1875 William Collins Whitney, perhaps the ranking social and financial grandee of the American scene, presented a letter of introduction from H. C. Cooper, Esq., whom Poole apparently recognized, and ordered a dahlia-colored velvet beaver frock coat with velvet cuffs and lapels and edges braided with the same material for $40 gold. More conservatively, J. P. Morgan ordered a black twilled Angora frock coat, superfine silk-lined for $35 gold. It is worth noting perhaps that the wide-skirted, tight-buttoned frock coat known as the Prince Albert had first been devised for the then Prince of Wales by Henry Poole.

The bright particular star of Poole's diadem on a transatlantic basis was, of course, Berry Wall, who had a wardrobe of 500 complete changes, wore a minimum of six distinct outfits daily, and was the beau ideal of masculine fashion, on an extravagance basis anyway, until he died during the second world war. At an absolute minimum estimate of $100 a suit, which is probably a gross understatement, Wall's investment in overcoats and ratcatcher suits, English walking coats, Inverness cloaks, opera capes, and morning trousers represented $50,000, which put him in the running at comparatively favorable odds with Mrs. Harrison Williams, the most expensive lady dresser of American record. Mrs. Williams achieved celebrity during the depression of the 1930s when, as a gesture of renunciation of extravagance to meet hard times, she cut her dressmaker's bill to an irreducible $20,000 a year.

It was Poole who seduced Berry Wall into the only recorded lapse of a long and devoted lifetime from strictest sartorial propriety. Wall was induced to appear one hot August evening on the ballroom floor of the United States Hotel at Saratoga in the first dinner jacket ever seen in public in the United States. An incandescent management commanded him to leave the premises, and that instanter.

"Feeling somewhat disgraced," said Wall in later years, "I was forced to leave and was only readmitted to grace after I had gone to my room and changed into an acceptable evening coat with tails. But my faith in Henry Poole remained unshattered."

When the author knew Berry Wall in 1921 he was very much one of the picturesque and admired institutions of Paris. Married then for the second or third time, he lived in a vast apartment in the Meurice Hotel handy to Charvet, Sulka, and the other shirtmakers and haberdashers whose best customer he was, and Zem, the cartoonist of the great world of sports and theater, did a sketch of him which hung in Charvet's atelier depicting Wall in one of the stock collars that were his hallmark and purchasing an exact duplicate which was being fitted to the neck of his inevitable chow dog.

296 ■ THE BIG SPENDERS

The Walls dined out every night of the year. In summer he especially enjoyed the open-air restaurants in the Bois de Boulogne where there was dancing, for, although well into his seventies at the time, he was reportedly one of the best dancers in Paris, not excepting the professionals, and he and Mrs. Wall seldom went home before daylight. Although his mustaches were gray he was a sprightly and dapper man to the end, his gray toppers, gleaming monocle, and old-world cravats a panache of elegance at the race tracks of England and the Continent, for he seldom missed a race of consequence. If necessary he would charter a private plane, a not frequent occurrence at the time, so that he might attend a meeting at Newmarket in the morning and be on hand at Auteuil after lunch, changing his attire en route if different clothes were required for each event. There were other beaus in the great tradition still around the boulevards, the King of Spain and Edward Center among them, but as he had been at Saratoga and Newport long ago, Berry Wall was still King of the Dudes. He died regnant.

While the supremacy of English tailoring for American gentlemen of fashion and secure social and economic position dominated the sartorial scene for many decades, it did not remain altogether unchallenged. There were, as there are today, flies in the ointment of British cutters and fitters, one of them being that English profiles and the design of English suits were not always suitable for American wearers, and another the unearthly weight of English woolens, eighteen ounces and up, which were admirably suited to a countryside without central heating, but which annoyed Americans living in a less rugged climate.

As a result there came into being in the United States a group of gentlemen's bespoke tailors which soon established a following as exacting as English exquisites, nearer to home and more adaptable to American standards. Their number included Wetzel, Bell, Schantz, and Raymond Twyeffort in New York, and Dunn in Boston. In many cases English cutters and fitters were employed by these emergent firms at least as fronts who came in contact with the customers, and, as an almost assured means of attracting a discriminating clientele, their prices were uniformly higher than those of the opposite numbers in Savile Row.

Most socially acceptable of these was, unquestionably, Wetzel, a firm with baronial offices on Forty-fourth Street just off Fifth Avenue, where dark wood paneling, creaky stairs, suits of armor and chain mail, and hunting trophies adorned the walls and the atmosphere was that of the feudal domain of a medieval seigneur who hadn't paid his light bill. Wetzel was launched, according to New York legend, by Sir Hugo de Bathe, ironically enough a British nobleman, who at the time was noted as the husband of Lily Langtry. Sir Hugo, the very archetype of a monocled English milord, widely advertised that he esteemed Wetzel to be a more knowing master of the morning coat than Poole and certified his loyalty by having the fifty-odd members of the crew of his yacht patronize Wetzel for their uniforms.

The faultless attire of Sir Hugo was matched by his faultless punctilio and observance of yachting protocol. Immortality at the bar of the New York Yacht Club was achieved by his resolute demeanor when faced with crises that would have unnerved lesser men. During one of Mrs. Langtry's New York stage appearances a group of gentlemen including Ned Center, Center Hitchcock, and one or two other sports were guests of Sir Hugo for an afternoon's sail down New York harbor at the terminal of which it was planned to dine at a well-known shore-dinner resort on Staten Island. Somewhere along Bedloes Island the owner contrived to fall overboard. As the vessel was moving at a gentle pace and the Baronet was known to be a strong swimmer, little concern for the contretemps was expressed by his friends and presently the yacht's cutter with two seamen at the sweeps was put over to retrieve the waterlogged nobleman.

As they came up with De Bathe, who was treading water with his yachting cap still in place and monocle adjusted, he was observed to be in a bad humor about something.

"Who the hell do you think I am?" was his greeting to the rescuers.

"Why, you're the owner, Sir Hugo, sir! You're the master!" the seamen replied in some surprise.

"That being the case, you can goddamned well go back and fetch out the long boat. And have the captain in command, you hear? And while you're at it you can get into your dress blues and show a little spit and polish. We'll have a little style around here when the owner falls overboard."

Charmed with this haughty conduct, a group of Sir Hugo's friends dreamed up a special pennant to be flown among the other signals at appropriate moments, signifying: "Owner Overboard."

Wetzel, so far as can be determined, was a pioneer in the field of subsidizing gentlemen of fashion to be socially acceptable shills for his sartorial products. For some years he dressed Harry Lehr, Mrs. Stuyvesant Fish's epicene court jester, quite literally on the cuff, outfitting him with all his suits, sports outfits, and formal clothes without ever presenting a bill. Lehr shared in similar degree in the regard of Kaskel & Kaskel, who outfitted him with shorts, shirts, pajamas, and underwear, and Black, Starr & Gorham, who supplied him with pocket watches, rings, cigaret cases, and other jeweled trifles with this difference: Wetzel and Kaskel & Kaskel donated their products outright to the cause of advertising and promotion. Black, Starr's were only on a loan basis and heavily insured.

The extent to which Lehr carried freeloading was by no means limited to his attire and furnishing. He paid no rent for a suite of rooms upstairs from Sherry's where he could entertain as many guests at any meal as might please him and receive no bill. The same was true at the Waldorf and at Delmonico's, but when the St. Regis opened in 1907 the management rudely insisted on payment when Lehr dined there, so he passed the bills along to his patron, Mrs. Fish. Mrs. Fish also stocked her cellars liberally with Moët & Chandon champagne on which Lehr received a commission amounting to $6000 a year from George Kessler even though it was not a brand Mamie particularly liked. He also traveled free on railroad passes supplied at Mrs. Fish's insistence by her husband Stuyvesant, president of the Illinois Central Railroad.

One of the most accomplished freeloaders and touch artists in the records of confidence games, Lehr never lost his peculiar fascination for Mrs. Fish. Years after his marriage to Elizabeth Drexel, a wedding night he spent locked alone in his own bedroom, Lehr had a mental breakdown and was living in almost complete destitution. "They say you are mad, poor lamb," Mrs. Fish wrote him. "But in the circles in which we move nobody would ever notice."

If the advantages of having Harry Lehr as a sandwich man for their clothes appears at this remove a curious choice on Wetzel's part, it must be remembered that in 1910 the facts of sexual life, aside from its superficial normal manifestations and most conventional attitudes, were virtually unknown.

By the 1920s Wetzel was established beyond all cavil as the best and almost the most expensive men's tailor in New York, which meant the world. His advertisements, meticulously drawn by Jim Williamson, of impeccable gentlemen in morning or evening attire, were institutional in *Vanity Fair* and Frank Crowninshield, its editor, warmly espoused Wetzel as the foremost perfectionist in his field. Wetzel pursued a curious policy and one that may very well have contributed to the eventual disappearance of the firm as an autonomous enterprise. Salesmen canvassed the better preparatory schools which might be expected to yield a bumper crop of future Wetzel customers and such eligible colleges as Yale, Harvard, Princeton, and perhaps one or two others. As an inducement to undergraduate patronage, a special price was offered in the $115 to $125 suit range, a price which immediately reverted to the firm's established and then astronomical $175 to $200 brackets the day a youth left college.

Observers remarked that the reverse might more prudently have been Wetzel policy, with a top schedule of tariffs when a young man was in college and, presumably, his parents were paying his bills, and a reduction when he took a job and was on his own.

In any event, Wetzel as an independent firm went out of business in the early 1940s. The suits of armor and stuffed foxes went to a theatrical warehouse and the company's name, patterns, mailing list, and other components were absorbed into the custom-tailoring department of Saks Fifth Avenue where they abide to this day.

There are, no doubt, still examples of Wetzel craftsmanship in the wardrobes of graying *boulevardiers.* His suits were built for the ages.

Berry Wall and the great New York beaus of the gas-lit years found few counterparts after the twenties with their emphasis on bathtub gin and the smoking jacket that had gotten Wall thrown out of the United States Hotel. The informality of a generation that had become accustomed to fist-fighting in public and falling on its face in the gutter found both occupations less inconvenienced by a short jacket and unstarched linen. The most effective agency of all in eliminating formality was the advent of the auto-taxi. The earliest models, available on cab ranks at Pennsylvania Station, the Plaza Hotel, and outside Shanley's and Delmonico's, like their British Vauxhall counterparts, were built high enough for a man to wear a silk top hat without inconvenience. The increasingly lower tops and the complete disappearance of open horse-cabs such as Victorias and hansoms spelled the doom of the top hat and, with it, all pretensions to sartorial distinction.

A thin red line of heroes survived, however, to maintain the flag of masculine decorum firmly nailed to the mast and to trail clouds of glory from a better time.

New York's Mayor James J. Walker was one of them. The dapper chief executive patronized a tailor with vaguely theatrical flourishes in his technique that suited Walker well, an artist named Jeann Friedman conveniently located next door to the Ritz-Carlton Hotel. The mayor changed clothes at City Hall, according to Gene Fowler, his biographer, a minimum of three times a day and four if he were dressing for evening or a civic ceremony requiring morning dress. His Derby hats were of a special design that was later copyrighted and marketed by a firm of hat manufacturers as

"The James J. Walker Model." Fowler later inherited one of the mayor's glossiest silk top hats, the one he had worn on countless occasions of civic rejoicing when welcoming Channel swimmers and war heroes in the name of the municipality. It reposed in Fowler's workshop in Hollywood until the time of his death, flanked on an adjacent peg by the collapsible gibus, or opera hat, that had been worn by Rudolph Valentino the night he was seized with the illness that was to prove fatal.

Another toiler in the vineyard of elegance was Otto Kahn, greatest of all New York patrons of the arts and almost singlehanded the benefactor of the Metropolitan Opera in its lean years. So institutional was Kahn's wardrobe that, upon one occasion when he was testifying on a complex matter of municipal finance before the New York Board of Estimate, the *New York World* devoted half a column to the quotation of his statistical remarks and three quarters of a column to a description of the witness' appearance, commenting lovingly on his pearl-gray English cutaway, ledger-ruled cashmere trousers, meticulously folded Ascot with its black-pearl tie pin, and the tiny orchid in his buttonhole.

Improbable as it sounds in a professional advocate of egalitarianism and democracy, one of the most costly man's fur coats in the United States at the time he occupied the White House was a sea otter lined greatcoat belonging to Franklin D. Roosevelt. An estimated value of $20,000 was set on it by Tracy Jaeckel, a leading New York fur consultant, although admitting that no precedent was available for comparison because, in his memory, no sea otter had ever been trapped and the sale of their fur was illegal.

Still another Beau Brummell of New York in the thirties was Charles Stanley Sackett, a hotel man whose best-remembered post was for more than a decade assistant manager of the very exclusive and now vanished Madison Hotel at 15 East Fifty-eighth Street. Because of his professional requirements, Sackett's wardrobe leaned heavily to formality, and an inventory of his dressing room once yielded a count of six morning coats and foreign-office short jackets and their appropriate striped trousers, seven dinner or smoking jackets, three evening tail coats, six silk top hats, one fur-lined overcoat, three Derbies, and one street suit of Harris tweed.

Dressiest representative of the New York fourth estate in the twenties and thirties was O. O. (Oscar Odd) McIntyre whose syndicated column "New York Day by Day" was purchased at the zenith of its popularity by 500 papers throughout the countryside and netted its author $5000 weekly as his 50 per cent of the syndicate fees. McIntyre was easily the best and most appreciative patron of Sulka, the exotic haberdasher and shirtmaker, both when they were located on Fifth Avenue at Forty-third Street and later at a further-uptown address on the same thoroughfare. He purchased Sulka's four-in-hand ties, which then retailed for between $8 and $12 each, quite literally 100 at a time, and lounging robes, for which he had a passion, on the same scale. With the author as a youthful reporter in tow, he once ordered no fewer than fifty elaborately brocaded, satin-faced, and silk-corded house jackets and full-length dressing robes of the heaviest and richest Sulka materials at a single sitting. The price range at the time was from $200 to $300 for one such magnificent garment, which would have made his day's expenditure at an absolute minimum $10,000, and probably substantially more. His apartment at 270 Park Avenue was constantly having to be enlarged to accommodate McIntyre's ever-growing collection of lounging attire in which, since he neither drank nor smoked, he only lounged.

A generous-hearted country boy who hailed from Gallipolis, Ohio, and singlehandedly created the column which made him famous and which contained neither scandal nor gossip of any sort, Odd's idea of affluence, in the days when he owned a single blue-serge suit and pair of high-button shoes, had been to have a Park Avenue address and own a limitless wardrobe. He lived to do both. His two favorite restaurants were the Colony and Monetta's Italian establishment on Mulberry Street and both Cavallero and Papa Monetta became rich on the strength of his constant mention of them. Odd's professional trademark was a homely twist almost as identifying as O. Henry's which equated the urban sophistication of which he wrote with terms of small-town simplicity. He would list an elaborate repast at the Colony, dwelling on the splendors of caviar, the mink, monocles, and champagne of the *mise en scène,* "but no pheasant *en plumage* ever tasted as good as the baked beans at the depot restaurant in Gallipolis, Ohio."

Other lavish spenders for personal adornment in the form of ties, shirtings, galluses, and gloves were members of a little group which included Roy Howard, the publisher, Prince Christopher of Greece, Alfred Knopf, and one or two other *boulevardier* types who were in revolt against the conventional white shirt and collar of acceptable masculine fashion in the thirties and patronized the Brothers McCrory on West Forty-sixth Street for shirts of pastel hue and other solid colors. A brace of amiable Cockneys, the McCrorys, Will and Sam, maintained during prohibition a lavish bar concealed from prying eyes behind a secret shelf full of bolts of shirting for the sluicing of special customers. The idea was to fill the patrons with liquid enthusiasm, and, while in a state of euphoria, to sell them a larger bill of goods than they would normally have ordered. It worked the other way. The McCrorys' got stiff as planks and gave away so much merchandise that they had to close the bar permanently in the interest of remaining solvent.

A field of endeavor which occupies the attention of a special brand of sartorial perfectionism is that of the gentleman cowboy whose admiration for the old West is so great that, amidst the heated swimming pools of Palm Springs and the plush gaming halls of Las Vegas, he must be clothed in an unreasonable facsimile of the cowhands who once drove beef critters over the long cattle trails from Texas to the Kansas railhead.

The original cow puncher was so called because when the herds were sent to market aboard the steamcars it was his duty to ride in the caboose and, at every stop, get down and with a pole inserted through the sides of the cattle cars, poke to their feet any animals that had gone to sleep on the floor where they might be smothered. Few items of his attire got more than his passing attention, but his boots and his hat when he hit Dodge City or Newton might cost him half a year's salary. Hand-stitched cowhide high-heeled boots of the softest imaginable manufacture might cost as much as a $100 from Herman Heiser of Kansas City, and a wide-brimmed Stetson half as much in the seventies. Today the best Stetson retails for $125 and almost anything can be spent on boots if the customer wants them elaborately stitched or finished with gold and silver heels and toes. Fred Lucy, an amiable Hollywood restaurateur of the 1930s with a large clientele from Paramount Studios, wore Texas boots with gold heels that cost him $350 from a Las Vegas dealer, not in footwear, but in jewelry.

The author's partner, when together they owned a newspaper in Virginia City, Charles Clegg, went Lucy one better with gold heels and toes which sadly baffled valets at the Savoy in London when they were told to take them to the silver-polishing department for cleaning.

The dapper Mr. Clegg owned but only infrequently wore what was probably the most expensive man's belt ever seen in the bar of the Riverside Hotel in Reno. It was fashioned from eighteen $20 gold pieces each framed and linked like the silver-dollar belts purchased by lady tourists, and stood the owner, including the coins and the workmanship, close to $2000. It was fastened by a massive gold buckle and weighed one pound twelve and one half ounces when delivered by Morgan Smith, the Reno jeweler. Except on occasions of frontier gala, its weight and value inhibited its frequent wearing.

Oddly, one of the most expansive of all admirers of things western was the late Jack Kriendler, one of the founding partners in Jack & Charlie's restaurant at 21 West Fifty-second Street. Equally oddly, his magnificent cowboy shirts of which he owned a reported ten dozen were made by a plainsman named Rodeo of Ben of Philadelphia at a cost of up to $100 each. Kriendler's saddle, which is on view at "21" to this day, was so massive as to stagger both the beholder and the horse assigned to its carriage. Often, if the beast's legs showed signs of buckling after being saddled, his intended rider walked beside him. Liz Whitney, one of Jock Whitney's wives, remarked that she had never seen a silver saddle with so many leather trimmings.

That being carefully shod was not always and only a human concern may be suggested by a cheerful footnote to the life and times of Lord Egerton, eighth Earl of Bridgewater:

> His carriage is frequently seen filled with his dogs. He bestows great care on their feet and orders them boots for which he pays as dearly as for his own. No less than a dozen of his favorite dogs daily partake of their master's dinner, seated very gravely in armchairs, each with a napkin around his neck and a servant behind to attend to his wants.

Styles in men's jewelry often derive from unpredictable origins. The masculine wrist or bracelet watch before the first world war would have been unthinkable on any man of approved masculinity and its wearer branded an utter fop or worse. When they became practicable articles of utilitarian purpose on British and, later, American army officers, they were retrieved from the category of effeminacy and elevated to the favor they enjoy to the present time.

Rudolph Valentino, idol of the silent-screen twenties, lent his stamp of approval to the slave bracelet, an approval confirmed in the second world war when they, like wrist watches in an earlier conflict, assumed a utilitarian aspect as identification tags. Valentino gave a short-lived boost to men's cigaret cases and matchsafes of platinum instead of the gold that had previously been favored for such articles. The platinum, however, was indistinguishable from silver, at least to the casual eye, and faded from favor almost immediately. Valentino's last purchase before his fatal illness was a $100 shaving brush of fine badger bristles which he bought from the chemist's shop at the New York Ritz-Carlton, a sum which,

306 ■ The Big Spenders

when it was reported, established The Sheik beyond all argument in the ranks of the big spenders of 1926.

Clarence Barron, the diarist of high finance and publisher for many years of the *Wall Street Journal* and the *Boston News Bureau,* as well as author of *They Told Barron,* was a dresser of an older school whose braided-edge morning coats, white-piped waist-coats, and jaunty silk ties set off a notable white beard in patriar-chal style. A devotee of the good things of life as well as a tireless reporter of the financially exalted world in which he moved, Bar-ron ate and drank well in the manner of the similarly bearded old kings of Europe who lived high half the year and spent the rest of it taking off their excess poundage.

He was well and favorably known to dining-car stewards on the New Haven Railroad aboard which he commuted between his newspaper properties, to waiter captains on the roof of an older Waldorf-Astoria on Fifth Avenue and the small but studi-ously attentive restaurant staff at Colonel Jack Bradley's gambling rooms at Palm Beach. Dinner was a ritual, a sacrament to be par-taken grandly, in leisure and luxurious attenuation. His taste in wines and food, especially the more princely vintages-and-orto-lan categories of culinary rarities, was of a ducal order and his tips were reputedly extravagant. Certain it was that he expected and received wherever he went the service accorded a regnant mon-arch in Europe. He once excited comment in Paris where he sat through a performance of the Folies-Bergères attended by three secretaries and paying no slightest heed to the show while dictat-ing to the scribes in strict rotation. The management was torn between admiration and outrage.

Barron kept track of his poundage, not through the conven-tional bathroom scales, but by the fit of six dinner suits of gradu-ated dimensions. Beginning with the smallest of these, he gradually ate his way through the intervening trousers, a process of enlarge-ment that took the better part of a year, until the most capacious of the six tuxedos strained at the seams. Then he headed for the Mayo

Brothers' clinic at Battle Creek to reduce to a point where he could start all over again.

A dapper and fastidious sartorial perfectionist in the tradition of another time when it was said that any San Francisco gentleman pretending to presentable appearance in public wore a fresh flower in his buttonhole every day of the year, Jake Ehrlich, dean of San Francisco trial lawyers, still wears detachable collars that have to be made to his order because nobody stocks them in California any longer. Ehrlich's suits, which have helped him gain a local reputation for urbanity to a degree where many people feel him to be "Mr. San Francisco," are locally tailored by Bullock & Jones at something better than $300 each. His shirts, which are all white with generous expanses of starched cuffs below the sleeve jackets, are made by Eric Nash at a cost of $20. The detachable collars stand him $3.50 apiece. He makes a practice of keeping about ten dozen shirts with their appropriate complement of collars distributed at his several residences in town and in suburban Marin County and at his office on San Francisco's Montgomery Street. Ehrlich has worn walking boots all his life which are made for him on alternate years by Lucchese of San Antonio and Jesse of Phoenix.

Celebrated, too, among Sunday supplement editors on the Coast is Ehrlich's enormous and valuable collection of cuff studs, of which upwards of 500 pairs remain in a bank vault while "The Master," as he is locally known for his amazing legal achievements, mostly in the realm of criminal defense, wears a couple of dozen pairs in rotation. They range from diamonds, rubies, and amethysts the size of pigeon eggs to a little pair of plated rocking horses from his grandsons, and include gifts from famous and infamous with fine impartiality. There are blue St. Christopher medal links from Pope Pius XII and a pair of opal-studded Buddhas from a bad-check artist doing time at San Quentin. It would have been longer time except for "The Master." There are gold horseshoes from Peter B. Kyne and a black-enamel top hat crossed with an ebony evening stick from Ted Lewis. Also in Ehrlich's safe deposit boxes are a number of presentation watches, most of them representing either an acquittal or a relatively light sentence. "There should be some sort of pun about people doing time giving me time," he says, "but I haven't figured it out yet."

It may be worth noting that the two most widely accepted dates for the total end of anything approaching civilization in the twentieth century both have overtones of men's dress. One period to the continuity of society as it once existed is unhesitatingly assigned by Hugh Cundey, head of Henry Poole & Company and first gentleman of Savile Row, to August 1914 when English gentlemen exchanged their civilian attire for uniforms. The other, pinpointed by Walter Lord in A *Night to Remember* was the sinking of the *Titanic,* an event in itself characterized by imposing sartorial overtones.

The *Titanic* sank under the highest imaginable social auspices, its sailing list having included such veritable grandees as Colonel and Mrs. John Jacob Astor and their personal servants, Sir Cosmo and Lady Duff Gordon, the Countess of Rothes, Harry Widener, Major Archie Butt, the President's military aide, the Isidor Strauses, Benjamin Guggenheim, Charles Hayes, president of the Grand Trunk Railroad, and other notables by the score. Because it was Sunday evening when not all passengers dressed for dinner, a number of fastidious persons who would have had it otherwise faced eternity in business dress. Unwilling to make an exit on this note of informality, the aged Benjamin Guggenheim summoned his valet and retired to his stateroom, presently to reappear in full evening dress with tails and his best pearl studs. "Now we are dressed like gentlemen," he said, "and ready to go." No nobler last sentiments are on record anywhere.

Worthy of a passing salute, too, is M. Gatti, maître d'hôtel of the *Titanic's* à la carte French restaurant. He was last seen aloof and self-contained on B Deck, his silk top hat adjusted at a decorous angle, a traveling shawl neatly folded over the arm of his satin-faced overcoat, formally and decorously attired to take passage across an even darker water. It was the gesture of a doomed emperor.

❧❧·❧❧·❧❧

Sex in its purest and, if the phrase may be pardoned, most naked aspect, which is prostitution, has proverbially been the world's oldest established commercial enterprise. It has also been less available to tabulation and documentation than any other and, as a result, obscured by evasion and euphemism in which the word "love" has become hopelessly involved. Then, too, the line between commercialized love and the amateur competition has tended to cloud the statistical facts, especially in the upper brackets of sexual gratification where the principals involved can avoid the sordid implications of cash on the bureau-top. Diamonds have become established as a girl's best friend with Rolls-Royce town cars, Park Avenue penthouses, swimming pools at Palm Springs, and charge accounts at Cartier running them a close second. Love is one industry which even the computerized Federal Bureau of Internal Revenue has never been able to reduce to a statistic.

The folklore of commercial love in the United States is an ample one but almost entirely unspecific. What the girls got, the going rates in the bagnios of New York, San Francisco, or Butte have been submerged in the probably exaggerated details of the beauty of the inmates or the eccentricities of their madams. The business affairs of Mattie Silks in Denver and Tessie Wall in San Francisco are well established in local legend but their basis of operations has vanished in the chaos of regional mythology. Julia Bulette is supposed to have imported culture to the primeval Comstock in the form of vintage wines and an absence of profanity on her premises, which, considering the time and place in the Nevada sixties, ranks with the Miracle of Canna. Veronica Baldwin of Denver had the airs of a grand duchess and carried, on her professional occasions, one of those tall ribboned walking canes associated with Gainsborough portraits. Mattie Silks, also of Denver's tumultuous tenderloin, once fought a duel under the formal conditions of the code with a rival madam, painfully wounding a bystander who happened to be her own fancy man.

The annals of prostitution are replete with everything except the economics of the profession. With a very few exceptions, nobody seems to remember the details of its bookkeeping.

One of the exceptions was the New York establishment maintained in the sixties on Clinton Place between University Place and Broadway by Josephine Woods. At a time when Manhattan night life teemed with parlor houses of advertised status, in many of which evening dress was required of patrons and only champagne was served from the bar, Josie Woods's operation was celebrated for its conservative conduct, the decorum of its premises, and the solvency of its clientele. It was, according to its patrons and partisans, the veritable Tiffany of love stores.

As when soliciting the recognition of superior British tradesmen, one had to be recommended to Miss Woods. She received no strangers and her list of regulars was so choice and her operation such a limited one that she never felt called on to expand. There were only twenty girls in attendance and the drawing room was achieved by way of an English butler of superior mien who was also a one-man admissions committee. The rooms of general assembly at Miss Woods's were sumptuously furnished with a profusion of richly upholstered sofas, velvet-covered chairs, and plush and ormolu *décor* generally. Gas light filtered through elaborately wrought crystal chandeliers and the formidable English butler supervised the service of vintage champagne only from a price list beginning at $8 a bottle. Only gentlemen in evening dress were received.

The services of Miss Woods's handmaidens were the most costly in town, which meant in the entire United States of the time, although as we shall presently see, an even more exalted tariff eventually prevailed in Chicago at the turn of the century. The girls paid $100 each a week in gold for their rooms, and their favors retailed for half that sum. It was occasionally possible for an energetic nymph to receive as many as four gentlemen in the course of an evening, but the proprietor frowned on any acceleration of operations which would have detracted from the dignity of her establishment.

When she took the air on Fifth Avenue, her soberly appointed carriages, sometimes with one or more of her commercial assets on view beside her, were indistinguishable from those of the great ladies who never would have mentioned her name. Josie, according to the admiring contemporaries, was at her ladylike best when, on New Year's Day, she held open house on terms of perfect equality of *ton* with the hospitality of her Fifth Avenue neighbors, the Lorillard Spencers and August Belmonts. On these occasions gentlemen drove up and mounted the front steps with no attempted concealment of their identities. They were merely fulfilling formal social obligations and it was widely reported that among her New Year's callers Miss Woods had numbered the younger James Gordon Bennett just before his fatal visit to the home of his fiancée, Miss Caroline May.

What Josie Woods represented in the New York night life of the sixties was re-created on an even more refulgent scale three decades later when the Everleigh sisters, Minna and Ada, established a pleasure dome that was to enter the folklore and mythology of Chicago on a scale comparable to the Great Fire and Mrs. Potter Palmer.

The Everleigh sisters, who were soon to be embraced in the national lexicon of sporting life at the most exalted level imaginable and whose premises were to be the setting for scandal of international dimensions, set up in business as brothel keepers at their first stand in Omaha, Nebraska, in the 1890s. Trailing an aroma of magnolia and other Deep South antecedents, they invested their operation from the very beginning with an aura of class which was to be associated with their memory long after Minna and Ada retired to anonymous gentility on New York's Riverside Drive.

Although the federal census bureau had formally declared the frontier a thing of the past in 1890, there were still unreconstructed communities where aspects of the old West flourished in unabated luxuriance, and Omaha was one of them.

A confluence of many railroads and a cattle-shipping and meat-packing center of importance, Omaha catered to the tastes of a varied and miscellaneous clientele of railroad boomers, cow punchers, gamblers, slaughterhouse workers, Chicago drummers, and other relaxed types full of exuberance and Saturday-night gold currency. Even here the Everleighs exhibited signs of the elegance which was to characterize their enterprise when they moved on to bigger and better destinies in Chicago. There was a gold-plated piano where, in place of the more accustomed stew-bum professor with a cigaret drooping above frilled sleeve suspenders, an accredited musician in a claw-hammer evening suit was in attendance. Minna and Ada themselves wore evening dresses and carried fans. Strict decorum was reportedly required of all the customers, but this may be discounted as an almost inevitable item of folklore. Omaha in 1895 would not have favorably impressed the Earl of Chesterfield.

The Everleighs' stand in Omaha was predicated on the momentary prosperity attracted by the Trans-Mississippi Exposition of 1898, and at the end of their first year in business they had doubled their original capital of $35,000. They decided to seek greener pastures and, to this end, made a personal survey of the prospects in a wide geographic variety of American cities. None of them seemed to be the sisters' dish of tea. Either the economic prospects were satisfactory, in which case the field was already crowded with competition or, in communities where there seemed an opening for foreign capital, the bagnio prospects were not alluring. San Francisco at first glance seemed, as it has to prospectors both before and since, to offer an almost ideal setting for amatory enterprise, but shrewder appraisal of the market disclosed that the town's carriage trade had already been sewn up by Tessie Wall and that the remaining sporting houses catered largely to the rah-rah college trade from nearby Stanford, of which the sisters wanted less than nothing. In Washington, Mahogany Hall was netting what was to be an eventual $1,550,000 fortune for its Spanish madam, but there were racial problems to be encountered even then and Minna and Ada with their southern background shrank from the added problems of segregation and a clientele with strong prejudices in one direction or another. Minnie Stevens in Boston was doing well enough, but there again the only suggestion of carriage trade derived from Harvard University across the Charles River, and the undergraduates, while long on manners, were short on cash. Belle Stewart in Pittsburgh said there was an opening but gave a far from reassuring account of the manners and taste of the Pittsburgh millionaires who were spending Andrew Carnegie's money like shore-leave sailors.

It was finally Chicago that seemed to the Everleighs the nearest thing to their ideal prospect. The town was loaded with money; it was wide-open and stunningly corrupt under the political sovereignty of Bath House John Coughlin, and there were no college boys.

On South Dearborn Street there was already in operation, although not on the exalted scale it was presently to assume, a parlor house run on progressive principles by Effie Hankins. The resort had been off to a gratifying start under the management of Lizzie Allen during the World's Columbian Exposition of 1893 and Miss Allen had sold out and retired at the close of the fair. Since then it had been a going concern, considering the density of the competition, and Miss Hankins was agreeable to selling out for $55,000 on terms: $20,000 down and the balance at the rate of $500 a month and interest.

Minna and Ada moved in and presently Chicago was aware that it had a new landmark, comparable in its way to the Bismarck Hotel and Mrs. Potter Palmer's turreted castle on the lakefront.

The first thing the sisters did was to publish a tariff schedule which, to Chicago eyes in 1900, read like a report of the income of Philip Danforth Armour: $50, $25, and a $10 minimum. Twenty-five dollars had hitherto been tops in Chicago. Colored southern help were introduced, southern cooking prevailed in the service of meals, and the attire of the ladies of the house was changed from soubrette costume to formal evening dress.

But the innovation that rocked the town's night life on its heels was not so much the visible and tangible upward nobility of *ton* as the change in the entire character of the operation. There was to be no rolling of drunken clients, no knockout drops in their drinks, no implications of blackmail, and no rough stuff of any sort. Young ladies proficient in these routines who held over from the previous regime were eliminated. Prospective clients were introduced formally to the members of the staff in small groups, and the long-established routine of undress parade in the front parlor on the summonsing call of "Company, girls," went into the discard. Prospective inmates were jointly screened by Minna and Ada in a manner of a headmistress of an exclusive boarding school examining applicants for admission. Once approved on a basis of personality, attire, deportment, and aspects of the trade which were given scant attention in other parlor houses of the time, inmates were told to remember they were ladies and hold out, as much as possible at least, for the $50 blue-plate special.

"You have the whole night before you and a single fifty-dollar client is far preferable to five ten-dollar customers," Minna told them. "Try and remember that you are ladies of the Everleigh Club and not hustlers."

The premises themselves shortly began to live up to this expensive billing. Customers were received individually rather than collectively in a suite of connecting parlors known from their *décor* as the Gold, Silver, Copper, Moorish, Chinese, Egyptian, Rose, Green Blue, and Oriental rooms. Here amidst a profusion of *bibelots* and ornamental oddments that included cushions, divans, love seats, thick carpets, and whatnots full of sea shells and travel mementos, the customers received a preliminary cultural indoctrination which might include polite conversation and usually presupposed a bottle of wine. Wine, according to Charles Washburn, official biographer of the sisters, meant only one thinkable beverage: vintage champagne. The price, regardless of brand, was $15 a bottle, $35 a magnum. This in a time when Mumm's and White Seal regularly sold at the Palmer House for $3.50 was a not inconsiderable markup. Although all the standard brands of the era were kept on ice, Piper-Heidsieck was the long-odds favorite and recognized as the bar brand if no marque was specified by the customer. This preference derived from the frequent presence of the Heidsieck agent for the region in a joint capacity as a patron of the Everleighs and as a promoter of his product. Often late evening found him purchasing for everybody present the very commercial product he had only that afternoon sold the management. "The Heidsieck man," as he was known, ranked high on the list of the big spenders.

Once the prospective customer had been gentled with wine and conversation, the inmate of his choice pushed a concealed bell which summoned a frilled and starchy colored parlor maid who showed the guest and his partner to an upstairs boudoir. Access to these was up a double grand staircase, its dimensions suggestive of opulence but its treads heavily muffled against the traffic of many feet. Each boudoir featured a large-size marble-inlaid brass bed. Many had mirrors in the ceiling. All were adjacent to an assortment of bathing facilities, showers, tubs, and, for the convenience of important customers, a gold-finished tub of superior esthetic design elevated on a mahogany sheathed dais or platform where the Everleighs' carriage trade was able to admire its gold clawed feet and superior gold spigots while mounting a brief stepladder.

Occasions of gala could be celebrated at the Everleigh Club not only in the privacy of the parlors and boudoirs, but amidst opulences of gastronomy. It was an era of four meals a day, and late supper wherever it was eaten was a feature of the abundant life. The Everleigh cuisine was notably southern in its overtones, featuring canvasback duck with rice cakes, Gulf lobster and oysters rushed from New Orleans on the overnight cars of the Illinois Central Railroad, and terrapin Maryland. Such entertainment, according to Washburn's recollection, ran to approximately $50 a cover, so that a spender in the mood that Minna and Ada admired to cultivate, with the aid of a few cronies, might run up a $2000 tab in the restaurant department alone. An evening's bill in the ordinary course of relaxation might well come to $500, exclusive of tips which were conventionally $5 to every domestic in sight. To rank in the upper brackets of philanthropy, a customer of seigneurial status was expected to tip his girl $100 for luck over and above fixed charges.

After the abolition of the $10 minimum when the sisters inaugurated a price scale that began at $25, the least possible sum on which an aspiring playboy could get through an evening of relaxation was in the neighborhood of $100. One party, which Sam H. Harris whimsically charged to George M. Cohan who indignantly denied he had ever been on the premises, was a flat $2000. Recipient of Harris', or, perhaps, Cohan's bounty, were listed as Julian Eltinge, the female impersonator, Eddie Leonard, and Richard Carle, although more casual and forgotten participants must have been recruited to drink up that much wine. The picture of Eltinge, for whom a theater was later named, cavorting with the authentic article is not without charm. Outraged, but appreciating the accolade, Cohan squared the bill.

Once established, the Everleigh Club became one of the recognized gentlemen's clubs of Chicago and an aspect of night life by no means to be missed by visiting firemen. The persistent rumor that Marshall Field, Jr., was shot there and died of the wound, although abundantly disproved by the record which fixes the place of the accident as his own Gold Coast residence, indicates the elevated social tone of its clientele. When Nathaniel Moore, son of James Hobart Moore of the multimillion-dollar Rock Island Railroad combine, was found dead of a heart attack in a lesser Chicago resort, his demise was automatically elevated to Everleigh estate. Even though he might have the bad taste to patronize the competition, contemporary sentiment suggested that a man of his social and economic standing with any regard for the proprieties should have died at the Everleigh.

When Prince Henry of Prussia, on tour of the United States in March 1902, was accorded honors suited to his station at Chicago, it was at his special request that a time lapse of three hours was incorporated in his official itinerary during which he was guest of honor at a somewhat less formal supper party at the Everleigh. He later reported to his imperial cousin the Kaiser that his Majesty's health had been drunk by the assembled guests from ladies' evening slippers instead of the conventional stem glasses. "What was the vintage?" the Kaiser asked.

Put out of business in a sensational crusade for civic morality which swept Chicago in 1911, the Everleigh sisters retired to well-heeled domesticity under other names on New York's Riverside Drive. They took with them, in addition to what can only be assumed to have been ample funds since they never worked again, the heavily gold-plated miniature piano and the solid-gold cuspidor that had been the prize ornaments of the Gold Room at their club. A carload of other furniture from Chicago's most widely publicized pleasure resort made their apartment overlooking Grant's Tomb a reasonable re-creation of the club's more public rooms of assembly. Old friends and patrons in Chicago's happier days, such as Charles Washburn, their biographer, Sam Harris, and Percy Hammond, the by-now graying drama reporter for the *New York Herald Tribune,* often had supper with the bright old ladies who had once made headlines. They retained their tastes for planked shad and champagne, but it was always necessary for one of their guests to do the honors when the wine was opened. Ladies to the end, and although they had sold thousands of bottles of the stuff to silk-hatted cutups, neither Minna nor Ada had ever in their lives learned to open a champagne bottle.

❧·❧·❧

Tonsorial whims are not frequent in the tally of expensive eccentricities, but here and there a diligent researcher can come upon pay dirt in the form of a favorite barber retained on a permanent basis by fastidious men of wealth, most of them notable for having very little hair so that what they have is precious in the sight of the owner.

John McCooey, venerable Democratic boss of Brooklyn in the days when James J. Walker controlled New York's affairs from City Hall, had a private barber on his payroll and, in that easygoing time, frequently made newspaper space for himself and his retainer by sending for him in tones of urgency from some distant place, say, San Francisco or London. Like many Americans of Irish ancestry, he delighted to twist the tail of the British lion, and like even more Americans, he had difficulty with the mores and mannerisms of English barbers who are known as hairdressers and insist on patrons booking time with them in advance. Walking into an English hairdresser's salon without appointment is unheard of.

Everything about getting a shave and haircut in London vexed Boss McCooey, including the oppressive British habit of shaving a customer sitting bolt upright in the barber chair, and McCooey's personal barber was constantly obeying a summons from his august master and packing his professional handbag to take immediate passage aboard the *Aquitania* or *Berengaria* for London. The circumstances that in those days a minimum of six days must elapse before he could get from New York to England made his presence the more urgently in request when he got there.

As well as soothing McCooey's nerves, the barber act served a twofold purpose. It got him favorable publicity at home where electoral favor was to be courted as a patron of native talent and a "buy American" advocate on a notable scale, and it got him more publicity, unfavorable to be sure, in England where it made no difference so long as they spelled his name right.

Perhaps the champion moonlighter of all time in the annals of barbering was Al Romano, for many years barber aboard the *Twentieth Century Limited* where he managed to attract a choosy clientele of celebrities whom he shaved, singed, and shampooed between runs to become, himself, something of a minor celebrity. First to perceive unusual talent in Romano was Cardinal Spellman of New York, a *Century* regular who undertook to persuade the man of clippers to leave the Vanderbilt employ and set up on a permanent basis at the Bishop's Palace on Madison Avenue behind St. Patrick's Cathedral. Romano was too much of a railroader for this, but he did make a good thing of the Cardinal between runs.

Al Smith promised Romano that if he should win the presidential campaign in 1928 he should become official barber at the White House, which proved illusory. Roy Howard acquired a taste for Al's special expertise with scissors and often had him visit his Scripps-Howard offices during business hours. Another patron who wanted his services was Bing Crosby who, on one memorable occasion, when he was unable to get properly barbered before the *Century* docked at La Salle Street, tried to get him to continue with him to Hollywood aboard the *Chief* when it sailed three hours later. Since the *Chief* in those days had its own barber and since, in any event, Romano was committed to make the return trip on the Central's No. 26 where he had an appointment with Senator Robert Wagner, he had to decline.

Still another stickler for a bravura performance amidst the Bay Rum flagons was William F. Kenny, a New York contractor of resounding wealth, a member of the private railroad car club and close friend of Governor Alfred Emanuel Smith who sometimes accompanied him on jaunts aboard *St. Nicholas* to the race tracks of Miami Beach.

Mr. Kenny had almost no hair at all and therefore required the ministrations of a very special barber indeed. His name was Louis Arico, proprietor of a basement barber shop on Reade Street, New York City. Finding himself in dire straits, tonsorially speaking, in Paris where he encountered the same obstacles to satisfaction in the hair-dressing parlors in the Crillon Hotel that Mr. McCooey had experienced in the Savoy in London, Mr. Kenny contacted Mr. Arico by transatlantic telephone, which in those days was more expensive than it was later to become, to take first-class passage on the *Leviathan* to his succor. The *Leviathan,* unhappily, was delayed by winter storms on this particular passage and when Mr. Arico arrived at the Gare du Nord, shaken but faithful, it was too late.

Mr. Kenny had heard of an expert in London and had imported him in Mr. Arico's stead.

The brother of the author of this book, the late Junius Oliver Beebe of Boston, a man of inquiring disposition and a devoted amateur of French military funerals, who couldn't learn of the death of an aged field marshal but he had passage aboard *Samaria* or *Laconia* intent on being in Paris in time for the funerary pomps, indulged a similar fondness for offbeat barbers. Hearing of a legendary master barber of Santiago, Cuba, who was reputed to be able to shave a customer in five strokes of a well-honed Solingen blade, he embarked for that distant seaport to see for himself. He returned two weeks later not quite a stretcher case, but bandaged like a Pharaoh's mummy and smelling powerfully of antiseptic.

It was some days before the scars were sufficiently healed for him to talk about his experience coherently, and then all he said was, "He did it in four!"

Another swaggering eminento in the private barber club was Colonel Oliver Payne whose sister providentially married William C. Whitney who, himself, even more providentially, was treasurer of the Standard Oil Company. A favored tonsor from one of the Colonel's New York clubs invariably accompanied him as part of his personal entourage when he visited his Thomasville, Georgia, shooting box.

Albert Keller, managing director of the Ritz-Carlton in New York as long as that sumptuous but ill-starred hostelry lasted and a *viveur* of ample splendors both in public and private life, with the knowledge and complete approval of his principal, Robert Goelet, maintained on the hotel payroll a full-time barber whose sole duty was to shave Keller in bed every morning, after which he was through for the day. Sometimes he was lent as a display of signal favor to special guests. Rudolph Valentino tried to hire him away from Keller but was rebuffed. No fool, the fellow moonlighted and held a full-time secondary job in the barbershop of the Madison Hotel on Fifty-eighth Street.

Closely allied to the pleasures of the barber chair, although the habit has declined in public patronage somewhat since the introduction of modest-priced Swedish type saunas for private residences, used to be the pleasures of the hamam or Turkish bath which in many older hotels such as the Biltmore in New York was located so handy to the barbershop as to be an adjunct of it.

Long favored as remedial therapy for overindulgence among the pots and at table, Turkish type baths reached their apotheosis in imperial Rome where the Baths of Caracalla were celebrated for their vast extent and architectural wonderments and where much of political importance transpired among the perspiring men of the toga, knights, and proconsuls on leave from Lybia or Dacia.

For many years the Biltmore Turkish baths, in a subcellar of the hotel under its Forty-third Street entrance and above the tracks of Grand Central so that the water in its pool rippled with the arrival and departures of the Stamford locals, were the scene of a weekly meeting of minds in the steam room worth a footnote in history. On Saturday afternoons Tammany was represented by Postmaster General James A. Farley, who never read a newspaper all week but had seven days' supply of all the important dailies stacked in chronological order by his bath chair, and by Governor Alfred E. Smith, who, when he was too old and feeble safely to navigate the treacherous marble steps and gangways, was attended by one or more of his grandsons.

Present on Saturdays too were former heavyweight champion and partisan of the Bard of Avon, Gene Tunney, Secretary of State Edward Stettinius, merchant prince Bernard Gimbel, George McManus of Jiggs & Maggie fame, and a handful of lesser eminenti of the Manhattan boulevards in the thirties. Both Gimbel and Farley were pronouncedly Roman of profile and the likeness was so enhanced by the togalike sheets in which they were swathed between *tediparium* and *frigidarium* and on the rubbing table that few who saw them in these attitudes failed to comment on their senatorial appearance.

Gimbel, a man of gregarious habit, was so fetched with his own Roman image that, when friends decided to honor the merchant prince on his seventy-fifth birthday, they conceived the notion of taking over the baths in their entirety as a component of a rout in the best manner of Trimalchio, albeit on a strictly stag basis. The Biltmore's bath department closed early on Saturday nights and room service took over when the rubbers and other attendants had left for the weekend, and decorators restyled the pool and its adjacent apartments in an approximation of the spirit of Caracalla. A relaxing period of cocktails and steam was arranged in the Turkish baths after which guests, still arrayed in togas and their brows twined with ceremonial chaplets, were transported on specially sequestered elevators to the Biltmore's Music Room for a more conventional dinner where a master of ceremonies read the courses from a papyrus scroll:

> *consommé double Sévigné, black diamond terrapin à la Biltmore,*
> *le filet de boeuf pique au lard frais Renaissance,*
> *le trou normande, la poularde en gelée Reine Pédauque,*
> *le plateau de fromages de France,*
> *les glaces de Rocaille sur socle lumineux.*

Things got tolerably Roman as the night advanced and the elevators shuttled between the Biltmore's upper floors and the steamy basement giving startled patrons a glimpse of senatorial revelry as they flashed by the lobby. Captains of finance went swimming balancing glasses of vintage Bollinger and carrying dishes of *le gâteau d'anniversaire* into the steam room with them. Since the baths didn't open Sunday, the assembled senators, Neros, and equites and others of proconsular dignity were able to sleep off the effects of Capitoline plenty undisturbed, but the returning attendants on Monday were busy retrieving highball glasses from under the rubbing tables and gilded wreathes of bay leaves from the light fixtures for days to come.

ᕈᕈ · ᕈᕈ · ᕈᕈ

In assigning the properties and caprices of wealth to their proper categories for purposes of classification, it is at once apparent to the student of expensive grandeurs that some are predominantly the perquisites of women, while others more or less automatically fall within the purview of masculinity.

In general terms, jewels, fancy raiment, titled sons-in-law, numerous and well-ordered domestics, cotillions, boxes at opera, debutante fetes, and spacious gestures of social aggrandizement like the entertainment of titled foreigners are the province and preoccupation of women. Seagoing yachts, shooting boxes, race horses, collections of old masters, fishing rights, private railroad cars, fine libraries, the ownership of newspapers, and membership in the United States Senate are masculine in their implications. True, there are sports in the biological sense in both classifications, like Mrs. Payne Whitney's fondness for racing stables and Cissy Patterson as publisher of the *Washington Times-Herald,* or James Hazen Hyde's fatal fondness for masquerade balls. Some expressions of expensive personalities are shared in about equal dimension by men and women: palatial town houses and vast country estates, elegant motorcars and the amenities of table, although it would be difficult if not impossible to name a celebrated lady amateur of Madeiras.

In one field of collecting and possessiveness as status-symbolism, there is no record of invasion or even passing interest by any women. Cows, although their gender is as feminine as chorus girls, like a taste in chorus girls, are for men only.

Cows and their breeding, as separated from cattle ranching for beef purposes, may not attract the attention of society editors in the degree that a $250,000 coming-out party can for a debutante daughter, nor are they as available to sensational headlines as jewel robberies involving stones of pedigree and pearls of price. Still less can they be incorporated in foundations and benevolences such as the Mellon art collection or the Frick Museum. Cows and their attendant appendages such as bulls, veterinaries, and accredited bloodlines can, nevertheless, run into such substantial money that Charles M. Schwab, who possessed most of the hallmarks of status of his generation including blooded cattle, once offered guests the choice of milk and vintage champagne at table.

"They cost the same, you know," he said.

The symbolism of cows as property is far older than the prestige of beef cattle, even when the descendants of the original longhorns are elevated to the degree of affluence represented by the King Ranch in Texas. The European aristocrat, as far back as the record can be traced, owned land and on it he owned cows. As *Fortune* magazine succinctly put it:

> The landed lord grew rich on his acres and bought a town house for pleasure; today's industrial lord grows rich in the town and buys a country place for his pleasure. The landed lord was rich because he had cattle. The industrial lord has cattle because he is rich.

Today's fanciers of blooded Jersey, Holstein, and Guernsey dairy cows often make the interest on their investment by selling dairy produce at the advanced prices justified by its pedigreed origins, but few of them would care to depend on their elegantly merchandised butter, cream, and cheeses to support their yachts and club memberships.

The precedent for bovine status symbols and cows as an ornament of wealth was probably set during the first decade of the century by Dr. William Seward Webb, a Vanderbilt-in-law who raised blooded stock on his magnificent Shelburne Farm on the Vermont shores of Lake Champlain. To justify his extravagant affection for fine Jerseys and Guernseys, he sold his butter to the dining-car department of the family's New York Central Railroad, where it appeared as a prestige item on the *Twentieth Century Limited* and other name trains of that princely carrier.

In the 1930s in much the same manner, the Atlantic liner *Majestic* on its every eastward sailing was serviced with 6000 quarts of super-grade milk from Wilfred Fry's Meridale Farms at Meridale, New York. Fry's herd, founded by his father-in-law, N. W. Ayer of advertising fame, in 1930 numbered 1000 well-upholstered Jersey milk cows and supplied more than 50 per cent of the milk and cream on all liners outbound from the port of New York.

That cows can run into money comparable to Van Cleef & Arpels cabochon emeralds is suggested by the price of $15,000 for a single Guernsey paid to start his personal herd by railroad tycoon William H. Williams. A short time afterward he paid $25,000 for a superior beast named Shuttlewick Levity (the names of circumstantial cows are as baffling as those of thoroughbred race horses) and, to service this haughty acquisition, he shortly afterward bought a bull, Langwater Eastern King, for $35,000.

Owen D. Young and Harvey Firestone were both cow collectors on a grand scale. Firestone's dairy products, on the combined basis of aloof origins and intrinsic superiority in butterfat, sold for 40 per cent more than similar products from adjacent Ohio dairy farms. The pride of his herd, Johanna Pieterje Artis Craemelle, the owner had purchased from the Jefferson County, Wisconsin, insane asylum. When Owen Young was in France as part of the Reparations Conference, a notable production record, sent him by cable, brought him what he termed the best news of any sort he had heard since landing in France.

As far back as 1913, Senator A. C. Hardy sold a bull calf out of his world-champion cow May Echo Sylvia for $106,000, while a Simsbury, Connecticut, fancier and his partner paid L. V. Walkley of Plainville, Connecticut, $65,000 for no more than a three-quarters interest in a Jersey bull inscrutably named Sybil's Gamboge.

William H. Williams, one-time chairman of the boards of both the Wabash and Missouri Pacific railroads, regularly visited his prize herd of Guernseys in Lyon Mountain, New York, aboard his private Pullman, and, wherever he might be on his professional occasions, talked every night by long distance with the superintendent of his herd.

Even the simplest kind of milk cow with pretensions to breeding brought $300 in 1930, a price that might well be three times as much in 1965. Land, barns, box stalls, trained dairymen, silos, all cost upper-bracket type money so that the basic cost of keeping a nice cow today runs upward of $1000 a head.

James Cash Penney of dime-store fame who, in his later lifetime, spent close to $1,000,000 collecting a herd of blooded dairy cattle at his Hopewell Junction farm in New York, halfheartedly attempted to justify the investment by saying that, since many of his dime stores were in rural districts, improving the breed to make richer farmers would create more potential customers for his merchandise.

Nothing quite equals the contempt of an eastern breeder and lover of pedigreed dairy cows for the cattleman and his beef critters of the western plains, except, perhaps, the attitude of Mrs. Payne Whitney as proprietor of Greentree Stables toward commercial raisers of horseflesh to provide dog meat. Curiously enough, no traffic exists in the portraits of even the most patrician cows, the veritable Mrs. Stuyvesant Fish matriarchs of butterfat, comparable to that in horses that enriched equine portrait painters such as Sir John Lavery.

A handful of dedicated buffs have ornamented their homes with the likenesses of favorite moo-cows. The bedroom of the Peter H. B. Frelinghuysens in 1930 was decorated with a pastoral scene of their dogs and Jerseys by Edwin Megargee, and J. C. Penney ruled over his 900 branch operations from a desk ornamented by the bronze bust of his first herd sire, Foremost, but no Sir William Orpen ever received princely fees from the dime-store magnate for court portraits of his cows Mixter May Royal or Valor's Fair May.

A well-to-do American cow fancier once was reported to have toured the art galleries and painting collections of Europe in search of cattle in deathless pigments to ornament his Ohio dairy farm.

He found a few in a Paris gallery that looked doubtful to him and called in a friend from Swift & Company to verify his suspicions that they weren't the best. The man of steaks and chops looked at the painted cattle with qualified approval. "Grade A canners," he said after a brief appraisal, "but nothing for the hotel trade."

⚶ · ⚶ · ⚶

New York newspaper readers of the 1920s and early 1930s, as long as the celebrated Beaux Arts Ball remained the most spectacular charity function of the Gotham season, were from year to year kept abreast of the progress in the direction of the next Beaux Arts Ball of an otherwise little publicized gentlewoman named Mrs. S. Stanwood Menken. From time immemorial, Mrs. Menken had been the floral centerpiece around which the Beaux Arts revolved. Her appearance climaxed its inevitable midnight pageant and what she was to wear was the central theme of the publicity which surrounded the occasion.

Mrs. Menken's costumes for this annual event were for many years confected for her by the Brooks Costuming Company. Popular legend maintained that each year, the morning after the Beaux Arts Ball, Brooks and Mrs. Menken started working on what she would wear 364 nights from then. Throughout the ensuing months such newspaper columnists as Nancy Randolph, Helen Worden, and Cholly Knickerbocker, when other inspiration lagged, reported on the progress of the creation under construction. Invariably the official publicity releases for the Beaux Arts committee placed the cost of Mrs. Menken's one-night appearance at $25,000. The figure varied little from year to year and her eventual appearance in feathers, furs, sequins, aigrettes, electric lights, court trains, peacock feathers, flounces, fans, and diamonds did little to discredit the publicity. As long as the Beaux Arts lasted, at first at the Astor Hotel and later at the uptown Waldorf, Mrs. Menken's $25,000 moment was institutional in the New York social calendar.

Thirty years after the Beaux Arts passed into history, Arthur Menken of Santa Barbara, California, is at pains to discount the reported costliness of his mother's fancy-dress attire.

"She never paid anything like the fortunes the gowns were supposed to cost," he writes. "These sums were the dream of the press agents for the ball and the hotels where they were held. She wore and paid for nothing more costly than Florenz Ziegfeld bought for top showgirls like Irene Marcellus. Mother may have spent $10,000 on the theory that the publicity would help the Beaux Arts which, together with the Alliance Française, was her favorite charity. The publicity probably cost my father, who was a hard-working lawyer, some of his conservative clients."

Nevertheless, the legend of Mrs. Menken is well established in the folklore of an older New York.

"I'll never forget the year she appeared in an outfit that resembled the feathers of a peacock in full fan formation," wrote Eve Brown many years afterwards, "and then, at the height of the pageant which was held on a huge stage in the Astor ballroom, she pressed a button and her entire person promptly burst into blazing glory like a Times Square electric sign. . . . The result was beyond Ziegfeld's wildest dreams."

The idea of lighting up like a Times Square electric sign might not seem completely irresistible to Mrs. Gloria Guinness, Mrs. Cornelius Vanderbilt Whitney, or any of a later generation of New York and London hostesses notable for the opulence of their personal attire, but the basic reality of expensive radiance is still valid. It is virtually impossible for a woman to spend really important money for clothes and not get some sort of return on her investment.

The ruling difference between being a well-dressed man and a best-dressed woman is the difference between amateur standing and that of a professional. A gentleman of fashion may represent a not inconsiderable investment of time, money, and effort, but the result is an aspect of his personality or perhaps even a component of perfectionism, but it is never a way of life in itself. Even such notably well-dressed public men as Berry Wall, the Duke of Alba, the Duke of Windsor, Sir Anthony Eden, or Grover Whalen never allowed their attire to dominate their over-all image or become a preoccupation, although in the case of professionals such as Adolphe Menjou, whose clothes were his reputation, the cut of a jacket or gloss on a hat assumed a dimension of importance.

Being a well-dressed woman has always been a preoccupation. Being a best-dressed woman is a career. Most of the women who annually make the lists of the internationally best-dressed are known for little else. Clothes are the essence of their being, a way of life and a professional attitude. A secondary aspect of making the best-dressed list may be that of a status symbol for husbands, one that is so well-recognized that it has a bidding price, although there is no record of a transaction being consummated. Eleanor Lambert, who annually compiles the accepted list of the ten best-dressed women in the United States, has been offered $50,000 to include the name of an aspirant, which puts at least a tentative value on the nomination, or perhaps a point from which to start bidding.

A few generalities may obtain in the field. A best-dressed woman has to be loaded. The entry fees alone are designed to exclude any but people of more than average affluence since, according to Eugenia Sheppard, the *New York Herald Tribune's* fashion editor, $20,000 annually is an absolute minimum on which a fastidious woman can cover her nakedness, while a really clothes-conscious aspirant for international consideration will spend upward of $100,000 a year on dresses alone, not counting furs and jewelry. Nor can a best-dressed woman be a total social or economic nonentity. Her name or that of her husband must be one which makes news, a requirement which sometimes catapults a total frump such as Mrs. Eleanor Roosevelt into the best-dressed tally simply because her husband was President of the United States or for shock value. Mrs. Jacqueline Kennedy, while no frump, would probably never have attracted attention in the realm of fashion if her husband had lost the election. Also a requisite for recognition is patronage of one of the established great names of the world of couture, Balenciaga, Givenchy, or Mainbocher. No anonymity ever dresses any of the ten best-dressed. Mainbocher charges a flat $1000 for the plainest and simplest tailored suit which presupposes, as mentioned above, a certain degree of solvency among his customers.

The basic minimum, according to Miss Sheppard, in the matter of wardrobes, anything less than which relegates a woman to the estate of Hetty Green, is six suits a year at $1000 to $2000 each, eight or ten matching coat-and-dress combinations, say $2500 each, six dinner dresses in the vicinity of $1000 a throw, as many floor-length ball gowns starting at $1500, three cloth coats, one sports fur (in Texas an ankle-length chinchilla), and a variety of odd fur pieces as well as one really de luxe fur coat, an item which in itself may stand the wearer's husband $75,000 at Revillon.

These are all items which presuppose being discarded or at least displaced at the end of a year. Jewelry is not included in Miss Sheppard's minimum requirements because it is more durable. Almost nobody nowadays discards an eleven-millimeter pearl necklace of two strands just because it's been worn three or four times and the headwaiter at the Colony recognizes it. In the same manner, diamond necklaces often last from one year to the next when they achieve the venerable status of family heirlooms and can't be thrown away just because they're dusty.

The ideal solution to the jewelry problem may well have been that evolved by Mrs. George Gould who had no fewer than five strings of matched pearls, each valued at more than $1,000,000. She wore three at a time while the others, much as thrifty motorists retread their tires, were at Cartier's being restrung and having their wrinkles ironed out.

Other women were even more casual about their pearls than Mrs. Gould. Arabella Huntington, widow of Collis P. Huntington of the Southern Pacific Railroad, once absent-mindedly left on the desk of Mitchell Samuels of the antiques firm of French and Company a handbag containing eleven pearl necklaces valued at $3,500,000. She explained the lapse by saying that she had an appointment with Lord Joseph Duveen to look at some furniture and paintings which were to cost her the more considerable sum of $8,000,000 for her California home and that the weightier matter had made her, momentarily, forgetful of trifles.

The best-dressed pitch, like most of the creations which were its essentials and components, originated in Paris no longer ago than 1933 when a group of top-flight designers including Mainbocher and Balenciaga, more or less for kicks, drew up a list of their favorite customers. The first year's favorite was Mrs. Harrison Williams, wife of a New York executive, who remained on the best-dressed list for so long thereafter that even after her husband died and she became the Countess von Bismarck, she was still receiving honorable mentions and awards in various categories.

The Paris Dressmakers' List received worldwide publicity, a circumstance which assured its perpetuation in years to come and also inspired imitations on a widespread scale. The following year the Associated Press got into the act and by the late 1930s every tong and association of bonnet designers, glove fabricators, and skirt smelters as well as all the important wire services and publications in the coated-paper field was clamoring for space and attention with its nominations of the best-dressed ten aspirants who, oddly enough, seemed to be among the best customers of the several arbiters. There were even best-dressed men lists, most reputable of which in the United States was sponsored by the Merchant Tailors Association.

When the Paris list was a casualty of the second world war, a reasonable facsimile of it was accorded the status of big business in the United States at the hands of Eleanor Lambert, top publicist of women's fashions, who organized it on an effective operational basis and as an institution productive of almost limitless ill will, frustration, and emotional chaos. Every fall the Lambert office conducts a survey of the important dress designers, importers, and fashion writers in Paris and New York. Ballots are circulated among lady editors, society commentators, manufacturers, and knowledgeable sources of an allied nature and the resulting evidence fed to computers, usually modified by a supplemental committee of fashion editors whose function is to abate public hysteria and water down "misguided enthusiasms." The need of such a clandestine board of equalization was never better demonstrated than the time the Associated Press list included Elsa Maxwell, Eleanor Roosevelt, and Amelia Earhart This is not remembered in the trade as a vintage year.

In addition to having the financial resources essential to making an all-out assault on the bastions of fashionable celebrity, a woman must get around a good deal. Not only is upward mobility a factor in the elegance sweepstakes, horizontal mobility is also an asset. Time was only thirty or forty years ago when the number of places a woman had to be seen to be considered of cosmopolitan status were comparatively limited: Sunday evening dinner at the Paris Ritz, luncheon at the New York Ritz and Colony restaurant, aboard the *Blue Train* to the Riviera, the restaurant of Claridge's in London, aboard the *Berengaria* or *Aquitania* during the right season in May and June, at the Everglades Club in Palm Beach and at the Hotel de Cap d'Antibes at Eden Roc. Today neither ocean steamers nor name trains figure in the fashion scene. Nor for that matter do airplanes, where nobody changes clothes, dines formally, or has room to move around. The right winter resort is still Palm Beach in the United States and Cannes on the Riviera, but there is in addition a whole new category of sports resorts where fashion editors and society reporters gather: at St. Moritz at Christmas, and Gstaad and Cortina the rest of the season, at Squaw Valley for western Americans and at the right charity balls and private entertainments in New York, London, Paris, and Monte Carlo, occasions which change each year and whose rating must be calculated in advance on the basis of their photographic potential and the favorable regard of powerful editors such as Diana Vreeland and Henry Sell of *Town & Country*. Sell is not, of course, a fashion editor as such, but has at his disposal enormously valuable resources of space and promotion in which fashions can be exploited in a highly enviable framework of social status.

Diana Vreeland is, in the sophisticated estimate of Eugenia Sheppard, perhaps the single most influential agent in the realm of women's fashions and their attendant expensiveness. Beginning her career on *Harper's Bazaar,* she switched to *Vogue* where she is editor-in-chief and herself on every best-dressed list of consequence. As Di-di Prest, Mrs. Ryan was Miss Vreeland's assistant at *Harper's* and has modeled her own styles on those of her enviable mentor ever since.

Barring such exotic confections as those of Mrs. Menken, the most expensive single dress within recent memory was a $3000 number by Balenciaga made of spangled sari material which left one shoulder bare. The identical model was purchased by at least half a dozen New York fashionables including Mrs. George Zanders, Mitzi Newhouse, and Mrs. William Paley. Since all of them moved in more or less the same social circles, confrontations between two or more owners of the same garment were inevitable with the ensuing bad feeling incidental to such contretemps.

The movements of Mrs. Loel Guinness, whose husband is an international financier and who for the past several years has been Mrs. Harrison Williams' successor as almost undisputed epitome of fashion elegance in international society, are conducted along lines of protocol and logistics as exacting as those which govern the movements of Queen Elizabeth. Mrs. Guinness maintains full-time homes, fully staffed with servants, in Paris, London, New York, Palm Beach, Deauville, and Lausanne. Between these she moves on split-second schedules either aboard one of her husband's several private jet planes or on the Guinness yacht *Caliste.* At each of these several residences when, metaphorically, the house flag reads "Owner on Board" one of the Guinness Rolls-Royces with a formally liveried driver on the box comes to the door at 8 A.M. every day and remains on instant call until it is dismissed, sometimes not until five the next morning.

Mrs. Guinness gives the approval of her patronage largely to Cristobal Balenciaga with occasional largess in the direction of Givenchy and Castillo and spends an estimated $200,000 a year to maintain her supremacy in the realm of women's fashions, although not all of this is represented by dressmaker's bills. Maintaining six residences and entertaining accordingly helps achieve this gratifying total.

The only woman within Miss Sheppard's memory who probably spent in the neighborhood of a quarter of a million dollars a year on clothes and their accessories was Mrs. Thelma Chrysler Foy who "bought absolutely everything that appeared." Mostly the fantastic spenders are a thing of the past, according to Miss Sheppard, while, with the generally leveling off of money that is a characteristic of the times, there are many more women who unhesitatingly spend from $10,000 to $20,000 a year on dresses. "The number of American women who spend in the neighborhood of $25,000 is really uncounted," is her estimate.

๑๖·๑๖·๑๖

When Mrs. Cortright Wetherill, a well-placed Philadelphia Main Line hostess whose grandfather was Joseph Widener, plans to wear her matching set of diamond and emerald ring, bracelet, and necklace, the smallest square-cut emerald of which weighs twenty karats, she gives twenty-four-hour notice by cable to Lloyd's of London and only takes them from her safe deposit box at the Girard Bank when a confirmatory wire has been received giving her permission to wear her own property for a period of no longer than another twenty-four hours. The premium involved is a modest $150 per evening of exposure to the public gaze, but if the understanding with Lloyd's is in any least detail violated, the insurance is void. Mrs. Wetherill could stand to lose in the neighborhood of $5,000,000 if some unprincipled person should appropriate her jewels during, say, the Hearts & Diamonds Annual Ball, of which she is president.

Mrs. Gilbert Miller, wife of the theatrical impresario and a daughter of Jules Bache who was, in his lifetime, one of Lord Joseph Duveen's best customers, inherited from her father Goya's celebrated painting "The Red Boy," a sort of companion piece to Gainsborough's "Blue Boy" which Duveen acquired for Henry E. Huntington. It is sometimes Mrs. Miller's whim to wear a diamond-and-ruby miniature of "The Red Boy" run up for her by Van Cleef & Arpels at a cost of no more than $50,000 which is approximately the interest on the Goya, but she was temporarily unnerved once to hear an acquaintance remark: "You know, Kitty Miller has a wonderful copy of her ruby pin made by some painter. It hangs in her drawing room at home." Mrs. Miller is, it should be added, seldom unnerved. A chilly and determined type who has sometimes been mistaken for an off-duty policewoman, she maintains three residences, one in New York, an American country home, and a town house in London, for each of which she has separate collections of jewels, feeling that what is suitable for one would not harmonize with the spirit of her other homes. "My diamond necklace," she says, "is only appropriate to London and would be quite out of place in the informal atmosphere of Metropolitan Opera in New York."

Other women who own great jewels have been more casual about them, as would seem to have been the case with the late Mme. Helena Rubinstein, who, while crossing to Paris aboard the *Queen Elizabeth* in 1956 inadvertently tossed two double-drop diamond earrings worth $70,000 through the porthole in what she imagined to be an empty cleansing-tissue box. Undismayed, Mme. Rubinstein, also a determined type who was described in her obituaries as "speaking eight languages, none of them well," searched around the stateroom until she found an aspirin box in the medicine cabinet in which reposed her stand-in earrings, pearl and emerald clusters of a value approximating the accidentally discarded drop diamonds. Neither the Kleenex set nor those that survived were insured.

The instances quoted here are the merest random and available anecdotes from the great body of legend and folklore that surrounds the jewel collections of America's wealthiest women. A survey of the top-ranking names in the tiara set conducted by Laura Riley in 1958 disclosed that an estimated thirty-six American heiresses and wives of important industrialists owned and regularly wore elements from collections worth $1,000,000 each. At least one of these, that of Mrs. Merriweather Post, is believed by knowledgeable informants to top ten times this sum. In the tally of their constituent parts such items as single pearls costing $50,000, while not a commonplace, are by no means isolated occurrences, and Harry Winston, the leading broker of great and costly jewel collections in New York, will gladly show an accredited potential customer $850,000 emerald bracelets from the vaults of maharajas and entire trays of emerald-cut diamonds suitable for engagement rings or whatever from $165,000 up.

If there were three dozen women with jewelry worth a minimum of $1,000,000 each in 1958, and although some of these, like Mme. Rubinstein, have since that time been received at a court where diamonds are not requisite, the bull market that rose unendingly until June 1965 is estimated to have increased this number to a minimal half hundred.

The owners of what are classified in the trade as "important pieces" are simply beyond counting or estimate. An "important piece" is defined by Winston as "a jewel or arrangement of jewels that kills every other piece within twenty feet." The possible consequences of this abundant fallout, socially at least, would seem to approximate those of atomic warfare.

It doesn't take any special originality to remark that the story of women's adornments is a clue to the larger implications of political and social history and that, from Cleopatra to Evalyn Walsh McLean and from the Empress Theodora to Mrs. William B. Leeds, how a woman glittered was an adequate index of who she was and, often enough, who her lovers were.

Fashions in jewelry have changed radically in the twentieth century, not only in styles and design, which have been subject to the mutations of caprice over the decades, but most dramatically in the status of their recipients. Sad to relate, the courtesan and extramarital love affair, at least according to the Dow Jones index of bracelets and earrings, are in decline. The best-dressed bosoms, throatlines, wrists, and hairdos today are, without any exception at all, those of women of married estate and of irreproachable moral facade.

The period when Liane de Pougy and La Belle Otero making an entrance at Maxim's in Paris on the arms of King Leopold of Belgium or Prince Orloff of Russia were so covered with emeralds, rubies, and diamonds that they were followed by personal maids carrying the overflow on velvet cushions never had any precise equivalent in the United States, although Diamond Jim Brady is certified in the record as having bestowed no less than $1,500,000 in gems on lady friends in the course of an animated lifetime. Rather, the trend in America was set by John Morrissey whose eye-popping $75,000 pair of opera glasses in Civil War times were a gift, as elsewhere remarked, not to a nymph but to Mrs. Morrissey.

Laura Riley's list of gem-encrusted names of 1958 included the great jewel collections in the United States of Mrs. Merriweather Post, Mrs. Horace Dodge, Sr., Mrs. Alfred I. du Pont, Mrs. Eleanor Searle Whitney, Mrs. William B. Leeds, Mrs. Chauncey McCormick; Mrs. M. Robert Guggenheim, Mme. Helena Rubinstein, Mrs. Ailsa Mellon Bruce, Doris Duke, Baroness Barbara Hutton von Kramm and her aunt, Mrs. James P. (Jessie Woolworth) Donahue, Mrs. William Randolph Hearst, Sr., Sonja Henie; Mrs. Ralph K. Robertson, the Duchess of Windsor, Mrs. Clarence (Anna Case) Mackay, Mrs. Frederick E. Guest, Mrs. Harry Winston, Mrs. Lauritz Melchior, Mrs. Horace Dodge, Jr., Ganna Walska; Elizabeth Arden Graham; Mrs. Buddy (Mary Pickford) Rogers, Mrs. Lorraine Manville Dresselhuys Baxter, Mrs. Perle Mesta, Mrs. Cortright Wetherill, Mrs. Gertrude Gretsch Astor, Mrs. Jacqueline Cochran Odium, Mrs. Basil Goulandris, Mrs. Stavros Niarchos, Mrs. Jock Whitney, Mrs. Jules (Hope Hampton) Brulatour, Mrs. William Woodward, Mrs. Horace G. (Marion Davies) Brown, and Mrs. George F. Baker.

Revision upward of this tally of emerald-cut chivalry would probably include Mrs. Henry Ford II and Mrs. Edsel Ford of Detroit, neither of whom have shown any sign of the preference in jewels for the stand-in fine arts which satisfied Henry Ford I, Mrs. Robert R. McCormick, widow of the opinionated colonel of the *Chicago Tribune,* Mrs. Lloyd Hilton Smith (Elizabeth Weiss) of Houston, Mrs. Thomas D. Thatcher of Philadelphia, Mrs. Stanley Marcus and Mrs. Clint Murchison of Dallas, Mrs. Alan Scaife of Pittsburgh and Mrs. Alma Spreckels of San Francisco, the ageless and durable widow of a sugar baron whose involvements in California family feuds included a well-attested shooting, are part of the folklore of the Golden Gate.

Many of the pieces owned by these favorites of fortune have long and almost invariably bloody histories, perhaps not as fatal as the Hope Diamond and certainly not menacing enough to inhibit their possession, but still dangerous enough to lend a macabre enchantment. The above-mentioned Mrs. Cortright Wetherill owns, among the other valuables covered by her $150-a-night insurance policy, a fabulous square-cut emerald once the property of the unfortunate Czar Alexander III of Russia who was assassinated late in the last century by an anarchist bomb within sight of his St. Petersburg palace. Mrs. Merriweather Post not infrequently comes downstairs to dinner in her immense Palm Beach establishment wearing diamond eardrops once the property of Queen Marie Antoinette and found on her person at Varennes when she attempted to escape the executioners of The Terror. Mrs. Horace Dodge's incredible rope of 389 matched pearls, each the size of a marble and forming a necklace as long as its owner is tall, was once part of the collection of Empress Catherine the Great of Russia and as such has as bloody a history as any bauble since Nero's emerald monocle with which he watched the lions have at the Christian martyrs in the arena. A single one of Mrs. Dodge's pearls is worth $50,000.

The largest sapphire in the world is in the collection of Mrs. Robert Guggenheim of Washington. Weighing 424 karats and adapted to a clip, its poundage makes it impracticable of wearing except with evening dresses that have been specially constructed with reinforced shoulder straps.

Among the well-placed American women who discount the possibility of hoodoo in their assorted brooches, clips, clusters, and necklaces is Mrs. Eleanor Searle Whitney whose fantastic matched string of pearls, each as big as a small pigeon egg and said to be of incomparable color, was at one time worn by the ill-starred Empress Eugénie, consort of Napoleon III. She also owns a frivolous diamond tiara that had first been doffed in the imperial presence of Franz Josef by the white-gloved hands of a favorite of one of the Austrian archdukes who had somehow gained admission to the Hapsburg court. Jewels and jeweled artifacts with a sinister ancestry, according to Winston, command a premium over diamonds and sapphires with blameless backgrounds and no associations of death or violence.

Many women, like Evalyn McLean, feel that buying jewelry has a therapeutic quality and that a visit to Cartier's can be as beneficial to health as taking the cure at an Arizona beauty ranch, as well as representing a tangible investment. Mrs. Gilbert Miller, upon one occasion back in 1956, was robbed of $36,000 worth of precious oddments while dining out in London and was so desolated by the loss that she wasn't the same until she had visited Mappin & Webb and replaced them with approximately twice their value in the form of a star sapphire bracelet. In her case, New Bond Street was as effective in its medicinal implications as Harley Street.

Mrs. William B. Leeds never has her diamonds or emeralds reset or adapted to new pieces. If she tires of them they go into a safe deposit box and are replaced by something new. If there's anything she can't stand it's a dusty star sapphire or string of pearls that is beginning to show its age. "If there's anything I need that I don't have, I just get a new one," she says.

In view of the fact that she inherited her maternal grandmother's collection, worth better than $8,000,000, replacement of even minor items can run into money. One of her grandmother's possessions that she has never tired of is a Kashmir blue sapphire weighing fifty-five karats.

Mrs. William B. Leeds, heiress to the great Leeds fortune in tin plate that was evolved early in the current century along with those of Daniel G. Reid and the Moore brothers, has so many diamonds and in such varieties of setting and combinations with other stones that she doesn't know the value of her own collection. She does know that when she has her photograph taken, wearing even a fraction of her diamonds, the reflected light from the photographer's flares makes it necessary to use the finest shutter opening available to press cameras. "Try it at one five-thousandth of a second," she tells newsmen from long experience.

"I'm jealous of my jewels," Mrs. Merriweather Post is frank enough to say. "Sometimes people look more at my necklace than they do at me." It is a circumstance which by no means prevents her wearing what looks at times like the combined window displays of Black, Starr & Gorham and Cartier's.

But, although the conscientious chronicler of today's most costly jewels including Mrs. Robert McCormick's peerless black pearls, Barbara Hutton's pigeon-blood rubies, and Mrs. Horace Dodge's Catherine the Great pearls should spend a month of Sundays looking over the sales receipts of Jules Glaenzer, Cartier's foremost salesman of tiaras and stomachers, he would not come up with a consequential sale for anybody's mistress. Diamonds may be a girl's best friend, but only nice girls, by and large, ever get a chance to know it.

Chapter Eleven
The Plutocrats of Pittsburgh

How to Live Well Though Only a Millionaire . . . A Brisk Market in Coats of Arms, Fine Bindings, and Mother-of-Pearl Toilet Seats . . . It Remained for Andrew Mellon to Raise the Business of Being Rich to the Status of a True Magnifico . . . Send Over a Vanload of Titians. . . .

ANDREW CARNEGIE WAS a man who translated his every random thought and vagrant fancy into its equivalent terms in hard cash.

"To make a drive like that," he said of his own game of golf, "is worth ten thousand dollars."

"Landing a big pickerel is as exciting to me as making a hundred thousand dollars."

"I would give all the millions I own ($492,000,000) to be a boy again."

"If I had my life to live over again I'd be a thirty-dollar-a-week librarian."

Uncle Andy was under no obligation to make good on his contemptuous references to wealth, and nobody ever showed less inclination to sell the dollar short. In fact, his parsimony in matters of personal expenditure was on a par with that of Collis P. Huntington and Hetty Green, two of the most notably prudent of his contemporaries where money was concerned, and his continued homilies on the uses of thrift finally alienated his one-time chief lieutenant, Henry C. Frick, who thought money was to be spent in great big sums as befitted a Pittsburgh magnifico.

But Carnegie had two great redeeming characteristics that set him apart from most of the archmillionaires of his time: he loathed and despised clergymen. His chief clerk, who occupied a third-floor office in Pittsburgh, had orders to literally kick all clerical panhandlers down the long flight of stairs leading to the street, and now and then the door to Uncle Andy's office on the second floor opened briefly as a ministerial mooch flew by and the heavily shod Carnegie foot added impetus to his going. And Uncle Andy was entirely willing that his associates should become, proportionally, as rich as he did when it came time for the eventual liquidation of Carnegie's steel empire.

Thrifty, tight-fisted, and filled to the Plimsoll line with bogus good works, Carnegie brought into being the most stupendous generation of spendthrifts America has ever known, a group of gorgeous parvenus who had money to throw at the birds and stunned man's feathered friends in so doing in a manner to alarm the SPCA.

Carnegie's division of the loot of his steelmaking dynasty created what were known as the Pittsburgh Millionaires. It was a name to freeze the marrow of conservative moneybags in Boston and Philadelphia but it made the Golden Triangle above the rivers a gold-rush town for tradesmen, whisky salesmen, dealers in old masters, disfranchised architects, heraldic experts, dancing masters, bankrupted dukes, upper-bracket prostitutes, and assorted representatives of Tiffany, W. & J. Sloane, Wetzel, and eventually the greatest con artist of them all, Sir Joseph Duveen.

Without the Pittsburgh Millionaires it is probable in retrospect that the art of engrossing coats of arms and the designing of porte-cocheres might well have become one with the building of chain mail and sedan chairs, a lost craft recorded only in museums. The Pittsburgh Millionaires gave the silk top hat industry, then, plucking at the sheets, a new lease of life that lasted until the automobile gave it the *coup de grâce*. Their consumption of Scotch whisky, in emulation of the master and benefactor, first made that article of commerce a major import into the United States. Throughout the Highlands stills that hadn't operated since the days of Robert Bruce reopened for business on the strength of the Pittsburgh trade and the Pennsylvania Railroad inaugurated service to New York and Washington aboard Pullman palace cars that shamed the Everleigh sisters' bagnio then in fullest operation in Chicago boasting a *décor* that was reported to have graveled Stanford White as a man smitten with stone. The Everleighs' layout included, among other stylish features, two gold upright pianos and they required full evening dress of their customers. Many of their best customers were Carnegie partners.

Carnegie's demoralization of the world of steel and the inflationary influence of his threatened monopoly had its dramatic and irresponsible consequences even before the creation of the new group of Carnegie millionaires. Small operators were bought out by larger industrialists for sums far in excess of the worth of their properties and a brisk market was created in smaller steel mills and accessory plants that until now had been beneath the notice of the large operators. Inflation at the higher industrial levels was already a reality. Small operators found themselves suddenly enriched beyond their fondest dreaming and spent their new wealth in the conventional terms of easy come, easy go.

John Moody relates the story of a group of industrial promoters en route from a tour of buying in Chicago and now headed for New York aboard the private car of one of their number, presumably John W. Gates of Bet-a-Million fame. The palace car was rolling through the Ohio countryside on a late-night express of the Pennsylvania when one of the celebrants, who were doing things with cards and bottles, glanced out of the window long enough to recognize where he was. "There's a nice plate mill we missed in the next town," he told Gates. "Why don't we stop off and buy it?"

The hour was late and Gates had trouble with the conductor about stopping at an unscheduled station, but the weight of his influence finally prevailed and the car was spotted on the freight track of a sleeping country town. The entrepreneurs, well along in wine, located the home of the mill owner and routed him out of bed long after midnight. They suggested $200,000 as a fair price and offered to write a check then and there.

"But my plant isn't worth $200,000 and anyway, it isn't for sale," protested the sleepy owner. "Why don't you gentlemen sober up and go home?"

"Let's not be small about it," announced one of the prospective purchasers, "we'll make it $350,000." On these terms the mill changed hands.

The acquisition, among other assets, by J. P. Morgan of the network of Carnegie properties for the sum of $492,000,000 reassured the industrial world, which had been alarmed by the threat of a Carnegie monopoly of steel, that order and reason would prevail in the nation's biggest business. The very name of Morgan imposed implicit confidence that things would be ordered on a tranquil and decorous basis and that the monopoly, if there were one, would be administered with paternal benevolence.

The sale also made millionaires, in some cases rich millionaires, of approximately thirty of Andrew Carnegie's associates in his various rolling mills, tubing plants, smelters, rail mills, coal and ore mining projects, and all the integral factors in the canny Scotsman's interlocking directorates. It made them millionaires suddenly, overnight and outright with no strings attached and no delay in liquidating their assets. Uncle Andy paid them off on the barrelhead before taking ship for his native glens where he pretended to like the music of a personal bagpiper at breakfast.

Almost all of the Carnegie beneficiaries were either Pittsburghers or viewed Pittsburgh as the nearest thing to heaven afforded by earthly geography and had been resolved from earliest times to set up residence in Sewickley Heights when they had made their pile. Now thirty absolutely uninhibited parvenus, many of them but a single remove from the open hearths at Youngstown and South Chicago who as a group had simultaneously found their wildest dreams of avarice abundantly fulfilled.

The impact on Pittsburgh was almost incredible.

Steel puddlers' wives, who only yesterday had been slaving over hot cookstoves to keep their husbands in Cousin Jack pasties at lunchtime, blossomed with English butlers and liveried house footmen. Bohunks from the open hearths at Youngstown and South Chicago whose sartorial tastes had hitherto been limited to a cast-iron Derby that afforded protection from the guided missiles of saloon brawls were confronted with a switch to French champagne for dinner and Scotch-and-soda between meals. The toughened offspring of Mesabi iron miners found themselves distressingly poured into Little Lord Fauntleroy suits and their Buster Brown curls ordered by exquisite barbers. Dressing for dinner came to mean something more than adjusting one's Police Special galluses over a woolen undershirt, and there were problems which arose from the multiplicity of eating tools at table.

The Pittsburgh Millionaires girded themselves manfully to do battle with the amenities of gracious living, and Americans not involved in the ensuing skirmishes with grammar and architecture were compelled to the spectacle as by a particularly sensational street accident.

Pittsburgh papers whose society columns had until now been devoted in their entirety to dispatches chronicling the balls of the Vanderbilts and Mrs. Astor's receptions in New York hastily promoted their bicycle editors to the post of society columnist and began listing the guests at *fêtes champêtres* on Highland Avenue that would have given pause to the Medici.

Owner of four of the Pittsburgh dailies was Harry W. Oliver, a Carnegie partner who started life as an immigrant from Ireland's County Tyrone and whose first job had been as a messenger boy in the Pittsburgh Western Union office. He eventually became a partner with Henry C. Frick and got $13,000,000 from the division of the Carnegie spoils. His first purchase with his newfound wealth was a $50,000 private car from the Pullman works named *Tyrone*.

Most picturesque of all the Carnegie partners to settle in Pittsburgh was Alexander Rollin Peacock who served no toilsome apprenticeship in mine or mill but walked into the Carnegie organization from behind a dry-goods counter and proved that selling steel plate was as easily done as dinner napkins. The two largest single orders for Carnegie steel were solicited by Peacock: 65,000 tons of railroad iron for Canadian Pacific and an equal amount of structural material for the building of the New York subway.

An extrovert to the core, Peacock got the news of his windfall from the Carnegie sale while on holiday in southern California. His first gesture of magnificence was to hire a special train over the Santa Fe that put him into Chicago in the then unheard-of time of fifty-seven hours and fifty-six minutes, a record that was to stand until the much publicized Coyote Special chartered over the same route by Death Valley Scotty.

Peacock was no man to let large sums of spending money burn holes in his expensive cashmere trouser pockets and his progress through Pittsburgh was a prolonged Neronic orgy of spending. At his command there arose on Highland Avenue a mansion which compelled attention even amidst the assorted facsimiles of Versailles and Blenheim Palace that surrounded it. It was called *Rowanlea* and the several acres of its formal gardens and rare shrubs and ornamental waters was surrounded by a nine-foot-high fence of the best Carnegie wrought iron with spearheads on top and matching wrought-iron gates so massive they were activated by machinery and rolled on wheels. Heraldic lions cast from the best bronze surmounted the gateposts and the front door was flanked by alternate round and square columns of Carrara marble and palm trees growing in enormous urns. All the devices of horticulture were insufficient to keep the palms either clean or alive in Pittsburgh and they were replaced at intervals from the two acres of greenhouses Peacock had built and maintained for that purpose.

Peacock was no snob and most of the guests at *Rowanlea* were his former associates, some of them from the slag pit, others from the front office, who held perpetual picnic amidst the vast marble halls, music rooms, and galleries of the eye-popping Peacock palace. Whisky was delivered at *Rowanlea* from the leading Pittsburgh grocer in four-horse vans and the master of the establishment was reputedly the softest touch in town. No old associate could be down on his luck but Peacock was good for the cost of a wedding, childbirth, or funeral. Mortgage-burning was a favorite pastime and the old gentleman liked nothing better than to scratch a kitchen lucifer on the seat of his expensive morning trousers and put the torch to the symbol of a friend's indebtedness. Often it was done with bottles and singing in the gallery of old masters that formed one of the wings at *Rowanlea*.

Now and then Mrs. Peacock indulged a womanly hanker for nicer associates and ventured a charity musicale or reception for whose accommodation her husband's friends were temporarily dispossessed. At one such matinee for the benefit of a Pittsburgh hospital, Mme. Ernestine Schumann-Heink grossed better than $6000. *"Ach, ist Schoenbrunn,"* gasped the diva at her first glimpse of *Rowanlea*. This was taken as the grossest sort of flattery by Pittsburgh's Four Hundred.

Peacock's next-door neighbor at the entrance to Highland Park was Thomas Morrison, a Carnegie partner who had begun life as a steel puddler at Homestead and built a red sandstone palace second only to the grandeurs of *Rowanlea* itself. Still further down the street was the home of Francis T. F. Lovejoy, a one-time Carnegie clerk who paused in Pittsburgh only long enough to erect a mansion with the town's finest private garage—it had stalls for sixty Packards and Appersons—before he drifted west to Denver.

Under the impact of the Pittsburgh Millionaires, Pittsburgh real estate soared both in the town's business and residential sections. An estimated $35,000,000 of the Carnegie money went for land which rose in value to three times what it had been before the big payoff.

On Fifth Avenue $15,000 a front foot was paid for property that only a few decades previous had gone for $200 and had few takers.

The vast sums available to reinvestment transformed the Pittsburgh Stock Exchange from a corner-store operation to a financial Golconda and when new seats were made available, thirty Carnegie partners clamored for admission, each with a check for $10,000 in his hand.

Not since the Spring Rendezvous of the Rocky Mountain fur trade had there been such a brisk trade in expensive trash as was attracted to Pittsburgh by its free-wheeling men of property, and wine salesmen, jewelers' representatives, interior decorators, art dealers, and confidence men filled its downtown hotels to capacity and drove up stylishly in rented rigs under the inevitable porte-cocheres of Sewickley.

Affable Alex Peacock, in the forefront of the spenders, heard that a rival in the elegance sweepstakes had installed two gold pianos in his music salon. Alex ordered four and had the music racks ornamented by a German artist who happened to be handy with cherubs and classical characters of mythology smiting harps and trailing diaphanous garments against Olympian backgrounds.

One Carnegie veteran advertised a thirst for culture and the police had to be called to maintain order among the book agents who thronged the portico of his mansion with sets of Zola in full levant bindings. Another had his wife's likeness painted by every foreign artist of note then practicing his arcane art in the United States and incoming trains for weeks disgorged eccentric geniuses in velvet smocks and Vandyke beards who tripped over paintboxes and stretchers as they headed for the *faubourgs* of fashion. A former stationary engineer who had been jockey to a donkey engine at Youngstown heard that a neighbor had eight bathrooms in his new home and promptly called on his architect to revise the dimensions of his own mansion to include ten such conveniences. Bathrooms, porte-cocheres, and coats of arms became a sort of legal tender or currency around Sewickley. Coat armor appeared on the bands of specially rolled dollar stogies which a new millionaire handed around to acquaintances like calling cards, while another with pretensions to being a gourmet built himself a $50,000 mushroom cellar so that his imported French chef might not lack fresh produce for his masterpieces.

One and all the Carnegie beneficiaries were pushovers for paid inclusion in the almost countless volumes then in vogue devoted to the biographies of "Famous Americans," "Men of Big Business," and "Leaders of Society." They fell over each other to pony up sums ranging from a few dollars to $2000 to assure laudatory biographies accompanied by steel engravings or halftones of themselves, their town houses, art treasures, and horses. Impresarios for bogus social registers and phony who's whos sported new fur-collared overcoats and ordered champagne for supper at the town's lobster palaces. Only the resourceful Colonel William D'Alton Mann of *Town Topics* and *Fads and Fancies* seems to have missed the boat for the Pittsburgh Klondike. None of the Sewickley magnificoes was tapped for the latter, which seems to have been a major oversight on the part of the Colonel.

Reticence had no part in the new order of things. Stewart Holbrook recounts how a Carnegie veteran spent hours covering reams of expensive stationery in the Duquesne Club with figures and ink spots "trying to figure out if its ten million dollars I'm worth, or is it twelve million?" Another was fond of pointing at a $15,000 painting in his drawing room and noting that, at the current rate of interest, it cost $2.00 a day to look at it.

Still another liked to itemize his wife and add up what she was worth on the hoof for his auditors. "What do you think of those pearls? Tiffany sold them to me for sixty thousand dollars but they're worth one hundred thousand any day! That dress! Came from Worth in Paris: fifteen hundred dollars and a steal! Her hairdresser gets one hundred dollars an appointment. And those sables. Got them from a man in Ottawa who really knows such things, a real bargain at seventy-five thousand!"

Salesmen for luxury products regularly commuted between New York and Pittsburgh the way, half a century later, Jules Glaenzer, Pierre Cartier's top salesman, commuted to the newly rich oil bonanzas of Houston and Dallas. George Kessler and Manny Chappelle, leading proponents of White Seal and Mumm's champagnes, respectively, made the rounds of the Pittsburgh night spots with profitable regularity, opening wine in magnums and double magnums for Carnegie playboys who could in future be trusted to order the right brands when their wives entertained at home. Automobile salesmen, a new race of promoters, arrived in the latest model Locomobiles with goggles and dust coats and found it more convenient to sell their merchandise in half-dozen lots than singly. Sewickley Heights wanted its motorcars in suites of color, eight or ten maroon Rolls-Royces or a dozen dark-blue Pierce-Arrows for every conceivable occasion.

It remained for the last word in Pittsburgh automotive splendor to be achieved many years later, and not by a Carnegie partner, in the person of Andrew W. Mellon who had built to his order at a cost of $40,000 a unique car, every single component of which from the aluminum cylinder block to the whipcord seat covering was the product of a Mellon enterprise. Not specially handsome to look at, the Mellon car was undeniably distinguished and easily identified around Pittsburgh. Traffic parted before its progress during the Secretary's lifetime like the Red Sea for the Children of Israel.

A few of the steel millionaires went in for politics as did Oliver but without conspicuous success. One of them, in the hope of eliminating fraudulent election practices, loaned his $100,000 home as a polling place and ward heelers and poll watchers alike drank champagne handed around by French house footmen until they fell in rows on the expensive sofas and needlepoint chairs. It was recalled years later as Pittsburgh's most elegant election.

At least one of the Pittsburgh group took up diplomacy. J. G. A. Leishman was appointed American minister to Switzerland and visiting friends reported back to Pittsburgh in awed accents that a lackey was behind every place at dinner and that the Minister spoke French like a Parisian. Leishman's daughter became the Comtesse de Gontaut-Biron.

In the matter of the entertainments dreamed up by the recipients of Carnegie's bounty, history is less specific, although writers for Hearst's Sunday *American Weekly* for years made guarded references to their splendor and Byzantine voluptuousness. Pittsburghers still tell in hushed accents of the local equivalent of New York's Awful Seeley Dinner which began as a stately enough banquet in a downtown hotel ballroom and increased in size and velocity until six entire floors in the hostel were given over to riotous excess for two full days. Toward the end of these rich disorders, the host hired the premises of a handy Turkish bath where his guests and their lady partners haunted the steam rooms and rubbing compartments in their birthday attire.

On the basis of the reputation thus established as a lively town after dark, Pittsburgh became an established tryout city for musical shows and revues contemplating Broadway. The Shubert Theater interests established a vedette there for the previewing of bedroom farces and it was while commuting to Pittsburgh that one of the three original Shubert brothers was killed in a Pennsylvania train wreck on the outskirts of the city.

Although he was no Pittsburgher, Diamond Jim Brady by a sort of process of natural association found himself tied in with the free-spending millionaires of the Carnegie group and an influence, for better or for worse, on their expensive tastes. A frequent visitor to the steel city and on terms of fraternal familiarity with many of the gaudy group, Diamond Jim became something of an Arbiter of Elegances and a paunchy Petronius on whom a number of the local Croesuses patterned their habits and appearance. Tailors told their customers that Diamond Jim, the beau ideal of the lobster-palace set, owned 200 suits, which approximated the truth, and such New York cutters to the world of fashion as Bell, Wetzel, and Nelson made a good thing out of their Pittsburgh contacts. Others imitated his famous diamond collections with evening studs and watch cases encrusted in precious stones. Still others, anxious to cut a figure as knowing fellows at table, learned from interested waiter captains that Brady was in the habit of opening quantities of White Seal, Moët & Chandon, and Mumm Extra Dry at his parties, although he himself notoriously touched no alcohol, and George Kessler and Manny Chappelle, who dealt in these commodities, found it easier to do business in Pittsburgh.

The most spectacular of the Carnegie partners were not, however, the Peacocks, Morrisons, and others of the group who made Pittsburgh their home and gave its authentic savor to the fame of the Pittsburgh Millionaire through the agency of dancing girls, champagne, and winding driveways guarded by heraldic lions. The true ambassadors of steel riches to the outer world were a smaller group of infinitely wealthier ironmasters comprising such names as William B. Leeds, the tin-plate king, Judge William H. Moore and his brother, J. H. Moore, of Rock Island fame, Henry Clay Frick who was to become Andrew Mellon's only rival as a magnifico of fine arts, Henry Phipps, and the most amiably extrovert of all the financial titans of the age, Charles M. Schwab.

For these men Pittsburgh may nominally have been home, but a wider stage was required for the epic of the cumulative millions they controlled and few of them in after years spent much of their time there.

Intimations of the impending retreat from the Pittsburgh scene by at least some of its rich millionaires were manifested as early as the mid-eighties and long before the division of the Carnegie spoils, when young Henry Clay Frick and his friend young Andrew W. Mellon were taking the air on Fifth Avenue and their cab paused in traffic outside the home of William H. Vanderbilt then arising in its solid magnificence on upper Fifth Avenue. The young men speculated on the probable cost of upkeep of such splendor and Frick came up with the suggestion that such a palace would cost about $300,000 yearly, say $1000 a day for safety. "That's the interest at six per cent on five million dollars and is all I shall ever want," said the steelmaster. Frick was eventually to do a good deal better than this preliminary estimate and place it in evidence twenty-odd blocks removed on the same avenue. Mellon remained a lifelong resident of Pittsburgh. But the conversation showed where the wind was blowing.

⚜ · ⚜ · ⚜

Nothing could better illustrate the unpredictable reaction to expansive gestures on the part of rich Americans than the tumult which accompanied a seemingly innocuous visit of Charles M. Schwab to the gaming tables at Monte Carlo in January 1902.

The ironmaster had only recently concluded the delicate negotiations with Andrew Carnegie which had made it possible for J. P. Morgan to bring into being the giant United States Steel Corporation and Schwab himself was president of the first billion-dollar corporation ever to be formed in the history of the world. U. S. Steel, with its fantastic holdings of mills, railroads, iron mines, smelters, and other components of steel production, was capitalized for $1,400,000,000 and this sum alone kept it very much in the public eye. Serious doubts were expressed in timid quarters as to the propriety of any such vast accumulation of the sources of wealth and the power to administer them in a single entity and, although Schwab failed at first to realize it, he was on a form of moral probation with the public. His every move and word were followed with an attention second only to that paid to Morgan himself and he was a far more conspicuous figure in the news of the world than he himself knew.

After the formation of the steel trust, Schwab embarked on a combined business and pleasure trip to Europe in the course of which he purchased a costly motorcar in Paris and drove it, in holiday spirit, down to Monte Carlo. In Nice he was joined by Baron Henri Rothschild and Dr. Griez Wittgenstein, head of the gigantic steel cartel in Austria and, roughly, Schwab's opposite number in Central European industry. Somebody remarked that the band at the Monte Carlo Casino was the finest in Europe and the jolly trio sat down to dinner there in bachelor style and made an evening of it.

After dinner they paused briefly in the private rooms of the Casino and, without even sitting down, followed the wheel for a few spins, throwing American double eagles and Austrian kronen on the green cloth as casually as they might at a church fair at home. Their presence attracted no attention and, after a nightcap at the bar, the three tycoons went their separate ways to bed.

Innocent as their evening had been, it was to have massive repercussions in New York within a few hours.

Monte Carlo in 1902 was at the zenith of its reputation for splendid wickedness. It was the resort of E. Phillips Oppenheim characters from every *faubourg* of fashion and gilded vice in the entire world, professional adventurers, Balkan spies, notorious mistresses of Old World noblemen, English milords, absconding treasurers from Latin America, deposed dictators, tottering royalty, and spendthrift industrialists with few personal reticences or none. Edward VII, who was widely hailed in the American press as a fellow of low if regal moral tone and the Russian grand dukes who reputedly swam in rivers of champagne were among its more celebrated patrons. Visitors of a gullible sort were treated by the Casino's press agents to tall tales of suicide benches and the colossal play at the tables.

To the impressionable American public, Monte Carlo was a dress-suit suburb of hell.

By the time Schwab had donned his Sulka pajamas and retired for the night in his suite at the Negresco, his name was warming the Atlantic cables. Next morning the *New York Sun* front-paged a dispatch from its Nice correspondent under the headline: SCHWAB BREAKS THE BANK:

> Monte Carlo, Jan. 12. Charles M. Schwab, president of the United States Steel Corporation, who has been playing roulette very high here during the past few days, broke

the bank this afternoon. He had backed 26 plain in various
ways in maximums and had won 50,000 francs. He left the
table amid great excitement and a large crowd followed
him. He resumed playing later at another table and lost
15,000 francs in five successive coups. He then resumed
his practice of backing a certain number and the contigu-
ous numbers on the cloth to the extent of 1000, 2000 and
3000 francs. He lost every time and his winnings almost
vanished. Although Mr. Schwab had occasional runs of
luck late in the afternoon in addition to his recent winnings of 75,000 francs on two successive coups, he has
already dropped several thousand dollars.

The following morning the *Sun* continued its story of the day
before, repeating the canard of "breaking the bank," and asserting
that Schwab had won 54,000 francs on No. 20. "The Casino was
thronged at the time and Mr. Schwab's feat was greeted with cheers."

By that time the American press was in full cry. The *World* and
Journal, handmaidens of sensationalism and inaccuracy, depicted
the steel baron as the central figure in scenes of Dionysiac license
with cheering mobs of duchesses and grand dukes elbowing each
other to touch his shoulder for luck and the Casino's servants
madly rushing hods full of currency from the vaults to stem the
tide of riotous loss. The conservative Schwab was linked in Sunday
features with that of Bet-a-Million Gates, Richard Canfield, and
variously delinquent Vanderbilts as a spectacular plunger in a variety of games of chance and he was depicted, in the jargon of the
time, as a red-hot sport generally. Stockholders in U. S. Steel got
the impression that the president of the outfit was going for broke
with their dividends.

Screams of anguish arose wherever investors held U. S. Steel's
handsomely engraved stock certificates. In the forefront of the outraged was mealymouthed old Andrew Carnegie, whom Schwab,
acting as Morgan's agent, had just bought out to the tune of
$225,000,000 net profit on his steel holdings. Carnegie's own

partners, rolling at the very moment in newfound and unexpected wealth, were making nights hideous in Pittsburgh with banshee screams and nude bathing parties for both sexes, but frosty Andy professed prodigious indignation at Schwab's conduct and wrote a note to J. P. Morgan disowning his former protégé and ablest lieutenant. He clipped to it a Reuters dispatch which had the President of U.S. Steel capering in private dining rooms with debauched scions of Rumanian nobility while dancing girls leaped from lamb potpies on the table. "I feel in regard to the enclosed as though a son had disgraced the family," Carnegie wrote Morgan. ". . . He is unfit to be head of the United States Steel Company, brilliant as his talents are. Of course he never could have fallen so low with us. His resignation would have been called for instanter had he done so. . . . He shows a sad lack of solid qualities, of good sense, and his influence upon the many thousands of young men who naturally look to him will prove pernicious in the extreme. I have never had anything wound me so deeply for many a long day, if ever."

The Laird of Skibo wasn't the only influential party to act as though set on by assassins. The *New York Times* took a dim view of Schwab's relaxed moments: "A man who is the head of a corporation with more than a billion dollars capital," said the *Times,* "which controls a great part of one of the chief industries of a great Nation, and of which the securities are offered to the public as a safe and profitable investment, is under obligation to take thought of some of his responsibilities."

While the righteous were clamoring for the tar pots and feather pillows, Schwab's friends, foremost of whom was George W. Perkins who was known as Morgan's most influential associate, lost no time in advising him of the situation at home. Perkins' cables summarized the attitude of press and public and suggested that Schwab make a statement to the press denying all and hurry home.

This Schwab was not in a position to do. He had played the tables in casual moderation and any denial would have to be a matter of degree and not of basic fact. That he had been in company with a

Rothschild, a very bulwark of banking probity, meant no more to newspaper readers in America than if he had been on a tour of Gold Coast bordellos with Boni de Castellane, the French adventurer who had recently taken Anna Gould to the tune of $12,000,000. French noblemen were selling at a discount at the moment.

What probably saved Schwab from the wrath of Jupiter Morgan was the fact that Carnegie, whom Morgan secretly despised, had turned against him. Carnegie had yet to commit the final solecism of addressing Morgan as "Pierpont" to his face, but Morgan had little enough use for the parsimonious Scot who professed a prissy morality about Schwab while his own associates were lending a new dimension to the opprobrious term "Pittsburgh Millionaire": EVERYTHING ALL RIGHT, cabled Perkins a few days later, ANDREW CARNEGIE AND SEVERAL OTHERS VERY MUCH EXCITED BUT DID NOT MAKE THE SLIGHTEST IMPRESSION ON MR. MORGAN. DO NOT GIVE THE MATTER ANY FURTHER THOUGHT OR CONSIDERATION. GO AHEAD AND HAVE A BULLY GOOD TIME.

Schwab shortly returned home, slightly chastened but by no means discredited with the boss, aboard the *St. Paul* and promptly repaired to the library at Thirty-seventh Street to make his report in person and do penance if necessary. In the interim he had been handsomely received by the Emperor Franz Josef of Austria and had made a great impression on German industrialists in Berlin.

"I did indeed gamble at Monte Carlo," he told Jupiter, "but I didn't do it behind closed doors."

It was then that Morgan made his famous remark: "That's what doors are for," and offered him a Prince de Galles fancy-tales smoke.

In approaching the saga of Andrew William Mellon, it is well to do so respectfully and with an open mind, for here was an authentic magnifico, one with Henry Clay Frick, his friend and business associate, William Collins Whitney, and John Pierpont Morgan, although in personality he was as different as may be imagined from the last of these. Where Morgan was overpowering, Mellon was diffident; where Morgan was direct, the impact of the Mellon authority was felt obliquely; where Morgan bought impetuously in the several fields of his collecting, Mellon thought long and soberly and wasn't to be hurried in his decisions.

That Mellon was a cold and remorseless tycoon devoid of either humor or sentiment was a legend induced by his almost measureless shyness and reserve and by a severe classical physiognomy. Even his son Paul used to refer guardedly to his father's "ice-water smile," but he possessed a nice sense of humor if not hilarity and was a notable author of good works performed in total secrecy lest praise should come his way.

The author of this book, a college contemporary of Paul Mellon, saw something of the old gentleman at the time he was Secretary of the Treasury and rejoices in some very human souvenirs of a rewarding personality.

There was, for example, the time at the Mellon home in Pittsburgh during these years and when the Treasury Department was nominally in charge of the outrages of prohibition. Mellon simply turned the other way when this aspect of his duties was brought to his attention. He owned Old Overholt Distillery and under the Mellon homestead were literally acres of cellars filled with the best of everything.

On the occasion in remembrance three separate parties, all involving bottled matters, were in progress at the Mellon manse. In one wing the Secretary was entertaining a group of personal friends; in another his brother Richard B. Mellon was conferring with a group of Pittsburgh bankers on topics so dry as to require liberal lubrication, and in Paul's personal apartments a group of friends from New Haven were simply drinking without the fabrication of any excuse for doing so. It was a time when drinking was admired among college boys as a full-time occupation.

So vast were the Mellon premises that three separate parties could be in progress attended by suitable servants without one of them infringing on the privacy of another, but during an only temporary lull in the chaos which reigned in Paul's room there was a timid knock at the door and there was the Secretary. We tried without notable success to look sober and intelligent but Mr. Mellon had no intention of joining us.

"I just thought to warn you, Paul, about throwing bottles out the window," he said in his mildest whisper. "You remember last Christmas when you had a party and when the snow melted in January there were all those bottles on the lawn. There was talk, you know."

That was all.

On another occasion at whose recollection the marrow freezes to almost total rigidity, the Secretary took a group of Paul's friends to Bermuda aboard the old Furness liner *Monarch of Bermuda* for the Easter holidays. Mr. Mellon stayed at a hotel suitable to his station and the rest of us put up at some remove in a premises called The Windsor which had the largest bar in town and a turtle reputed to be 100 years old. We went our ways and the Secretary went his until it was time for us to return to New York, where whisky in those days, if it was at all potable, sold for $12 a bottle.

Our liaison with Mr. Mellon was through his personal valet, an admirable English gentleman's gentleman named Flore, and some of us including Paul took counsel with this functionary in the matter of importing a few bottles of shellac, say a couple of cases, in the Mellon luggage which would, of course, escape scrutiny as a courtesy of the customs.

Flore doubted the feasibility of stashing a substantial amount of Old Chivas Regal among the Secretary of the Treasury's dress shirts, but in a moment of inspiration suggested that perhaps something could be done with the Mellon golf clubs. These traveled in an imposing leather case several feet long and of construction sufficiently sturdy to stand the weight of considerable contraband. It was a labor of love accomplished with the aid of the house carpenter to saw the heads off Mr. Mellon's cherished putters and mashies, fill the case with Scotch and newspapers, and replace the heads to protrude from the top in a fraudulent facsimile of Abercrombie & Fitch relaxation.

"He won't be playing any golf the day he gets back from vacation," argued the conspirators, "and we'll be staying at the Biltmore where it will be easy to slip across the street and buy a new set of clubs at Abercrombie's!"

Once safely on its way to New Haven, the whisky hadn't cost more in replaced sporting tools than three or four times the going bootleg price, but the admirable Flore was a bundle of nerves for days. The merest mention of the word golf on the part of the Secretary caused him to twitch in a manner painful to behold.

Mellon's great ivy-grown Tudor type mansion on the outskirts of Pittsburgh was built and inhabited by the Secretary and his family in the years before the Golden Triangle had its face lifting which removed the pall of soot that towered above the city and made its whereabouts visible to incoming airplanes for literally hundreds of miles. Shifts of cleaning women worked the clock around merely removing the traces of soot from walls, furniture, and carpets that made the wearing of men's dinner linen possible for a single night only without laundering and women often changed their white gloves every time they left the house. Many of the celebrated paintings that later became part of the Mellon bequest to the National Gallery were enclosed in glass frames when they hung in Pittsburgh, a practice that excited comment among viewers until they were apprised of their protective purpose.

Like many of the great mansions of the time and place, the Mellon household had its own night watchman who prowled the dimly lit corridors during the dark hours and admitted late guests after he had identified them through a massive front door held by a chain lock. Mr. Moon, for such was indeed his name, was a benevolent old party who wore dinner clothes on duty with a watchman's clock on a strap around his neck, and a well-kept snow-white beard which might well have stamped him one of the nabobs rather than a retainer. When Paul's friends from Yale arrived home at advanced hours from Christmas holiday dances, Mr. Moon would assist them in preparing late snacks or impromptu breakfasts in the vast kitchens downstairs where rows of ranges crouched, as Gene Fowler once said in another context, like spavined dinosaurs.

On one such occasion a house guest who had never met the Secretary of the Treasury, awed by Mr. Moon's imposing mien and attire, called Paul Mellon aside and whispered: "Don't you think you ought to introduce me to your father? You know I haven't met him yet."

Because of the overpowering Mellon wealth and the native diffidence of Andrew Mellon who lived protected on every hand by janizaries to ward off impertinence and solicitation, access to the Secretary was reportedly more difficult to achieve than audience with the elder Morgan. Mellon was not a mixer and even at the august Duquesne Club in Pittsburgh where today his austere likeness easily dominates the expensive portraits of his contemporaries and social, if not economic, peers, he was not on first-name terms. Nobody who got to him with a hard-luck story was ever turned away; the problem in this case was to effect a meeting. Few, except in the Secretary's own exalted sphere, were able to do so.

Most lordly of Mellon's generation of purveyors of costliness to the very rich was Sir Joseph, later Lord, Duveen, a ducal hawker of old masters, mostly paintings but with occasional skirmishes into statuary, miniatures, and ceramics, whose transatlantic traffic in Titians and Rembrandts was for years a one-way street of the most rarefied commerce.

Duveen's philosophy of fine arts was once expressed in his remark to a customer: "You can get all the pictures you want for fifty thousand dollars apiece; but to get pictures for a quarter of a million dollars each, that wants doing!"

No other operative in the stealthy jungle warfare of fine arts so succinctly expressed the motivation behind the acquisition of old masters unless it was Duveen's customer, Henry C. Frick. "Railroads," said Frick with unerring sense of the *mot juste,* "are the Rembrandts of investment."

Time meant nothing in the Duveen scheme of things until toward the end when the impending presence of the Reaper accelerated his pace. He had sold millions upon millions of dollars' worth of fine arts to rich vulgarians and aloof magnificoes ranging from Henry Huntington to J. P. Morgan and from Elbert H. Gary and H. C. Frick to P. A. B. Widener, Jules Bache, and John D. Rockefeller, Jr. The biggest fish in the Duveen pool, whose luring would be the consummate triumph of a notably successful career and the capstone of his professional achievements, was Andrew Mellon.

Other archmillionaires sought out Sir Joseph and begged for his favor and the resulting status of being allowed to do business with him. Duveen often let them wait for years, figuratively and literally cooling their heels in his anterooms while the prices of his merchandise mounted and unworthy applicants for recognition earned his reluctant approval. Frick and Morgan had come to Duveen, perhaps not as humbly as Henry IV at Canossa to do penance in 1077, but still more or less hat in hand and as customers. Duveen had a way with the rich, especially rich widows, so that Arabella Huntington, widow of the great Southern Pacific Railroad nabob, had been so precipitate to keep an appointment with him that she had absent-mindedly left a handbag containing eleven pearl necklaces valued at $3,500,000 on the desk of a competitor.

Mellon moved in spheres that were difficult of access even for Sir Joseph who otherwise had entree everywhere.

Duveen (according to S. N. Behrman in his masterly biography) had experienced singular success with upper servants as instruments of forwarding his campaigns of salesmanship and diplomacy. A fee of $100 to the deck steward aboard the *Mauretania* had found Duveen seated on the sun deck next to Alexander Smith Cochran, a Yonkers, New York, carpet baron who panted for the finer things of life and to whom Duveen, later and under pressure, consented to sell $5,000,000 worth of miscellaneous art objects. No paintings. Duveen had nothing available at the time that would have been appropriate but some nice miniatures and brocades that looked well in the parlor whatnot in the Cochran mansion. On another occasion Duveen had found the services of a Fifth Avenue butler, not identified by Behrman but believed by some to have been the major-domo in the household of Jules Bache, so helpful that remembrances in the sum of more than $100,000 changed hands and the butler was able to retire in comparative affluence to Santa Barbara.

Butlers and valets who saw to it that competitors with paintings to sell their employers never, somehow, achieved their master's presence found Sir Joseph particularly grateful.

Duveen was greatly wishful to have the pleasure of an acquaintance with Mellon and his earlier success with Cochran suggested the efficacy of adjacent steamer chairs. Finding himself crossing on the *Berengaria* with the Secretary, the usual consideration to the deck steward found his steamer rug neatly rolled next to the Mellon steamer rug every morning, but the results were disappointing. The Secretary, a believer in shipboard exercise in an alarming degree, never sat down. Instead he circumnavigated the deck for a certain interval in the morning and after each meal and then disappeared into his suite on A Deck. Fortunately the suites on *Berengaria* were sufficiently commodious to meet with Mellon's favor. Once, when taking passage for an Easter vacation with Paul Mellon at Bermuda, the master suite on the elderly Furness Withy liner *Fort St. George* was found too small and had been summarily enlarged by knocking down the adjacent partitions and converting half a deck into a single apartment. The impromptu carpentry had weakened the structure of the already aging vessel to such a degree that on the very next trip out of New York she sank while passing through the Narrows.

Thwarted aboard *Berengaria,* Duveen found himself again handy to Mellon when each occupied a suite at Claridge's on West Brook Street. Mellon was on the third floor; Sir Joseph had a permanent flat on the fourth. In the course of their duties Duveen's valet found an opportunity to cultivate the acquaintance of the invaluable Flore. "The two valets seemed to have wished the contagion of their friendship to spread to their masters." The phrase is Behrman's.

Alerted to the impending departure from his apartment of the Secretary, Duveen's valet was also, by judicious timing, enabled to get his master into hat and overcoat just in time to ride down in Claridge's perfumed lift with his prospect. Pleasantries were exchanged about the weather and Sir Joseph was able, with the utmost propriety, to introduce himself on terms of equality to one of the world's richest men. Duveen suggested that, instead of taking his constitutional around the park, Mellon accompany him to the National Gallery, a matter of ten minutes' walk through the most socially eligible part of London, and the beginning of a profitable relationship was laid through the diplomatic agency represented by the two contracting valets.

That it was not immediately to bear fruit was evidenced in a manner that would have been considered downright discouraging by any dealer less optimistic than Duveen. Sir Joseph had been in negotiation with the Soviet Government for the purchase of a vast quantity of paintings from the collection at The Hermitage which he planned to sell to Mellon as the beginning of the collection that should eventually be the National Gallery.

One morning he awoke to discover that Mellon had purchased $7,000,000 worth of The Hermitage art from Knoedler's, Duveen's bitterest rival.

Far from being dismayed, Duveen was enchanted. "It shows that he's ready for me," he said modestly. "Only Duveens will do now that he has had a taste of what his money can really buy him."

Duveen was right. Shortly thereafter Mellon purchased various other items from The Hermitage for $3,000,000, this time from

Duveen, and subsequently another $21,000,000 worth which jointly and with still further additions to come became the basis of the National Gallery which is the Secretary's most enduring public monument.

Long after his triumphs in selling the future National Gallery to Mellon, Duveen was still of disposing mind when it came to upper servants. Waiter captains and hotel managers were careful to salute him as Sir Joseph even in democratic America, none more so than the dining-car steward on the New York Central's *Detroiter* which Duveen frequently boarded when doing business with customers in the Motor City. On one such occasion the diner steward gave him his accustomed "Good night, Sir Joseph," with the usual $10 result, and, after his car was closed, turned for relaxation and instruction to the pages of the *Detroit Free Press*. What he learned there enabled him at breakfast to salute his prize passenger with "Good morning, Lord Duveen." In the interim he had learned of Duveen's elevation to the peerage. It rated a $50 fee, the difference between a knighthood and a baronetcy.

Whatever sums Joseph Duveen may have collected from Andrew Mellon for the paintings that are Mellon's last memorial in the National Gallery must, on a pro rata basis anyway, pale in comparison to the toll he exacted from Jules Bache for the storage in Duveen's Paris atelier of the Bache cigars.

Many legends have come into being about the costliness of various rarely aromatic and princely cigars. Alfred de Rothschild of the English branch of the family made presents to departing house guests at his country estate, Halton House, of bundles containing 100 each of his celebrated guinea ($5.00) panatelas. The elder J. P. Morgan smoked a specially handmade super-corona-size oscuro Havana that stood the financier $1.50 each. Few, even of the world's wealthiest men, paid the price ponied up by the international banker Jules Bache for the storage of his favorite smokes.

Bache, a monocled and Teutonic connoisseur whose uptown offices in New York occupied the space in the Plaza Hotel now occupied by the men's stand-up bar, was a favored customer of Duveen's who, as a mark of special esteem, was permitted to keep his supply of cigars for smoking in Europe in the properly humid-ified cellars of Duveen's Paris art gallery. There, nestling cosily among the temporarily homeless Rembrandts and Vermeers await-ing a purchaser, Bache's Hoyo de Montereys and Belindas matured and were withdrawn as their owner required on his frequent visits from the United States.

On one occasion when he was taking the boat train to Cher-bourg preparatory to boarding the *Mauretania* for New York, Bache found himself in short supply for the Atlantic crossing and bade his chauffeur detour by way of Duveen's place of busi-ness en route to the Gare du Nord. Time pressed and Bache kept looking nervously at his watch while an emissary procured the cigars, but in the course of his pacing up and down his eye was caught by a Vandyke without which, on the spur of the instant, the collector knew he could not live. In a matter of less than five minutes he had purchased the Vandyke and had it wrapped up, and just managed to catch the boat train with the painting and the cigars under his arm. There was no charge for the storage of Bache's cigars but the Vandyke cost him $275,000, which made the various perfectos and coronas perhaps the most expensive in the annals of smoking.

The tie-in sale involving Jules Bache's cigars was by no means unique in the history of the collection of fine arts by American millionaires where oblique considerations, furtive campaigns of attrition, and intrigue to amuse a Florentine prince were the accepted order of the day. In the heyday of miscellaneous acqui-sition in the seventies, William Henry Vanderbilt, following the example of other wealthy Americans, was wishful to have his like-ness painted by the French portraitist and depicter of spirited bat-tle scenes Ernest Meissonier. No matter that Meissonier scorned to flatter his subjects to such a degree that Mrs. John Mackay, wife of the Comstock bonanza king, on the completion of her portrait immediately withdrew it from view and reportedly destroyed it, a gesture which provoked international tension and bad feeling.

Vanderbilt, who fancied himself a knowledgeable art critic, admired the meticulous detail of Meissonier's warriors and statesmen but was unable to induce the artist to book him for a sitting. Vanderbilt's time in Europe was brief and the master was fully booked for months in advance. Not for nothing was Vanderbilt the most successful railroad operator of his generation. At a cost of $188,000 he purchased seven Meissonier paintings of grenadiers at the battle of Austerlitz and other stirring Napoleonic moments and, charmed by this courtesy, Meissonier found he could accommodate his sitting book to the magnate's schedule. It was a very good portrait indeed and figured in all the obituary articles when Vanderbilt died.

After the death, full of years and honors, of Andrew Mellon, his place as the supreme hidalgo of Pittsburgh came to be occupied by his nephew Richard K. Mellon, a grandee in his own right who exercised much of the power of the Secretary but lacked the old gentleman's personal sense of splendor. Once when a newspaper reporter spoke of him as "the King of Pennsylvania," Richard Mellon complained to associates of what he regarded as an impertinence.

"Do you really think it proper for this fellow to refer to me as the King of Pennsylvania?" he asked at luncheon at the Duquesne Club. "Do you think I ought to take umbrage?"

"It may have been taking liberties, Mr. Richard," he was told, "but how would you have felt if he had described anybody else as 'the King of Pennsylvania?'"

Mr. Mellon confessed himself answered.

Chapter Twelve
Bonanza Bazaar

To Rich Texans, Neiman-Marcus Is a Way of Life . . . It Solves the Problems of Men and Women Who Have Everything . . . When the Store Burns Down, the Debris Sells at a Markup . . . Mother-of-Pearl Regency Armchairs Are Always in Stock, So Are Mink-Covered Pocket Flasks, but Vicuña Blankets for Horses Are Frowned on . . . Neiman-Marcus Raises His and Hers to the Ultimate Elevation with His and Hers Airplanes at $176,000 . . . "It's a State of Grace," Says a Historian. . . .

WHEN, ONLY A few days before Christmas 1964, a four-alarm fire, fortunately during the midnight hours, caused an estimated $5,000,000 worth of damage in the nationally celebrated store of Neiman-Marcus in Dallas, Texas, very little of the damage was structural or architectural. Despite the reasonably plush amenities which surround customers at Neiman-Marcus including elevators sprayed at frequent intervals with a special perfume calculated to loosen fiduciary inhibitions, a Zodiac Restaurant that is one of the more agreeable gastronomic premises of the Southwest, and escalators that waft moneyed patrons between floors through bowered arches of tropic blooms, it is doubtful if the entire Neiman-Marcus plant would have assayed out to the gratifying sum estimated by the management and triumphantly carried by wire services all over the world.

It was the stock that was so costly. In normal seasons just an ordinary mid-summer inventory of Neiman-Marcus' stockrooms and display cases would come to a total to strain credibility. At Christmas, when merchandise is placed in availability for oil-rich Texans in full flight of their most splendid delusions of grandeur, Neiman-Marcus simply transcends the imaginable. The fire hoses washed out tide rips of mink, sable, and ermine in sufficient quantities to renew the state robes of all the peers of England. Matched pairs of his and hers airplanes at $176,000 the set contributed to the expensive combustion. Ermine bathrobes at $6500 and men's lounging pajamas at $650 fed the flames. The fire axes made kindling out of kiddies' model Rolls-Royces at $75 and mahogany bars for the home at $3000 complete with sterling-silver drinking tools. As, in the case of an early and more comprehensive catastrophe, when Lawrence Harris wrote about the destruction of San Francisco by fire in October 1906, it produced "The damndest finest ruins, nothing more and nothing less."

Some of the debris turned up later in various discount houses and distress merchandise marts throughout the countryside. A large consignment of almost undamaged furs went to Filene's automatic bargain basement in Boston where they caused such riotous conduct among the customers that police were summoned. Elsewhere, Neiman-Marcus castoffs retailed wildly, sometimes at prices in excess of their original tags in Dallas, so great is the prestige of the firm's name. Neiman-Marcus would have nothing of it. A spot of chemical or even a trace of the smell of smoke was enough to condemn men's $250 chesterfield overcoats as surely as though they had the sleeves burned off. Neiman-Marcus has no truck with damaged goods.

Some of Neiman-Marcus' stock in trade was not available to resale on any terms, such as the shipment made daily by air express from Los Angeles of specially flavored ice cream from Wil Wright's, the most expensive ice-cream foundry in the world, whose water ices are flavored with vintage Bollinger champagne and where the price wholesale of something called Nesselrode

Bula is $3.00 the quart. Other gustatory delicacies recruited from all over the world and in their several repositories in the Zodiac Restaurant were beyond salvage.

With typical Neiman-Marcus flair for opportunism, the management converted the Christmas fire of 1964 from a disaster into an asset in the field of promotion to a degree where almost as much newspaper space was devoted to the resulting "world's most elegant fire sale," as was usually achieved by his and hers items in the holiday season. Texas newspapers were glad to announce that it was the "biggest department-store fire in U.S. history," and the prices fetched by such items as slightly scorched opium beds and singed Burmese idols added to the already established luster of the store as an abode of *richesse* under happier conditions. Even the ruins at Neiman-Marcus were worth $1,741,502.97, a gratifying figure by any standards.

Thirty-three would-be buyers sent representatives to Dallas from as far away as Boston, Atlanta, and Los Angeles (not to mention Mexia, Texas) to rummage through the miles of smoky, sooty goods and figure up the sealed bids which were opened in the Dallas Room of the new First National Bank Building.

Six of the thirty firms which eventually bid were successful—not including two firms with intriguing names, Pizitz of Birmingham, Alabama, and Nothing Inc., of Buffalo, New York.

The successful bidders were:

- Weinstein Company of San Francisco, which bought "men's hanging goods," retail-priced at $799,242.88 for a high bid of $392,013.13, "women's hanging goods," priced at $1,617,664.87, for $510,030.13, and cosmetics priced at $225,192.12 for $89,128.13.
- Railroad Salvage Company of New Haven, Connecticut, which bought children's clothing priced at $107,990 for $21,011.
- Ben Bail of Los Angeles, which bought men's furnishings priced at $495,899.96 for $190,039.

- Jordan Marsh Company, an Allied store in Boston, which bought luggage priced at $133,468.63 for $33,462 and handbags and umbrellas priced at $178,179.33 for $55,636.
- Bargain Center of Quincy, Massachusetts, which bought stationery priced at $105,317.25 for $24,705 and lingerie priced at $746,477.03 for $225,605.
- Tillman & Levenson of Birmingham, Alabama, which bought linens, gifts, china, and glass priced at $326,346.21 for $62,126.

Miscellaneous odd lots brought the total up to the gratifying total named.

Only two companies submitted bids on the entire eleven lots of merchandise. Weinstein Company offered $1,544,413.13 and the Bargain Center offered $1,663,899.99.

But the total of the highest bids on the eleven lots added up to $1,741,502.97 and the Underwriters Salvage Company of New York, acting for some sixty-odd insurance companies that had carried the fire risk on Neiman's merchandise, took the individual bids.

All of the merchandise was sold on "as-is and where-is basis with the inventory guaranteed as to quantity but not as to quality, price, or condition." It might not be resold within 100 miles of the Dallas city limits, and in advertising to the public it could be identified only as "formerly owned by Neiman-Marcus." The Neiman-Marcus labels remained in the merchandise.

Thousands of items were sold. Each inventory ran to 706 legal-size pages and listed dresses priced up to $1800, purses to $1000, exotic items such as an opium bed, a $5500 silver pineapple, and a Burmese goddess priced at $8500.

At the afternoon sale, jewelry, silverware, and antiques priced at $220,135 went to Breier Sales Company of Houston for $26,979.97 and toys priced at $12,566.50 went to Tillman & Levenson of Birmingham for $2126.

A lot of wigs priced at $20,067 failed to sell. The bids were rejected as too low.

When Friday's fire sale was over, the Underwriters Salvage Company found it had taken in $1,946,831.94 on the damaged merchandise. Neiman's price tags on it all—including the furs previously sold to Filene's of Boston—added up to $6,417,701.40.

The Neiman-Marcus fire left traumatic scars on Dallas beyond those that could be inflicted by a comparable conflagration elsewhere for the abundant reason that it is the biggest thing in the community, the town's chief claim to fame and very nearly its only one. The community, for a brief moment of panic, envisioned what it would be like to live without Neiman-Marcus and found it unthinkable. Stanley Marcus reassured it on that score before the fire engines had left the scene, but Dallas got the fright of its life for a short time that fatal morning six days before Christmas. If Jordan Marsh in Boston or even Marshall Field in Chicago should disappear utterly and not be replaced, the loss, while massive, would not be fatal. Dallas, for all its oil companies, banks, insurance, Sheraton hotels, and a minor university wouldn't exist without Neiman-Marcus. It would be Waco or Wichita, which is to say: nothing.

That is why the Neiman-Marcus fire, although it might be hard to get a responsible resident to say so, upset Dallas far more than the assassination of President Kennedy there a scant year earlier. The assassination could have taken place anywhere. Neiman-Marcus can only burn down in Dallas.

One of the first calls from the outside world to come through to Stanley Marcus was from the White House. For years President Johnson has bought the western hats he wears and gives away as souvenirs there. The late Amon Carter of Fort Worth gave away ten-gallon hats, too, but rather than patronize a Dallas shop he bought them directly from Borsalino in Italy at nearly double the price.

When President Johnson called he was assured that inaugural gowns being prepared by the store for Mrs. Johnson and the Johnson daughters were still being designed in New York and therefore were not damaged in the blaze. But ten young ladies of Dallas who were to be married that Saturday lost their dresses in the fire. The

Store (as it is often called by Texas writers) rose to the challenge by renting a suite in the Statler-Hilton Hotel for refitting the brides.

The first wedding was scheduled to be held at 4 P.M. At 2 o'clock a wedding gown from the N-M store in Fort Worth arrived at the hotel by truck. A fitter measured the bride-to-be and the dress, and at 2:22 P.M. departed for the N-M store in Preston Center, a Dallas suburb. There seamstresses set to work on alterations. The fitter then brought the altered dress to the church. She arrived at 3:40 P.M. and found the bride waiting in her underclothes. The wedding began on time.

One of the brides-to-be whose dress was lost in the fire was Ginny Lou Martin, a Baylor University senior who had been chosen by *Glamour* magazine as one of the ten best-dressed girl students in 1963. Ginny wept when the N-M bridal director broke the news that her dress had burned. But she, too, was refitted at the hotel and married in style.

Commenting on the bridal rush, a woman official of Neiman-Marcus said that it was (no pun intended) a fitting challenge to the all-round wedding service that the store provides.

"Why, we even hold the hand of the father if he gets nervous," she said.

The idea of all-round service has been the philosophy of the store ever since it was established in 1907 by Herbert Marcus, his aunt, Mrs. Carrie Marcus Neiman, and her husband, A. L. Neiman. When they opened their specialty shop in a small two-story building in Dallas, Herbert Marcus remarked that any fine store could dress a few women beautifully.

"Our idea is to dress a whole community that way," he said. Now, after more than fifty years, it is generally conceded that Neiman-Marcus has done more than any other store to influence the dress of Texas women, especially urban women and the rich.

As it has grown to institution status, various writers have tried to chronicle the Neiman-Marcus essence. George Sessions Perry, a native Texan, wrote: "Many folks look at Neiman-Marcus and see only a breathtakingly beautiful store. This is like a rancher looking at wild flowers and seeing only cow feed. Neiman-Marcus is a state of mind. Almost a state of grace."

A University of Texas professor made "Tales of Neiman-Marcus" part of his doctoral thesis.

"One of the earliest Neiman-Marcus tales," he wrote, "concerns a woman from Electra, Texas, an oil town near Wichita Falls. About 1927, this woman appeared in the Neiman-Marcus store barefooted and in a sunbonnet. She announced that she wished to purchase a mink coat. When she had selected a coat, she paid for it on the spot with currency. The sales force at Neiman's, sensing an exceptional opportunity, also sold her a pair of shoes."

There are few barefoot women in Texas today. How the scene has changed—and with it the sales pitch of the store—was shown by an N-M newspaper advertisement that appeared shortly before an opening of the Metropolitan Opera in Dallas a few seasons ago. The ad was titled "Neiman-Marcus Opera Libretto," and purported to give information no operagoer should be without: what to wear, and even what the husband should wear. It read:

> Opening Night. *Il Trovatore,* by Giuseppe Verdi. You wear a full-length dress (here, Dior's yellow lace sheath, $495); your escort, white tie and tails. Saturday Afternoon, the beloved *La Bohème* by Giacomo Puccini. Attend it in a sophisticated print, such as this Traina-Norell dotted surah, $210. Your husband should wear his newest dark silk suit. Saturday Night, hear Renata Tebaldi in Verdi's *La Traviata.* Go gala in short, flowing chiffon by Traina-Norell, $485. Your husband? In dinner jacket, of course. Sunday Afternoon, the delightful *La Périchole,* by Jacques Offenbach. Plan ahead—wear a silk ensemble like this Blotta design, $265. You'll shed the jacket for a final opera celebration Sunday evening.

In noting this classic instance of fashion direction, John Bainbridge, in his book about Texas, *The Super Americans,* observed that the Dallas opera lover who wanted to attend in N-M style would spend $1455, not counting the price of admission. Also, the question arose as to whether the husband could attend the Sunday performance at all, since Neiman-Marcus had not told him what to wear.

Neiman-Marcus' world celebrity of today was originally predicated on the same philosophy that motivated gamblers, saloonkeepers, and the managers of bagnios in the old West, a belief that was radiantly justified by events that there was more money to be made by supplying the amenities of life to the miners than there was in the diggings themselves. Smack dab in the diametric center of the richest flowering of multimillionaire Texas oil producers, cattle ranchers, real-estate tycoons, cotton kings, and railroad barons, Neiman-Marcus aimed to supply the wants of these several enviable categories of potential customers at the source of their wealth and before it could be siphoned off to undeserving recipients in New York, London, and Paris.

The idea proved so sound that it wasn't long before the store and its ever-growing body of folklore, like the Alamo, the Bowie knife, Davy Crockett, and Big Foot Wallace, transcended the mere boundaries of the Lone Star State and became a national and then an international institution. Its fame, like anything else, grew in the Texas telling of it and soon the management was in the dilemma of trying to live up to its billing. It can only be said that it rose to the challenge.

Today, Neiman-Marcus is one of the truly great mercantile institutions of the world, one with Selfridge's and Fortnum & Mason in London, Wanamaker's in Philadelphia, and, perhaps, Marshall Field in Chicago, although on a scale and magnitude greatly abated from the last of these. It attracts its customers from as far away as New York and San Francisco and has mail-order accounts throughout the free world. Now and then its celebrity involves inconvenience such as customers who, at Christmas time, when delivery wagons are at a premium and outside expressmen are employed, won't accept delivery except in conveyances with Neiman-Marcus name in sight, preferably occupying the whole side of the truck.

There are also women who send their furs and evening wraps back to have the Neiman-Marcus label inside the collar reversed so as to be legible to those sitting behind them at the theatre.

These are whims of snobbishness the management is glad to humor.

No commercial venture in the record ever received free publicity comparable to that which every year at Christmas gladdens Neiman-Marcus and delights or outrages, as the case may be, uncounted millions of the newspaper readers of the land.

Now and then the tally of $1500 mother-of-pearl Regency armchairs and mink-swathed pocket flasks raises the blood pressure of social consciousness as it was reported to do in an army sergeant on active duty during the Korean War who sent for fifty copies of the Christmas catalogue to distribute among the troops as evidence of what they were fighting for. The intent was subversive. The soldiery, it is pleasant to report, were enchanted and many of them expressed the sentiment that the first place they'd go when they got out of the Army was to Dallas to buy something at Neiman-Marcus.

Neiman-Marcus' Christmas catalogue is a widely sought item in the merchandising folklore of the land, and nowhere more so than in the editorial rooms of the Texas press and the wire services, which accord the store free advertising and promotion only before achieved by one commercial venture: the circus. What the old-time mail-order-house catalogues from Chicago and St. Louis used to be in lonely farmhouses in Maine and distant ranches in Arizona, the Neiman-Marcus Christmas book is to the Rolls-Royce-and-opera-season trade in San Francisco, Omaha, and Atlanta, a sort of Social Register edition of Sears, Roebuck.

Mention has already been made of the his and hers airplane which led the list of Santa Claus's suggestions for 1960 and $176,000 the pair with one's own choice of color, style of curtains, and cabin furniture. The year before that there was available for $1925, FOB Chicago, a live prize Black Angus steer, together with a solid-silver rolling table to serve him from when cooked. If you were not prepared to butcher the animal, it could be had dressed and ready for the deep freeze at $2230, still with the serving cart.

"We're not against conspicuous consumption," Stanley Marcus once remarked, "as long as it doesn't show."

Another year the money-is-no-object gift was either a complete cellar of French vintage wine, 144 bottles in all, in a self-contained cellaret that could double as room divider for people with no basements, at $5000 or an ermine bathrobe at $6975, federal tax included, good to wear outdoors, as one wag suggested, in case of a revolution.

That was the year they featured a stuffed toy tiger fur-deep in $1,000,000 worth of cut diamonds, and a complete beach-party setup including a pink Jeep for $1848, FOB Detroit, an Empress chinchilla coat at $25,000, and a vicuña rug to spread on the sand for $295. Now and then, just to show that it is human, Neiman-Marcus loses its footing, trapped in its own superlatives and delusions of grandeur. This was conspicuously so the year it featured a his and hers combination, a pair of Chinese junks made to order in Hong Kong with mahogany decks, silk sails, and a concealed thirty-horsepower motor, FOB Houston, for $11,500. The eleven customers who bought them got bargains. Neiman-Marcus had forgotten to add its own markup.

The featured his and hers gift for 1964, the year of the big fire, was a pair of hot-air, free-flying sports balloons, painted to resemble the original Montgolfier models and available to being filled with pink hot air at $6850 each. Lesser items on occasion have been ladies' pipes set with rubies, emeralds, and sapphires at $1250; white mink flask covers, $100; bulletproof vests, $195; sets of seven gold buttons for men's blazer jackets, $205; and a sort of Christmas cocktail served in a huge champagne glass whose ingredients included a $10,000 mutation mink opera coat frosted with a $75,000 diamond necklace and topped with a bottle of French perfume.

Because it likes to paint itself as occasionally being fallible, Neiman-Marcus admires to publicize its own infrequent lapses like the no-profit Chinese junks. Once, during a Christmas season when special emphasis was being laid by the promotion department on the elaborate and costly nature of the available gift wrappings, a hurried salesgirl discovered she had absent-mindedly wrapped her own luncheon in a fetching bundle of gold lamé and tinsel cord and that it had already gone out on the truck, consigned to some forever-unidentified customer. Nobody ever did find out who got it.

The management structure of the world's most glamorous store and perhaps its most costly in over-all terms (there are impious Texans who speak of it as "Neiman-Markup") is vested in Stanley Marcus, its president, and his three brothers, Edward, Herbert, Jr., and Lawrence Eliot. Until her death in 1953, chairman of the board had been the brothers' aunt, Mrs. Carrie Marcus-Neiman, wife of one of the founding fathers. To the outer world, Stanley Marcus is very emphatically Mr. Dallas. There may be other industrialists, bankers, and oil men of consequence in the community whose names are locally known, but visiting dignitaries always call on Mr. Stanley the way ambassadors call on heads of state to present their credentials.

In his lifetime, jovial and flamboyant Amon G. Carter of nearby Fort Worth gave Mr. Stanley a run for his money as the best-known Texan of his time, but their personalities were somewhat different. Carter's notion of showing good will, and one that was widely approved by its beneficiaries, was to arrive in New York's Waldorf-Astoria for the annual newspaper publishers' convention, take over an entire floor, and throw all the keys out the window into Park Avenue. He then kept open house like a maharaja for the duration. Mr. Marcus' idea of a big evening is an after-dinner discussion of Picasso with a visiting art critic.

The first of Neiman-Marcus' regular accounts averaging more than $100,000 in merchandise a year was that of Mrs. Electra Waggoner Wharton whose husband ran up a modest stake into an oil fortune of $100,000,000 in the first world war. The day she discovered Neiman-Marcus, Mrs. Wharton spent $20,000 and liked what she'd bought so well she came back the next day and spent another

$20,000. Later she bought a home in Dallas so as to be near Neiman-Marcus and furnished it with a $42,000 Persian carpet and $55,000 antique tapestries on the dining-room walls. Sometimes Mrs. Wharton would take weekend guests to the family oil farm in Wilbarger County and, if a gusher came in that blew the crown block and head rigging off the well, the party was a success. Many of the Wharton guests carried firearms which they sometimes pulled from under their dinner jackets and fired miscellaneously as the soup was being served at table. The $55,000 tapestry got more antique every time this happened, but the hostess didn't like the hot shells ejected from her guests' six guns to burn the $42,000 Persian rug so, at each place along with the ash trays and place settings, she placed a woven gold-mesh empty cartridge basket. They cost $1500 each.

Mrs. Wharton had a new pair of shoes sent out from Neiman-Marcus almost daily until she had 350 pairs in her shoe closet, most of which had never been worn, but she refused to wear a dress that had been tried on by anyone else. Neiman-Marcus sent them to her, eight or ten $500 frocks at a time in the original packages from Paris with the customs seals intact.

Neiman-Marcus, among its other superlatives, is the largest single American purchaser of vicuña, according to the store's official annalist, Frank X. Tolbert, who doubles as a columnist for the *Dallas Morning News.* Even so, only about enough of this exotic and supercostly cloth, so soft that among the ancient Incas it was worn only by royalty and so durable that it wears like Levi's "only we don't advertise that," says Lawrence Marcus, comes in every year to make a garment for each of 500 fortunate customers.

Hearing about the fabulous cloth, a well-heeled Borger, Texas, cowhand wrote in and ordered a vicuña blanket for his horse. Neiman-Marcus was stern; they told him it wouldn't be fair to their waiting list of customers to make up a vicuña horseblanket.

A year or two ago the window department placed in one of the display cases $150,000 worth of vicuña coats ranging in price from

$375 for a man's sports jacket to $1500 for a full-length skirted woman's coat. "Nobody even in Texas will pay $1500 for a cloth coat," was the word that went around. The window was empty next morning. All had been sold.

Neiman-Marcus has a favorite customer for vicuña coats of which he regularly buys one a year. He lives in Peru where the camel-like beasts breed from which the wool is clipped. "You gift-wrap my purchases so prettily," was the customer's explanation.

Captain of industry or not, Stanley Marcus himself greatly admires to make sales in person in his store and materializes out of well-perfumed nowhere when a particularly dough-heavy customer paws at the threshold. "There's a legend around Dallas that salespeople summon him on a secret whistle that only Mr. Stanley can hear," says Everett De Golyer, himself a Dallas hidalgo of stature who collects railroad trains, full-size, as a hobby. Last year Mr. Stanley personally sold $420,000 worth of mink alone. It's not in the record if he took a commission.

Legend clusters more thickly around Neiman-Marcus than around any other store in the world for the ample reason that its traffic is indeed in the fabulous and that nothing so fascinates and delights people as money and the things money buys. It is present in vast quantities and it buys almost anything at Neiman-Marcus. Also the management is acutely aware of the uses of publicity. Tiffany in New York, a comparable name in the field of quality merchandise, is so standoffish about publicity that it is upset by the merest miscalling of its name. It likes to be known as Tiffany, not Tiffany's, so that when Truman Capote wrote a book called *Breakfast at Tiffany's* the management was haughty about it. "Not our store," they said, making hand-washing motions. "Must be somewhere else."

As long as the name is even approximately correct, Neiman-Marcus is happy to get newspaper and magazine space, although they weren't entirely glad to be identified in a coated-paper periodical as "The Lord & Taylor of Texas."

There are traces of the Neiman-Marcus *mystique* everywhere that legend can penetrate. During the battle of Salerno, a one-time army stenographer remembers being summoned by a lady major to take some dictation. An intense bombardment was going on with high explosive blowing people to smithereens on every hand. Overhead a number of planes were engaged in a dogfight. Troops were being deployed to man essential positions and the man of pothooks expected a terse military communication concerning replacements of at least the logistics of combat.

"Neiman-Marcus Company, Dallas, Texas, U.S.A.," said the major in measured accents while thoughtfully buffing a nail. "Please send me as soon as possible a four-ounce bottle of your Woodhue perfume which is unobtainable in these parts just now."

Perhaps the best-known article of Neiman-Marcus faith, or at least the one that appears most frequently in anthologies of the store's folklore and anecdota, concerns the customer from East Texas who was agreeable to buying the entire window display of one of the shop's main windows if it could be arranged intact in the drawing room of his home. Measurements were procured, disclosing that the room assured the proper dimension, and the entire miscellaneous layout of fur coats, jewelry, Steuben glass, bed linen, perfumery, chinaware, and men's lounging robes was dispatched in a delivery truck and reassembled as ordered. The cost was a cool $86,000 but the man was happy. He wanted members of his family when they arrived to celebrate the holidays to get the feeling of window-shopping at Neiman-Marcus without having to go to Dallas.

Usually and by preference of the management, the sales staff is refined to a degree provocative of wonder and disbelief among some of the cowhand and oil-rigger customers. One such was the salesgirl who rose to the occasion when a waddy from Waco wondered if $9.50 wasn't a bit high for an embroidered handkerchief.

He was reassured when the young lady looked him in the eye and said: "But sir, this item is *hand-did.*"

Less susceptible was the young man of modest means who wandered in one morning near Christmas just as a matron was purchasing something she desperately needed: a diamond-mounted swizzle stick for champagne for $265. At another counter a folksy customer who looked as though he ate at counter lunches was casually peeling $12,000 off a bank roll for an emerald bracelet for his little girl in high school. Down the aisle somebody was completing an order for twenty dozen of Romanée Conti Burgundy at $22.50 the bottle.

Asked by a salesperson if there was anything he saw that he liked, the young man said resolutely: "No, ma'am, there isn't. I just have never seen so many things in my life I can plumb do without."

Perhaps the all-time Neiman-Marcus inspiration was the occasion when, as a present from the management and without charge, the store sent a member of its own staff a chauffeur and footman for his car. The store's shoe buyer, Robert Alexander, was, in his spare time, a collector of vintage motorcars, which will give you an idea of the sort of people Neiman-Marcus hires. Lawrence Marcus, noting that one morning as he came to work Alexander parked a magnificent vintage Bentley that had once belonged to a film star in the company lot, remarked that it was really the sort of car that ought to have two men on the box. On Christmas morning Alexander found his car parked in front of his home with a chauffeur and footman in full livery, gloved, visor-capped and putteed at attention. "You cannot discharge them as they are hired for a full week and paid in advance," read the Christmas card from his employers. At the end of the week they returned to less exalted occupations, driving one of Neiman-Marcus' delivery trucks.

While Neiman-Marcus basks warmly and approvingly in the radiance of some of the best free publicity in the world, there is an ever-present hazard, occupational among bankers and merchants of expensive properties and artifacts, against which elaborate security precautions are maintained. This is the violation of the anonymity of the firm's customers. Strictest secrecy shrouds who bought his wife the $75,000 cabochon emerald and diamond bracelet that was the prize of the Christmas jewelry collection. Closely locked in the company's corporate breast is the identity of customers for Chinese junks and hot-air balloons even though such properties may not escape notice in the home to which they are delivered. That many of Neiman-Marcus' best patrons would be enchanted to have their purchases and their prices trumpeted to the winds makes no difference. There are also those whose habits of extravagance must, for a variety of cogent reasons, be kept from employers, wives, mistresses, bankers, and credit-rating agencies.

To shield these from the bright light of publicity, Neiman-Marcus maintains what amounts to military security regulations. Compared to its credit department, the grave is a chatty source of informative gossip. Sales personnel, shipping-department help, and billing clerks are made to know that their jobs depend upon a degree of taciturnity becoming domestics at Buckingham Palace. Popular legend holds that a Neiman-Marcus executive in the higher echelons of the hierarchy was given his congee for being seen at lunch at Henri Soule's in New York with Inez Robb, then gossipy lady columnist of the *New York Daily News,* although this may well be part of the folklore that surrounds every aspect and activity of Dallas' foremost institution.

When the author of this anthology petitioned Stanley Marcus for material on which to base even the friendliest appraisal of Neiman-Marcus, the president of the firm at once assumed the protective coloring and the evasive tactics that have long characterized his contacts with the press. An interoffice memorandum from Mr. Marcus to an underling, included, one may surmise by error, in the ensuing correspondence, read: "I'd be very careful what I sent him."

Now and then Neiman-Marcus makes a halfhearted effort to promote the idea that it really isn't the well-to-do Texas oil man that keeps the firm in business so much as the more modest purchases of the oil man's secretary. On the basis of this estimate Texas secretaries live fairly high on the hog. In a single year they were offered such secretarial necessities as an emerald and diamond necklace at $65,000, a cookout set with appropriate beach jewelry, Chinese jade wind-screens and a handpainted Jeep to carry them in for $150,580.70, a lucite paperweight filled with real Texas oil for $7.95, sterling-silver diaper pins, $6.20 each, gold-plated mice for favorite kittens to play with, $35, fourteen-karat gold dog bones for $45, beaver and mink cowboy hats for $250, and an alligator handbag that opens into a writing desk for $330. Then, too, if you wished to equip your ever-loving St. Bernard dog with accessories appropriate to his mission in life, there was a gold-washed brandy keg with harness to suspend it around faithful Towser's neck, $450. Extra was a smaller but similar flagon for holding crème de menthe at $175. That was in case any-body being rescued from a snowdrift wanted a Stinger.

As Neiman-Marcus points out every year at Christmas, there are a lot of things that can be had from its catalogue at "under $1,000,000."

Lest it be assumed that Neiman-Marcus and the gold-plated cowpoke trade its name evokes have any monopoly on gift sugges-tions of debatable worth but well-established cost, it may be well to consider in passing the Christmas offerings of Shreve & Com-pany of San Francisco. Shreve has been court goldsmith to San Francisco since the days of the Mother Lode and the gold service plates essential to the peace of mind of such early-day nabobs as James Ben Ali Haggin, Darius Ogden Mills, and Lloyd Tevis were supplied by them. In the seventies the wives of Comstock million-aires were known to make a beeline for Shreve's diamond coun-ter directly they crossed the Bay on the ferry without bothering to check in at the Palace Hotel.

Nowadays readers of the *San Francisco Chronicle* look forward to an annual survey compiled at Christmas by Herb Caen, the com-munity's headlined columnist and town crier, in which he under-takes to demonstrate that the Bay City's resources of costly nutti-ness rank with those of Dallas.

Recently he was able to report that Shreve, ever aware of social change, was supplying its proletarian patrons when they arrived in their Bentley Continental convertibles with solid sterling-silver lunch pails at $650, ideally contrived for hard-hat stiffs on bridge construction jobs in the traditional pattern with sandwich and thermos compartments. Shreve's stock of solid-gold shoehorns at $400 disappeared the day they were advertised and other fast-selling items were solid gold-headed golf clubs at $750 and silver-plated shovels, presumably for ground-breaking ceremonies, at $125.

Shreve's less socially exalted but still solvent competition, I. Magnin & Company, was also in the running on the basis of an Audemars-Piguet gentleman's evening pocket watch in platinum and diamonds that remembers to change the date at leap year and tells the phases of the moon. Mr. Caen noted thoughtfully that it is called "The Grand Complication," and carries a price tag of $11,600. Everybody should have one.

As a coda to this recital of amiable ostentations, it may be remarked that signs abound that Neiman-Marcus is tiring of its own image as the bonanza boutique of the gold-bearing waddies from Waco. Evidence comes to hand in the form of the firm's 1965 Christmas catalogue where the most costly expression of gilded whimsey was a para-sail for elevating its recipients behind a moving car or motorboat through the agency of a nylon parachute. It sold for $365.

That the management of Texas' most refulgent mart had not, however, capitulated unconditionally to such mediocrities as gold bubble-bath paddles and kocktail krutches for inkapacitated drinkers is suggested by the inclusion of a full page in four seductive colors advertising "Romanoff's Golden Caviar as Reserved for the Czars of Russia," of which the entire year's catch is less than fifty pounds. Neiman-Marcus was willing to part with a fourteen-ounce tin of this essential commodity, delivered with dry ice anywhere, for $130 with a Baccarat glass dish for its service thrown in. Connoisseurs of Neiman-Marcus felt that the firm's surrender to reason had not been without reservations.

Chapter Thirteen
Misfortune's Darling

Evalyn Walsh McLean Moved Through Life Amidst Diamond-Studded Disasters, an Allegory of Tiaras and Tragedy . . . But She Was the Most Lavish Hostess Ever Seen in Washington . . . A Lady Bountiful of Homeric Dimensions . . . And, by Way of Contrast, a Few Footnotes on Hetty Green. . . .

ALTHOUGH THEY WERE contemporaries in that their lives overlapped in the calendar and in the social history of the United States, this was about the only common bond between two of America's richest women: Hetty Green and Evalyn Walsh McLean. They complemented each other as do the two sides of a medal, but there was no resemblance save that each had within her control vast sums of money at a time when money entailed few taxes and no responsibilities. Hetty hoarded her money. Evalyn McLean spent it like a drunken sailor. Hetty died rich in impoverished surroundings; Mrs. McLean died comparatively a pauper and surrounded with the utmost elegance.

The contrasts and paradoxes of these two remarkable women are among the most fascinating in the record of American wealth and its expenditure.

Largely our concern in this book and in conformance with its title is with the Lady Bountiful of the Hope Diamond, but for the sake of contrast it can do no harm to gaze in awe at the spectacle of embattled parsimony represented by the Witch of Wall Street.

Henrietta Howland Robinson was born in 1834 at New Bedford, Massachusetts, an ancient citadel of whaling and New England thrift, appropriate as the natal setting for an incarnation of acquisitiveness who was to die eighty-two years later richer in liquid assets—and she had no others—than John Pierpont Morgan. In her thirties she married a Vermonter named Edward Green from whom she derived the name that was to become in the ensuing decades a household synonym for being what Yankees call "near" with money, but that is all the importance Green ever achieved. Hetty distrusted anything even suggesting a community of property between husband and wife and before she would permit the minister to pronounce the binding and holy words on their wedding day, she made Green sign an agreement by whose terms, though they might be man and wife in the sight of God, they were to maintain separate accounts at the bank and there was to be no nonsense about common access to the safe deposit box. What Hetty had, Hetty proposed to hold on to.

Thus empowered to act on behalf of nobody but herself, Hetty effected a descent upon the jungle life of New York's financial district in the capacity of Lady Wolf of Wall Street in comparison to whose greed and audacity the operations of whole generation of later "Wolves of Wall Street" such as Dave Lamar and James Keene were to pale.

The New York Stock Exchange had hitherto been a closely guarded preserve of purely masculine rapacity, but Hetty, in the guise of a sort of reverse Florence Nightingale, was soon stacking the maimed and dying like cordwood as a result of her ruthless operations, and bears and bulls alike were licking financial wounds that were pitiful to behold. Even such hardened participants in speculative street accidents as Jay Gould were awed by the carnage that followed in her wake, and Gould had reason to shudder, because Hetty chose as her favorite field of operations the railroad fliers that were Gould's special preserve.

Fairly early in the game, Hetty's claim to being a bombshell in black bombazine was validated when she came into open conflict with the archrobber baron of them all, rich and powerful Collis P. Huntington of the Central and Southern Pacific Railroads, in an encounter from which Huntington retired scarred and bleeding as from fisticuffs with a panther.

Huntington was at the time in mortal combat with Jay Gould for control of the railroad picture in Texas, and the Southern Pacific was laying rails across the Lone Star State for a photo finish of the first transcontinental between California and the Gulf of Mexico. Huntington was buying up branches and short lines that might impede his progress and consolidating them into what was to become the Sunset Route, not exactly regardless of cost, for it pained him grievously to spend an unnecessary two bits, but still from a fairly lavish treasury.

As she often did in cases involving wide geographic distances which might separate her from the shadow of Trinity Church, Hetty sent her son, Colonel E. H. R. Green, to represent her in the lists. She had a double motive in this particular operation; first, she smelled a nice potentiality of profit, and second, she might be able to make it out of the tough hide of Collis P. Huntington, of whom she had a low opinion. This dim view of the feudal overlord of California derived from Hetty's investment of a considerable sum in a streak of rust called the Waco & Northwestern, in Texas, which she claimed had been so signally mismanaged under Huntington ownership that she had lost all when the railroad finally folded.

Colonel Green arrived in the remote town of Terrell, Texas, to do battle with the Southern Pacific's widely renowned general manager of lines in Texas and Louisiana, Julius Kruttschnitt, a towering figure in railroad circles who was later to achieve national celebrity in rebuilding the Union Pacific–Southern Pacific system under Edward H. Harriman. The bone of contention was control of the Houston & Texas Central, a subsidiary of which had been the ill-fated Waco & Northwestern. Hetty had a stake via her shares in the bankrupted branch line.

Colonel Green, although his mother was a nationally known figure already famous for her threadbare umbrella and hand-me-down dresses, was not personally known in Texas, and when he presented a certified check for $500,000 signed by his mother, the Terrell bank wired North for further identification.

"Have him remove his hat," was the reply. "If there's a large mole on his forehead, he's the McCoy. Also, Colonel Green has a wooden leg."

The Colonel obligingly removed his silk top hat, and there was the mole as specified. He also asked the cashier to kick him in the shin as further evidence of authenticity. The bank was glad to cash his check and make him a vice president as well.

Thus financed, Colonel Green turned up at the referee's sale where he faced Kruttschnitt, a representative of the Rock Island Railroad, which was also building into the territory and felt there might be some sort of pickings, and a Mr. Gold, acting for party or parties unknown.

The Espee man of money opened with a bid for $800,000.

The Rock Island raised him $50,000.

"Nine hundred thousand dollars," said the unidentified Mr. Gold.

Colonel Green topped everybody with $1,100,000, or about three times the value of the property in question from an operable standpoint.

Kruttschnitt met him with $1,250,000.

"I'll give you one million two hundred fifty-*five* thousand," said the wooden-legged competition.

In the end, between the Rock Island and the mystery man Gold, they parlayed the price to $1,365,000 at which it went to Hetty Green.

Huntington, apprised of this Waterloo, was numbed and muttered something derogatory about the "mad mud hen." Mud hen was a local term in San Francisco for the frowsy old beldams who played the market in Comstock shares on a shoestring.

It was this sort of thing that caused even big-time operators on Wall Street to dodge into doorways and seek out the men's room when Hetty Green put in an appearance.

In her personal economy, Hetty was as hot on the trail of a bargain shirtwaist as she was for a short-line railroad. Living in shabby rooming houses, she did her own cooking off a gas ring and lived for months on end off graham crackers which she purchased in barrel lots to save the grocer's profit. A single black dress, threadbare from age and now turning a poisonous green, was her only wardrobe and her frayed umbrella, when she put it up, admitted the elements through rusty ribs from which fluttered the remnants of silk covering.

She presented so scarecrow an appearance that once on encountering her sorting out the contents of a trash barrel on Fifth Avenue, Edward Hatch, one of the executive staff at Lord & Taylor, told her that if she'd come by he'd give her a fine black veil from stock.

"Would you?" she said, happy as a kid with firecrackers. "That would be real nice."

Soon afterward there was a disturbance among the merchandise counters devoted to female furnishings at Lord & Taylor and Hatch was informed by a courier that Hetty Green was raising unmitigated hell with the sales staff and claiming she'd been promised a veil for free. The man of garments saw to it that his promise to Mrs. Green was kept, whereupon she asked if by any chance there was any damaged merchandise in the skirt line that she might have at abated prices? Hatch gave her several in last year's mode for fifty cents each and always afterward Hetty told anybody who would listen that Lord & Taylor was a fine place to shop and her favorite outfitter.

Since Hetty's appearance was that of one of the three witches in the first scene of *Macbeth* this was an endorsement to ponder over.

In 1916, Hetty suffered a stroke after a knockdown argument with the housekeeper in the home of a friend over her extravagance.

The cook, Hetty claimed, was bankrupting her employer by using whole milk where the skimmed article would do, and in the ensuing exchange of insults, Hetty burst a blood vessel. Her last hours were spent attended by nurses hired by Ned Green to ease his mother's passing, but they were never allowed to appear at her bedside in nurse's uniforms, only in street clothes. Trained nurses got as high as a dollar an hour in wartime and knowledge of such expense would, Colonel Green knew, have killed her out of hand.

As it was, she left an estate of $100,000,000 which, as Stewart Holbrook points out, is more than the net liquid assets of J. P. Morgan and a resounding monument to what a diet of whole-wheat crackers can accomplish.

We come now to the story of Evalyn Walsh McLean, born under as evil a star as could have been evoked in a manic-depressive moment by Evangeline Adams, a seeress so omniscient that she foretold with split-second accuracy the exact moment of her own death. For although Evalyn Walsh went through life in a snowstorm of currency, envied as a darling of fortune and the associate of reigning monarchs, she was, in fact, a lightning rod for disaster, the sort of Typhoid Mary of the gods dreamed up by Greek tragedians in moments of Athenian hangover.

Evalyn Walsh was born at four on a Sunday afternoon, the first day of August 1886 at Denver, but the urban scene of her first appearance is of little significance because, for the next decade or so, she was to know the most romantic background within the American experience, the mining towns of Colorado in great moments of bonanza, at a time when Central City, Leadville, Creede, Ouray, and Silverton were, in synthesis, the beating heart of the American dream of illimitable wealth for all, or, at least, almost everybody.

Nearly fifty years after she had first known the steeply cobbled pitch of Eureka Street in Central City as a little girl, Evalyn Walsh McLean, owner of the Hope Diamond and the nation's foremost hostess, was escorted by the author of this book to a first night at Central's storied opera house, where the surviving pioneers of those now distant times crowded to do her honor as a symbol of the old days and the good days in the Shining Mountains.

"The magic is still here," she told me. "The magic of a mining town in Colorado never dies for those who knew it when they were young."

The next night she gathered the now graying and stooped companions of her girlhood around her in a setting of wealthy splendor at dinner in the Brown Palace Hotel. Those who had survived the decades were the successful ones, and diamonds and evening dress and formal livery bespoke a way of life they had all known together. Together these elderly gentlefolk, who had once been the pioneers, and the finders, most of them, retraced the trails above the mine at Camp Bird, lived again the wild night life of Creede. It was Evalyn McLean's last return in worldly triumph to the Colorado of her youth.

Her father had been Irish Tom Walsh of Clonmel in Tipperary, who had left the Old Country in the famines of the fifties and drifted west as a woodworker, carpenter, joiner, and builder of bridges on the Colorado Central Railroad. He had gone to the Black Hills in the fevered seventies and there were, until only a few years ago, false fronts in Deadwood that people said he had hammered into place. Inevitably, in that time and place, he prospected for gold with the varying luck of the seekers, once turning a neat $75,000 on a claim in the Black Hills and on another occasion rejecting a partnership that would have made him one of the owners of the great Homestake from which the heirs of Senator George Hearst took $266,000,000 over the years. Tom Walsh took a sort of Irish pride in the magnitude of this bad judgment.

He turned up in Leadville in the bright noontide of the carbonate kings as third owner of a saloon and, a little later, as owner of the Grand Hotel in that frozen suburb of hell. The Walshes were a cut above the rough sourdoughs and a contemporary described Mrs. Walsh as "a rather refined lady," adding that "although the Walshes do well enough from roomers and boarders, they do not attain bonanza rank during this boom."

But essentially Tom Walsh was a miner, perhaps one of those rarely fortunate possessors of an authentic second sight that enabled him to look deep into the heart of the reluctant mountains and sense the presence of true fissures and rich colors where no eye could see. There were such men in the West of the time; their number included bearded old Senator Hearst himself, Bonanza Mackay of Virginia City, for a time the richest man west of William Henry Vanderbilt, and knightly Senator John Percival Jones, also of the Comstock Lode. They were all men to build many mansions on Dupont Circle, on Carlton House Terrace, on the rue Tilsitt. They were the finders.

Tom Walsh's pot of gold, when it finally revealed itself, was even more inaccessibly located than most discoveries in precious metals. It was a conversational cliché of miners that God put valuable things where they were uncommonly hard to come by.

Over behind Red Mountain in southwestern Colorado, where the Imogene Basin near today's town of Ouray was a desolation that had been impervious to man since the dawn of geology, Walsh had a partner. Andy Richardson boasted that he had been the first white man to cross the high divide and prospect the Imogene and he was torn between the true prospector's love of solitude and secrecy and the urgent belief that somewhere in those remote fastnesses there was wealth unutterable to be had for the mere asking and a little luck.

Tom Walsh and his family were living in Ouray in 1896 while Richardson was taking samples from a claim called the Gertrude, samples that Walsh stowed away in canvas sacks under his brass bed at night and finally, when he had enough to fill two saddlebags, started with them for Silverton where there was an assay office.

Three days later, gaunt from the trail where today's Million-Dollar Highway takes you from Ouray to Silverton in minutes, Tom Walsh returned, his eyes feverish with excitement.

"Daughter," he told Evalyn, "we've struck it rich!"

The Camp Bird Mine was a sport in the geological sense that it was a vast true fissure of tellurium gold in a region where only silver-lead carbonates had been found previously. Within a few days of the assay, Walsh and his partner were recovering ore with values of $3000 a ton from the tailings they had discarded in digging their original shaft. With ore such as that around, Tom told his family, any fool with an ice pick could have knocked off a decent living for his family. Tom was no fool with an ice pick; he was a sophisticated miner with very big ideas.

A true discovery in a mining region is never a secret for long, but the fantastic inaccessibility of the Camp Bird kept it from being overrun by come-lately opportunists until Walsh had established his legal right to the claim and gotten protection for it. In time, the Denver & Rio Grande would run its narrow-gauge track into Ouray from its junction at Ridgway with Otto Mears's fantastic and equally narrow-gauge Rio Grande Southern, but in 1896 even the heaviest mining machinery had to be dismantled into its smallest components and packed in on burros.

When the burros came down the mountain they brought saddlebags filled with what was known as "sugar quartz," a delicious phrase for ore that was practically free-milling gold. Few mines of such magnitude and potential production were developed more expeditiously than the Camp Bird. Within a year it was one of the greatest producers in the Western Hemisphere, and Irish Tom Walsh and his family, lately the boardinghouse keepers of Fryer Hill in Leadville, were living on the sunnier side of Easy Street and becoming accustomed to dining well above the salt.

The Camp Bird was pouring out $5000 a day in clear profit.

"Each morning we Walshes arose richer than when we had gone to bed. Mine and mill ran day and night."

The ever richer Walshes had no intention of settling for the rank of local nabobs in the howling wilderness of the Colorado mountains. The mine began producing in 1895 and the season of 1896 saw the family in a vast suite of rooms at the old Cochran Hotel in Washington, a city which for political reasons and because of the presence there of senators and congressmen they knew, held more appeal in

those days for newly solvent westerners than rock-ribbed and impersonal New York. Where the Vanderbilts and Belmonts were impervious to *arrivistes,* a senator who had been assisted into office could
always be counted on to help the socially ambitious on their way up
the ladder, and the Walshes were socially ambitious. Not wildly or
vulgarly so, but in a prudent and cautious manner. They knew that
money existed to buy nice things and they had the money.

More of it by the minute, and some insight into Tom Walsh's
character may be gleaned from his first large investments of the
Camp Bird profits which were $433,850 worth of United States
Government gold bonds at 3 per cent and $102,957.50 worth of
the same yielding 2 per cent, fairly conservative investments for a
self-made American millionaire of the period. He also bought for
$125,000 the Oxford Hotel in Washington, thus maintaining con-
tinuity with his days as hotelier at Leadville, and kept a sharp eye
open for bargains in Washington real estate.

Mrs. McLean's first real splurge was a set of furs from Gunther's for $1800, and it was this tangible evidence of ready cash
that prompted Evalyn McLean to beg for, and get, a blue victoria
drawn by a span of sleek sorrels with a colored coachman in livery
to take her to school. The carriage was assigned to the twelve-year-
old girl for her own occasions and wasn't to be requisitioned by
other members of the family except in emergency.

Evalyn Walsh was determined to travel in splendor until the day
she died.

The Walsh political affiliations were of the right sort. Tom
made contributions in places that were helpful, and in 1899 was
rewarded with an appointment from President McKinley as one
of the commissioners to the Paris Exposition of that year. This was
just the Walshes' dish of tea. Another commissioner to Paris was
Mrs. Potter Palmer, effulgent wife of Chicago's foremost businessman and himself an innkeeper on a somewhat more exalted scale
than Tom Walsh. But no matter. The Walshes embarked for Paris
on the White Star liner *Majestic* and in no time flat were settled in

the Paris Ritz in a state suite facing on the Place Vendôme and giving dinner parties, in the name of the United States commissioners to be sure, but paid for out of the Camp Bird, for 300 and 400 persons at a time.

The Walsh entertainments soon achieved an enviable reputation, and their guest lists at the Ritz even had the approval of cynical Olivier, the monocled maître d'hôtel who separated the sheep from the goats among his customers as arbitrarily as might a highly intelligent Ward McAllister. Olivier was court chamberlain to the great world of before 1914 and his approval probably was more important to the Walshes than the friendship of the American ambassador could have been. When Olivier observed that regulars at the Walsh dinners on Sunday evening included Mrs. Potter Palmer and M. Georges Nagelmackers, president of the *Compagnie Internationale des Wagons-Lits et des Grands Express Européens,* he allowed them to be served the Cheval Blanc '78 from the hotel cellars. When Olivier found himself walking backward to escort Leopold, King of the Belgians, to the private dining salon reserved for Tom Walsh's guests, he brushed off the Margaux '65. The Walshes were in.

The Walshes had become acquainted with bearded old Leopold through the kind offices of M. Nagelmackers who took them to visit that well-heeled monarch at the Châlet du Roi at Ostend. They went by private train made up of *wagons-lits* cars ordinarily reserved for royal personages in what Evalyn was later to describe as "truly palace cars as wide as rooms in houses with costly paintings, fine oriental rugs, and a swarm of liveried servants who seemed to spend two thirds of the time serving foods and wines."

The liveries of the *wagons-lits* attendants may have seemed ostentatious to a girl brought up in Ouray and Leadville; they included white silk stockings with crimson knee breeches, blue tail coats with immense gold *fourragères* looped across the front, frilled lace shirts with trailing cuffs, and white wigs. No conductor on the Colorado & Southern had been so attired, and it gave Evalyn Walsh ideas. Many years later her house servants on Wisconsin

Avenue were the handsomest and best uniformed in Washington, although knee breeches had largely gone out of style by the time the author of this book was her guest.

King Leopold's interest in the rich American mining man was neither altogether social nor wholly impersonal. His mistresses were enormously expensive; the Châlet du Roi needed central heating and new plumbing; and some of his Congo rubber plantations weren't doing as well as anticipated, as it later turned out, because shortsighted overseers had executed numbers of workmen necessary to their maintenance. Leopold knew that nothing was more reassuring to a man of extravagant tastes than a nice gold mine in good working order, and Tom Walsh was entirely agreeable to giving him a cut in the Camp Bird. Having a king for a partner never did any harm around Colorado in those days.

To conclude his services as American commissioner at Paris, Tom Walsh gave a dinner party still remembered by chroniclers of such matters as one of the most sumptuous on record. Frederick Townsend Martin, the generally acknowledged leader of the American colony in the French capital, brought the Countess Spottswood Mackin, a rare social catch that year, and Mary Garden, who was at the Opera Comique at the time, sang to enormous applause. The only event marring an otherwise memorable evening was that Mrs. Potter Palmer lost a $40,000 teardrop emerald from her stomacher. It was never recovered and Walsh wanted to replace it as the responsibility of a host, but Mrs. Palmer wouldn't hear of it. Later she told friends she made up the loss by personally penciling in raised prices on various items at the Palmer House menu when she got home to Chicago, ten cents on the strawberries, a nickel on the coffee, little things that nobody would notice but which in no time paid for a new emerald.

Leaving Paris on a note of resounding triumph, the Walshes sailed for home aboard the *St. Paul* and here the malign star under which Evalyn had been born began to warn of its presence. Already the Walshes had been involved in a railroad accident while en route to Denver, in which a number of less fortunate passengers had been killed, and now, in mid-Atlantic, the *St. Paul's* engines broke a moving component which drove a large hole in the hull, letting in quantities of North Atlantic seawater and delaying her four days in getting to port. It was a day before wireless and the vessel was feared lost. It was annoying more than anything else, but an ominous foretaste of the mischance that was to play so large a part in Evalyn Walsh's life.

While recuperating from the strain of near shipwreck, the Walshes put up at the Waldorf and went shopping. Mrs. Walsh improved her fur closet with purchases at Gunther's coming to $12,000 and a pair of monster vases to the tune of $5000 at Tiffany's. They left $1000 owing when they were able to tear themselves away from Altman's and similar sums at Stern Brothers and Wanamaker's. They returned to Washington aboard the *Congressional Limited* exhausted but happy.

At fifteen, Evalyn experienced her first affair of the heart. She fell in love with the coldly ascetic profile of William Gillett who was then playing Washington in one of his endlessly recurrent farewell tours in *Sherlock Holmes*. Evalyn and a school friend went to six matinees hand-running to shudder at the gas-chamber scene and laugh heartily at Billy, the Boy in Buttons, and sent Gillett innumerable mash notes on embossed, heavily scented stationery. Nothing came of them.

By now, the rich Walshes, once of Ouray and Leadville, were really beginning to feel their oats and looming large in the Washington scheme of things social and dynastic. The modest home at the corner of Leroy Place and Phelps Place that Tom Walsh purchased when he first came to Washington from Conrad Jenness Miller for $58,129.21 cash was no longer suited to their now secure social status which was in a few years to make Evalyn Walsh McLean one of the firmly established old-time cliff dwellers of the Federal City.

At 2020 Massachusetts Avenue, the Walshes started to rear a palace that was to bug the eyes of a metropolis where the presence of embassies, the homes of high government officials, and the mansions of Silver Senators from Nevada and California made ostentation a commonplace.

Cab drivers pointing out the Walsh home to impressionable visitors invariably estimated its cost at a flat $5,000,000, a figure somehow associated with western mining kings since the homes of Nevada's silver-maned Senator William Morris Stewart and that of Montana's equally acquisitive William Andrews Clark always received the same conversational price tag. Actually, the house, when completed, stood Tom Walsh $835,000 in the hard dollars of 1902 when a fine overcoat cost $10. It was a figure sufficient to establish Walsh in Washington folklore as the "Colorado Monte Cristo" just as elsewhere the Comstock's peerless John Mackay was known as "Bonanza" Mackay.

The house contained sixty rooms and included in its facilities a reception hall with a well that extended four floors upward to a dome of many-colored glass, a grand staircase guarded by two marble nymphs in classical dance, a theater in which Evalyn's brother, Vinson Walsh, could give sleight-of-hand performances, and, on the third floor, a regal apartment with a veritable throne room achieved by a $5075 hydraulic elevator against the possible arrival for a weekend of the family friend, King Leopold of the Belgians. There was also a ballroom to accommodate 300 on the third floor and a roof garden.

To assist in furnishing the premises, the Walshes retained Anna Jenness Miller, who had sold them their first Washington home, on a commission basis, and for two years this industrious lady traveled abroad as their agent, buying paintings and bric-a-brac, Persian rugs, fine bindings from Rivière in Paris, statuary, furniture, grand pianos, and all the costly properties with which the time and place admired to create an atmosphere of security and possession. Sometimes the admirable Mrs. Miller was gulled by unscrupulous dealers in *objets de virtu* and, after Evalyn McLean's death in the 1940s, supposedly solid-gold saltcellars and butter dishes from

2020 Massachusetts Avenue, when they arrived at the auctioneer's for appraisal, were found to be base metal thinly gilded.

No matter; the gold machine at the Camp Bird was functioning without interruption and the output had increased many times over since the first yield of $5000 a day back in 1896.

No. 2020 Massachusetts Avenue was inaugurated with a small ball in honor of Alice Roosevelt. Evalyn was thought to be too young to associate with such fast company as that represented by the Nicholas Longworths and the President's daughter, who was known both to use rouge and to smoke cigarets in public. She was seventeen.

It was a time and place in American social evolution when no well-to-do young woman was thought to be properly educated until she had had musical schooling of some sort and of necessity in either Paris or Vienna. Serious-minded young ladies with thick lenses in their pince-nez glasses went to Vienna. Evalyn didn't wear thick lenses. She went to Paris.

It was arranged for her to stay, together with a paid companion, with a family friend known as "Aunt Fanny" Reed, a sister of Mrs. Paran Stevens of New York and an aunt of Lady Paget who was a favorite of the jaunty King Edward VII. Fanny Reed had already had experience with Americans of great wealth and it was her contribution to the foreign-aid program of the nineties when she introduced Count Boni de Castellane to Anna Gould at her Paris salon in the rue de la Pompe. De Castellane had thought Fanny's singing was terrible and had told her so, after which (and after his divorce from Anna) their friendship had cooled. Now the temperamental French singing instructor who had been engaged to run scales with Evalyn listened to her for the first three bars of an aria from *Carmen* before he turned to Fanny Reed, tearing his hair and holding his head in anguish.

"He says he wouldn't teach you singing for all the gold in Colorado," Miss Reed translated in a way that suggested that she was pleased about something. Perhaps she was thinking about Boni de Castellane.

If a career in grand opera wasn't indicated for Evalyn Walsh, no matter; she had a $10,000 letter of credit on Baring Brothers for basic expenses and credit in all the best shops, including Cartier's. She began going out in Bohemian society, despite the chaperone, and picking up the checks for dissolute young men in spade beards and velvet smocks who assured her they were the heirs to the genius of Rembrandt or, anyway, Titian. On one of these unauthorized excursions into the great world where unchaperoned young ladies were a novelty, she encountered Frank Munsey, whom she told all about what a good time she was having and pointed out several of the claimants to the mantle of Leonardo.

Munsey was sailing for home next day with an eye to discharging a substantial number of staff members from his various periodicals, and appears to have run into Tom Walsh soon after the *Deutschland* docked. At full-day rate Evalyn received a cable: STOPPED YOUR LETTER OF CREDIT: AM SENDING MRS. WICKERSHAM TO BRING YOU HOME. Evalyn had just time between the cable and the arrival of a replacement in the chaperone department to hurry around and buy some things she really needed on tick: a sable muff, coat, and scarf and eight trunks full of dresses from Worth and Paquin, and then have her hair dyed a bright henna.

Tom met her at the boat and, after denouncing the new hairdo as something that wouldn't have been tolerated on Myers Avenue, Cripple Creek, took her to the Waldorf for the night. The next morning there was a call from the customs house for Thomas Walsh.

"Are you sure you declared everything yesterday at the dock, my dear?"

"I declared a great deal, considering how much I brought in!"

Tom Walsh paid $1475 in fines and told Evalyn not to do it again.

"You aren't cut out for the smuggler scene in *Carmen*," he told her, "and you know now that you can't sing it anyway."

The next time Evalyn visited Europe, Tom Walsh went along to look out for things and she found herself moving in a society that was somewhat removed from the seedy Rembrandts, but no less aware that she wasn't exactly destitute. She had a mild flirtation with an Italian prince of the same downgraded Colonna family that had gotten into John Mackay by marriage, but friends rallied to Tom's assistance in pointing out the matchless Colonna record for worthlessness and Evalyn struck a bargain with her father.

"I'll tell him to go roll his hoop," she said, "if I can have a red Mercedes roadster."

Still surrounded by swarming Italian title,s but now proof against their fascinations, Evalyn and her father went on to Monte Carlo in the well-ordained circuit that was *de rigueur* for wealthy Americans, in the course of which they encountered in each new premises of fashion the faces they had left the night before on taking the *Blue Train* out of Paris.

At the Hôtel de Paris, conveniently situated just across the way from the Casino, and boasting the most resplendent guest list of titles of any hotel in the world, they encountered another rich American with time on her hands in the person of Mrs. John W. Mackay who had been born Marie Hungerford Bryant, the daughter of the town barber at Downieville in the California Mother Lode before she married the richest member of the Bonanza Firm of the Comstock.

Mrs. Mackay was by now a mountain of fat who remained in bed until the Casino opened for business, when she donned a dark red wig of outsize dimensions, took a checkbook with her, and sat at the roulette table until they closed the place over her head that night.

"But Mrs. Mackay, you always lose," Evalyn said to her.

"I am buying wares you do not see," replied the weary old woman. "I am buying excitement when I gamble and that makes my blood run faster than the doctors are able to. Perhaps it will prolong my life."

The next year was 1905 and it saw the Walshes, now sufficiently established in Washington society and with the polish of continental contacts, at Newport, ultimate citadel of copper-bottomed,

upper-case New York society with its overtones of foreign aristocracy, a community by no means as hostile to new money, provided it came reasonably accredited, as it had been painted. The
Walshes took a big place next to Mrs. O. H. P. Belmont's *Beaulieu*
on Bellevue Avenue that had once belonged to William Waldorf
Astor and subsequently been occupied by Mrs. Potter Palmer for
two brilliant seasons. The place was popularly supposed to reek
with bad luck, which promptly effected an alliance with Evalyn's
unlucky natal star to demonstrate that, for all Tom Walsh's daughter was one of the most envied heiresses in the world, she was also
Misfortune's Darling.

The automobile, at that time, was still in the stage of being a rich
man's toy and, as such, was heartily damned by young Dr. Woodrow Wilson of Princeton University. It was also one of the most
effective executioners of the well placed since the guillotine and
the list of its blue-blooded victims in those years of inherent structural vice, defective tires, and highways that were an invitation to
suicide, read like the guests at a Vanderbilt ball.

Evalyn was returning from a Clambake Club luncheon in her
chauffeur-driven Mercedes, with Harry Oelrichs and Herbert
Pell, Jr., on the rear seat beside her and her brother up front with
the driver when the car blew a tire. The Mercedes was crossing
a wooden railed bridge at the time and turned over in a shallow
stream on top of Evalyn Walsh, who was nearly drowned before
passers-by were able to effect her rescue. Never was a street accident attended by better names: Alfred G. Vanderbilt helped drag
the women from under the overset car; Blanche Oelrichs, Hermann's sister, and their mother were among the first arrivals; Fifi
Potter Stillman took off a coat of priceless Irish lace and laid it over
Evalyn while they waited for the ambulance. But her brother Vinson was dead, his body transfixed by an enormous splinter that had
been sheared off the guard rail by the impact.

The evil star that had burned fitfully in the heavens the night of
Evalyn's birth was now well established as a prophetic agency in

the destinies of the Walshes, where it was to be an omen of violent death for three full generations.

Evalyn Walsh never entirely recovered from the effects of the Newport disaster. Incompetent surgeons improperly set the bones in a fractured leg that had to be reset months later when her life was despaired of and she had become hopelessly addicted to morphine for the pain it gave her. When a delicate and highly dangerous operation, performed at 2020 Massachusetts Avenue, because she refused to chance dying in a hospital, was successful, it left her a nervous wreck and the back of her head as bald as a duck egg. Always thereafter she wore a succession of wigs and was available to narcotics on provocation. She used them, with some restraint, for the rest of her life.

In a family council convened after Evalyn had begun to move around, it was felt that perhaps a return to Colorado might change the Walsh luck, and Tom Walsh bought for $150,000 an estate named *Wolhurst* of 500 acres south of Denver that was part of the estate of Senator Edward O. Wolcott. Tom thought it would be nice to rename the place *Clonmel* for the county of his Irish origins and President William Howard Taft, a family friend who happened to be in Colorado at the time, presided at a ceremony attended by the ranking county families and deluged in champagne. Evalyn's close-fitting lingerie hats, which she wore to conceal her wigs, became a standard article of Denver fashion and at Colorado Springs, and for a brief time, the Walshes relaxed among familiar scenes of old friends from other days.

But the Walsh luck hadn't changed and just to let them know that its malign influence was hovering offstage, Tom Walsh was nearly killed in a railroad wreck en route to inspect reported new gold diggings at Hartsel in the Colorado mountains. The train crew of fireman and engineer were killed outright when their special collided head-on with an unscheduled freight in a narrow cut, and Tom Walsh was severely cut from window glass and sustained a mild concussion.

With this overt incident for a curtain raiser, the stage was now set for the full-dress series of calamities that were to derive from Evalyn Walsh's marriage, not the least of which was destined to be the marriage itself, to her childhood companion and family friend, Edward Beale McLean. Fate was reserving its Sunday punch concealed in a bridal bouquet.

The John R. McLeans of Washington and Cincinnati, where they owned the *Washington Post* and the *Cincinnati Enquirer,* were people who were accustomed to money in large, encouraging quantities, having had it for generations. John R.'s father, Washington McLean, had been a titan of nineteenth-century newspaper publishing and had built up the *Enquirer* from a paper of miniscule consequence to a position of national importance and influence. Mrs. Washington McLean had delusions of social grandeur in which she sometimes identified herself with an imperial autocrat, say, Catherine the Great of Russia, sometimes with lesser mortals, perhaps Mrs. William Backhouse Astor. In Cincinnati, which only a few years previously had been known as Porkopolis and the hog-butchering center of the universe, her equipages attracted attention. The most familiar of them was a *grande daumont de visite* in which no coachmen were permitted to share the seats with its regal occupant, but rode two of them on the dickey out behind while two mounted postilions in jockey suits and matching caps rode two horses of the four that drew it.

The John McLeans, at the time they enter the Walsh story, were a rich, powerful, well-established family whose authority and greed for power were slightly perfumed with corruption. John R. made a specialty of acquiring secret dossiers on people of public consequence, many of whom had private lives of an interesting nature, and using his knowledge in the game of power politics and social domination. He lived in a vast palace on I Street that had been designed by John Russell Pope, where the luncheon service was solid gold and the champagne glasses had stems a foot long. On H Street, around the corner, John R. McLean had a private hideaway that would have done credit to Professor Moriarity in *Sherlock*

Holmes, where his shadier and more profitable transactions were implemented. Later on, during the scandals of the Harding administration, the H Street house found dubious fame as the love nest of Harry Daugherty.

Like many of the great generation of robber barons, John R. McLean was vulnerable in a single matter, and that was his wife, whom he adored and for whose pleasure and comfort no concern was too great, no expense to be considered. When ordering a new carriage for her, McLean had written personally, holograph, to the Brewster firm in New York concerning its details, and the letter has survived, a monument to the meticulous courtliness which was a part of even business relationships in that now distant time. The name Emily was to appear in raised silver letters at so many specified positions on the interior of the carriage, the upholstery was to be of dove-gray hammercloth; Mrs. McLean weighed 140 and the springing was to be adjusted accordingly; salts, pincushion, hand mirror, address book, hatbrush, and memorandum pad, each was to be in its specified place.

"Remember, Mr. Brewster, I want this to be very nice and I look to you to make it so for me."

At another time he wrote Tiffany & Company as follows:

> I have just received by U.S. Express Company this morning the emerald-and-diamond pendant, which I ordered from your company in Paris. But the combination collar and bracelet which I ordered at the same time for Mrs. McLean has not yet reached me, and as my time for giving it is getting short, won't you kindly cable over there and find out when it will arrive in this country and when I will get it here, Washington Gas Light Company, D.C.

When Mrs. McLean was dying years later at Bar Harbor, it was suggested that a certain doctor who specialized in her ailment might be helpful.

"Get him," said John R.

The doctor was located by telegraph on vacation at Lake Tox-
away in North Carolina and his fee was $1000 while practicing
away from home.

"Get him."

It would take three special trains routed from the South to
Washington, from Washington to New York, and from New York
the length of New England to fetch him in time.

"Get him," was the command, and he came.

The third generation of the feudal McLeans, and one which
was destined to prove the shirt-sleeve aphorism in the form of
canvas straight-jacket sleeves, took the form of Edward Beale
McLean, a wastrel of the first chop who married Evalyn Walsh in
one of the sensational matches of the century, fathered a so-called
"$100,000,000 baby," and died a victim of the bottle as horribly as
any of the characters in Hogarth's Gin Lane.

Evalyn Walsh had met Ned McLean in dancing class, when she
first moved from Ouray to Washington, and had maintained a
boy-and-girl flirtation with him ever since. Ned had first proposed
before he was able to grow a mustache and had done so periodi-
cally ever since. Mrs. McLean was the sort of mother who paid her
son's companions in sandlot baseball or games of Parcheesi to let
him win. He was as spoiled as a mackerel three hours in the sun.

Now in the summer of 1908, with wild oats behind both the
contracting parties, Evalyn Walsh and Ned McLean took up where
they had left off in dancing school and agreed that each was made
for the other. Driving in a chauffeur-driven car a few miles from
Denver in July of that year, even as the prospective groom's mother
was making plans for a wedding ceremony of cosmic dimensions to
be celebrated at Bar Harbor, Ned suddenly suggested to his fiancée
that they get married then and there, thus avoiding all the tiresome
sentimentalities of well-wishers and the pagan ritual of nuptials in
the upper brackets of society and finance.

The chauffeur was instructed to stop at a telephone and young
McLean called Crawford Hill, a man of standing in at least that

portion of Denver which read the *Denver Post,* who agreed to set in motion the machinery of practically instant matrimony if the prospective bride and groom would meet him in an hour at St. Mark's Episcopal Church.

Hill was secure in the respect of *Denver Post* readers because his wife was rated in its columns as the Queen of Denver society, an elevation that received upper-case treatment in the time and place. Like many royalties, this was achieved through the agency of merger. Mrs. Hill's father, a geology professor from Brown University who had turned his special sapience to account in the milling of precious metals, had bought the *Denver Republican* with some of the proceeds and as long as this paper lasted, Hill's wife was, naturally, Queen. When Hill died, and his estate merged the *Denver Republican* with the *Denver Post,* Mrs. Hill was one of the properties that went along with the reference library and the presses, still in the capacity of Queen.

Because there were only that number of people in Denver who didn't pick their teeth at table, Mrs. Hill's list of acceptable socialites was limited to thirty-six and, in time, these fortunate ones came to be the hard inner core of local society and known as "The Sacred Thirty-Six." Over those who recognized her sovereignty, Mrs. Hill ruled despotically down the decades attired in a tiara of emeralds said to have belonged to the Romanoffs, which gave her the appearance of a stage duchess in a Shubert road company musical.

Alas, not everyone in Denver acknowledged the Crawford Hills as anointed with holy oils. The impious *Rocky Mountain News,* which seldom saw eye to jaundiced eye with the *Denver Post,* made a practice of flinging editorial dead cats in the direction of the throne. Worse, it presented a rival slate, hailing, in appropriate capitals, as the True Queen a Mrs. Claude Boettcher, wife of a cement millionaire who had been known as "Piggy" Boettcher while at Yale in the twenties. This porcine appellation prevented Mr. Boettcher from sharing his wife's throne as King, but he functioned satisfactorily in the role of royal consort and, as owner of the Brown Palace Hotel to boot, received the approval of the community as a whole.

To return to the principals of this story, however, Crawford Hill was as good as his word and a wedding that had been projected to combine the most sensational features of the Burning of Rome and the Field of the Cloth of Gold was accomplished in an inconspicuous and private manner. In place of a convocation of divines which in Bar Harbor would have numbered, at the very least, Bishop Henry C. Potter of New York, Bishop William Lawrence of Massachusetts, and the Rev. Endicott Peabody, headmaster of Groton School, had Ned's mother been consulted, the bonds were sealed by a humble clergyman, whose name Evalyn Walsh McLean was never able to remember in later years.

The wedding trip on which the McLeans departed as soon as the dust had settled from their clandestine marriage was of the sort dreamed about but seldom realized by the gifted staff writers of William Randolph Hearst's *American Weekly,* where heiresses whirled in perpetual snowstorms of $1000 bills pursued by gyrating youths in tail coats and monocles, proffering goblets of champagne and diamond necklaces. Not even the most gilded playboys of the Sunday supplements and their brides had started on their honeymoon with a joint budget of $200,000 and parental assurance that when this was gone, there was more where it had come from.

The father of the bride and the father of the groom each came up with letters of credit for $100,000. Tom Walsh assured his daughter that this was merely designed as pin money and that if she wanted to make any really substantial purchases, the Riggs Bank in Washington would provide.

Evalyn took him at his word. Within sixty days she was doing her own version of Oliver Twist via the Mackay Cable with a request for "More." This sort of thing in 1909 was the measure of a really gifted spender. The modern equivalent of Evalyn and Ned's combined $200,000 would be more than $1,000,000. It takes diligence and application to spend $1,000,000 in two months and have nothing more to show for it than three or four Mercedes roadsters and an outsize case of the shakes.

To minister to their needs, the bridal pair took along a chauffeur named Platt and Evalyn's old-time nurse, now promoted to lady's maid, who was improbably named Maggie Buggy.

Although the McLeans had brought along a yellow Packard roadster with red fine lining in the hold of the steamer, they wired to Paris for an additional Mercedes when they landed in Holland and it turned up two days later as specified, 15,500 guilders C.O.D. They headed for Berlin, while Platt and Maggie followed in the Packard. In Berlin Evalyn did little shopping; she was waiting for Paris, but found time to purchase a $40,000 chinchilla wrap—"so soft that I can imagine no more delicate sensation than the feel of it against my cheek"—which she usually wore decked with fifty marks worth of fresh hothouse violets.

Ned bought her a present, price unspecified, a traveling case fitted in solid gold and the twin of one that had just been delivered at the command of one of the royal German princesses. It was given to Maggie Buggy to fetch along with the rest of the luggage and Evalyn forgot about it until she found it years later gathering dust in an obscure closet at 2020 Massachusetts Avenue.

"One day, in Leipzig, we lost patience with the fact that we had only one Mercedes and went to Paris that night and bought an extra one for twenty-four thousand francs."

From there the McLeans went on to Constantinople where they immediately, in the manner of important Americans of the time, demanded of the United States ambassador, John G. A. Leishman, that they be presented forthwith to the Sultan Abdul-Hamid. The Sultan was having troubles enough of his own; the Young Turks were shooting up the Bosporus nightly and Constantinople was an armed fortress, but they got to see the Sultan, whom Evalyn found to be a fat man "with paunchy, bilious eyes, an ugly nose, and lots of trimmed bristles, red with henna, for a beard. He was stoop-shouldered and kept on his head a fez ornamented with an emerald for which my fingers itched."

Evalyn's fingers also itched for the Sultan's coffee cups, tiny eggshell vessels of fantastic value, each one in a golden filigree-and-meshwork holder set with diamonds. There were so many and the Sultan seemed to have so much of everything including wives, that Evalyn was half of a mind to slip one of the eggshell coffee cups and its diamond setting into her muff but at the crucial moment thought she saw a palace eunuch looking hard at her and desisted.

In the Sultan's harem, however, she saw something else that she couldn't have, at least not right at the moment, but which was eventually to become the hallmark of her being and possibly an evil talisman in league with her malign natal star. It was a great blue stone at the throat of the Sultan's number-one favorite of the moment and it, too, made Evalyn's fingers itch, but again there were eunuchs all over the place. She had yet to hear of the Hope Diamond.

Leaving Constantinople resounding to gunfire and the screams of the Young Turks, the McLeans went to the Holy Land where they bought appropriate Arab costumes for riding camelback, Ned's attire including a small and very holy green hat that could only be worn by pilgrims who had been to Mecca.

"My favorite saloon in Cincinnati is a marble barroom called the Mecca," he explained. "I've been there frequently."

One gets the impression that the McLeans' honeymoon was largely an extension of Ned McLean's visits to the Mecca in Cincinnati. He kept falling off camels and looked terrible in the morning.

It was at this point, quite unaccountably, that Ned and Evalyn discovered they were without funds. They took Tom Walsh at his word and cabled for help and headed for Paris where one could cash a letter of credit at Morgan, Harjes without any trouble, that is, if there was that much money in Paris. It was in Paris that Evalyn remembered she still hadn't bought herself a wedding present and happened to drop in to Cartier's just as a frock-coated functionary was taking from the vault "an ornament that made bright spots in front of my eyes."

The Star of the East was a pear-shaped diamond of ninety-two and a half karats that was well known to lapidaries everywhere and had made bright spots in the eyes of beholders before Evalyn McLean. It was supported in a triple loop of platinum links by a thirty-four-karat emerald, also a stone with an international dossier, which in turn depended from a magnificent pear-shaped oriental pearl weighing a mere thirty-two and a half karats.

Evalyn knew then and there she couldn't live without the Star of the East. The price was 600,000 francs, or $120,000 U.S., and they didn't have that much money in their pockets so they charged it to Tom Walsh. After that there was nothing to do but go down the street to the Ritz bar, wearing the crown jewels, of course, to celebrate their purchase.

"Father will see what a bargain it is right off," said Evalyn. "He knows I wouldn't spend that much money foolishly."

In order to save further expense in connection with their purchases, they smuggled it past customs in New York and once more Tom Walsh had to square things with Uncle Sam. The word compulsion had not come into the language then so Tom couldn't tell the Collector of Internal Revenue about his daughter in Freudian language.

"I told him my daughter is a little bit crazy," he said.

Once the Camp Bird had settled the various accounts standing when Ned and Evalyn returned from their wedding trip and Mrs. McLean had expressed her emphatic and unqualified disapproval of the Star of the East, the stage was set for the advent of what the press of the nation was forever afterward to refer to as "the $100,000,000 baby."

Evalyn's child, born at 2020 Massachusetts Avenue in 1909, was obviously something special even among the issue of the very rich. Dr. Harvey Cushing arrived in the cab of a chartered locomotive from Baltimore when a blizzard had halted conventional train service, to see to his head formation, and the child was placed in a gold crib in which it was sheltered from drafts by a canopy depending from a gold crown quite as though royalty were involved. In a manner it was; the crib was a gift from thoughtful King Leopold who so much admired the production graphs of the Camp Bird Mine.

Nurses, bodyguards, and night watchmen, as well as a full-time twenty-four-hour-a-day doctor were in attendance on the child Vinson Walsh McLean, named after Evalyn's dead and much loved brother. As soon as it was possible, the McLeans had to leave the infant to speed to the bedside of Tom Walsh, who was finally dying of cancer of the lungs in Texas, and Evalyn did so with reluctance because she was in terror of possible kidnapers. Obviously, a great deal of newspaper space had been accorded the richest baby in the world and a commensurate number of crackpot and threatening letters resulted. A telegram every hour from Massachusetts Avenue, day and night, was filed by the chief bodyguard reassuring the McLeans of the continued welfare of their son.

There was no hope for Tom Walsh and it was decided to move him back from Texas to Washington to spend his final days in his own home. To transport him in ease, together with a suite of doctors and nurses, another of the special trains that were the hallmark of truly significant wealth in an age before private planes was chartered on a special schedule, where speed was sacrificed to the comfort of the dying man. A baggage car rode ahead to give a cushion and stability between the engine and the rest of the train, followed by a coach for the working crew, then John W. Gates's private Pullman palace car which he had won from sanctimonious Arthur Stillwell along with the Kansas City, Pittsburgh & Gulf Railroad, and finally the McLean family car, *Ohio,* also a Pullman palace conveyance.

It is difficult to ascribe Tom Walsh's death, met in an ordered and tranquil world amidst his own loved ones, to the McLean evil star. Sixty was not old by contemporary standards, but among the pioneers who had known sleeping on frozen ground and enduring the hardships of the old frontier, it was not an altogether untimely age. Tom Walsh had few regrets.

After Tom's death, with no parental restraint, the Ned McLeans took to their respective vices in a big uninhibited way, Evalyn to the poppy and Ned to the sauce, and there were wild orgies of travel and even wilder dissipation in the fashionable places frequented by people they knew and whose toleration of everybody's vices was mutual and a way of life: Claridge's in London, the Ritz in Paris, Biarritz, Nice, yachting in the Mediterranean, gambling in the Casino of the Bains de Mer at Monte Carlo. It was here that Evalyn one evening won $70,000 at Russian bank, which disappeared with the speed of light from her place at table when they stepped to the bar for a quick one. Ned and Evalyn were the most vocal members of the I-Was-Robbed Club ever to put in an appearance in those golden antechambers to bankruptcy and the management was making shushing motions to no avail when a saintly-looking old gentleman with a monocle and long white beard turned up and presented her with the missing money. He had taken the liberty, not knowing if she was to return to the table, of cashing her winnings into large banknotes and here they were. He was the Angostura Bitters king.

In such glittering and heedless surroundings, where ancient titles and newly printed money, fantastic fortunes and little responsibility, were all merged in a wonderful farrago of tail coats, tiaras, and motorcars as big as locomotives, the Hope Diamond gravitated toward Evalyn Walsh McLean as the most natural thing in the world. They were made for each other.

True to the whim of the Fates, its acquisition was heralded by tragedy and death as a curtain raiser to its purchase. With her Monte Carlo winnings in her reticule, Evalyn headed for Paris with Ned, and the *Blue Train*, being too slow for their taste, they undertook to beat it with a yellow Fiat that happened to be handy, in which the chauffeur rode in a dickey seat behind. Ned made it to the Bristol Hotel in ten minutes less than the scheduled time of one of the fastest expresses in Europe, quite an achievement on the French country highways of the time, but when they drew up at the porte-cochere of the hotel, the chauffeur was dead on the floor. Ned's driving had been too much for his heart.

As if on cue, the Hope Diamond came on stage the morning after this contretemps.

The McLeans were breakfasting in their apartment at the Bristol, and Ned, in a peacock-colored lounging robe and two-day beard, was having trouble with the eggs.

"Try a brandy milk punch, darling!"

With the brandy milk punch there was announced the arrival of an old friend, Pierre Cartier, whose timing was almost psychic and who knew that, in Evalyn's case, there was no hangover cure like a nice diamond necklace. M. Cartier's silk hat was as glossy as though it had come from Lock only the hour before, his morning coat hung in folds of somber and decorous opulence over lavender-striped trousers, and he had in his hand a small package sealed with the red wax court jewelers find irresistible.

"You know about the Turkish revolution?" asked the man of rings and brooches, as soon as he had made his manners. Ned said grumpily they had been there when it was going on.

"You may remember, when you visited the Sultan's harem, seeing a remarkable stone at the throat of his number-one favorite?" continued Cartier imperturbably.

Evalyn had total recall where jewelry was concerned and said brightly that she did.

"We hear that she was stabbed to death in the palace," said Cartier, tapping the package ("with fingernails that resembled his own show window," Evalyn later recalled). "And sometimes royal jewels of consequence come to Paris in times of trouble."

By now Evalyn had a pretty fair idea of what was in the package.

The Hope Diamond was a legend in the world of precious stones, part of whose record is factual, part speculative, and part almost wholly mythical. The stone's first appearance in Europe was in the time of Louis XIV of France, when a man named Tavernier brought it to the French court and sold it for an unrecorded price. It weighed sixty-seven karats when it was appraised for the royal regalia of the Bourbons and was reputed to have been worn by Queen Marie Antoinette. Even then its baleful reputation was well established as Tavernier is supposed to have, in some unexplained manner, been eaten by wild dogs, while the fate of the unfortunate Queen is well established.

Along with the other properties of the crown, the Tavernier diamond was nationalized by the French revolutionaries and, in the manner of the properties of the people in republican governments generally, disappeared from view, never to be seen again in its original dimensions.

In 1830, however, a London diamond dealer named Daniel Eliason, offered for sale a still enormous diamond that weighed forty-four and a quarter karats, and whose color was uncommonly like that of the missing Tavernier gem. Dealers reflected that the original stone couldn't have been sold with a clear title anywhere and nobody was surprised when, many years later, a still smaller stone of the identical blue was placed on sale that might very well have been cut from the missing weight of the Eliason diamond.

The larger stone was purchased by a London banker, Henry Thomas Hope, from which its eventual name derived and whose daughter was in possession of it when she became Duchess of Newcastle. From the Duchess, via her daughter, it passed to her grandson, Lord Francis Pelham Clinton Hope, a fellow of abandoned habits whose genius for picking losers at Epsom and other race tracks was a legend in English sporting circles. When his fortunes were at low ebb, Lord Francis married an American actress named May Yohe, who wore the Hope Diamond along with her costume jewels on the stage. Since it was part of an entailed estate, Lord and Lady Hope were unable to sell it, and when after a devastating season at Newmarket, he was declared a bankrupt, the stone again disappeared from human ken.

Again years passed until an old trader in odd lots of estate jewels turned up with the Hope Diamond in the office of Sir Caspar

Purdon-Clark, one of the curators of the Metropolitan Museum of Art in New York City. The dealer had a shrewd notion of the value of the gem which had come to him in an odd lot of stage diamonds and Sir Caspar at once recognized it for what it was and suggested that the dealer get in touch with the Hope Estate to which it legally still belonged. Once returned to the Hopes, it was sold to a customer who simply identified himself as Selim Habib and who was known to specialize in *sub rosa* deals with Middle Eastern potentates who had no aversion to a bargain. Travelers in Turkey said they heard of a fabulous blue diamond at the Court of the Sublime Port and Evalyn McLean saw something like it in the last days of the old Sultan.

Now the Hope lay on a breakfast table in the Bristol Hotel and Pierre Cartier was suggesting that it was the proper complement in Evalyn McLean's collection to the Star of the East. He added, honestly enough, that it had a long reputation for bad luck and that the mysterious broker, Selim Habib, had been drowned at sea soon after consummating the sale to the Turkish Sultan. Tavernier, Marie Antoinette, the bankrupted Lord Hope, Selim, the dethroned Sultan, and the favorite with a throat cut, all added up to what some people might feel was a jinx.

Evalyn wasn't impressed. "Bad-luck objects are lucky for me," she told Cartier, but she didn't like the setting and for the time being the deal was off.

A few months later, Pierre Cartier, who knew Evalyn like a checkbook, sent her the Hope in a new setting, edged in a square frame of diamonds and with a heavy diamond neck chain, much like those worn by lord mayors, to go around her neck. M. Cartier hoped Mrs. McLean would wear the thing over the weekend, to try it for size, as it were, and Evalyn was lost.

The price was $154,000, $40,000 down and the balance over a three-year period.

Even if Evalyn didn't believe bad luck was associated with the Hope Diamond, she wasn't one to take chances and, climbing

into the family electric victoria with Maggie Buggy, she set out to
a nearby church to have the stone blessed. While the priest was
robing himself for the ceremony, a fearful tempest arose, thunder
crashed, lightning, possibly attracted by the batteries of the electric,
shattered a tree nearby, but there was no rain. Everything pointed
to a show of elemental displeasure toward the Hope Diamond, but
as the man of holy orders recited a benediction in Latin, the clouds
rolled by and the sun came out. Evalyn and Maggie acknowledged
a miracle and the clergyman got $100. The author of this book has,
upon occasion, worn the Hope Diamond at various McLean residences and experienced no evil save the outsize hangovers that were
the conventional consequences of any sort of party at *Friendship*.

To celebrate the acquisition of the Hope Diamond, the McLeans
gave a dinner party at 2020 Massachusetts Avenue whose cost, had
they applied to payment for the diamond, would have substantially
reduced the amount they still owed Cartier. There were forty-eight
for dinner, which was served off the gold service with the foot-
high champagne glasses and the bill, which rocked even Evalyn on
her French heels when she saw it, came to $40,000, or just under
$1000 per place. One element in the total was 4000 yellow lilies
sent from London for the occasion and ranged around the dining
room at a tab of $2.00 per blossom.

These were the years of the ortolans so far as the McLeans were
concerned, while Ned McLean's personal income ranged upward
to $900,000 a year and Evalyn's was perhaps double that amount.

They bought country places and town houses as ordinary folk
buy a new hat; the Sears place at Bar Harbor, *Black Point Farm*
at Newport because it was adjacent to their friends the Reginald
Claypoole Vanderbilts, and, for $90,000, a retreat called *Belmont
Farm,* at Leesburg, Virginia, where Ned was able to spend the same
amount over again on guns, dogs, horses, carriages, and the country equipment expected of a squire.

The household staff at *Black Point Farm* had aggregate salaries of $2700 a month. There were thirty people in the house,

cooks, butlers, house footmen, nurses, bodyguards, chauffeurs, maids, laundresses, and cleaning women, and as many more on the grounds and in the stables.

When her son Vinson wanted to see the circus, Evalyn bought out an entire performance of Ringling Brothers so that the child might be the only audience and have all the acts played to him. Every Christmas there was a party for Vinson, the least of which cost $15,000, the more elaborate ones more. Each guest received an electric train or expensive doll, and on one occasion Admiral Dewey sent a pastry cook's version of the battleship *Olympia* in spun sugar. Vinson's things came from Worth, his little carriage robes, hats, diminutive jackets for outdoors, all arrived from Paris and all in ermine.

At one time it was the McLeans' whim that Vinson should have for a companion a little colored boy playmate of his own age and a search was instituted for a five-year-old Negro with respectable antecedents who might be rented for this purpose. Eventually, the article in request was turned up and, after exhaustive ministrations with soap and scrubbing brush, arrayed in one of Vinson's suits and started for Palm Beach aboard the McLean private car, *Ohio*.

"The colored Pullman porters all the way to Florida were just about hysterical," Evalyn was to recall.

The experiment was not, alas, an unqualified success, "and we canceled ourselves out of the deal with money."

One Fourth of July, Ned and Reggie Vanderbilt decided late in the afternoon that it would be a fine thing to go from Newport over the Narragansett pier to continue their drinking in a different setting.

"The last ferry's gone."

"No matter, hire a ferry," and with Evalyn with "about a pound of diamonds and some evening clothes in a bag," they steered an Isotta-Fraschini onto the hired ferryboat "and went ashore in the whizzing manner of a skyrocket."

The first place they hit was an illegal gambling joint where Ned lost $54,000 with almost the speed of light, but Evalyn, whose knowledge of drugs and their effect was at first hand, was of the mind that he had been given a mickey, and got him off the premises before he was further looted.

If there was one department above all where Evalyn saw little merit in economy, it was in the matter of her personal wardrobe. The entire top floor at 2020 Massachusetts Avenue, a space about as big as a small ball park, which had originally been dedicated to the royal apartment for King Leopold, was set aside for her clothes and the several tiring women charged solely with their maintenance and preservation. The south hundred was reserved for ball gowns and evening dresses, the north forty for furs.

The winter of 1912, which saw the Hope Diamond come to Washington, Lady Duff Gordon was in high favor with Evalyn as court *couturier* and made for her a superb coat of tailless ermine with a deep-shaded flounce of broadtail that draped from the wearer's shoulders to her ankles. The collar was a strip of fur finished with a heavy tassel designed to be twisted around the throat like a hunting stock and Evalyn wore it with a smart little black velvet hat trimmed with black aigrettes. The outfit was billed at $60,000.

The imperial manner came easily to the mother of the $100,000,000 baby, and cablegrams, special trains, and couriers were pressed into service when something new to wear was in urgent request. Lady Duff Gordon did business in New York under the style "Lucile" and Evalyn sent her a typical wire: PLEASE HAVE LADY DUFF GORDON MAKE FOR ME THE LOVELIEST DRESS SHE CAN, HAVE 200 IMPORTANT PEOPLE COMING TO DINNER DECEMBER 31. And again: PLEASE MAKE ME AN ORANGE THEATER GOWN, AM DESPERATE. And on still another occasion, she ordered Mme. Tappe put a man or girl on the train and send MY HATS AND DRESSES TO ME RIGHT AWAY AS I MUST HAVE THEM TOMORROW AT LATEST.

Years later, when she was attempting some sort of inventory of her properties before closing the house at 2020 Massachusetts

Avenue and moving to *Friendship* permanently, Evalyn McLean found an enormous wardrobe trunk to which she had no key and about whose contents she was curious. When the locksmith had come and gone, it was found to be "filled right to the lid with sable collars and a gross or more of ermine tails that my maid at the time had just put away and forgotten."

The regular weekly visit of a dog *coiffeur* to bathe and frizzle Sarto, Evalyn's poodle, was $5.00, not a princely fee today, but in 1912 not exactly hay. Sarto's clothes were as fashionable as Evalyn's; they came from Lucile's, too.

Evalyn McLean had nothing but the best throughout a long life-time, and, although philosophers may now and then raise tired voices to proclaim that the most expensive things aren't always the most desirable, they always find it difficult, when challenged to point to examples. She paid $4000 a pair for the sheets in which she slept and considered them bargains because "as any woman knows, forgetful, restful sleep will take out the wrinkles." When she stopped overnight away from home and was forced to put up in a hotel, such as the Waldorf in New York, she took a $350-a-day suite in the Towers because the servants knew her and, as she said, "there was room to swing a cat." Her idea of swinging a cat was up to 100 people in for cocktails and two full rows of ringside seats at a world's championship boxing match afterward, and the manage-ment of the Waldorf made this possible.

One day in the *Friendship* era she set out with her small daugh-ter, Evalyn Beale McLean, to buy the little girl a white poodle she had been promised. They rode in the little Rolls-Royce, the dimin-utive Hooper-built town car with just two seats in the back and the chauffeur out front enjoying the weather, but when they reached the source of poodles there were none available, at the moment, the management not having been apprised sufficiently in advance, and Evalyn was at her wit's end how not to disappoint the little girl. The chauffeur was helpful; his brother-in-law bred St. Bernards and, by happy chance, the world's champion of champions, a noble beast of the most exalted lineage, was available to Mrs. McLean at a special of only $5000. They put the dog in back with little Evalyn, and Mrs. McLean and the Hope Diamond rode out front with the chauffeur. "The dog's tongue alone was as big as a boiled ham."

It is pleasant in retrospect to think of the St. Bernard in the little Rolls starting for a home that was indeed heavenly and fit for a Saint, because, for once in her life, Evalyn McLean hadn't been had. No amount anyone can pay for a St. Bernard is too much, and she was wise enough to know it.

The private golf course at *Friendship* was considered by professionals who were privileged to play it to be finer than that at Chevy Chase, perhaps because the grass on the greens "was far more costly than any oriental rug in the house." When her children wanted a diminutive coach to drive around the grounds in, Evalyn paid a museum price for three midget horses and the carriage, brightly lacquered and daintily upholstered, that had once belonged to General Tom Thumb.

In 1926, Evalyn read the sports sections of the *Washington Post* to discover that one of her horses was running that day at Cincinnati, a fact that had slipped her mind so that it was now too late to get to the track in time to cheer her colors. Chartering private planes in 1926 was not the commonplace it was to become in later years and Evalyn wasn't quite certain how to go about it. "But I called up New York and told them to send me the biggest plane they had and the best pilot and best mechanic." In due time a tri-motored Fokker arrived at Washington Airport and Evalyn sent one of the Rolls-Royces out to bring in the pilot and mechanic for her personal inspection before entrusting her life to their hands. "I wished to discover if the pilot was sober and in other ways all right." It was a time when almost nobody, passenger or crew, boarded an airplane without one for the road. "The pilot proved to be very nice and quiet; his name was Wilmer Stultz." Thus reassured, Evalyn and her maid hastened to Cincinnati and were at the starting post along with her horse.

Most women, when assailed with morbid doubts about life, death, eternity, and the meaning of it all, brighten perceptibly when it is suggested they go out and buy a new hat. A new hat lends a new dimension to depression. With Evalyn McLean, jewelry performed the same function that in lesser women is supplied by a smart bonnet.

One day she was blue from all the trouble making $1,000,000 ends meet—she was being dunned for $800,000 by some of Ned's creditors—so she boarded the Pennsylvania's *Congressional Limited* and went to New York where she took a taxi to Cartier's. Mr. Cartier himself happened to be in the United States and, when she had described her symptoms, promised to find something extra fine and sent an assistant to rummage through the vault to this end.

He came up with a dazzling ruby-and-diamond bracelet whose principal stone was a sixteen-karat diamond known as the Star of the South. Evalyn already had the Star of the East and the prospect of boxing the compass made her feel better right away. There were also sixteen rubies and sixteen other diamonds. "How much?" she asked.

The price was right, $135,000 because it was in the midst of the depression of the thirties, and she took it right home with her.

"I felt like a new woman the moment I put it on," she recalled. "There's nothing like spending money as a cure for not having it!"

Another thing besides buying jewelry that relaxed Mrs. McLean was fussing around with electrical installations. An early admirer of the films, first-run movies were shown nightly for many years at both *Friendships* and she had made friends with David Wark Griffith who put an entire film laboratory at the I Street house where she personally supervised the processing and cutting of countless miles of film she had herself exposed.

James B. Duke, the tobacco king, was as a rule impervious to social entertainment and resisted parties to the death, but once he was lured to *Friendship* where Evalyn gentled him after dinner with a double feature in the great drawing room. Duke was happy as a child at Christmas and saw in the cinema the solution of all his own domestic problems. "I'm going to get a couple of projection rooms set up in each of my houses," he said. "That will be eight, no, ten altogether. Hereafter when my wife has a dinner party, we won't have to sit around and talk."

Evalyn, who never went to bed if she could help it before six or seven in the morning and not then sometimes, used to rewire both *Friendships* from time to time and in person. Not wanting to be known as a no-bill, she took out membership in an appropriate electrical union in Washington and clipped a union cap badge to the Hope Diamond when actually handling the pliers. When sometimes a guest at second *Friendship,* a partner of the author of this book was an electrician in the Navy, and often turned up among the admirals and statesmen in sailor suit at her better parties. To be sure, he had been expensively educated by the Navy in counter-radar, but Evalyn was entranced with his knowledge of more ordinary electrical techniques as well.

On one memorable occasion, after the rest of the guests at a Christmas party for the members of the diplomatic corps had departed, he was specially asked to stay and spent the entire night on a step-ladder handing insulating tape and copper wire to his hostess who was assisted in rewiring her ballroom by two night watchmen, Thurman Arnold and Cissy Patterson, publisher of the *Washington Times-Herald.*

When at length the Old Man With the Scythe caught up with Evalyn Walsh McLean in 1947 and she died of pneumonia at the age of sixty-one, she had almost achieved the boast of her lifetime that she would die bankrupt, for her estate was probated at $606,110.80, scarcely more than she was in the habit of raising in an afternoon to settle Ned McLean's bad checks in palmier times. The Hope Diamond was valued at $176,000 and household effects were appraised at $85,337.90 and her jewel collection was picked up by a New York broker in rare gems, Harry Winston, who had them mailed to him by the estate lawyers for the sum of $152.50 postage.

Although its value as appraised was far lower, Winston paid a round $1,500,000 for the Hope and undertook in a reticent sort of way to sell it to somebody impervious to its reputed bad luck.

Nobody, apparently, wanted the Hope Diamond at a price which would satisfy Mr. Winston, and, as a bravura gesture and perhaps to show a tax loss, he presented it to the Smithsonian Institution where it reposes to this day, not many blocks removed from the scene of its final and most glittering triumphs at the two *Friendships* and at 2020 Massachusetts Avenue.

While talking in terms of truly important jewels, it may be worth noting that the most talked-of earrings during the Deauville season of 1965 were the diamond pendants of Mrs. Eric Loder which cost a cool $1,000,000 for the pair and were as big as teaspoons. Because of their weight and the consequent strain of wearing them, Mrs. Loder detached them at intervals during the evening to give her ears a rest.

Only a short time before Evalyn's death, the Hope had accomplished what superstitious folk liked to believe was one final act of tragedy in the long line of death, disaster, and mischance that had followed its known record through the world. Evalyn's only daughter, Evalyn Beale McLean, who had married a man many years her senior, Senator Robert R. Reynolds of North Carolina, died of an overdose of sleeping tablets. The news reports and those circulated in private in Washington society had little hesitation in describing the death as suicide.

Thus lived grandly and expensively and died in what she herself would have considered straitened circumstances, the most spacious of all the lady spendthrifts in the American legend. From the Colorado mining towns of the eighties to the ballrooms and embassies of the great world, her way had been paved in gold pieces and cushioned in a snowstorm of banknotes. Few women in her century had kept the faith more devotedly with Gene Fowler's dictum that money was something to be thrown from the back platform of trains.

Never a downright silly woman, Evalyn Walsh McLean's costliness gave her the stature of greatness and her last gesture of magnificence was in keeping with the good will that throughout her lifetime had somehow been betrayed and made to seem frivolous by her unlucky star.

Always concerned for the men of the armed services, during the final months of the second world war word was brought to her that a number of seriously wounded Marines in a Washington hospital were sadly lacking in amusements with which to while away the tedium of recovery.

Apprised in the middle of the night of this unhappy circumstance, the old firehorse snorted and started from her stall, intent on answering an instant and imperative call to duty. A manufacturer of musical jukeboxes was awakened at two in the morning and his entire stock of melodeons purchased in the grand McLean manner with no argument about prices, while a Washington teaming firm was instructed to send a capacious wain at once to pick up the music boxes and deliver them forthwith to the neglected soldiery.

Alas, the hospital to which they were consigned shortly after daylight refused to accept delivery and it took a telephone call from the Surgeon General of the United States to explain to a furious old woman the reason her good offices had been thus summarily rejected. The patients to a man were the most grievous cases of shell shock to whose survival absolute tranquility was the first essential. The tumults of Evalyn's generosity would have killed them like flies. It was a fitting farewell to her lavishness that Evalyn Walsh McLean should, at the end, invade the premises of urgent quietude with well-intended chaos.

Chapter Fourteen

Game Preserve for the Rich

Palm Beach Was and Is a Wildlife Sanctuary for Millionaires . . .
Here They Browse in Ruminant Herds on Diets of New-Mown Ban-
knotes . . . Money Begets Money and Standard Oil Begot the Florida
Gold Coast . . . $8,000,000 Villas and Forty-Car Garages That Got
Misplaced . . . A $500,000 Carpet and a $1,000,000 Dinner Table . . .
Gold Lighting Fixtures Emplaced While You Wait . . . All the Table
Silver Is Gold . . . Send for Another 100 Electric Gondolas. . . .

O F ALL THE great American fortunes, the Rockefeller billions were productive of less fun and games and more grimly determined good works than any other. The founding patriarch, John D. Rockefeller, was a type, perhaps the archetype of Dives, who was also on chatty terms with his maker and justified his every activity by invoking God as a silent but apparently enthusiastic partner. Nothing frivolous characterized the early conduct of John D. Rockefeller. Perhaps he was exhausted at the very idea of the magnitude of the frivolities available to his wealth. Translated into yachts, dancing girls, Paris divorces, vintage wines, old masters, racing stables, and dinner parties at Maxim's, a tithe of his money would have turned North America into a continental version of Belshazzar's Feast. In terms of mistresses, Rolls-Royces, diamond necklaces, terrapin ponds, shooting boxes in Scotland, private railroad cars, boxes at the Metropolitan Opera, and debutante parties at the Waldorf, the old gentleman's caprices, had they leaned in these directions, could not have accounted for the interest on the interest on the interest of his fortune.

In very desperation he was forced to turn to good works. It is a melancholy commentary on great wealth, apparently justifying all that moralists have had to say of it since earliest times. Where Rothschilds purchased the world's finest vineyards as the merest incidental to their supply of table wine, Rockefeller would have had to buy up the entire beverage industry. Where J. P. Morgan might transport his Episcopal bishops aboard five- or six-car trains of private cars, John D. would have been forced, to hold up his end, to have chartered trains hundreds of cars long. Dancing girls in a proper dimension would have had to come popping out of acres of potpies and all the navies of the world been bought up as his private fleet of yachts.

Confronted by such a depressing prospect of voluptuary dedication on a truly astronomical scale, the elder Rockefeller found refuge in a diet of soda crackers and the benevolent regard of the Baptist Church. Even his comparatively modest wish, for a Rockefeller, to live to be 100 was denied him. One wonders if it was all worth while.

Nor did his immediate heirs fare any more happily. The prophecy of his adviser Frederick T. Gates to the elder Rockefeller that, unless he took thought for its disposition on an epic scale, his money would destroy him came too late even for the second generation. If the competitors of Standard Oil who were bankrupted and ruined by the South Improvement Company wanted a vision of revenge, they had only to contemplate the fate of John D.'s heirs and assigns even to the third generation. No Rockefeller in the record is ever known to have had a good time.

Afflicted with social awareness, overwhelmed with their obligations to society, cursed with conscience, their lot has been a melancholy one, their inheritance half money, half misery.

But if neither fun nor games attended the accumulation, let alone the dispersal, of the greatest single American fortune which bears the Rockefeller name, such was by no means the unhappy fate of John D. Rockefeller's several partners in Standard Oil, including his own brother William. Within the domain of the founding father a degree of sanctimonious decorum was enforced almost without parallel in the annals of big business. Attire, conduct, and the conversation of the partners were those of a vestry meeting in a particularly solvent parish. Domestic discord spelled instant banishment. Drink was unthinkable. At one time John Archbold, a notable man with a bottle, was coerced by the elder Rockefeller into taking a pledge of temperance and reporting to the senior partner once a month like a criminal under suspended sentence. He took to whistling "Onward, Christian Soldiers" in the corridors and kept a supply of cloves in his waistcoat pocket in self-protection.

Although such an objective was patently unobtainable, William Rockefeller, Henry M. Flagler, Archbold, Henry H. Rogers, Oliver Payne, Edward Harkness, Charles Pratt, and some of the lesser grandees of the organization strove valiantly to stem the flow of spending money deriving from Standard Oil from going down the rat hole of good works.

That this was as impossible in the partners as it was in the case of John D. himself is suggested by the circumstances that many of their expenditures, simply for want of more amusing and worthy objectives, automatically went to philanthropies and benevolences. Harkness in particular found it useless to attempt to evade high-mindedness and gave away most of his fortune to Yale and other worthy recipients simply because its magnitude prevented its expenditure on more endearing objectives.

Even John D. Rockefeller's father, William Avery Rockefeller, although he died too early to get in on his son's bonanza, was a merry scoundrel given to larcenous practices on a modest scale, flowered waistcoats, and tipping a companionable elbow. The curse of complete sanctimoniousness was acquired by John D., and transmitted directly into his own bloodline. It had no comparable counterpart among his associates.

The impossibility of making a serious dent in Rockefeller money without resort to good works was illustrated in 1922 when John D.'s brother William died at the age of eighty-one and left, in a casual sort of way, a fortune of $200,000,000. Even the Payne Whitney estate of $175,000,000 and the Thomas Fortune Ryan bundle of $135,000,000 paled beside the awful grandeur of the amount that William Rockefeller, a genial and generous man much given to entertaining and good living, had been unable to spend on the amenities of a rich man's scheme of things. Without either the most intense sort of application to expenditure as a career, such as characterized Henry Flagler, or the indulgence in wholesale philanthropy, Standard Oil money tended to multiply faster than it could be directed into channels of disbursement.

Perhaps the best evidence that the Rockefeller fortune was not altogether an allegory of futility is the state of Florida, a merest by-product of Standard Oil but still on a scale to refute the notion that the entire concept of monopoly was a chimera. Standard Oil money created and brought Florida into being precisely as though it had been ordered from a dealer in such commodities and fashioned to the specifications of its purchaser. Rockefeller money, by indirection, set in motion the machinery of the world's most embracing pleasure dome. It built a stunning series of luxury resorts and the railroad to serve them. It redeemed swampland and worthless real estate in terms of a playground for a nation. Everything about Florida and its creation by one of his partners must have been offensive to John D. Rockefeller and yet, ironically, he died there, beguiled by its climate and, possibly, by the legend of Ponce de León.

The agent who transmuted money made in Rockefeller partnership into yacht harbors, luxury resorts, Colonel Jack Bradley's roulette tables, and Saturday fetes at the Everglades Club was a man of more or less blameless personal life named Henry M. Flagler. True,

Florida's great patron and creator without encountering whose name it is impossible today to turn on any hand in the Palmetto State, was on the uxorious side; he had a habit of marrying, but in comparison to the vistas of indulgence open to him, it was a microscopic weakness. He neither drank nor smoked. Profanity never passed his lips. His toleration of gambling in connection with his Palm Beach projects was always puzzling to his associates, but he knew how to spend money where it did the most good. He was a tireless and dedicated spender.

Florida first swam into the ken of Henry M. Flagler, then a senior partner in Standard Oil, in 1874 when he visited Jacksonville in search of health and a restful, semitropical surrounding for his first wife, a partial invalid. The rest of the United States had only vaguely heard of the Palmetto State at this time and its celebrity rested on the Seminole wars, a few ranges run with scrawny cattle, and the fact that, some time back, Ponce de León had landed precisely where *El Mirasol,* the villa of Palm Beach's greatest spender, Mrs. E. T. Stotesbury, was to rise in the twentieth century.

When Flagler first visited Florida, there was no railroad connection beyond Jacksonville, Miami was a fishing village without a post office of its own, and Palm Beach had not yet grown the first of the tall coco palms for which it was named. Not until 1878 did the Spanish bark *Providencia,* with a cargo of coconuts and a drunken seaman at the helm, go aground where the Bath & Tennis Club would one day dazzle beholders. The coconuts that floated ashore when the vessel broke up took root and became identified with some of the most expensive real estate in the world.

Flagler saw merit and limitless vistas of possibility in Florida which he visited again after his first wife had died and he had married her nurse. At St. Augustine it was his whim to undertake the finest resort hotel in the world. The Ponce de León, built of Spanish Renaissance architecture, at a cost of $1,250,000, had 540 rooms, all illuminated by electricity, a great advertising angle at the time, and it was also asserted that the furnishings of each room had cost the builder $1000. In a time when resort hotel bedrooms from Franconia, New Hampshire, to Phoenix, Arizona, were conventionally furnished with a brass bed, a rocking chair, and a commode, this was Babylonish luxury.

There was nothing of the absentee owner about Flagler. When the widely advertised suites of furniture arrived late for the scheduled opening, he took off his jacket and smashed open the crates alongside his hired hands. The pouring of the cement of which the structure was built in the absence of building stone presented problems so Flagler engaged an army of 1200 Negroes who tamped the liquid coquina gravel into the forms with their bare feet while musicians played them on. At the grand opening the first guests to register at the Ponce arrived in a vast six-horse omnibus borrowed from the circus which was wintering nearby.

The operation of the Ponce de León was of a piece with its construction, namely the best of everything. Flagler shared the philosophy of another great hotelier of his generation, Fred Harvey, that a hotel or restaurant was obligated to lose a certain amount of money to establish it as a bona-fide operation. The Ponce was crowded with fashionable guests and was losing money nicely when a new manager, unaware of its deficit policy, wired the owner in New York for permission to discharge the costly French chef and an equally costly dance band in the interest of economy.

Flagler wired back: HIRE ANOTHER COOK AND TWO MORE OF THE BEST ORCHESTRAS.

In the meantime, Flagler had retired from active participation in the assaults and ambuscades upon the ramparts of finance that characterized the affairs of Standard Oil with a fortune estimated at $150,000,000, not as large as that of William Rockefeller or Harkness, but sufficient for his purposes of the moment, which was to make Florida the acknowledged playground of the American people. Nor were all his expenditures available to chalking up on the red-ink side of the ledger. In time, many of his Florida investments, including the Florida East Coast Railroad and much of its adjacent real estate, made heavy returns upon their seemingly casual and openhanded investment. Despite a lifetime of dedicated spending which included his fantastic residence at *Whitehall* in Palm Beach, a gift of $15,000,000 outright to his third wife, and similar caprices of a costly nature all along the line, Flagler left an estate in excess of $100,000,000. His career proved the thesis that, after a certain point of no return, it is virtually impossible to become disembarrassed of a Standard Oil fortune. Money that he had hoped to see the last of kept coming back with interest. It was all very discouraging.

The interlocking fascinations of Flagler's railroad, the Florida East Coast, and the resorts which sprang up along its well-ballasted right-of-way were a perfect example of the ageless metaphysical problem of which came first, the chicken or the egg. The railroad was built primarily to serve the resorts, and the resorts were envisioned as furnishing the passenger traffic for which the carrier was designed. Further ambiguity, to orderly minds at least, is suggested by the entire Flagler scheme of things which was first conceived as a personal caprice and subsequently turned out to be an enormously profitable real-estate venture. The more extravagantly the empire builder sought to unburden himself of his original Standard Oil fortune, the more millions rolled in from the operations of the complex of transportation and hotels and their peripheral investments in ever-booming real estate. There is reason to believe the whole thing confused its proprietor and guiding genius, so that his last years were spent as a split personality, half philanthropist, half highly successful real-estate developer. In Florida they were regarded, of course, as the same thing.

As his railroad continued in the only direction available to its survey, southward from St. Augustine, Flagler's eye next lit on Palm Beach, a tropic spit of land separated from the mainland by a pleasant lagoon which would presently provide an anchorage for some of the most expensive of the world's seagoing yachts. For $75,000, a sum which caused the natives to tap their heads significantly, he purchased a vast tract of property on the ocean side of the lagoon and announced that here he would once more build the world's finest resort hotel, thereby undertaking to surpass his own previous triumph at the Ponce de León.

The Royal Poinciana eventually lived up to a vast number of superlatives, although there are dissidents who feel that it soon lost its primacy as "finest" to such other and even more swaggering ventures at the Negresco at Nice, the Hôtel de Paris at Monte Carlo, and Cap d'Antibes at Eden Roc. Patriots liked to name Spencer Penrose's Broadmoor at Colorado Springs and even the Del Coronado at San Diego as competitors in the elegance sweepstakes.

But for a time the Poinciana held the blue ribbon among resorts much as Mrs. William B. Astor held down her self-identified mission as head of New York's social Four Hundred, by virtue of sheer, overpowering grandeur and the density of its potted palms, food, and entertainment.

Like other authentic magnificoes such as Spencer Penrose, as is recounted elsewhere in this monograph, Flagler took a long view of the most massive transactions and expenditures while working up blood pressure over trivialities. Informed that a federal court, in the course of the Government's attacks on Standard Oil in 1906, had levied a fine against the corporation of $29,000,000, a sum that might well be reflected in his own holdings, Flagler brushed the matter off as unworthy of his attention. "Have you got those plumbing estimates for the bathrooms at Whitehall?" he asked the bearer of bad tidings. It is possible although not probable that Flagler foresaw that the dissolution of Standard as a holding company of which Judge Landis' fine was an incidental would vastly increase the value of Standard Oil shares in private hands so that in a period of ninety days more than $200,000,000 was added to the worth of Standard stock in the wildest bull market of all time.

If the plumbing estimates for *Whitehall* might have loomed large in Flagler's awareness, they were indeed trifling compared to the expense to which he went with utmost casualness in the construction of a monument which was to prove expensive even by Florida standards of the pre-income tax era. Much of the expense of his residence at *Whitehall* resulted from Flagler's preoccupation with the time element involved. In 1901, when he undertook the project, he was seventy-one, and although his estimate was mistaken, he felt that, like William Henry Vanderbilt in the construction of his Fifth Avenue mansion, he hadn't long to live and that work must be pushed with the greatest possible expedition. Henry C. Frick shared this preoccupation with mortality and chafed under delays at building his Fifth Avenue museum piece.

In 1901, as at a later date, foreshortening of the time element in any major enterprise advanced the cost in geometric proportion. *Whitehall,* by Cleveland Amory's estimate, might well have taken five years for its completion. Instead it was finished in eight months. The total cost as a result was $3,000,000, take or leave a few thousand, depending on whether the estimate was made before or after the installation of gold plumbing fixtures in the master bathroom. Today, a museum to the memory of the empire builder and the Palm Beach region he brought into being, *Whitehall,* in its seventh decade under the Florida sun, is still a monumental contriving.

Stately bronze doors cunningly balanced to turn on their massive hinges at the touch of a child's hand gave onto a marble foyer or great hall 110 feet long, 40 feet wide, and finished in seven shades of delicately veined marble ranging from cream-yellow to dove-gray and from sea-green to off-pink, rich brown, and pure white. Sixteen bronze-topped pillars of solid marble supported a vaulted roof engrossed with frescoes symbolic of such attributes of the mind as "Knowledge," "Happiness," and "Prosperity." The owner's ever-present preoccupation with the hurrying footsteps of Chronos was represented by an ornate clock with dials showing month, year, and day as well as the hours, in elaborate symbolism. It stood nine feet tall like a tapered campanile where nobody coming down the grand staircase could escape its implications. The theme of its message was "Time Riding the World in a Cloud." When the author visited *Whitehall* in 1959 as a consultant in aspects of its restoration as a museum, the allegorical clock was still in service, having marked the passing of the owner and the several incarnations of *Whitehall* itself as private residence, public resort hotel, and finally a monument to its original builder.

The general assembly apartments of *Whitehall* left beholders breathless not only for their size but for the rich and ornate furnishings which filled them. There was a profusion of tapestries which Paris Singer, himself no amateur as a spender, said must have been ordered by the square mile. Rugs big enough to accommodate a polo field and costing as much as $35,000 each were thrown around like scatter carpets in lesser homes. Jewel-studded mirrors, vast crystal chandeliers, Buhl cabinets, Boucher panels, allegorical murals executed by master craftsmen, maroon velvet portieres so tall that their tops disappeared toward a ceiling shrouded in perpetual gloom, vast Spanish chairs and chests, Carrara marble benches to match the walls, where they were visible under their profusion of hangings, and love seats, refectory tables, and sofas in which whole platoons of occupants could become lost without trace, made the downstairs a branch office of Sloane's with overtones of some of the bigger Spanish royal palaces.

"What a course for a point-to-point meeting!" exclaimed Devereaux Milburn, the polo player, on first encountering *Whitehall*.

Upstairs Flagler's profligate tastes ran to even greater chaos of costliness. Sixteen guest suites each with its bedroom, drawing room, dressing room, bath, and foyer were decorated in motifs representing epochs in the history of civilization. Mrs. Flagler's personal apartment was draped in silk damask, its bed canopied in gold cloth with panels of Cluny lace at a cost that must have given even a Standard Oil millionaire pause. The bathroom was seventeen by eleven feet in dimension with a sunken marble tub which may or may not have cost the $25,000 attributed to a similar fixture in the Long Island Home of Mrs. Clarence Mackay, but was certainly cut from a single prodigious piece of rare yellow Carrara.

The several clothes closets and mothproof presses were designed to accommodate an even 100 dresses each and it was Mrs. Flagler's boast that she never wore the same garment twice.

Mrs. Flagler's appointments of hospitality were of a piece with the general *décor* and dimension of *Whitehall:* she stated for the record that she could entertain fifty guests a night at dinner for a week and never use the same article of china, silver, flat plate, vase, or epergne a second time.

The glory years at Palm Beach, the years of the ortolans just before the 1929 stock-market debacle, were also the age of a triumphant plutocracy when all, or almost all, old-line standards of social status and family gave way to the impact of sheer, unadulterated wealth.

Privacy and property at Palm Beach were assured by the simple erection of barriers of costliness. It was so expensive either to live there on a seasonal basis or visit briefly that the well-to-do whose playground it was in vast, ruminant herds were never embarrassed by the presence of anyone with less money than they had.

A double room in the Royal Poinciana during the winter season, and for the massive resort hotels of Florida there was then no other, was $50 in the hard gold currency of the time, the equivalent of, say, $250 in the inflated money of a later generation, and the Poinciana covered thirty-two square acres. Much of this space was, of course, occupied by the hotel's public rooms, restaurants, verandas, corridors, its famous Coconut Grove tearoom, and eight tennis courts, but even a fraction of this square footage stacked six floors high with private apartments at astronomical rents represented a tidy citadel of money in its own right. The staff of 1400 remained unabated from the days when the founding Flagler had built West Palm Beach as "a city for my help," and distances were so great that prudent guests living in the more remote wings allowed two hours to dress for dinner, half an hour coming and going each way, and an hour to struggle with corsets and hairdos.

Everything about Palm Beach in the 1920s was superlative. Everything was solid gold, extra large, outsize, the most expensive, the most ostentatious, and the most opulent. Palm Beach real estate, like that in the non-residential sections of New York City, sold by the square foot instead of the acre. Jewel robberies, elsewhere considered a hallmark of status if the gems involved could be quoted at a value of a few thousands of dollars, hardly made a ripple in the day's news if they were not in excess of $100,000. The yachts anchored up and down Lake Worth at Washington's Birthday, the apex of the Palm Beach season, were estimated to have an aggregate value of well over $100,000,000. This didn't include some of the more pretentious seagoing vessels which could understandably have been taken for Cunarders on a dark night, whose dimensions prevented their anchoring in the inner harbor. C. K. G. Billings' 240-foot *Venadis* had to anchor three miles out to sea on the edge of the Gulf Stream and its house guests and visitors were ferried to and from the shore in a fleet of brass-bound, mahogany-finished small boats running on the hour and half hour. Uniformed stewards served highballs and cocktails aboard the Billings conveyances, and on the master's own dinghy, a shallop approximating the size of the more modest yachts in the harbor, a Hawaiian steel-guitar quartet played tropical music during the transit as guests and the owner sipped equally tropical rum drinks served in hollowed coconut shells.

One seagoing private yacht that most emphatically never saw Palm Beach was the most pretentious of all private vessels, *Savarona*, built to the specification of a Philadelphia Main Line Cadwalader.

When Mrs. Richard Cadwalader of Philadelphia commissioned the building at Kiel of her 408-foot-long *Savarona,* a private vessel just under half the length of the *Queen Mary* and more than twice the dimension of the *Britannia,* first Cunarder to go into the Atlantic service, the cost, although never ascertained precisely, can scarcely have been less than $5,000,000. *Savarona* was a source of trouble and inconvenience to its owner from the beginning. Although it contained gold-plated plumbing fixtures, priceless

Gobelin tapestries, and a house organ two stories tall, when it was ready for delivery it was found to be lacking in elevators. Outraged that she should be owner of the world's largest private seagoing vessel and still have to walk up and down its grand staircase, Mrs. Cadwalader, figuratively, sent it back to the chef with her explicit disapproval. In vain the builders and architects pointed out that to install the conveyances she wanted would require the virtual reconstruction of the entire ship. Stresses and structural aspects had to be accommodated that were not present in landbound architecture. It would cost $1,000,000 to rebuild *Savarona* with elevators. It was rebuilt.

Savarona never anchored in an American harbor. It was too big for either Newport or Lake Worth and, anyway, the owner refused to pay the taxes the American government claimed if she took delivery in her native land. It remained under foreign registry and Mrs. Cadwalader had to go abroad to board it. The nearest harbor where she might be welcomed aboard her own private *Berengaria* was at Bermuda.

Those visitors to the gilded purlieus of Palm Beach who did not, in a pre-airplane age, arrive aboard their own oceangoing vessels came by rail aboard the all-Pullman extra-fare luxury name trains of the Florida East Coast and the Seaboard Air Line railroads. From December to the end of March these magnificently appointed runs originating in New York, Chicago, Detroit, and Kansas City ran in two, three, and sometimes as many as six sections daily and their names were household words wherever wealth and sophistication compared notes on the amenities of international travel: *Orange Blossom Special, Florida Special, Flamingo, Havana Special, Palmetto Limited, Floridan, Dixie Limited, Miamian, Royal Palm* and *Royal Palm de Luxe, Ponce de León, Seminole, Florida Arrow,* and, honoring the founding father of the whole solid-platinum carnival, the *Henry M. Flagler.*

These were not ordinary run-of-the-mill conveyances, but tightly scheduled fliers made up of specially selected Pullmans, mostly entirely room cars, with the latest and smoothest-rolling diners, club cars, buffets, libraries, and observation lounges. Like such crack year-round extra-fare runs elsewhere in the land as the *Twentieth Century Limited,* the *Broadway Limited,* and the *Chief,* they carried a full staff of trained personnel, valets, lady's maids, manicurists, secretaries, barbers, bartenders, lounge stewards, and maîtres d'hôtel.

Palm Beach was the most concentrated of all aviaries for those most exotic birds of feather, the private Pullmans which, until 1929, continued to be the crowning panache and supreme hallmark of status and social and financial achievement. These were rolled across the Flagler Trestle over Lake Worth from West Palm Beach in the early morning hours and spotted on the private-car siding of the Royal Poinciana Hotel so that their privileged occupants, when they raised the shades of their staterooms in the morning, could look out upon a serene vista of sumptuously maintained lawns and ornamental waters with coco palms waving gently in the Gulf breeze and sailboats with multicolored canvas on the nearby waters of Lake Worth.

Mostly the Palm Beach regulars of private-car status moved from their Pullmans into their own homes or hotel suites, but many kept them spotted and in full service on the Poinciana house track for a fee of $100 a day for convenience in giving cocktail parties and, most of all, for the attenuated poker games which their owners so much admired and which were not permitted in the rigidly formal purlieus of Colonel Bradley's Beach Club.

Visible under the palms in the latter twenties were the properties of some of the most ornamental members of the private-car club: William F. Kenny's *Skipaway,* Paul Block's *Friendship,* Mrs. James P. Donahue's *Japauldon,* Harry Payne Bingham's *Pawnee,* Harry Payne Whitney's *Wanderer,* Charlie Clark's *Errant,* Edward B. McLean's *Inquirer,* and A. K. Macomber's *Seminole.* There were also noted by the *New York Herald Tribune's* Palm Beach correspondent, Dr. and Mrs. John A. Vietor aboard *Vietwood,* Princess

Barbara Hutton Mdivani's *Curley Hut* occupied by her father Franklyn L. Hutton, and Edward S. Harkness' *Pelham.*

Each of these magnificent private residences on roller-bearing trucks represented an initial investment of from $100,000 to $400,000 for the basic car alone from the Pullman Company. Again as much could easily be lavished on their furnishings, but, as Mrs. E. T. Stotesbury was fond of pointing out, the gold plumbing on her car was really an economy; it saved constant polishing.

Especially celebrated were the long-drawn-out games of stud poker aboard *Roamer,* the private palace car of Joshua Cosden, the oil Midas, as was the opposition game on another oil magnate's car parked on the same track, Harry F. Sinclair's *Sinco.* It was aboard J. Leonard Replogle's *Westmount* on the Royal Poinciana house track that Cleveland Amory relates how George Loft, the New York candy magnate, appeared one evening and asked to buy his way into the game already in progress. He produced a roll of crisp $1000 bills as evidence of solvency and Cosden pushed over to him a single white chip. On Harry Payne Whitney's car on another occasion, John Studebaker, the motorcar manufacturer, regretted that he had no ready cash in the pockets of his dinner jacket. He had just lost $200,000 to Colonel Bradley in a roulette game and was temporarily out of funds.

That some, at least, of the members of the private-car club mentioned here survived the economic Waterloo of 1929 and were still practicing the ancient rituals is suggested by a dispatch of March 10, 1935, to the *New York Daily News* by its society editor, Nancy Randolph, a post at that time occupied by Mrs. Inez Robb, under a Palm Beach dateline.

Despite a dash of rain and soupçon of wind all the horsy folk went down to Miami today (wrote Mrs. Robb) to attend the running of the Florida Derby. Joe Widener, the Pete Wideners, George D. Widener, Isabel Dodge Sloane, Col. E. R. Bradley, George Marshall, and Jay F. Carlisle are only a few of the folksies-wolksies who made the trip to see the last day's racing at Hialeah this season. Lots of Palm Beachers went in a train marked "strictly private." It was composed of three private Pullmans, the *Japauldon,* owned by Jessie Woolworth Donahue; the *Curley Hut,* owned by Princess Barbara Hutton Mdivani, and now in use by her papa, Franklyn L. Hutton, and her stepmama, Mrs. Hutton, and *Vietwood,* the property of Dr. and Mrs. John A. Vietor. A Fourth car, just a day coach, was added to the train, but only to give it weight and ballast and make it ride more easily. No one was permitted in the coach but auxiliary members of the train crew. It didn't really cost a fortune to make this grand gesture. By chipping in $95 apiece, Mrs. Donahue, Mrs. Vietor, and the Huttons were able to make the trip in pomp and privacy. In other words, the cost of the private train down and back was exactly $100 round-trip fares to Miami, and an r.t.f. to Miami is worth $2.85. This is exclusive of the light snack, sandwiches, Scotch, and champagne which the hostesses served both goin' and comin'. The train was about twenty minutes late in getting started this noontime because, when Mrs. Donahue arrived at the private train, her Pullman held the rear, or caboose, position. And Mrs. Donahue doesn't like to ride last. Car sways too much, she feels. So there was much switching until the *Vietwood,* in first position originally, right behind the empty day coach, could be switched to the rear. The delay was a lucky break for the Munn party, which arrived late and a bit breathless. In the midst of the switching, Mrs. Vincent Astor, Mary and Frances Munn, and Charlie and Gurnee Munn swung aboard the *Japauldon.* George Marshall, his plaid race-track coat alight with a red carnation, was a member of Mrs. Donahue's party. He almost always is these days. Frank Hutton took motion pictures of the guests as they arrived. Some bystander obliged Mrs. Vietor by cranking a movie camera of herself and her guests. Pierre Barbey, Jr., and Mr. Carlisle bought a few magazines to study on the way down. Eventually, everyone on board and everybody happy, the train rattled off down the tracks for Miami.

Quite aside from the private-car trade which converged on Palm Beach, some idea of the seasonal wealth that rolled toward

Florida and the volume of traffic to the luxury resorts of Palm Beach, Miami, Hobe Sound, and the lesser but still costly resorts of the West Coast may be gleaned from the statistic that in 1926 when railroad travel was at its all-time high and neither the flying machine nor automobile figured as an agency of long-distance travel, 1000 Pullman sleeping cars were in service every night en route to or from Florida.

First and last, money in appreciable availability was the key to Palm Beach's every activity. Almost none of the great hostesses whose names are associated with the resort's golden years before the market debacle of 1929 or with its brief but gratifying revival just before the second world war pretended to social exclusiveness in the antecedent Newport and Fifth Avenue tradition of Mrs. William B. Astor, Mrs. Vanderbilt, and Mrs. Stuyvesant Fish. The basic hallmarks of status were the same: yachts, motorcars, legions of house servants, sumptuous dinners and entertaining, and vast arrangements of real estate including private zoos and bathing beaches; but the entire structure was frankly, and with engaging honesty, predicated on solvency, and if a more patrician social background was available to some of the participants in the circus they seldom mentioned it, for as currency it was valueless.

A clue to the cost of even the most modest accommodations in the Palm Beach twenties for visitors who didn't want the responsibility of property and its attendant problems of management was the rent paid at the Everglades Club by the Frazier Jelkes: $3000 a month for four rooms. When the Jelkes moved to the Breakers Hotel, by now a contender for honors with the far older Poinciana, they paid $6000 for the same accommodations but with a difference: the Breakers was on the American plan. In the hard currency of 1925 the sum was considerable.

Palm Beach cottages ran, of course, to more money. *Playa Reinte,* built for oil man Joshua Cosden in 1923 by architect Addison Mizner, cost $1,800,000, the equivalent of perhaps $6,000,000 in today's currency, and featured a flowered rug which was valued at

$500,000, or $1,500,000 in the same terms of appreciation. The rug was in the living room which was almost never occupied.

Two years after the Cosden cottage was completed, Cosden's fortune of $75,000,000 had vanished to a point where Palm Beach could no longer feature in his scheme of things and it was purchased by Mrs. Horace Dodge for $2,800,000 which Mrs. Dodge could well afford, having just sold the motorcar company that bore her husband's name for $150,000,000. A story went the rounds of the Sunday papers at the time that the sale was accomplished because the thirty Cosden servants wouldn't stay on the job. They were frightened by a herd of elephants which was realistically featured in a painting in the drawing room by José Sert who was later to decorate a room named for him in the new Waldorf-Astoria. A new butler who had not been indoctrinated, suddenly faced with the menace of an ambuscade of snorting elephants, dropped an entire tray of highballs and the footmen likewise panicked.

When Mrs. Merriweather Post, who was then Mrs. Edward F. Hutton, built what was generally considered Palm Beach's most notable villa, adjacent to the Bath & Tennis Club, she was for some forgotten reason not on the best terms with either Mizner or Maurice Fatio, who were then the resort's favored architects, and instead called in Joseph Urban, stage designer for Florenz Ziegfeld. Urban was told by his patron to shoot the moon on this project and create a residence that would outrank everything else in Florida in magnificence and put a capstone to Mrs. Hutton's previous extravagances. This was a not inconsiderable order, as Cleveland Amory points out, since Mrs. Hutton's various *pieds-à-terre* included a seventy-room triplex apartment on Park Avenue in New York, a magnificent estate at Roslyn on Long Island, a 16,000-acre shooting lodge in South Carolina, and her *Topridge Camp* in the Adirondacks where tired guests, fatigued by a day's hunting, were wafted from the wharf at water level to the main residence by an escalator an eighth of a mile long.

Urban, with a proper sense of the theatrical, built *Mar-a-lago,* as Mrs. Hutton's Palm Beach home was known, around a dining-room table which cost a basic $1,000,000 for its marble inlaid with eighteen-karat gold tracery. There was a good deal of gold elsewhere around the premises, everywhere, as one inquiring guest reported, but on the front door. By the time he left the premises this oversight had been rectified and a pair of handsome gold-plated griffons lit him on his way into the Florida night with gold battle lanterns suspended in their beaks. When the Huttons entertained at *Mar-a-lago* they did it in the best tradition of importing a full Broadway production of *Stepping Out* to amuse their guests for the evening. Usually such troupes of entertainers were returned next morning to continue their Broadway run. Not so the fortunate cast of *Stepping Out* who remained for a week with all expenses paid as Mrs. Hutton's guests before returning to New York.

Mar-a-lago's $1,000,000 dining-room table seated thirty-six, which was sometimes more than Mrs. Hutton found it convenient to entertain at the moment. One such occasion is remembered by Schuyler Parsons who recalls that at the time he was staying with Mrs. Harrison Williams whose other house guest was Mrs. Lytle Hull. Mrs. Hull was uncommonly anxious to see the Hutton establishment but refused an invitation to a large dinner party on the grounds that she was in mourning for a member of her immediate family. That would be taken care of, Mrs. Hutton assured her, and it wouldn't be necessary for her to meet more than six or eight people, all of whom she knew already, an arrangement in keeping with Mrs. Hull's strict sense of propriety. When they arrived at *Mar-a-lago*, a special entrance had been breached by stonemasons into the patio and the patio itself divided by screens and hedges into ten separate rooms seating only eight at table in each. The little gesture of privacy for a guest cost, on Parsons' estimate, $10,000 for a single intimate meal.

In keeping with the disregard for cost that characterized the Florida twenties, there remains intact to this day as a museum across from Key Biscayne the site where an heir to the Deering harvester fortune undertook to build *Villa Vizcaya* out of what had been, until then, a mangrove swamp. This palatial scheme was forwarded without regard for expense by Burrill Hoffman, a Beaux Arts graduate from Paris, who created gardens filled with classic statuary, balustrades, courtyards, waterways, and canals overhung with rare trailing orchids through which guests were floated aboard a fleet of electrically powered gondolas imported from Venice. In front of the house was a huge stone ship's prow, symbolizing the ancient Vizcayans who had been merchant princes and sea rovers, a landfall used to advantage by bootleggers during prohibition for the storage of case goods awaiting distribution.

Deering had, in the initial stage of the project, suggested that perhaps $4,000,000 might be a sort of target sum for the construction but somewhere along the way money ran out and the architect submitted a revised estimate of $6,000,000. Deering batted no eye, but said to be sure there were plenty of orchids and parrots in the swamp and it might be a good thing to send for another 100 gondolas.

In its time and place the Augustan era of American extravagance with money and the things money can buy, the Palm Beach twenties must seem to observers to have been characterized by a sameness and prevailing common denominator which was invariably expressed in terms of $1,000,000, occasionally in fractions of this sum. Joshua Cosden's living-room rug with its beautiful raised flowers on which nobody ever walked, was worth $500,000. Mrs. Hutton's dining-room table, which was sometimes inconvenient because of its implacably fixed dimension seating just thirty-six persons, cost an even $1,000,000. *Villa Vizcaya* with its preliminary estimate of $4,000,000 and eventually $6,000,000 worth of parrots, orchids, and electric gondolas comes in even figures as if to avoid tiresome bookkeeping. In the end, the researcher among many millions comes to yearn for something that came out in less scrupulous decimals and cost, say, $1,345,678.25.

The long view also must suggest that the magnificoes who moved in such an exhilarating cloud of currency didn't always get their full money's worth and that somewhere along the way there were architects who split fees with contractors and butlers who got more than the conventional butler's markup of 20 per cent added to all bills from tradesmen they favored with their employers' custom.

If Addison Mizner didn't die the richest man in Palm Beach, which he did not by a wide margin, it must be attributed to his absent-mindedness with money, both his employers' and his own. It was an absent-mindedness that embraced his architecture as well, so that the hallmark of a Mizner villa came to be the absence in the blueprints of some essential of domestic economy, perhaps a stairway to the upper floors, a master bathroom, or even a front door through which to gain access to the premises as a whole. When he built *El Mirasol* for E. T. Stotesbury, the cost was something in excess of the conventional $1,000,000 and Mizner forgot to send a bill. Mr. Stotesbury had to look him up and ask for an accounting. Even when submitting the accounts for the main structure of *El Mirasol,* Mizner contrived to forget the charges for a forty-car garage which he had included at the last moment. For one client Mizner designed a fairly commonplace Palm Beach home whose economy embraced a Mooresque tower in the garden. When Mizner characteristically forgot to include a stairway by which to gain access to the apartments and roof of the structure, he hastily added a circular flight of steps on the outside and made the place a landmark.

Some idea of the upkeep cost of a Palm Beach establishment of a fairly de luxe order may be gleaned from the revolt of E. T. Stotesbury against the ever-mounting costs of maintaining *El Mirasol.* Although his resources still topped $75,000,000, the depression was having its sobering effect on Stotesbury's fondness for expensive good cheer and he found himself forced to budget his wife for the Palm Beach season. She was not to spend more than $50,000 a month on entertainment. This was in the midst of the same lean years that saw Mrs. Harrison Williams voluntarily limiting her dressmaker's bill to $20,000 a year for the duration of hard times.

The moneyed sameness of life at Palm Beach in its golden years may be suggested by the accounts of the day's social excursions which were filed each evening by their Palm Beach stringers for the two New York morning newspapers, the *Herald Tribune* and the *Times,* Day after day the identical names of Stotesburys, Horace Dodges, Cosdens, Jelkes, Munns, Sanfords, and Biddies came over the wires, were scrupulously proofread and captioned by the *Tribune's* Howard White and the *Times's* F. L. (Free Lunch) Baker, and run through all editions. Because of their social and financial implications and the involvement of the paper's respective owners with the names which figured in these dispatches, they were regarded as sacred copy, immutable and not to be cut or tampered with in any least degree.

One late evening in 1932, Ogden Reid, conning the first edition of the *Herald Tribune* in Bleeck's saloon, remarked to Howard Davis, the paper's diminutive business manager, that the Palm Beach dispatches read much the same to him from day to day and couldn't telegraph tolls be saved by running the identical story throughout the Palm Beach season, thus making one column of typeset do for sixty or more? The order was given and for a solid week the *Herald Tribune's* Palm Beach intelligence was identical from day to day. Neither readers nor the names involved ever remarked that the same people were doing the same things in the paper for seven days running.

Although the Edward Stotesburys were reported to have fallen short of complete acceptance by many old-line Philadelphians like the Lippincotts, Morrises, Newbolds, Peppers, and Robertses, some of whom not merely downgraded wealth but actually embraced the cult of financial irresponsibility, there never was any doubt about their absolute and undisputed supremacy in Palm Beach or at Bar Harbor. In both of these rarefied precincts the legend of their expensive ways may have been exaggerated, as it certainly was in Philadelphia where the newspaper reporters could never agree if *Whitemarsh Hall* comprised 272 rooms or a mere 172, although a general concensus held to fourteen elevators, seventy inside servants, and a maintenance staff of approximately twenty carpenters, electricians, and handymen, and forty gardeners.

It was at *Whitemarsh Hall* after a brief visit that Henry Ford is credited with having remarked that it was interesting and instructive to see how the rich lived. Social commentators at once saw the parallel with Queen Victoria's exclamation on coming over one day from Windsor Castle to call on a particularly superb member of the Rothschild family: "I have come from my residence to stay at your palace."

In the great tradition of princely hostesses of another age where complete transformations of grounds, gardens, and even major architectural innovations were accomplished at night when the coming and going of artisans might not discommode the owners, Mrs. Stotesbury once had the entire downstairs of *El Mirasol* at Palm Beach done over between midnight and breakfast. Stotesbury, who had dined uncommonly well the evening previous, came downstairs to breakfast in a house he failed to recognize as his own, where a complication was added by two new footmen and a change of butlers taking part in the service of the eggs.

"Tell your master it was kind of him to have me for the night," he instructed the major-domo.

The experience left scars. Shortly thereafter Mrs. Edward Hutton told Stotesbury of a surprise, an innovation of some magnitude that she was planning for her husband's impending birthday. "Don't do it," advised Stotesbury. "Husbands don't like surprises."

The Stotesbury housekeeper dating from the great days in Palm Beach, Mrs. Logseton, recently told Schuyler Parsons that her employer really kept a comparatively small domestic staff but that since all its members were available on twenty-four-hour call it necessitated a larger personnel than ever met the eye at one time: one secretary at Palm Beach, one at *Whitemarsh Hall,* one butler, four house footmen, two *chefs de cuisine,* two kitchen assistants and "necessary maids," and three chauffeurs. It was her practice, however, to send for outside help when occasion demanded in almost unlimited numbers and George Lamaze recalled lending her an extra sixty housemen for a single dinner while as many as six extra butlers might be borrowed at double wages from neighboring establishments. When Alfred Barton took the author to lunch with Mrs. Stotesbury in 1939 in the declining years of her fortunes, the meal was served for six guests by four liveried housemen and two butlers while the outside staff had shrunk to a mere fifteen gardeners.

In one aspect of staffing, Mrs. Stotesbury topped all the competition by maintaining a full-time personal fashion designer and costume secretary whose talents included sketching her employer in her projected attire for an evening even down to the last clip and finger ring so that she might see how she was going to look without the trouble of dressing and could amend the whole arrangement without inconvenience. The same staff artist kept a complete record of all Mrs. Stotesbury's entertainments with seating charts of dinners and luncheon parties, notes on what place settings, flatware, and flowers were used, and a file of menus. If a guest complimented the Stotesbury chef on a *mousse au chocolat* he might well be served the same dessert on coming to dinner after a lapse of years.

Nor was Mrs. Stotesbury willing to play second fiddle to Palm Beach hostesses who went to elaborate lengths to rotate their jewels and avoid appearing on successive occasions with the same combinations of necklaces, tiaras, and bracelets. In a dressing room specially assigned for the purpose adjacent to her private apartments, her entire fabulous collection of ornaments was arranged, as in the window of a jewelry store, on the necks and wrists of mannequins with heavily annotated memoranda as to the dates and occasions when they had last been worn.

At Bar Harbor the Stotesburys lived no less palatially at *Wingwood House,* always spoken of as a cottage although it comprised eighty rooms, twenty-eight baths, twenty-six open fireplaces kept with logs blazing on all but the hottest nights of summer by a special staff of firemen, fifty-two telephone extensions, and a servants' wing with thirty-eight rooms for inside domestics.

On one occasion, when Stotesbury acquired the place from Alexander Cassatt of the Pennsylvania Railroad, it was extensively remodeled at a cost of $450,000. Mrs. Stotesbury didn't like some of the new woodwork and it was redone a second time, presumably with satisfactory window frames and doorways, for $650,000.

Survivors of the years of the ortolans at Bar Harbor such as Colonel Haskell H. Cleaves, a retired army officer, remember the high point in Ed Stotesbury's career as one of the three or four undisputed grandees of the American resort scene. The occasion was in honor of the banker's eightieth birthday when a small dinner was given for him at the Bar Harbor Club in August 1929. "I have today achieved my life's ambition," Stotesbury told those present with all the pride of a small boy who had been honored by the members of his high-school class. "I have just received a letter from my financial adviser telling me I am worth a hundred million dollars."

Life could hold no more.

Chapter Fifteen
Fun with Real Estate

Platinum Portals for Economy and $25,000 Rose Trellises... A Running Brook in the Library Is Nice... The Wendel Sisters and Their $5,000,000 Dog Run... Everyone Should Have a Gold Dinner Service... Charlie Schwab Liked a Private Turkish Bath and Organ Music... Jack & Charlie Knew How to Leave Home in Style....

IN THE YEAR 1900 there arose in the predominantly iron-producing city of Marquette, Michigan, the noble, all-stone, sixty-room mansion of John M. Longyear, one of the original pioneers of the Mesabi iron region whose home was to be a monument to his shrewdness and success in uncovering some of the richest metal deposits in the then wildly booming Northland. Unlike many of his contemporaries, Longyear was a man of taste and cultivated habits. His residence boasted a fine library where the retired magnate passed away happy hours actually reading, and the rest of the house was in keeping, an abode of civilized discrimination.

Came the day, however, when the location stakes for the tracks of the Duluth, Mesabi & Iron Range Railroad, an ore carrier of which in any other circumstances Longyear would have warmly approved, were driven right under the windows of the Longyear library. For reasons of geography there just wasn't any other right-of-way available, and although the ironmaster fought the carrier to a finish in the Michigan courts, he was unable at long last to prevent the snorting locomotives from waking his household in the night and sooting up his fine bindings.

A man who didn't know the meaning of defeat, Longyear snorted right back at the locomotives. He called for photographers who made a pictorial record of every room, angle, approach, facade, profile, and elevation of the house and all its shrubs, trees, fountains, ornamental waters, hedges and drives, its gatekeeper's lodge, porte-cochere, greenhouses, and stables. Every last minute component of all these properties was then dismantled and the whole magnificent shebang loaded on flatcars, requiring, according to Stewart Holbrook, two long trains of highest tonnage rating. The conductor signaled a highball, the hoggers whistled off, and the cars began to roll, not to come to rest until they were in the Brighton yards of the Boston & Albany Railroad handily adjacent to the aristocratic Boston suburb of Brookline. Brookline was then widely and respectfully known as the richest village in the world and here, atop the equally patrician eminence of Fisher's Hill, once more arose the Longyear mansion, its every prideful pinnacle snarling architectural insult in the general direction of Marquette, Michigan.

Here beyond all threat of invasion by bells and whistles, Longyear resumed where he had left off reading Gibbon's *Decline and Fall,* inconvenienced but not discomfited. Marquette, Michigan, was never the same again.

Comparable in the record of architectural whimsey was the vast Gothic castle constructed at Pebble Beach on California's Monterey Peninsula by the late Templeton Crocker, one of the heirs to the enormous fortune made in the early days of railroading by San Francisco's Charlie Crocker. Boasting three-foot-thick walls and doomsday masonry, with apartments impervious to sound and perhaps to armed invasion, it rose like Arthurian Tintagel above the surf and breakers of the Pacific, a not inconsiderable monument to the eccentricity of extreme wealth. To finish the interior

Crocker ordered several thousand tons of rare and expensive travertine to be specially quarried in Italy. It was brought over as ballast in ships and unloaded in Monterey Bay, but through some oversight or misunderstanding an entire shipload of stone arrived in excess of the builder's requirements. This Crocker ordered jettisoned offshore in the deep waters of the Pacific. Nobody else was going to lay hands on any of the special Crocker travertine.

ৡ৽·ৡ৽·ৡ৽

Dr. Preston Pope Satterwhite, a resounding eminento of the New York thirties whom Maury Paul, "Cholly Knickerbocker" of the Hearst newspapers, unhesitatingly assigned to the category of café society as separated from old-guard cliff dwellers, had what must have been one of the largest apartments even seen on Fifth Avenue, a duplex with every known style of architectural *décor* represented, Louis XIV, Louis XVI, Regency, Restoration, Empire, Colonial, and Cape Cod. There were Chippendale powder rooms and Roman peristyles, Queen Anne breakfast apartments and Mooresque music rooms, Indian throne rooms and English Tudor banqueting apartments, sixty rooms all different.

Mrs. Satterwhite had only recently moved into this formidable ménage when, as a newspaper reporter in the early 1930s, the author was sent to interview her about some matter of passing concern to readers of the *Herald Tribune*. She hadn't seen a map or a floor plan. It was approaching one o'clock and he was courteously asked to remain for luncheon.

"Madam is served in the Sheraton luncheon gallery," announced a starchy personage.

"Where is it?" asked Mrs. Satterwhite.

Admirable too, in the grand manner of real-estate yesterdays, was the social awareness of Charles T. Yerkes, the traction king who in the nineties built himself a swaggering Fifth Avenue mansion to house one of the greatest collections of old masters in the United

States. Times were bad and worried friends pointed out that such ostentation as a $5,000,000 home when space was at a premium for sleeping under railroad bridges might contribute to unrest or resentment among the lower orders.

Especially singled out for disapproval were a pair of magnificent bronze doors from a Venetian palace which, fronting as they did on the main thoroughfare of the city, openly flaunted the wealth of their owner.

Yerkes listened attentively and said he'd give it his consideration. He didn't want to do anything to contribute to bad feeling between the classes. A few days later the friend encountered him and Yerkes, beaming, told him that as a concession to the times, he had had the offending bronze disguised under a duller coat of less opulent-appearing metal.

"What is it?" he was asked.

"Platinum," said Yerkes proudly.

When Yerkes died he left an estimated fortune of $50,000,000 in cash and fine arts to his widow, a woman largely addicted to champagne in double bottles and not especially interested in the cultural pursuits represented by the Rembrandts and Frans Hals that highlighted her picture gallery. In a moment of vintage enthusiasm she overwhelmed Wilson Mizner, then fresh from the Klondike, with matrimony. Finding herself in possession of a celebrated husband of gregarious personality and not minded to lose him when he sobered up, she kept him confined to a well-upholstered suite in her inherited mansion while she held his trousers and nether garments under lock and key. Mizner could have anything he wanted, plovers' eggs, Moët & Chandon in crystal bottles, musicians if he were so minded, anything but his freedom.

Mizner pined for enlargement.

He sent piteous messages beseeching succor to his brother Addison Mizner who consented to visit the prisoner and was so permitted after he had been searched by an English butler to be sure he was carrying no concealed rope ladders or other jailbreaking tools.

He found his brother in a two-acre square gold and mahogany bed that had been fashioned to the order of the Mad King of Bavaria. At the headboard a swarm of gold cupids covered up an allegorical female figure in diaphanous garments representing Night, while at the footboard they tore the clothes off her again.

Wilson was attired in a woolen undershirt that had shrunk. A million dollars' worth of point lace covered him to the middle and he was rolling a Bull Durham cigaret. A footman arrived with breakfast on a set of solid-gold flat plate with a solid-gold coffee pot that Addison Mizner at once coveted with an eye to making a whisky still of it.

Wilson wanted out, but Addison had a better idea. Mrs. Yerkes wasn't allowing her husband pocket money for fear he would somehow escape and make good his getaway in a hired hack, and Addison gentled him with vintage cognac and sage counsel. Wait a few days, he begged his brother, and he would come and see him daily, bringing news of the outer world and plans to gain him his liberty.

Mizner's prison cell was hung with masterpieces of a variety of schools of painting, Flemish masters, Romneys, Rembrandts, and Titians, any one of which would keep the brothers in an apartment at the Waldorf-Astoria for a year. For several days Addison dutifully visited his brother, being searched on arrival to prevent the smuggling of forbidden contraband such as hacksaws but being shown out with what amounted to the freedom of the city.

Whenever he went Addison Mizner departed stiff-legged. A Titian or Velásquez, removed from its frame and rolled tightly, was in his trouser leg. By the time Mrs. Yerkes had tired of her husband and consented to a divorce, which was only a matter of weeks, the Mizners were on Easy Street.

The final chapter to the Yerkes mansion was written when Thomas Fortune Ryan, a piratical freebooter of the financial main at the turn of the century, built himself a town house on the adjoining Fifth Avenue real estate. Spacious as it was, a matter of fifty-odd rooms and a vast conservatory, it wasn't big enough for Mrs. Ryan whose whim it was to have more space to lay out a rose garden. There's nothing so homey, she told Ryan, as roses, so Ryan bought the Yerkes mansion, which happened to be on the market at the time, and tore it down for garden space.

All except a circular marble staircase that had cost $50,000 when the traction king looted it from a doge's summer house and which now spiraled up into nowhere. Ryan left the staircase where it was so that his wife's roses could grow over it. The kind that liked to climb.

He was fond of pointing out the retention of the staircase as evidence of his native thrift and acumen. "That sort of thing can run into money if you build it from scratch," he said.

ঙ⊹∙ঙ⊹∙ঙ⊹

Like all arbiters since the days of Petronius, *Arbiter Elegantiarum* to the court of Nero, Maury Paul, or Cholly Knickerbocker as he was known to readers of William Randolph Hearst's *New York American,* dearly loved making a list. Cholly's annual catalogues of the best-dressed women, best-dressed men, most acceptable hostesses, and most bejeweled society women caused anguish or exaltation in rarefied circles, none more so than his all-time definitive Medes-and-Persians decree of who was old-line New York society and who fluttered hopefully on the outer fringe.

Number-two name on the list of old-guard New Yorkers was August Belmont, presumably August Belmont II since his father had died before Maury Paul was born, but that the second of that swaggering name came honestly by his inheritance is amply attested by the record.

The first August Belmont, who took society in his stride, was the town's first and one of its greatest and least questioned of magnificoes, peer of the almost peerless William Collins Whitney and J. P. Morgan, Sr.

Belmont, *père,* arrived in the United States in the early years of the century under the very best auspices for a career as a grandee.

He had been the protégé of the Rothschilds, serving this imperial banking family first in Naples and later in Havana for an interlude that compared favorably to the chapter with this affluent setting in *Anthony Adverse*. Within three years of the time he had hung out his shingle on Wall Street, and acting as the Rothschilds' proconsul, he had established himself as one of the country's most influential bankers. From there to its first authentic magnifico was, in the light of his training and antecedents, the natural consequence of his ever-increasing wealth. On the way up the ladder he offended many, so that in 1841 he fought a duel with a hotheaded South Carolina gentleman over "a subject too trite to be mentioned," and as a result limped slightly the rest of his life. It in no way detracted from the Belmont legend.

A little more than a decade after his arrival in New York, Belmont secured his position with what Mr. Dooley was pleased to describe as "gilt-edge bonds of matrimony," by marrying the daughter of Commodore Oliver H. Perry, who had been instrumental in opening the ports of Japan to Western commerce after centuries of unavailability. The marriage brought him not only a well-endowed wife and unassailable social position but a father-in-law who turned out to be one of the most accomplished wine butlers in the record, a capacity in which Belmont had no hesitation, at his magnificent entertainments, in employing the affable old diplomatist.

Belmont was American minister to the Hague, president of the American Jockey Club, one of the founders of the Manhattan Club and is remembered for a variety of New York landmarks that included Belmont Park and the now vanished Belmont Hotel, and the famous Belmont Circle at Island Cemetery in Newport, all of which were monuments to his son first but to his progenitor by indirection and family name. In his own time, the senior August Belmont was one of the most successful turfmen in the country, having the satisfaction of seeing two colts of his own breeding, Potomac and Masher, run first and second, respectively, in the great

Futurity Stakes and finishing a single year's track operations with a profit of $170,000, an almost unparalleled feat in the 1880s.

As an outstanding financial magnate August Belmont undertook to do a great deal of his business in the continental manner he had learned from his Rothschild patrons, and entertained in a style that was termed regal at the time and would be considered imperial today at his great mansion on lower Fifth Avenue. It was the purest incidental to its owner's purpose that Belmont's mansion should in his lifetime become a sort of spite house in much the same manner that Henry Clay Frick's palace three miles up Fifth Avenue in a later generation had been consciously devised as an affront to Frick's archenemy and neighbor, Andrew Carnegie. Frick set great store by shaming his former associate. Belmont couldn't have cared less about the feelings of James Lenox, but he was popularly reputed to have hastened that elderly curmudgeon's end by the spectacle of his magnificence.

James Lenox occupied the Fifth Avenue corner opposite the Belmont manse and had ringside seats at a bravura production of which he most heartily disapproved. Lenox was one of New York's archetypal cave dwellers and, like Levi P. Morton, Lorillard Spencer, and a few other entrenched patricians of an older generation, clung to his lower Fifth Avenue address long after the trend of fashion had moved farther uptown. Lenox was celebrated for his parsimony, a veritable Hetty Green of the patroon inheritors. Parting with the smallest sums caused him acute physical anguish and he proudly stated for the record that in twenty years none had taken dinner at his table who were not immediate relatives. Like the draperies that were to occasion comment a full century later in the last Vanderbilt home on Fifth Avenue, Lenox's portieres were notably shabby and torn, lending a Charles Addams aspect to a mansion inhabited by haunted inmates. Old man Lenox peered furtively from behind his musty curtains to survey the activities of his neighbor. What he saw filled him with dismay.

To begin with, while minister to the Hague, Belmont had studied the Flemish and French schools of fine art and, as soon as he had the means for gratifying so expensive a taste, set about their collection. He bought with liberality and in time became the first collector in New York to construct a gallery in his own home lit by other than artificial illumination. His introduction of the skylight started a trend. His collection was catholic in its purview and included examples of Madrazo, Meyer, Rosa Bonheur, Munkácsy, Vibert, Meissonier and especially the French painter of robust and uninhibited nudes, William Bouguereau. Bouguereau's nudes were not, in the phrase of William Henry Vanderbilt, a magnifico second-class, created with "chaste intent." They were the scandal of the age and the last word in dashing sophistication.

James Lenox heard about the Bouguereaus, as who did not, and stared in fussy disapproval through his seedy peephole at the expensive people who drove up on Belmont's visiting days to peer at them, peek-a-boo fashion, through decorously mitted fingers. When Belmont heard of his ancient neighbor's disapproval, as a personal invitation to go to hell he ordered a particularly undraped and flauntingly luscious Bouguereau nude hung in the foyer of his home where it would be unavoidable whenever the front door was open.

James Lenox never entertained beyond his immediate family. Belmont thought nothing of 200 at dinner where sumptuously liveried footmen in knee breeches rolled a carpet down to the sidewalk and the carriages of arriving notables stretched three blocks down Fifth Avenue and required special police. He set a table that caused admiration and envy in a time when epicurean doings were taken for granted, and it was an achievement to arouse favorable comment on dinner. As formidable a critic as Lorenzo Delmonico, who seldom allowed himself to be quoted about his customers, described Belmont as a "Maecenas of gastronomy."

"The secret of Mr. Belmont's success as an epicure," said Delmonico, "is that he makes his cook give him a good dinner every day."

Thus kept in training, the Belmont cook, a disciple of the ineffable Careme, now in the employ of one of Belmont's De Rothschild patrons, thought nothing of turning out masterpieces for

200 who were served off the Belmont gold service, the first such in New York excepting only that of Mrs. William B. Astor. Under Delmonico's supervision the Belmont cook was able to enchant his employer's guests with a novel *aspic de* canvasback, a positively supernal creation, which was served with a salad of string beans and truffles. The meal terminated with one of Lorenzo's novelties, a truffled ice cream which everybody anticipated would be awful and which turned out to be heavenly.

Tidings of these costly scuffles with gastronomy when carried to the palpitant James Lenox caused his nates to quiver with indignation, but they were nothing to an account of the Belmont cellars and their conduct. If the army of house footmen found itself taxed with the service to a large number of guests of *la gigue de chevreuil poivrade,* Belmont was in the habit of enlisting his father-in-law to assist in opening the wine. "There's a good fellow," he would address the good-natured old gentlemen. "Run down to the cellar and see if there are six more of the *Rapid* Madeira. Try not to shake them on the stairs." The dignified Commodore whose courtly diplomacy had so charmed the stern-visaged Japanese would trot down to the cellar and return with his arms filled with dusty bottles cradled as a royal infant to the baptismal font.

This was enough of an affront to the ancient proprieties to set Lenox to gnawing his knuckles and rolling his eyes to heaven. He aged perceptibly, and heirs began to gather from as far away as Albany. When he heard that Belmont's wine bill alone came to more than $20,000 a month, he failed to survive the shock. The end came, fortuitously, on an evening when August Belmont was entertaining Sam Ward, "King of the Lobbyists," at a small stag dinner at which Ward disclosed to the fascinated financier the secret of his celebrated *pâté de foie gras de canard de Toulouse.* "Never lift the lid of the casserole while it is simmering," said Ward.

❧·❧·❧

Often it proves that the simplest pleasures in lives of the really well-to-do are the most costly. Many a Yankee countryman in Maine or Vermont and probably numbers of Pennsylvania Dutchmen, living in countries where small brooks are a commonplace, has built his home astride a small stream for the pleasure of its sound and that of living near running water. Paul D. Cravath, an eminent New York corporation lawyer of vast professional prestige and recognized social position in the twenties, built himself a $300,000 home on the North Shore of Long Island and then decided he had omitted what he wanted most, a nice, lively brook running through his drawing room.

"What kind of a brook do you want?" asked the Cravath architect when summoned to resolve this crisis. "One that mutters, babbles, murmurs, or purls? The last of these costs more than the rest."

"I'll take all four," said Cravath, and got them. The bill was another $75,000.

❧·❧·❧

Bostonians in the early years of the current century were familiar with the persons and stylish whims of two bachelor brothers, Frank Huntington and J. Arthur Beebe, no relatives of the author, but great patrons of music in general and Boston Symphony in particular. Another brother, E. Pierson Beebe, is remembered for his vast robin's-egg blue Pierce-Arrow limousine with a pink interior to match his whiskers and two men in robin's-egg blue on the box to match the car. There was also a radiator-cap mascot: a large metal bluebird for happiness.

All the Beacon Street Beebes were wealthy, having been heirs to a Boston dry-goods fortune deriving from a store that made headlines when, in the great Boston fire of 1871, it was one of the first structures to burn and in so doing spread the flames with the largest stock of women's silk lingerie which showered down on neighboring roofs and carried the flames as they blew downwind. Frank Huntington Beebe, listed in his obituaries as "philanthropist," liked to redecorate houses. He owned two, one next the other on Beacon Street. One he lived in and never had redecorated; the other he redecorated twice a year and never lived in. The better part of an inherited fortune of $3,500,000 was spent on the house where he never slept.

ᲘᎩᲘ·ᲘᎩᲘ·ᲘᎩᲘ

John Markle, a coal operator who made an enormous fortune in the New River and Pocahontas coal regions of West Virginia, disliked being fenced in and had built to his order a thirty-two-room apartment on a duplex plan on New York's Park Avenue, It was too small by far. Two years later, in 1928, he moved into a co-operative apartment on Fifth Avenue with forty-one rooms and fifteen baths. He had a private telephone switchboard installed with twenty-six extensions and a round-the-clock operator. This was before large numbers of extensions were a commonplace, or the Princess handset had been dreamed of. A black and white staircase of tessellated marble connected the two floors of the duplex at a cost of $25,000. When an impertinent newspaper reporter asked how he could use fifteen baths at once, Markle snapped, "It's nobody's goddamned business."

ᲘᎩᲘ·ᲘᎩᲘ·ᲘᎩᲘ

Few *beaux gestes* in the record of expensive real estate can top that of Thomas Fortune Ryan's rose arbor, but its peer surely was the later departure from their original stand-in business as a speakeasy of the partners of Jack & Charlie's "21" Club, easily the most austerely maintained and most sumptuously upholstered of the many plush refuges from prohibition. The partners, Jack Kriendler and Charlie Berns had prospered greatly at the premises they liked to call the Puncheon Grotto at 42 West Forty-ninth Street. The brownstone seat of their operations, like many of its competitors in the West Forties had, in former times, been a home of consequential people, in the case of the Puncheon of the family of Benedict Quinn, Yale '26, whose patronage of the premises on a sort of inherited basis was one of the assets of the management, since he brought along well-heeled and influential classmates such as John Whitney, Peter Arno (then known as Curtis Arnoux Peters), Rudy Vallee, Avery Rockefeller, Nicholas Saltus Ludington and Henry C. Potter, a descendant of the Episcopal bishop of New York who brought with him few overtones of religion.

So greatly did the partners Kriendler and Berns prosper at the former Quinn residence that late in the 1920s they sought more commodious quarters at 21 West Fifty-second Street, an address slated for immortality in convivial annals. The removal called for a grand opening at the new address, a conventional gesture of good will to old patrons and freeloaders, but why, in the present special circumstance, shouldn't there be a grand closing as well? The suggestion was made by Robert Benchley and found instant favor with the management. Many of the fixtures of the original premises it had been found expedient to duplicate rather than remove including mirrors, chandeliers, and fittings that were incorporated into the architecture and didn't lend themselves to relocation.

On a given evening, therefore, a select group of invited regulars assembled at the original Puncheon Grotto. On their arrival they were handed with the compliments of the management an assortment of fire axes, crowbars, and other approved wrecking implements and told to do as they would, the joint was theirs, and for the smashing of glass and destruction of furniture for this one evening there would be no charge.

The list of celebrants reads, even at this remove, like a synthesis of Dun & Bradstreet and the Social Register. It included as its bright particular star John Hay Whitney, head of the august house of Whitney and future American ambassador to the Court of St.

James's, Edward Reeves, heir to a fortune of grocery-store millions, Tommy and Bill Laughlin of Jones & Laughlin Steel, men of letters Benchley, Ernest Boyd, and Donald Ogden Stewart, art patrons Bill and Nick Ludington, Gilbert Kahn, Otto Kahn, Jr., William H. Vanderbilt, Frank Hunter, Elliot Sperber, George W. Marshall, the Washington socialite laundry-man who took in the White House washing, Valentine Macy, and a member of the house of Harriman who is unavailable to posterity because, in his haste to have at the supply of fire axes, he omitted to sign his first name to the guest register. It merely and regally reads "Harriman" much as Mrs. William Backhouse Astor was accustomed to sign herself "Mrs. Astor."

It is improbable that so much destruction was ever accomplished by so blue-blooded a wrecking crew as that which closed one era of Jack & Charlie's and inaugurated another.

By virtue both of social and financial primacy, Whitney was accorded the honor of smiting the first blow and chose as his objective a twelve-foot expanse of plate-glass mirror behind the back bar. The satisfying carnage which followed inspired Joe Sheffield, heir to a name large in the annals of Newport, to take an overhead swipe at a massive crystal chandelier in the center of the main restaurant after which Nick Ludington commenced an embattled assault on the door to the men's room which had once worsted him in a late evening encounter when propelled from within by Ernest Hemingway. After that the destruction became so general that the noise attracted the mounted officer on the beat. He was bidden to enter and join the party by Jack Kriendler on condition that he bring his horse, an elevation which gave him an advantage in having at the light fixtures in the foyer with a bung starter provided by the management.

When at last the main stairway was sawed through, leaving Benchley and Roger Wolf Kahn stranded on the second floor and cut off from the basis of supply, it was agreed no greater disaster could be contrived and everybody went up the street to the new address. Gilbert Kahn to this day cherishes a toilet seat that was ravished from the men's room and a bar flap of solid mahogany, probably the sole surviving tangibles from one of the most celebrated of all speakeasies of New York's drinking years.

The damage, Charlie Berns later was wont to assay at between $25,000 and $40,000. "It was worth every penny of it," he says. "I wish we could do it all over again."

It seems worth noting as a footnote to this most resounding of all grand closings that the engraved announcements of Jack & Charlie's at their new address where they became the town's most spectacular speakeasy read: "Luncheon at 12, Tea at Four and Until Closing."

❦·❦·❦

Barter was not unknown in the rarefied circles frequented by the wealthy and powerful of the world in the days before the market debacle of 1929. Shortly before the crash Mrs. Morton Plant, mother of playboy Philip Plant and Leland Hayward the producer, negotiated the sale of her town house on the southeast corner of Fifty-second Street and Fifth Avenue to Pierre Cartier of Paris for his jewelry store, which now occupies the building. Just as the negotiations were being terminated with $1,000,000 as the going price, Mrs. Plant's eye lighted on a pearl necklace that was in Cartier's stock, priced at an even $1,000,000. Instead of cash she accepted the necklace. Oriental pearls have declined on the market and Mrs. Plant is long since dead, but Carrier's real estate is worth many times the $1,000,000 in pearls for which he bought it.

Many stories are told of the vivacious Mrs. Plant who had originally run a boardinghouse at New London. After Morton Plant's death, when she inherited an estimated $20,000,000, suitors for her hand were numerous. One of them proposed that she marry him and settle on him the equivalent of what she could then save annually on a joint income-tax return. Another, whose name was West, Mrs. Plant prudently rejected on the grounds that it would be inconvenient to be known as Mae West.

❦ · ❦ · ❦

Difficult of assessment because his pathway led with nicely cal-culated ambivalence halfway between the screaming vulgar-ity of such parvenus as Bet-a-Million Gates and the Corinthian aloofness of such authentic grandees as William C. Whitney, was the course of Charles M. Schwab, golden boy of the steel industry at the turn of the century and organizational genius by turns for Andrew Carnegie and J. P. Morgan.

Schwab enjoyed ostentation. The mother-of-pearl call buttons in his wife's bedroom aboard his second private car *Loretto* were seven in number, certifying to the domestics available to her sum-mons. The refrigerator in his château when he came to build on Riverside Drive was designed to hold twenty tons of meat, a con-siderable poundage if translated into terms of tenderloin available to the three French chefs always on duty for rendering it palatable as *filet de boeuf Mirabeau.* A seventy-five-room mansion in 1905 was nothing to be sneezed at, or, for that matter, sneezed in if the three low-pressure steam boilers serviced by two licensed firemen with six tons of coal a day were performing properly. Many of the rank-ing nabobs of Fifth Avenue got by without their own private Turk-ish bath with a husky rubber in twenty-four-hour attendance and some were able to rough it without their own private chapels with a ten-ton Carrara marble altar installed at a pious cost of $35,000.

Ostentation, it was generally admitted, was part of the Schwab scheme of things, but it was on every hand tempered by a certain degree of taste and appreciation of what his money bought for him. When Schwab retained Caruso to sing for his dinner guests at a reported $10,000 fee, he enjoyed the music and knew the operas from which the arias derived. The books in the library had their pages cut and their bindings showed signs of wear. He preferred Moët & Chandon's bottlings of champagne and knew a vintage wine from a non-vintage without asking the butler. More than most *arrivistes* who consulted pocket notes before showing guests through their art galleries or entrusted them to trained curators who could be relied on to know a Corot from a Rembrandt, he knew his own possessions. His favorite portrait in his well-chosen collection was Titian's likeness of Cardinal Pietro Bembo and the owner could talk with informed intelligence about the character of the churchman and the details of his being painted.

That Schwab was a photo-finish contender in the expensiveness sweepstakes was undeniable. His Riverside Drive mansion was a synthesis of various elements that had pleased his architect, Maurice Ebert, of the Château de Chenonceaux, Elois, and Azay-le-Rideau. The structure itself had cost $2,000,000, little enough in comparison to the Palm Beach villas of Cosdens and Stotesburys twenty years later, but the dollar was more valuable in 1905. The grounds had set the ironmaster back another $800,000; there was a $50,000 pipe organ and an art gallery which, together with incidentals, brought the value of Schwab's establishment to just under $8,000,000.

Joseph Pulitzer's *New York World* was able to work up quite a head of socialistic blood pressure about an $8,000,000 residence whose finishing touches were being applied just in time for the panic of 1907. Pulitzer's most agonized spasms of anguish on behalf of the downtrodden, it was noted by the cynical, always coincided with his own more expansive gestures such as building a sound-proof mansion on upper Fifth Avenue with $2,000,000 worth of extra marble to keep out the noise of traffic. If the editorialists of the *World* were particularly exercised about the arrogant gestures of the capitalist classes, it could with a minimum of research be discovered that Pulitzer, in his role of the people's friend, had just bought himself a new seagoing steam yacht whose dimensions only allowed it to anchor at Bar Harbor on a spring tide.

Schwab's Riverside Drive home had about it other things that Joseph Pulitzer bitterly envied the owner besides his limitless capacity for fun extending even to crap games in the stable and his lighthearted views about money. They included the Schwab gymnasium, somewhat larger than that of the YMCA in Schwab's native Pittsburgh and its sixty-foot swimming pool set amidst columns of Carrara marble in a Tuscan motif, private bowling alleys and a billiard room with an even dozen Brunswick-Balke-Collander tables. He might also envy the three passenger elevators (no New York town house to date had boasted more than one such convenience) with their heavy bronze doors and crimson cushioned banquettes for repose while riding between floors.

There were those who suggested that what Schwab had built himself wasn't a home but a hotel, an impression in no way diminished by its night-and-day attended telephone switchboard, its $100,000 self-contained power plant, and its fully equipped laundry capable at any time of taking care of a potential of seventy guests occupying its bedchambers. Obviously the self-made ironmaster who had started life only a few years back as a $3.00-a-week dry-goods clerk had none of the social urges which motivated his less affluent neighbors downtown on Fifth Avenue and wasn't about to make overtures in the direction of Mrs. Stuyvesant Fish or Bellevue Avenue, Newport. Mrs. Schwab, in spite of the seven bell pushes on the railroad car, was in fact a homey type who took more pleasure in attending her husband's wants than in what *Town Topics* was thinking that week.

Schwab's tastes were actually a long cut above the intellectual aspirations of Fifth Avenue, always excepting the remarkable William C. Whitney who was equally at ease with the Poet Laureate of England and the head trainer of his stables. William Henry Vanderbilt admired art with a capital A but qualified it, in the case of nudes, with admiration "only if the intent were chaste." August Belmont's fondness for the nudes of Bouguereau took no account of their chaste intent and was obviously indulged for their shock value to his parsimonious neighbor James Lenox.

Schwab's interest was in neither letters nor fine arts, but music. His costly pipe organ was often played for him by a full-time professional named Archer Gibson. Schwab could read music and sang passably himself and his $10,000 checks to Caruso were in the nature of honoraria rather than fees, princely gifts between equals and not a stipend for services rendered. Mme. Ernestine Schumann-Heink, Zimbalist, and Sembrich were friends who made Sunday afternoon in the great hall at Riverside Drive melodious, and the New York newspapers, always excepting the churlish *World* whose owner couldn't abide the spectacle of other people having fun with their money even though he himself would be in today's 90 per cent tax bracket, had a wonderful time with Charlie Schwab and his musical friends. They were awed that a practical steel man who could talk production figures with the redoubtable Captain Bill Jones, the master working stiff of Homestead, could be on equally easy professional terms with operatic tenors in discussing the merits of Mozart.

Not all relationships between artists and their patrons were conducted at such elevated levels of mutual appreciation.

Irene Castle of the once top-ranking dancing team with Vernon Castle in the years before the first world war remembered when she and her husband were not invited to dinner, but only after dinner to entertain, once being commanded to appear at Mrs. Stuyvesant Fish's to dance for a few choice guests at a time when their standard fee for such appearances was a flat $5000. Less than Caruso, par for Paderewski. Due to some misunderstanding in the correspondence, the Castles were under the impression that they were merely to offer their usual repertory of ballroom steps; Mrs. Fish had specified that they were to execute and introduce a new dance that was to be named for her. Thomas W. Lawson had just paid $30,000 to have a newly evolved carnation named for his wife and Mamie wanted a waltz or perhaps the Fish Glide named for her.

When, just before they went on, the Castles were apprised of this additional obligation, they remonstrated with their hostess, saying that there had been a misunderstanding and that they were not prepared to evolve a whole new dance routine on such short notice.

"But you've got to, Mr. Castle," snarled Mamie in her Port-wine voice. "Releases have already gone out to the newspapers saying the new dance is a *fait accompli!*"

Experts at improvisation as both the Castles were, they went on with the performance, merely executing a number of routines in complete reverse, which, to the unprofessional eye, gave them an appearance of novelty. For this accommodation, the Castles upped their fee from $5000 to $10,000 and Mrs. Fish was able to have the expensive satisfaction of a dance created in her honor.

Carnegie and Schwab (to resume) notably failed to see eye to eye in many matters, but one thing found them in agreement. Sanctimonious Carnegie deposed that "to die rich was to die disgraced." Charles M. Schwab, the first executive in America to achieve a $2,000,000-a-year salary, died with liabilities some $400,000 greater than his assets.

ᴓ⚜·⚜·⚜

Not usually considered a dealer in real estate, although the acreage of old masters sold by him to American art collectors might well have relegated him to that category, Sir Joseph Duveen, who bridged the cultural lag between the Old World and America with a profitable torrent of Titians, Vermeers, and Rembrandts, occasionally ventured into the field of what may be termed interior landscaping. One such venture was the renovation of Mrs. E. T. Stotesbury's *Whitemarsh Hall* outside Philadelphia, a premises so vast and maintained by such hierarchical hundreds of servitors that when, upon a recorded occasion, she personally encountered and spoke to her head gardener, that usually sober Scot took the bottle and was unfit for duty the rest of the day. He was as unnerved as though he had encountered the Holy Ghost among the petunias. Mr. Stotesbury was senior partner in both the banking houses of Drexel & Company in Philadelphia and Morgan & Company in New York and ran up an excellent clam chowder at meetings of The Farmer's Club.

Mrs. Stotesbury wanted *Whitemarsh Hall* done over by Duveen in its entirety, which the fine-arts impresario agreed to for a fee of $2,000,000. The undertaking may not have been altogether a profitable one since its magnitude necessitated moving the entire Duveen staff and much of his tangible establishment to Philadelphia for half a year with a resulting loss of much business that Sir Joseph could have transacted in the meantime.

When it came time for a settlement Stotesbury obviously disapproved of his wife's expenditure. No question was raised, however, about the bill. Simply it was paid over a long period of time in checks for varying amounts, the largest of which was $25,000.

❧·❧·❧

Perhaps the most overpoweringly prodigal big spender in the real-estate sweepstakes was William Randolph Hearst, a client of whom Sir Joseph disapproved on grounds of his megalomania and lack of direction. Duveen firmly believed in concentration among his customers in a given field of collecting. Hearst fired shotgun charges of currency all over the landscape, purchasing in the same shipload Cellini salt shakers, Welsh baronial castles, papal altarpieces, and Spanish mission dining-room suites. With fine impartiality he bought, dismantled, crated, shipped, and reassembled at San Simeon English Episcopal palaces, hunting lodges from the Black Forest, Dutch windmills, and classical swimming baths from the Greek islands of the Mediterranean.

Although offended by this disordered expenditure of money that might have, with more resounding effect, been concentrated in a narrower field of endeavor, Duveen played ball with Hearst to the extent of selling him an occasional $5,000,000 worth of ibexes, llamas, and Welsh castles. Hearst, on the other hand, like many of Duveen's clients of whom Sir Joseph himself disapproved, felt that doing business with Duveen was perhaps the loftiest status symbol of all. Surrounded as he was with debased and slavish sycophants

who regarded the Chief's most idiot caprice as Medean law, Hearst
found it a novel and even refreshing experience to be treated like
dirt by a dealer in secondhand merchandise who regarded him as
the veriest parvenu.

A rival of Duveen's in New York upon one occasion was able to
offer Hearst, with no more than the conventional markup of 1000
per cent for himself, for $50,000 the components of a room from
a Venetian doge's palace on the Grand Canal. Hearst couldn't have
cared less and turned his attentions to attempting to purchase one
of the minor pyramids from the Egyptian Government. A short
time later Duveen acquired the doge's breakfast nook and sold it to
Hearst for $200,000. Hearst was overwhelmed with gratitude for
this crumb of recognition.

Long after the publisher's death, when San Simeon had become a
part of the California system of public parks and a signally successful tourist attraction, the story goes that two lady visitors, within
the hearing of their guide, were discussing in heated tones the pros
and cons of a story they had heard to the effect that, somewhere in
transit on the way to California, an entire Gothic castle had disappeared, presumably the fault of the express company.

"If you will excuse my interrupting," broke in the guide, "I can
verify the story for you ladies. Only it wasn't really a castle; more
on the lines of a château."

☙ · ☙ · ☙

Almost nobody in the United States who could read in the
early thirties remained in ignorance of the Wendel sisters,
who lived in an uncompromising and expensive residence at the
northwest corner of Thirty-ninth Street and Fifth Avenue. On
every hand the uptown movement of Manhattan reared itself in
towering office buildings, clubs, and department stores. The Wendel house of ancient peeling brownstone, no more pretentious than
thousands of other mid-town homes of brownstone, rose a scant

four floors. Its front door on Fifth Avenue hadn't been opened in a generation and its lower windows were permanently barricaded against impertinent sight-seers. An atmosphere of forlorn desolation might well have provided inspiration for Charles Addams. At the rear of the house and around an ample expanse of back yard bare of any sort of vegetation or ornament, a high board fence along Thirty-ninth Street kept out the stares of the curious, some of whom day and night kept track of the least sign of activity in the Wendel house.

Well might they be intrigued by this seedy mansion, for although its haunted appearance and tattered window curtains suggested extreme poverty, its occupants were two of the richest old ladies in town who at any moment could convert their corner lot into cash ranging upward from $5,000,000. Until recently Miss Ella and her equally ancient sister, Miss Rebecca, had occupied the premises with their bachelor brother, J. G. Wendel, a dusty old party who might have been mistaken for a mendicant if everyone hadn't known him to be one of the largest owners of Manhattan real estate since John Jacob Astor. Wendel resented the publicity which attracted to his decrepit home and spent most of his time at the Union Club, and the cobwebby old house was occupied by the spinster sisters, a couple of aged harpies masquerading as domestics, and the world's most expensively maintained dog.

Tobey, a small animal of chaotic ancestry but much loved by his owners, was one of a long line of Tobeys reaching backward into historic times so that reporters assigned to the Wendels speculated that the first primeval Tobey may well have had marks of Indian warfare upon his person.

Some idea of the long obscurity which the Wendels had contrived for themselves may be suggested by the fact that, until the interest aroused by their refusal to sell their property to the Union Club for a new clubhouse for $5,000,000 in 1929, no mention of their existence could be found in the public record for thirty-two years. In 1897, the Elite Directory, a forerunner of the Social Register, briefly noted that "The Misses Wendel" maintained a domicile at 442 Fifth Avenue. From then until 1929, all was silence.

There was really no very great mystery about the Wendels. The sisters had been born at that address some seventy years earlier, had lived there all their lives, and weren't minded to move out for any such trifling consideration as $5,000,000. They were too wealthy to be available to inducement and far too rich to care about appearances. Most potent of all reasons for their intransigence was that nowhere on Manhattan Island would $5,000,000 have begun to afford such an extended private exercise ground for Tobey.

All the old ladies wanted was a little privacy, which was the one thing denied them by circumstances. The curiosity of their fellow citizens only confirmed them in determined eccentricity and for years their wealth and seclusion were grist to the Sunday editions. The Wendels' seclusion and insistent anonymity, in an age when publicity was perhaps the most valuable of all commodities, was a challenge to every newspaper in town. Reporters had long since tired of pushing the front door bell which hadn't been connected since Dewey took Manila, but photographers still tried to get a foot in the areaway door when groceries were delivered, and lady journalists attempted to bribe the cook for interviews. All in vain. The nearest thing to penetrating the Wendels' cobweb curtain were pictures taken with telescopic lenses from adjacent office buildings showing Tobey lifting a leg in solitary grandeur in the world's most expensive dog run.

The Wendel sisters, besieged on every hand by the twentieth century, continued their strategic retreat from reality. Had they but known it, most New Yorkers admired them intensely, but their gentle upbringing in another era convinced them that the interest they aroused was hostility. They also resented inevitable comparisons to Hetty Green.

So far as the newspapers were able to discover, neither Wendel sister ever left the house on any occasion of pleasure or relaxation. About once a month Miss Ella in a poke bonnet and carrying a

capacious reticule made the perilous journey of four full blocks up
Fifth Avenue to the equally old-fashioned premises of the Bank of
Fifth Avenue for household expense money. The Bank of Fifth Avenue required a standing balance in checking accounts of a minimal
$25,000, which proved no burden to the Wendels, and it provided
the reassuring atmosphere to which they were accustomed.

In its counting room in inclement weather a vast and cheery fire
of logs burned in a red-brick fireplace. Bank officials sat in positions of easy availability at old-fashioned roll-top desks and secretaries in Gibson-girl hairdos and shirtwaists pounded on Oliver
typewriters, a make that elsewhere had disappeared about 1915. In
its concealed offices and accounting departments the bank staff
worked under conditions of flawless modernity with up-to-the-
minute electronic equipment, but its front apartments were maintained in a facade of obsolescent gentility to encourage just such
patrons and depositors as the Wendels. Old ladies who arrived
in Baker electrics and were helped out of Simplex cars fit for the
Smithsonian found its services courtly, its atmosphere conducive
to tranquil contemplation of agency accounts and trust funds.
Vice presidents in morning coats and cashiers who knew everyone
of consequence gave the Bank of Fifth Avenue a cachet of George
F. Baker respectability. Even the guardian of the safe deposit vaults
far below the surface of Fifth Avenue wore muttonchop whiskers.
The place was obviously as safe as houses.

When at last and to the dismay of many New Yorkers the Wendel house yielded to the wreckers and was replaced by a glaring
Kress dime store, the Wendel sisters had gone down with colors
flying before a stronger foe than the real-estate barons or the New
York City tax assessors. Their obituaries, while inevitably recapitu-
lating the story of their long siege, were respectful in the extreme,
as are all obituary writers confronted with a personal estate well
over $100,000,000.

The long shadows of departed Tobeys, too, were admitted to
probate by the clerk of court. Sometime in the forgotten past an

ancestral Tobey had been taken ill in a time and place where no veterinaries were available and a kindly member of the staff at Flower Memorial Hospital, whose larger concern is with human ailments, had ministered to his doggy needs. In the Wendel will, it was not forgotten and 32/200 of $100,000,000 went to Flower Hospital. Sixteen million dollars was probably the largest veterinary's fee in the record.

ઓજ઼ · ઓજ઼ · ઓજ઼

Only a block or two removed on Murray Hill from the penurious Wendel sisters, the spacious gestures of J. P. Morgan, the most effulgent hidalgo of them all, were in radiant contrast to all the parsimonious spinsters stood for. An example will suffice.

The elder Morgan, ever the grand seigneur when it came to rewarding his associates, was in the habit of showing his esteem with two categories of gifts: blooded collie puppies which he presented to those who enjoyed his special financial favor, and his famous special cigars which went to those who had done social or personal services. Morgan partners-to-be were always alerted to impending promotion by coming home to find a new dog in the house, while agents who had added to his collections or otherwise been deserving sometimes got a sufficient supply of cigars to last a lifetime even if they weren't smokers. In still a third category, that of feminine favors, he inclined to build theaters named for the happy recipients as witness the Maxine Elliott in New York.

Schuyler Parsons, the squire of Palm Beach and one of its most accurate social chroniclers, recalls being with his father in Morgan's London home at Prince's Gate in the opening decade of the century where he witnessed a typical exhibition of the Morgan magnificence.

As they entered the front door the butler was just turning away an old woman who was demanding to see the financier and whose attire and comportment did not recommend her to the trained eye of the servitor.

"She has a basket and showed me a china figurine," the elder Parsons told Morgan. "It was a sailor with ribbons down his back."

"Mr. Morgan, a passionate collector of fine porcelain, quite literally ran down the street after the old lady," Parsons recalls. "He brought her into the house and kissed her excitedly as he sat her down in his great drawing room. 'Now let's see him!' he commanded. It appeared that the sailor was one of a famous pair to which Mr. Morgan already owned the mate and for whose companion piece he had been searching for years.

"The old woman's mother had inherited them from some titled woman to whom she had been a lady's maid. Mr. Morgan presented her with a nice cottage in her home township in Wales and a life income to go with it. Father, for having saved the day, as it were, got so many boxes of the Morgan cigars that they had to follow our four-wheeler to Brown's Hotel in another cab. They lasted into my day and I only smoked the last of them a few years ago."

In the domestic arrangements of the well-to-do in the age of ostentation no component of luxury was held in greater regard than gold table service, and the weight of gold plate and sterling silver both in the form of eating tools and in flat service as well as vases, epergnes, and ash trays was a ponderable element in the elegance sweepstakes. It has been recorded elsewhere how Electra Waggoner of Texas, vexed because her guests ejected hot cartridge cases during dinner on her priceless oriental rugs, resorted to woven gold baskets at a cost of $1500 each at each place setting to receive the discarded brasses.

Both the Palace Hotel in San Francisco and the St. Regis in New York had heavily gold-plated table service, by Shreve and Tiffany respectively, for special dinners and state occasions, resources of luxury which usually required the presence of private detectives when they were in use to supervise their counting and return to the vault.

The Palace gold service was very nearly the occasion for an international incident when in 1945 a banquet of major dimenisons was served to the various delegates to the United Nations in the hotel's celebrated Garden Court restaurant and its gold place settings were laid at the head table where heads of state and ranking ambassadors were seated. The Palace was then owned in the name of the Sharon estate by Mrs. William B. Johnstone of Reno and Chevy Chase, a Queen Mary type with a whim of iron who regarded the hotel as a family trust and watched the conduct of its slightest detail with the proverbial eye of a hawk. During the course of the state banquet, which she viewed from a concealed vantage point, she was alarmed to observe, while the general attention was directed elsewhere, Mme. Chiang Kai-shek, wife of the Chinese generalissimo, slip a gold ash tray into her reticule with the absent-minded gesture of an expert collector. Elbowing her way through the august diners, Mrs. Johnstone took a determined stance immediately in front of the offending guest and leveled an accusing finger.

"Put it back. I saw you!" she said in tones of menace.

The ash tray was returned, instanter, to circulation.

No aspirants for honors as a social or financial grandee in the years before 1914 but prided themselves on gold table service in more or less comprehensive dimensions. Mrs. Whitelaw Reid in her Madison Avenue town house could accommodate 100 on the service she had used when her husband was American ambassador at London. Most services were heavily plated gold on silver, solid gold being impractical as both too heavy for maneuverability and too soft for washing, but William Collins Whitney was supposed to have had a solid-gold service watched by a special custodian with no other duties than its handling and protection. As a gold-plated service ran well above $1000 a place setting, depending on the number of components, it staggers the imagination to estimate the value of a solid-gold parure of plates, knives, forks, spoons, butter chips, and incidental tools suited for a ten-course dinner. Since the rules of the game required that each place setting be complete at the beginning of the meal, there was no chance to rotate a given suite of tools or use them as ringers.

The Joseph J. O'Donohue family of People's Steamship Company wealth in New York possessed a gold service of almost legendary splendor as did Mrs. Henry White of Lenox whose husband, like Mrs. Whitelaw Reid's, had once been ambassador to the Court of St. James's. Mrs. Julia Berwind of Newport scorned to serve guests off anything less than heavily plated gold as did all Vanderbilts worth recording, although observers reported that toward the end, just before she abandoned her stately address at the last of the eleven Vanderbilt mansions that once lined upper Fifth Avenue, Mrs. Cornelius Vanderbilt's flat service which could once have accommodated 100 now strained to suffice for half that number and was badly worn to boot. The Vanderbilt curtains in the Fifth Avenue French windows also showed unmended rents in their fabric which occasioned unfavorable mention in the public prints.

Perhaps the most celebrated of all gold table services in the years of the ortolans was that of Mrs. Stuyvesant Fish, an intricate and beautifully fashioned service for 300 which had been made to order by Tiffany and was one of the breathtaking sights, when laid for full-dress occasions, at Mrs. Fish's Newport villa, *Crossways*. Many of the set pieces, candelabra, epergnes, and the like were in several sections which screwed together and could be dismounted for storage or cleaning. A disgruntled butler took his revenge on Mrs. Fish by taking his leave a few hours before one of her major social triumphs at table, leaving behind him the entire service taken apart on the dining-room floor. Happily, a Tiffany representative was in town working on somebody else's eating tools and the disjointed place settings were reassembled in the nick of time. It was her resourcefulness in the face of such potential disasters that gained for Mrs. Fish the unquestioned primacy among Newport hostesses of her era.

For some reason not altogether apparent to students of the legend of hauteur, the exchange of insults between men of the world has more frequently been a matter of record than the *beaux gestes* and affronts between females, so it is worth reporting that an epic encounter once ensued between Mrs. Jack Gardner of Fenway Court, Boston, and Mrs. Potter Palmer, undisputed Queen of Chicago's Gold Coast in the early years of the century. Each woman was legendary in her home town and a *grande dame* of formidable dimensions who was not apt to be easily impressed with the other. Neither was.

On a tour of the Potter Palmer castle being conducted by Mrs. Palmer's son, Honore, Mrs. Gardner was eventually shown the kitchen offices and pantries where young Palmer ostentatiously displayed to her the family gold table service which contained complete place settings for fifty people.

"And what do you do when you're having company in for dinner?" asked Mrs. Gardner.

That the standard of private entertainment for as commonplace an occasion as Sunday dinner in New York in the early decades of the current century was fully as opulent and painstakingly regarded as any great public function is suggested by the recollections of Mrs. Joseph J. O'Donohue of a Manhattan family of long-established wealth that had had its origins in the Brooklyn ferryboat traffic in the days of the People's Steamship Line. Mrs. O'Donohue recalls that these occasions, which were largely peopled with relatives and only a comparative handful of guests from beyond the family circle, never saw fewer than forty at table and often twice as many.

Shortly after breakfast on Sunday morning an expert would arrive from Bellows & Company, the wine merchants and, after being handed by the butler a list of the wines and spirits to be served that day, would spend an hour or more, sometimes alone, sometimes with the assistance of a footman, in decanting wines of sufficient age to require this ritual, drawing the corks of those which merely needed a few hours' breathing at a room temperature, and icing in the appropriate silver buckets the champagnes and any other wines that must be chilled. He also saw to it that Port, Madeira, and cognac were set out in cut-glass decanters, each with its appropriate gold chain and identifying tag.

By the time the man from Bellows had finished, there arrived a Mr. Humphrey from Charles Thorley's flower shop, usually with an assistant to check the floral displays of the day, see to it that the American Beauty roses were in sufficient water in their four-foot silver vases throughout the main salon, music room, and entrance hall and that the table centerpiece was in order with its violets, roses, and white orchids. At every lady's place there was a matching orchid corsage and at every gentleman's a boutonniere.

At twelve thirty, just as the musicians were unpacking their instruments and setting up their music behind the screen of palms in the foyer between the main salon and the dining room, Mr. Charles Thorley himself, top-hatted and morning-coated, would arrive for a final inspection of the floral arrangement, seldom pausing to remove his overcoat unless something required his personal touch of adjustment, because he had similar offices to perform at the residences of half a dozen other regular customers where Sunday dinner was a ritual of comparable formality.

When Sarah Bernhardt, an old friend of the family, was in New York, Sunday dinner at the O'Donohues' was ritual and the family's chef, without special order but as a matter of course, prepared for her a favorite dish of capon and *foie gras*. Before being made into *chaudfroids,* the several elements of the bird, breast, wings, and legs, were boned and stuffed with goose liver and then reassembled in the shape of an entire fowl. The evidence of the chef's special expertise was that the joints where the bird had been dissected were not visible to the naked eye.

On one occasion, Mme. Bernhardt brought with her a pet lion on a gold and emerald lead, and, as it was a cold wintry day, the lion was wearing a fine sealskin overcoat. The footman on duty to receive the wraps of arrivals being terrified to approach the beast, Mme. Bernhardt undertook to remove the garment herself, and during the course of the ensuing battle of personalities, the animal escaped into the library where Grandfather O'Donohue was having a preliminary gin-and-vermouth. It is part of the family

legend that the start he received took years off the old gentleman's life.

These fairly elaborate preparations, it will be noted, were not for
any occasion of special rejoicing but merely a weekly family dinner,
and had their equivalent in scores and hundreds of New York homes
of men and women as comfortably situated as the O'Donohues.

J. J. O'Donohue IV more than half a century afterward recalls
that at Christmas time it was the pleasant custom of his great-grand-
mother to drive from her home at 5 East Sixty-ninth Street down
Fifth Avenue to Washington Square, pausing at each intersection,
in a day before traffic lights, to distribute $20 gold pieces to the traf-
fic policeman on duty. The shades of her Pierce-Arrow were drawn
so that she might not be recognized, a naïve precaution since there
must have been ample identification about the car itself, but still a
pleasant gesture in a gentler New York than it was ever to be again.

Pet lions by no means disappeared from the New York scene
with the over-all decline of elegance. As late as 1943, Miss Tallulah
Bankhead, then resident at the Elysee Hotel on East Fifty-fourth
Street, kept in her apartment a partly grown lion cub, the gift of
an admirer, and known as Winston, after the British statesman for
whom Miss Bankhead entertained a lively admiration. Winston,
Miss Bankhead assured everyone, was gentle as a kitten, but on
one occasion while his owner was busy with the vermouth, with a
single swipe of his paw Winston clawed an entire leg off the din-
ner-jacket trousers of an interviewing reporter. A good deal of leg
went with it. Grafton Wilcox, then managing editor of the *Herald
Tribune,* flatly refused to validate the reporter's expense account of
$350 for a new dinner jacket and $2.00 for iodine until the episode
had been confirmed by a phone call to the Elysee. "People don't
have lions around nowadays," said the managing editor. "Doesn't
she know there's a war on?"

A nicety in the conduct of private homes in large cities in the
years of upholstered comfort, comparable in its way to the perpetual upkeep that came with Ettore Bugatti's Royale cars and the

long-running warranty of Rolls-Royce, was the maintenance by jewelers and clock merchants of a clock-winding service for patrons whose clocks were too numerous or delicately adjusted to be left to the domestics. For a minimal fee of a few dollars a week, the owners of fifty or a hundred clocks in the home were visited at stated intervals by a professional clock winder who saw to the perpetual activation of the timepieces in his care and made the delicate week-to-week adjustments to keep them reasonably in harmony with the stars or Greenwich.

A veteran employee of Garfinckel's specialty shop in Washington, dealers in a variety of costly furs, fashions, and artifacts who eventually took over Brooks Brothers in New York, recalls that the store's official winder, a small, mousy man, as became his special calling regularly made the rounds of Georgetown and other eligible *faubourgs* attired in a formal morning coat of office and carrying his own miniature step-ladder for gaining access to tall clocks without inconvenience to the servants of the house.

Upon one occasion a valued client of Garfinckel's who lived at some remove, on North Astor Street, Chicago, to be exact, purchased a costly mantel clock which was in due course forwarded by express with its pendulum, as is customary in such cases, disengaged and separately wrapped. Soon there arrived from Chicago a letter saying the clock had arrived but it wouldn't go. Garfinckel's wrote back with precise instructions for hanging the pendulum and setting the works in motion. Back came another letter to the effect that the customer didn't buy $1000 clocks on a do-it-yourself basis and what was Garfinckel's going to do about it?

Garfinckel's clock winder boarded the Baltimore & Ohio sleeping cars and went to Chicago, performed the ten-minute operation of setting the clock in motion, and returned the next day to Washington.

That messenger service of a casual degree of grandeur at one time went out from Chicago as well as in, is suggested by Anita McCormick Blaine of the Chicago McCormicks who once, in the course of remembering friends at Christmas, contrived to overlook one who, as it chanced, lived at Huntsville, Alabama. Never one to hurt feelings where it could be avoided, Mrs. Blaine retained the services of a Western Union boy at the then (1922) going rate of fifty cents an hour, plus carfare and eating expenses en route, to deliver the gift at Huntsville where it arrived right on Santa Claus schedule on Christmas morning.

ᏫᏫ·ᏫᏫ·ᏫᏫ

Among the more picturesque ostentations of affluence in the era immediately preceding the stock market debacle of 1929 was the $50,000 privilege of smiting a groom over the head with a polo mallet. Those familiar with the personality and temperament of Frederick H. Prince of Boston's North Shore and Newport were not surprised when the bill for this indulgence was presented, still less when payment was refused in terms of outrage and indignation.

Prince, credited at the time with being in all probability the wealthiest man in New England, was owner outright of the Chicago stockyards, a director in twenty-odd Class I railroads and interlocking directorates past counting. The hallmark of his personality was the formidable riding crop which he carried at all daylight hours whether associated with horses or mere bankers and which he was only with difficulty restrained from regarding as a component of formal attire in the evening. Quite late in the game and after telephones had been perfected so that conversational tones could carry across the Atlantic, Prince rejected modulation of speech in the belief that a telephone when loudly addressed carried his message to better effect. In making local calls he merely shouted; on long distance he bellowed, larding both types of communication with frequent invocations of God as witness to the rectitude of his sentiments. He also was germ conscious.

A victim of this particular phobia was Mrs. Prince, a diminutive and dutiful woman who was never permitted by her husband to handle money in any form lest contact with currency convey the Black Death or chronic septicemia. To facilitate her progress in a world where money was often required, Mrs. Prince was at all times accompanied by a combination major-domo and bursar, a French-born Irishman named Thomas who was never seen by anyone in other attire than a hard Derby hat, riding breeches, and canvas leggings. He was reputed to sleep in them. To combat the menace of germs Mrs. Prince never slept two nights running in the same bedroom, but sought repose in an oversize child's cradle which was every evening scrupulously disinfected and then wheeled to the apartment she might select for slumber. The walls of the bedroom of her choice were draped with fresh sheets also doused with antiseptics.

Mr. Prince did not always sleep at home. Riding crop in hand, he was fond of dancing at whatever pavilion was for the moment graced by Florence Walton of the dancing team of Maurice & Walton. Sometimes he insinuated a pearl necklace in a bowl of roses which was ceremoniously brought to their table by a respectful maître d'hôtel. Absentminded in such matters, Prince gave Miss Walton so many pearl necklaces that she was unable to wear them all at one time and eventually suggested that diamonds were equally acceptable.

The $50,000 blow with a polo mallet was alleged to have been struck by Prince in a moment of vexation on the afternoon of July 29, 1929, within the perfumed precincts of the Myopia Hunt Club at Hamilton on Boston's patrician North Shore. On the receiving end was Arthur Mason, a groom and polo professional who had incurred the millionaire's anger by riding him off the field in the excitement of a practice match. Prince had thereupon, according to later court testimony, loudly called on God to vindicate his cause and had grievously smitten the offending Mason with the polo mallet.

In a suit filed the following year in Salem Superior Court, Mason, with a restraint that would have seemed commendable in a later age of $1,000,000 awards in parallel circumstances, asked $50,000 damages to cover medical expenses and professional incapacity resulting from the polo mallet assault. Prince's lawyers countered with a charge that "a deliberate fraud was sought to be imposed on the court and the defendant."

The ensuing trial and the evidence it produced packed Essex County Superior Court with the mink, monocles, and emotions of some of Boston's most resoundingly blue-blooded names. The audience was largely recruited from the spectator seats adjacent to the polo fields at Myopia and at Prince's own estate, *Princemere*, and court attendants and the jury were edified with fine points of polo technique as well as social feuding of Hatfield-McCoy dimensions in the *bon ton* of the North Shore.

Much of the testimony tended to suggest that, although by every social and financial standard eligible, Prince was not overwhelmingly popular among either his peers or dependents. At one point in the trial Mrs. Albert C. Burrage, wife of a towering magnifico of Boston finance, splintered the railing of the jury box with a polo mallet to indicate the violence of the assault to which the complainant had been subjected.

Defense attorney asserted that Mrs. Burrage was motivated by an overwhelming urge "to be the star witness in what to her is the social drama of the North Shore."

"I'm sure that Mr. Burrage knows what to do if a polo mallet is within Mrs. Burrage's reach," declared James M. Sullivan, counsel for the defendant, who also asserted that Mrs. Burrage had been seen swinging on inanimate objects with a polo mallet in obvious rehearsal for her courtroom appearance.

Umbrage within the membership of the Myopia Club was suggested when the defense charged the entire suit was a frame-up and had been devised in malice by Quincy Agassiz Shaw II, of Pride's Crossing, a grandee of the inner circle at Myopia who disapproved of Prince. "Shaw scowled and twisted the cloth cap in his lap as Sullivan asserted that he had instigated the suit," reported the *Boston Herald*.

Charges and countercharges in Essex County Superior Court continued to attract what the Boston newspapers described as capacity audiences of irreproachable social standing. For once this was no exaggeration and Robert Choate, managing editor of the *Boston Herald* and himself an accredited member of the Beacon Street elect, at one time had the hearings covered by reporters from the paper's society department as well as by more conventional newsmen from the city staff. A jury's award of $20,000 to Mason was appealed by Prince and the litigation dragged on for another four years, flaring now and then with an exchange of cultured insults between legal counsel and witnesses recruited from the Somerset Club and other precincts of privilege. In the end, in 1934, the difference was settled out of court with a figure variously reported but commonly believed to be the full $50,000 mentioned in the original complaint.

The amount could not have been of concern to Frederick H. Prince whose income in the depth of the depression was estimated at $5,000,000 but it at least established a going price on being beaten around the ears with a polo mallet.

Bibliography

Abels, Jules. *The Rockefeller Millions.* Macmillan, 1965.

Allen, Frederick Lewis. *Lords of Creation.* Harper & Brothers, 1935.

Altrocchi, Julia Cooley. *The Spectacular San Franciscans.* E. P. Dutton, 1949.

Amory, Cleveland. *The Last Resorts.* Harper & Brothers, 1952.
Who Killed Society? Harper & Brothers, 1960.

Andrews, Wayne. *The Vanderbilt Legend.* Harcourt, Brace, 1941.

Barrett, Richmond. *Good Old Summer Days.* Houghton Mifflin, 1952.

Barron, Clarence. *They Told Barron.* Harper & Brothers, 1930.

Beebe, Lucius. *Mansions on Rails.* Howell-North, 1959.

Beebe, Lucius, and Charles Clegg. *U. S. West, The Saga of Wells Fargo.* E. P. Dutton, 1949.
Legends of the Comstock Lode. G. H. Hardy, 1950.

Beer, Thomas. *The Mauve Decade.* Vintage Books, 1960.

Behrman, S. N. *Duveen.* Random House, 1952.

Bird, Anthony, and Ian Hallows. *The Rolls-Royce Motor Car.* Crown, 1964.

Bowers, Claude G. *The Tragic Era.* Houghton Mifflin, 1929.

Brown, Eve. *Champagne Cholly.* E. P. Dutton, 1947.

Burt, Nathaniel. *The Perennial Philadelphians.* Little, Brown, 1963.

Cromie, Robert. *The Great Chicago Fire.* McGraw-Hill, 1958.

De Castellane, Count Boni. *How I Discovered America.* Alfred A. Knopf.

Fowler, Gene. *Skyline.* Viking Press, 1961. *Timber Line.* Covici Friede, 1933. *Beau James.* Viking Press, 1949.

Glasscock, C. B. *Lucky Baldwin.* Bobbs-Merrill, 1933. *The War of the Copper Kings.* Grosset & Dunlap, 1939.

Holbrook, Stewart. *The Age of the Moguls.* Doubleday, 1953.

Hoyt, Edwin P. *The Vanderbilts and Their Fortunes.* Doubleday, 1962.

Josephson, Matthew. *The Robber Barons.* Harcourt, Brace, 1934.

Lehr, Elizabeth Drexel. *King Lehr and the Gilded Age.* Blue Ribbon Books, 1938.

Lewis, Arthur H. *The Day They Shook the Plum Tree,* Harcourt, Brace & World, 1963.

Lewis, Oscar. *Bonanza Inn.* Alfred A. Knopf, 1939. *The Big Four.* Alfred A. Knopf, 1938.

Lord, Walter. *A Night to Remember.* Holt, 1955. *The Good Years.* Harper & Brothers, 1960.

Lundberg, Ferdinand. *Imperial Hearst.* Equinox Cooperative Press, 1936.

McLean, Evalyn Walsh, and Boyden Sparkes. *Father Struck It Rich.* Blue Ribbon Books, 1938.

Matz, Mary Jane. *The Many Lives of Otto Kahn.* Macmillan, 1963.
Meyers, Gustavus. *The History of Great American Fortunes.* Modern Library, 1936.

Minnigerode, Meade. *Certain Rich Men.* G. P. Putnam's Sons.
Morrell, Parker. *Diamond Jim.* Simon & Schuster, 1934.

Morris, Lloyd R. *Incredible New York*. Random House, 1951.

Morton, Frederic. *The Rothschilds*. Atheneum, 1962.

O'Connor, Richard. *The Scandalous Mr. Bennett*. Doubleday, 1962. *Gould's Millions*. Doubleday, 1962. *Courtroom Warrior*. Little, Brown, 1963.

Purdy, Kenneth W. *Kings of the Road*. Little, Brown, 1952. Ross, Ishbel. *Charmers and Cranks*. Harper & Row, 1965. *Silhouette in Diamonds*. Harper & Brothers, 1960.

Seitz, Don C. *The Dreadful Decade*. Bobbs-Merrill, 1926. Sichel, Pierre. *The Jersey Lily*. Prentice-Hall, 1958. Sprague, Marshall. *Money Mountain*. Little, Brown, 1953. Swanberg, W. A. *Jim Fisk* Charles Scribner's Sons, 1959.

Tebbel, John William. *The Life and Good Times of William Randolph Hearst*. E. P. Dutton, 1952.

Tolbert, Frank X. *Neiman-Marcus*. Holt, 1953.

Tully, Andrew. *Era of Elegance*. Funk, 1947.

Walker, Stanley. *Mrs. Astor's Horse*. Stokes, 1935.

Warshow, Robert Irving. *Bet-a-Million Gates*. Greenburg, 1932.

Washburn, Charles. Come *Into My Parlor*. National Library Press, 1936. *Mahogany Hall*.

Wecter, Dixon. *The Saga of American Society*. Charles Scribner's Sons, 1937.

Wendt, Lloyd, and Herman Kogan, *Bet-a-Million*. Bobbs-Merrill, 1948.

Winkler, John. *Morgan the Magnificent* Star Books, 1932. *Incredible Carnegie*. Star Books, 1934.

Index

A

Abdul-Hamid II, Sultan, 411
Adams, Evangeline, 193, 392
Aldrich, Nelson, 127
Alexis, Grand Duke, 253, 258
Altrocchi, Julia Cooley, 64
Amory, Cleveland, 240, 270, 271,
    443, 446
Andrews, Wayne, 3
Archbold, Ann, 120
Archbold, John, 431
Arico, Louis, 319
Arlen, Michael, 247
Armitage, Merle, 242, 243
Armour, Philip Danforth, 313
Arno, Peter, 467
Arnold, Thurman, 425
Arthur, Chester Alan, 211
Aspinwall, William H., 26
Astor, Gertrude Gretsch, 337
Astor, John Jacob, 126, 131, 266,
    308, 477
Astor, Mrs. John Jacob, 148, 149,
    308

Astor, Mrs. Vincent, 444
Astor, Mrs. William Backhouse,
    62, 136, 406, 436, 445,
    464, 468
Astor, Vincent, 163
Astor, William Backhouse, 16

B

Bache, Jules, 335, 362
Baer, Bugs, 74
Bagot, Lily, 185
Baker, F. L. (Free Lunch), 450
Baker, George F., 17, 479
Baker, Mrs. George F., 337
Baldwin, Lucky, 46, 62
Balenciaga, Cristobal, 334
Bankhead, Tallulah, 486
Barbey, Pierre, Jr., 444
Barnes, Albert C., 241
Barnum, P. T., 140
Barrett, Richmond, 10, 120
Barriger, John, 229
Barron, Clarence, 197, 306
Barrymore, Ethel, 1

D

E

F